DRUGGING THE POOR
LEGAL AND ILLEGAL DRUGS AND SOCIAL INEQUALITY

MERRILL SINGER
UNIVERSITY OF CONNECTICUT

WAVELAND
PRESS, INC.
Long Grove, Illinois

For information about this book, contact:
Waveland Press, Inc.
4180 IL Route 83, Suite 101
Long Grove, IL 60047-9580
(847) 634-0081
info@waveland.com
www.waveland.com

Cover design: Jacob Singer
Interior art: Bonnie Atwood

10-digit ISBN 1-57766-494-9
13-digit ISBN 978-1-57766-494-9

Printed in the United States of America

16   15   14   13   12   11   10

To James Ernest Gonzales III,
a teacher, close friend, and fellow activist,
in celebration of his 60th birthday

Contents

Preface

This book is the third in a series of volumes I have written on drugs using a critical medical anthropology (CMA) perspective. All three books have a common origin in a paper I wrote in 1986 entitled "Toward a Political Economy of Alcoholism: The Missing Link in the Anthropology of Drinking Behavior" published in the journal *Social Science and Medicine*. It was there that I first began to grapple with understanding drug use from the vantage of the CMA perspective. Additionally, all three books are rooted in the street drug research carried out by the Center for Community Health Research at the Hispanic Health Council in Hartford, Connecticut, where I have worked and been involved in research for the last 25 years. This and the previous two books (published by Waveland Press also) are informed by a long series of federally funded (primarily, NIDA, CDC, and SAMHSA) street drinking and other drug use studies carried out by the center's research team and reflect ongoing discussions and input from the committed research, service, advocacy, and policy staff at the Hispanic Health Council.

In the first book in this series, called *Something Dangerous: Emergent and Changing Illicit Drug Use and Community Health* (2006a), I focused on *drug use dynamics*, the processes of change in drug use patterns, including the appearance and spread of new drugs and ways of using drugs, and the social conditions and structural relationships that drive such changes in drug use behaviors. The objective of the book is to present an historic examination of the nature and health effects of changing illicit drug use practices in American society and globally and to assess the ways that drug use changes in response to transformations in the social structures and cultures in which it is embedded.

In the second book, *The Face of Social Suffering: Life History of a Street Drug Addict* (2006b), I applied the CMA approach to a life history examination of a single drug addict, an individual I interviewed multiple times over the course of a seven-year period beginning in the late 1990s. By placing his life in social and historic context, the book is intended to affirm the insight of the path breaking sociologist C. Wright Mills in his classic book *The Sociological Imagination* (1959) that "Neither the life of an individual nor the history of a society can be understood without understanding both."

The current book extends the CMA understanding of drug use beyond illicit drugs to the fuller pattern of intertwined legal and illegal drug use, with a special focus on the social groups or *drug corporations* involved in the production and distribution of mind altering substances, the economic system in which these entities operate (*drug capitalism*), and the impact this system has on maintaining the dominant structure of social inequality among the wealthier and poorer social classes. Drug use matters, not just in terms of the significant problems it can cause for the emotional and physical health of users, not only in terms of the damage it can do to the fabric of involved families and communities, nor even solely in terms of the fiscal and other costs it imposes on the wider society; drug use matters because it plays a significant role in blocking the eradication of vast inequalities, injustices, and disparities in society while helping to generate specific kinds of disparities of its own. Examining how and why this is so is the purpose of this book.

Together, these three volumes constitute alternative reflections produced by shining the light of inquiry on drug use through the same theoretical prism. They are united also in having a common ultimate objective, namely challenging the assumption that how things are is how they always have been or how they need to be, and acting on that challenge. In the words of social activist Daniel Berrigan (1971), "One learns, I hope, to discover what is right, what needs to be righted—through work, through action." In this sense, this book addresses something that *needs to be righted*, the drugging of the poor.

Structure of the Book

Chapter 1 provides an overview of the system that promotes and supports drugging the poor. Building on the concepts and themes presented in chapter 1, chapter 2 explores the nature of drug capitalism and its impact on contemporary U.S. society within the context of globalization. The chapter demonstrates that the licit and illicit drug industries comprise two sectors of a common mode for the production and distribution of desired but risky consumer goods, namely psychotropic drugs. Nonetheless, while the producers of legal drugs are honored, those behind illegal drugs are vilified. In short, legal and illegal drugs, their respective producers, and their use are assigned to opposing conceptual worlds. The chapter argues that these two worlds are not as different as they might at first appear; they have many shared features and common strategies for achieving their goals.

Chapters 3–5 construct the world as seen by legal drug producers, as well as their role in helping to insure their vision of the world is realized: Chapter 3 examines the corporate production and worldwide sale of tobacco products and their role in drugging the poor; chapter 4 presents a parallel examination of the global alcohol industry; and the pharmaceutical industry is the focus of chapter 5. Chapter 6 scrutinizes the underground drug corporations that produce and bring to market a wide array of illicit drugs, including heroin, cocaine, methamphetamine, and Ecstasy. A goal of chapters 3–6 is to draw parallels and reveal connections between companies that produce, distribute, and promote the use of legal drugs and those that produce and traffic illegal ones.

Chapter 7 moves from the supply to the demand side of drug capitalism, based on field research on the everyday lives of street drug users and the growing body of literature on low-income drug consumers. The chapter is structured around the theme of self-medication as a socially determined motivation for psychotropic drug consumption in a context that includes: (1) the War *for* Drugs, (2) the unlevel playing field and significant social inequality that characterize America and other societies, and (3) the resulting experience of social suffering among the poor. Based on this foundation, the chapter addresses the specific role played by all psychotropic drugs and the dual drug industry in the creation and maintenance of the existing unequal structure of society, including as a central feature of that inequality the emergence of health disparities among by the poor.

The concluding chapter examines grassroots efforts to build a people's war on drug capitalism as part of the struggle for social equality and freedom from the burdens of both drug abuse and the official War on Drugs. The challenges of the people's war are considerable because legal and illegal drugs are the source of enormous global profits, and thus insuring their availability is strongly defended by those who reap the economic benefits of drug use, abuse, and addiction.

Preface, 2010

At the time this book was completed in late 2007, the U.S. economy, as indicated on p. 13, appeared to most financial observers to be strong, primarily because gross domestic production was increasing. In fact, the economy was in trouble, as soon became evident. The signs were there far earlier but were not taken seriously by lenders, analysts, and the government. For example, by 2006 the U.S. trade deficit had reached $70 billion and the country was almost $9 trillion dollars in debt, including to foreign nations like China. By early 2008, the value of the dollar had dropped by 18% against other major world currencies and the budget deficit was nearing $3 trillion. By 2009, all categories of U.S. loans (except, at least initially, commercial real estate) were defaulting at record levels. The debt burden on households and business was rising quickly. Soon, the mortgage giants Fannie Mae and Freddie Mac were bankrupt because many people with subprime mortgages could not repay their loans. Before long, giants of the U.S. economy, including banks, other financial institutions, the car industry, and others were standing on the edge of collapse and seeking (and getting) government bailouts. Among working people, or "Main Street" as it came to be labeled in the media (as opposed to Wall Street), layoffs became widespread, people began losing their homes in record numbers, and life savings were disappearing. At the same time, the level of corruption and accounting scandals among increasingly unregulated U.S. corporations was revealed to be extreme. Exposure began with Enron, the largest corporate bankruptcy in American history. Despite their huge salaries, Enron executives launched a number of off-the-books spin-off partnerships to enrich themselves at the expense of stockholders. The end result was the implosion of the corporate giant. After Enron, the country was rocked by case after case of similar illegal corporate greed and financial collapse. More broadly, movement of production overseas, elimination of pensions, and layoffs of workers, have further contributed to a rising level of social suffering among the poor (especially) and working classes.

As discussed in the pages of this book, these are the very conditions that push the poor (old and new poor alike) to seek temporary relief in drug use. Consequently, the current turn in the U.S. economy, and the economies of other developed nations, suggest the potential for rising rates of drug abuse, for the reasons specified in the pages to follow.

Jim Gonzales has been an inspiration in my life since I was 18 years old. There is an old activist slogan that urges: "each one, reach one, each one, teach one." Jim reached me and has taught me important things for almost 40 years, including the importance of always trying to be a decent human being in an indecent world. In my life, I have never met a more decent person than Jim.

Some of the ideas presented herein were tested in a series of lectures given at the University of Melbourne and the Australian Research Centre on Sex and Society, Latrope University during the winter of 2006. These talks were arranged by Hans Baer, another long-time friend and colleague who, too, has enriched my life in immeasurable ways. I can't quite imagine having lived my life without his friendship.

Special heartfelt appreciation, for this and for all three of my "drug books" with Waveland (and for much more), goes to Pam Erickson. She watched it happen, aided the process in many ways, and kept a quiet, loving smile through it all, yet again. To borrow e. e. cummings' words, "i carry your heart (i carry it in my heart)."

I want to express appreciation to Philippe Bourgois for helping me select the final title of the book. Finally, I would like to thank Nobel Prize-winning economist Amartya Sen for having said during a 2001 interview on Alternative Radio, "I believe that virtually all the problems in the world come from inequality of one kind or another."

CHAPTER 1

The Global Dual Drug Industry and Drugging the Poor

> The hearts of the poor do not beat, they are beaten.
>
> —Brazilian proverb

Illegal and Legal Drug Use in America

Drugs—substances that affect your brain and alter your mood, and, in some cases, your body—are everywhere and Americans use a lot of them daily. Moreover, the drugs Americans use come from everywhere, passing across many borders and through many hands on their way to market. They are big business, capture enormous profits, and exemplify patterns of globalization in the modern era. Yet their full impact on society and their unique role in the social order remain obscure.

Some drugs, of course, are illegal and must be purchased clandestinely and potentially at grave personal risk. Despite being banned, they usually are available and not particularly hard to acquire in most locales across the land. In the year 2004, over 19 million Americans, or about 8 percent of the population over the age of 12 reported using illicit drugs during the 30-day period prior to being interviewed in the National Survey on Drug Use and Health, an annual study of the civilian, noninstitutionalized population of the United States (Office of Applied Studies 2005). Marijuana is the most widely used illegal drug, with almost 15 million current users. The survey also found that there are two million cocaine users (about one-fourth of whom use crack cocaine), just under a million hallucinogen users, and several hundred thousand heroin users. The effectiveness of this study in reaching homeless and marginally housed street drug users is uncertain. Thus, the study's figures may underestimate the actual number of impoverished street drug users, many of whom do not use a "single" psychotropic drug but are users of multiple drugs, legal and illegal, often in combination. The number of heroin users, for example, has been estimated by others to total several million nationally. The actual number of users of any particular drug is never precisely known and varies over time. Although illicit drug use is found among all social classes, negative consequences fall disproportionately on the poorest members of society.

Many of the drugs used by Americans are legal and can be purchased at the neighborhood supermarket or pharmacy. It is estimated, for example, that 70 percent of males and 60 percent of females in the United States drink alcoholic beverages, although geographic differences in drinking patterns are significant (e.g., 70 percent of adults over the age of 18 in Wisconsin vs. 30 percent in West Virginia) as are gender differences, although the latter have been diminishing in recent years. One indicator of the significance of alcohol consumption is the finding that in the year 2000 there were almost 64,000 deaths in the United States attributable to dangerous drinking practices such as binge drinking (Zalin 2004). While each year 1,400 college students die from alcohol-related causes, including alcohol-involved motor vehicle crashes, the negative effects of excessive drinking tend to be disproportionately concentrated among the lower classes (Hingson et al. 2002).

The level of tobacco use, like alcohol use, has been found to be inversely related to socioeconomic status in numerous studies. As Rogers and coworkers (1995) point out, daily cigarette consumption is 14 percent higher among smokers with a high school education or less than among those with more than 17 years of education, an educational divide that tends to parallel class background. As Bobak and colleagues observe:

> Since the poorer groups in developed countries appear to smoke more than the rich, tobacco-related deaths would be expected to be more common among them than among the rich. Smoking is, therefore, a powerful mediator of the association between poverty and mortality. (2000:22)

Thus, the risk of death associated with smoking is 4 percent for wealthier people compared to 15 percent for the poor in the United States (Bobak et al 2000). Moreover, not only are the poor and those with lower levels of education less likely to attempt to quit smoking, their chances of succeeding in smoking cessation have been found to be lower than is the case with wealthier smokers (Jones 1994). Additionally, smokers from lower socioeconomic strata tend to smoke for a longer portion of their lives than do wealthier smokers, resulting in a longer period of bodily exposure to the stew of toxic substances in tobacco smoke (Siahpush et al. 2005).

Overall, it is estimated that the *combined drug toll* in lives lost to tobacco, alcohol, and illicit drugs approaches one million people a year in the United States. As documented in the pages to follow, this loss disproportionately befalls people of lower socioeconomic status.

Why do the poor smoke more and have a harder time quitting than other social classes? While various theories have been proposed to account for this disturbing pattern, there is no agreed-upon explanation. Graham (1987, 1993, 1994) proposed that for poor women tobacco consumption is a form of self-medication to regulate mood, to manage social stress, and to cope with the emotional strains of social marginalization and material deprivation. Smoking, in other words, functions as a coping mechanism for handling the daily indignities and injuries of social inequality. Significantly, the tobacco industry appears to agree with Graham's conclusion about the relationship of stress to smoking.

Young adults, for example, always an appealing market for the tobacco industry, have been found in industry-sponsored research to increase smoking levels in response to perceived increases in the level of stress in their lives. According to an industry memorandum: "For young adults who smoke, the use of cigarettes is seen as a mechanism to help ease the stress of transition from teen years to adulthood" (quoted in Ling and Glantz 2003:125). Ironically however, nonindustry research suggests that

> much of the stress that cigarettes relieve is caused by nicotine withdrawal; it is common for people who stop smoking, once they are past withdrawal, to feel less stress than they experienced while smoking ... the use of smoking for "stress relief" as supported by tobacco marketing is really self-medication for nicotine withdrawal. (Ling and Glantz 2003:125–126)

In other words, existing research supports the interpretation that people may start smoking to cope with the pressures and strains of life—forces that are persistent, pressing, and enduring among the poor—but as they become addicted to the nicotine in cigarettes they continue to smoke primarily to avoid the painful effects of nicotine withdrawal. At the same time, it bears mentioning, the "financial and health burdens of smoking coupled with social inequalities in smoking behavior suggest that smoking may exacerbate social class differences in health and standards of living" (Siahpush et al. 2005:1105).

In short, smoking, indeed all psychotropic drug use among the poor, juxtaposes immediate, short-term relief and longer-term, negative consequence. In the context of *structurally imposed distress*, what has been termed *social suffering* (Kleinman 1997; Singer 2006b), the poor seek relief. In seeking remedies for their distress, like all people in need, the poor look for what works, what is available, and what is accessible. Drugs meet all of these needs; drugs offer immediate relief, they are on hand from local distributors, and many of them are affordable even for the poor. That they also have long-term serious health, fiscal, and emotional costs does not diminish their short-term benefits.

While no one begins psychotropic drug use with the intention of developing dependence or addiction, these, and a wide array of other health problems they facilitate, are common outcomes of continued use. Once dependence (emotional attachment to a drug) or addiction (physical need for a drug) develops, however, motivation for drug use is driven as well by a powerful new factor: relief from drug craving and the pains of withdrawal. In the end, a *vicious circle of commodity-mediated causes and effects* is produced: the desire for relief from inequality and social suffering reproduces inequality and social suffering. This is but one of the many complicated issues in the often murky world of human interaction with psychoactive drugs, a relationship that has a long history and far greater impact on the conduct of human affairs through time than is usually acknowledged (Courtwright 2001, Singer 2006a). This interaction, and the use of drugs for self-medication among the poor will be examined more closely in chapter 7.

Theoretical Perspective: Critical Medical Anthropology

Unlike many other social science books that have focused on substance abuse in the United States, such as James Spradley's classic *You Owe Yourself a Drunk* or Philippe Bourgois' more recent powerful achievement, *In Search of Respect: Selling Crack in El Barrio*, this book is organized around the development and presentation of a *unified framework* for all kinds of drug use, from tobacco and alcohol to heroin and cocaine, among low-income and impoverished populations in the United States. Moreover, the book addresses both the aboveground and underground markets for mood- and mind-altering pharmaceutical drugs. This unified framework, as noted in the Preface, is derived from the theoretical orientation known as *critical medical anthropology* (CMA) (Baer et al 2003).

CMA is a scholarly and applied approach concerned especially with the political economy of health, including understanding the social origins of sickness, health-related beliefs and behaviors, and healing systems and treatment practices. While it is concerned with the impact on health of the exercise of power and social inequality, its approach is not "top down." Rather, it focuses attention on the relationships between on-the-ground (i.e., observable) health-related actions and the actors who perform them, as well as associated beliefs, attitudes, and experiences, on the one hand, and macro-level structures and forces, such as modes of production, social hierarchy, and hegemony, on the other. In other words, with reference to drug use, CMA theory orients researchers toward the manner and degree to which trends, patterns, and consequences of drug consumption are influenced by such factors as: social class and other structural relations, policies enacted and actions taken by state institutions, including court rulings, the enactment of laws, and the use of physical force through the activities of the police, national guard or other military bodies, and social effects registered by the prevailing economic system.

Thus, the framework that guides the analyses presented in this book links together all mind- and mood-altering drugs as commodities produced and distributed by what is referred to here as *licit and illicit drug capitalism*, or more simply *global drug capitalism*. Drugs become commodities when they are put into circulation or exchanged (e.g., sold). As Appadurai argues:

Economic exchange creates value. Value is embodied in commodities that are exchanged. Focusing on the things that are exchanged, rather than simply on the forms or functions of exchange, makes it possible to argue that what creates the link between exchange and value is politics, construed broadly. (1986a:3)

Given its concern with the relations between politics, or more broadly, political economy, and everyday life, a CMA approach to drugs draws attention to both the supply and demand sides of the drug equation. As Courtwright (2001:113) notes, "Casks of rum, bundles of kola nuts, bricks of opium, and kilos of cocaine are so many commodities." Specifically, all of these, as well as bales of marijuana, bottles of methamphetamine, sheets of LSD-laced paper, and jars of Ecstasy pills, are *consumable psychotropic commodities*, chemical substances that are industrially produced through a system of wage labor (although, like many agricultural products, some begin with the work of small independent farmers) and are commercially distributed (again through a system of wage labor) in a market economy, where they find their way into the hands and bodies of consumers who share relatively similar consumption motivations. In addition to paying attention to both sides of the supply and demand equation, CMA is also concerned with the material item—the commodity—that is supplied and demanded, or sold and consumed.

Drugs as Commodities

Why is it important to understand commodities? Are they not, for the most part, just "things" we buy and use? These questions reflect "the powerful contemporary tendency [which] is to regard the world of things as inert and mute" (Appadurai 1986a:4). This is not the approach taken here. Anthropologists Sidney Mintz (1985) and Eric Wolf (1982), in their respective writings, argue that the production and sale of things of value is far more than the mere economic exchange of inert objects because, while society makes commodities, the opposite is true as well.

As Alfred McCoy (1995) notes, "[s]ince the rise of the modern world economy, commodities have—in a fundamental sense—shaped the politics, culture, and social structure of peoples around the globe." Further, as Mintz (1985) argues, with general reference to the class of commodities of particular concern to this book (i.e., things we imbibe, inhale, ingest, inject and otherwise consume), the social adoption of a certain commodity can be a momentous historic event. For example sweetened hot tea, which is a stimulant, was a mainstay of the diet of the British working class, and it signaled a society's economic configuration; its culturally constituted patterns of consumption, perspective, and social relationships; and daily routines of life and the cultural definitions of pleasure. In the same way, beginning in the late 18th century, opium emerged as an essential global commodity that played a key role in expanding the intensity of commerce and social exchange between Asia and the West. The same can be said of cocaine with reference to trade and other interactions between the North and the South. As a result, drugs like opium and cocaine became deeply entangled and helped to reconfigure not only the economies but the cultures of most if not all sectors of the contemporary world. Observes McCoy (1995) with reference to opium:

> Above all, it is opium's long history as a global commodity that has given its traffic a unique and little understood dynamic. During the 18th century, when it first emerged as a commodity, opium production grew as one part of a rising long-distance trade in natural stimulants—coffee, tea, tobacco, and coca—that tied First World consumers and Third World producers together in a global commerce. As demand for opiates rose in the 19th century, opium cultivation spread across the Eurasian land mass from Yugoslavia to Manchuria. Simultaneously, the pharmaceutical manufacture of opium products developed in the world's industrial centers.

In short, psychotropic commodities have come to be deeply entrenched in the world economic system (Baer et al. 2003; Jankowiak and Bradburd 1996), in its variant regional and local expressions (Marshall 2004), and in the diverse ways of life of the far-flung peoples whose socioeconomic structures comprise the over-arching global system. People use drugs precisely because they produce experiential and bodily effects, but drugs are not physically or socially inert. They shape social life and social conception as they, in turn, are shaped by it.

Blurry Boundaries between Legal and Illegal

A key objective of this book is to analyze the corporate structures involved in legal and illegal drug production and marketing—a complex that is here termed the *dual drug industry*. This industry is bifurcated with one segment involved in aboveground drug production and distribution, such as casks of rum or cartons of cigarettes, and the other segment involved in belowground drug production and distribution, such as bricks of opium or kilos of cocaine. Rather than being elements of two different systems these industries are more closely linked and aligned than is commonly imaged. Further, both can be analyzed as integral if somewhat different components of drug capitalism and the wider capitalist economy. While the aboveground sector of the dual drug industry tends to be wrapped in a "cloak of social legitimacy," the underground sector generally suffers the "stain of illegality." Their contrasting social positions have significant consequences, such as the ability to use the police to control unruly labor forces and access to the mass media for product promotion.

Functionally, however, they are but two sides of the same coin. They have common impacts on individuals and on society: they both provide drugs to the poor, drugs that are often mixed together in various ways (e.g., cigarettes commonly are smoked by heroin users immediately following injection; diverted pharmaceutical tranquilizers and heroin are used jointly), and thereby help to maintain the existing pattern of pervasive social and health disparities among the socioeconomic classes that comprise society. Thus, while recognizing the importance of legality, it is appropriate to use the term *global drug industry* to encompass both the above- and belowground corporations involved in drug manufacture and trade.

The development and structural implications of the role drugs play in containing social unrest merit careful assessment. A starting point for this endeavor is a perusal of the borderlands between legal and illegal drugs. Contrary to official understandings that separate good drugs (medicinal substances) from bad drugs (nonmedicinal, so-called recreational substances), the border is quite blurry. Some drugs are legal in one context, but are commonly diverted for clandestine use in other settings. This happens in a variety of ways. On college campuses, for example, students with a prescription for drugs to treat attention deficit disorder may give or sell a few of their pills to friends, who, in turn, use them to stay awake during exam week or to prolong periods of celebration and "partying." In fact, a kind of folk pharmacist has emerged whose personal knowledge of drug effects puts him/her in a position to acquire and dispense pharmaceuticals to others in response to expressed emotional needs for mood alteration. In an effort to secure drugs for resale or redistribution, some people submit fraudulent prescriptions to pharmacies and others fake pain or other conditions and present themselves to several different doctors in order to receive multiple prescriptions for the same condition. Legal drugs are also stolen from medicine cabinets in people's homes, from pharmacies, from hospitals, and from pharmaceutical manufacturing companies for illicit sale and consumption.

Like heroin, cocaine, and marijuana, diverted pharmaceutical drugs also can be purchased on the street in inner-city areas from illicit drug dealers. These street drug salespeople are sought out both by people with pills to sell and by those who wish to buy prescription drugs (e.g., Xanax to mix with heroin, a popular drug combination among street drug addicts). The end result is that a sizeable amount of legal pharmaceuticals is sold illegally and is gaining an increasing share of the underground drug market. As Anne Lovell (2006:156) remarks, a legal medicine "becomes a dirty commodity" without changing content, shape, size, color, or any other physical attribute. In France, where Lovell did her research on diversion, Burprenorphine (a pharmaceutical pain killer used to treat opioid addiction), "has become a [street] drug of choice for injection" (2006:158). Users want it partly because they know that as a pharmaceutical drug it does not have adulterants, has fewer side effects, and is reliably pure, unlike nonpharmaceutical street drugs.

Legal drugs, like alcohol and tobacco, do not require a prescription and can be easily acquired in numerous locations like neighborhood liquor stores, bars, convenience shops, and corner grocery stores—outlets that are disproportionately common in poor neighborhoods. Nonetheless, local, state, or federal laws may restrict these stores' hours or days of legal sales or their range of potential customers. For example, the Synar Amendment is a federal law passed in 1992 that requires states to enact and enforce statutes banning the sale of tobacco products to minors. Research conducted by the Centers for Disease Control and Prevention (1999) along the U.S.–Mexico border several years after passage of the law found that the percentages of retail stores that illegally sold cigarettes to minors was 6 percent in Las Cruces, New Mexico, and 18 percent in El Paso, Texas. Such violations open the door to the producers of the legal products (e.g., cigarettes and beer) to market them to illegal buyers.

Another example of how certain drugs may be legal (or at least accepted by the powers that be) in one context but not in another is the use of steroids and amphetamines, "performance-enhancing drugs," an issue that has been reported in the national media and the focus of congressional hearings. Although major league baseball began testing for various drugs, including steroids, in 2002, there has been considerable resistance to addressing illicit drug use within baseball. According to retired baseball player Larry Walker:

> Steroids weren't even illegal in the game. . . . They [owners, managers and coaches] didn't say "Don't take them." Even though they were illegal in society, they weren't illegal in the game. . . . The problem is, we know why they weren't illegal, and why they didn't say not to take them. They were performance-enhancing substances, and it was good business for performances to be enhanced. Steroids were the best business move for baseball since Joe DiMaggio, or maybe Babe Ruth. (Arthur 2006:12)

Some commentators have even suggested that steroids saved baseball after the devastating strike of 1994–95 left many fans disillusioned with the game. As sports commentator Mark Spector observes:

> Somehow clubhouses full of baseball people—from players to owners and everyone in between—buried their heads. The [illicit drug-driven] home-run derbies were good business, and none chose to get to the bottom of what we know now was the genesis of the most dire predicament baseball has ever faced. (2006:1)

After major league baseball began testing for steroids, between 5 and 7 percent of players tested positive. How many were using steroids before testing was implemented remains unclear, but it is believed that steroid, amphetamine, and other illicit drug use was quite prevalent among players. Illegal use of legal drugs is another aspect of the blurry line dividing the licit from the illicit in drug consumption.

Drugs and the Emergent Global Social Order

Psychotropic substances are everywhere and, for motivated individuals, getting them is really not difficult, even in the poorest sectors of society with only the minimum of disposable cash. Why is this the case? This text explores the nature of the socioeconomic system that insures that massive quantities of psychotropic drugs are easily available, if always for a price. More precisely, it addresses the fact that while both legal and illegal drugs are used by people of all social classes, the prevalence of drug use and the consequences of drug consumption are not equally distributed but fall disproportionately on the poor.

Like other sectors of capitalism, the dual drug industry has been reshaped by processes of globalization in recent decades. *Globalization* is a complex term, but some of the critical elements of the globalization process—including the vital roles of corporations, commodities, and countries—are illuminated by the following example:

> Some models of Honda automobiles are designed in Japan and assembled in the United States with American labour and with parts manufactured in Europe, the U.S., and Japan. Is this Honda a Japanese car? In truth it is a global car coming from a Japanese company which has become a global company. (Roy 1997:48)

According to Waters, globalization involves the "creation of new economic, financial, political, cultural, and personal relationships through which societies and nations come into closer and novel types of contact with one another" (2001:8). While this definition provides a broad outline, it does not quite capture the essence of globalization. It does not, for example, explain why some commodities, and not others, including both legal and illegal drugs, have universal appeal and distribution.

As used in this book, globalization refers to transnational, capitalist economic processes, including resource extraction and trade, which override local decision making, traditional ways of life, and indigenous cultural histories and promote uniformity, impose externally devised social changes, and elevate the market and the needs of transnational corporations as the socially legitimized determinant of social values and ways of life. Some of the key features of globalization are identified by Greaves (2006:154):

> At its heart, globalization involves corporations, technology, and capital. More precisely, it is a process of rapid internationalization and integration of commercial enterprises, supported by global communication technologies, and global deployment of financial capital.

Globalization builds significant pressure for: the rationalization of productive and social processes; commodification of an ever-widening array of objects, relationships, and activities; and standardization of labor, markets, finances, consumption, governance, and transportation and communication systems. Consequently, as James Scott (1998:8) stresses, "Today, global capitalism is perhaps the most powerful force for homogenization" across nations, regions, and ways of life. Over time, the pace of globalization has sped up considerably: for the 15-year period leading up to 1995, for example, the flow of financial capital between countries never exceeded the growth of the world's gross domestic product (GDP). In the ten years since 1995, the flow of capital across national borders has tripled and is now 16 percent greater than the world GDP (Gittins 2006).

The pharmaceutical industry, which is the source of an increasing proportion of the illicit drugs sold on the street, exemplifies current patterns of globalization. As Bodenheimer explains, "A pharmaceutical company might have its corporate headquarters in the United States, [test its drugs in Uganda], produce its drugs in Ireland, assemble its capsules in Brazil, and sell the products in Bolivia" (1985:190). Adds Mehrabadi:

> Pharmaceutical/biotechnology companies cannot be pinpointed to one location as they function as any transnational corporation would; globally. As with any corporation that is transnational in scope, operations are carried out depending on where labor is cheapest, raw materials are the least expensive, where taxes can be most easily evaded, as well as where market regulations are the least strict. (2005:1)

Wherever components of the business are located, pharmaceutical companies establish corporate hierarchies. Rules, standards, norms, and styles are taught to workers formally and informally and are re-created in varying degree across countries, regions, and the cultural systems of the local peoples employed in corporate facilities. While the flow of corporate cultural elements is not unidirectional, and even in their performance of corporate roles people retain values that reflect local, regional, and national orientations, corporate culture writ large has become increasingly universal. In the metaphor of journalist Thomas Friedman (2006), changes in the pharmaceutical industry reflect a broader "flattening of the world."

Importantly, globalization has contributed not only to the development and extension of the legal drug industries but to the illegal drug industry as well. Notes Pamela Thomas (2006:5), "Globalisation has supported the expansion of the illicit drug trade making the transboundary movement of money, drugs and precursor chemicals quicker and easier and increasingly difficult for individual countries to identify and control." Globalization facilitates the illicit drug trade in multiple ways: (1) reduction in the cost of transportation; (2) unification of financial markets through the rapid electronic transfer of money; (3) creation of offshore tax havens; (4) relaxation of border controls for the movement of commodities; (5) opening of new markets for trade; and (6) improved worldwide communication systems. As a result, illicit drugs and the precursor chemicals used to produce them move quickly from point of production

to point of use, while the profits they generate flow back to illicit producers despite national and international control efforts.

One of the critical features of contemporary globalization has been a
widening gap between the rich and the poor (Bezruchka and Mercer
2004). During the modern period of globalization, the stretch of time
from the 1970s to the present, global economic disparities have widened
considerably. According to UNICEF (2004) there is a 100–fold difference
today in the per capita gross national income between the least and most
developed nations of the world. In 1960, the difference between the richest 20 percent of the world's population and the poorest 20 percent was
30 to one, by 1990 it had reached 60 to one, and by 1997 was 74 to one,
at which point the wealthiest 20 percent of the world's population was
consuming 86 percent of the world's gross domestic product and the
poorest 20 percent had access to only 1 percent (Kim and Millen 2000;
United Nations Development Program 1999). How the growing ranks of
the poor have responded to these dramatic changes, including turning to
licit and illicit drugs as a means of coping, is the focus of this volume.

Resocializing Understandings of Globalization

One shortcoming of many analyses of globalization is that they offer
a desocialized account of the processes involved, presenting them as an
almost mechanical progression driven by economic forces that transcend
human decision making, indigenous worldviews, and the existing structures of social relationship. As Vincent Navarro stresses, in contemporary globalization discourse, "Governments appear as prisoners of
international economic forces that determine what they can do. This economic determinism is imposed on the world's western, eastern, northern, and southern populations" (2002:82).

As Navarro argues, however, even global corporations "rely heavily on
the government of the country in which they are based for creating the
national and international conditions favorable to their reproduction and
expansion" (2002:90). In the case of the legal drug corporations, for example, there has been a consistent pattern of mobilizing organizational
resources to influence government policies. Legal drug companies spend
enormous amounts of money on lobbying, including campaign contributions, donations to political parties, and the financing of social activities and
travel by politicians, as well as on the less publicly visible bribes and payoffs,
all directed at specific individuals with the power to influence policy. Politics,
which is always a social process, remains a central aspect of globalization.

Philosophizing Globalization

The economic philosophy unpinning globalization, known in the literature as *neoliberalism*, asserts that everyone, rich and poor, benefits

from the unrestricted free trade of commodities and the free flow of capital around the planet. By removing structural hindrances to the movement of capital (e.g., restrictions on foreign investment, tariffs), new production occurs, new wealth is created, and money trickles down the elongated socioeconomic hierarchy from the super-rich corporate elite to working people to the poor to the super-poor. Although capital can move rapidly to take advantage of regional differences in labor costs, the availability of needed resources, or other conditions that promote production, is "sticky" (Haar 2006). Workforces are composed of real people enmeshed in social relations; they cannot relocate easily, jettisoning family ties, homes, belongings, and emotional attachments to socially meaningful places (e.g. "hometowns"). As a result, "rather than workforce mobility matching capital fluidity" (Haar 2006:D2), a global competition among labor markets unfolds, with the places that have the greatest number of disparate workers who will accept the lowest wages, fewest job benefits, and least protective regulation of working conditions attracting capital investors. The result is a general devaluation of work below the rank of middle management and a general shrinking of working-class salary levels, a process that has been going on in the United States for several decades.

Notes Haar (2006:D2), "In the United States today, working class salaries are stagnant—despite a strong economy—and the average weekly pay of nonmanagement workers is losing ground to inflation." An assessment of full- and part-time workers in the United States from 1979 to 1999 reveals approximately a 7 percent decline in wages earned. A similar decline occurred in work-related fringe benefits (e.g., health insurance, pension). The percentage of U.S. workers who receive job-related health insurance dropped from over 70 percent in 1979 to 69 percent in 1993. Each year, one million workers in the United States lose their job-related health insurance. Pension benefits provided by employers declined from 48 to 45 percent during this period (Navarro 2002). Since 1999, the slide in working-class salaries has continued. As the Economic Policy Institute's *The State of Working America*, a report on the economic status of working families in the country, shows:

> Despite the fact that the most recent economic expansion began in late 2001, the real income of the median family fell each year through 2004, the most recent available data. Between 2000 and 2004, real median family income fell by 3%, or about $1,600 in 2004 dollars. (2006:38)

In short, the old economic adage, "a rising tide raises all ships," is no longer true. Rather, the pattern has been increasing *wage polarization*. Corporate profits rose sharply during the 1990s, but wealth did not trickle down, it floated up. The average salary of U.S.-based corporate CEOs—now at approximately $12 million a year—continues to climb, while the difference in pay between the average worker and the CEO of a large corporation exceeds a ratio of 300 to one. The annual income of a three-person family living at the poverty line ($15,577) is now lower than a CEO might spend for a top-of-the-line Philippe men's gold watch ($17,600).

The source of the increased wealth of the wealthy is the corresponding decrease in the income and social benefits received by the poor and working classes. Meanwhile, the income status of the middle class has begun to slide downward as well. The income of the middle class reached a high point in 1999 after adjustment for inflation; by 2005 the median family income was over a $1,000 a year lower than this peak. This drop occurred even among households with college-educated members (Sklar 2006). As Navarro (2002:68) argues, "This transfer of income from labor to capital has been one of the explicit purposes (and consequences) of neoliberal policies, and has been responsible for the unprecedented growth in social inequalities." The end result is not just impoverization but the demoralizing impoverization of the workforce, creating a demand for relief, one that is met, in part, by the drugging of the poor.

Indigenization and Overstated Homogenization

No doubt, it is possible to significantly overstate the homogenizing or flattening effects of global capitalism and to obscure the continued importance of local particularity. Anthropologists, especially, have demonstrated that local culture, while subject to change, does not disappear, nor does its fail to impact corporate operations and markets (Friedman 2003). Efforts, for example, to use standard advertising slogans and concepts in the marketing of products cross-culturally often have failed miserably because, when translated into another language and used in foreign cultural setting, they are either meaningless, or worse, send the wrong message. For example, when Coors attempted to translate one of its slogans developed for the U.S market—"Turn It Loose"—for use with Spanish-speaking customers, the slogan was mistranslated into "Suffer from Diarrhea." Similarly, Pepsi's slogan "Come alive with the Pepsi generation," was initially translated for use in China as "Pepsi brings your ancestors back from the grave." Because homogenization is only useful to corporations if it is profitable, from the site of production to the language of marketing, globalization has meant corporations have had to adapt to local conditions.

At the same time, anthropologists have stressed that culture does not diffuse in pristine form. As cultural patterns and products—including those of corporate origin—are introduced to and adopted by new social groups a process of "indigenization" occurs (Appadurai 1996). Indigenization is the common practice of "local level adaptation of social institutions to fit a distinct sociocultural milieu" (Coreil and Mayard 2006:135). Indigenization is seen most readily on the consumption side of the drug use equation. Globalization has not displaced the significance of local processes, patterns of interpersonal relationships, and understandings. There is considerable social and geographic variation, for example, in illicit drug use style and frequency. Inner-city injection drug users in some locations, for instance, inject two and three or more times as often as do their counterparts in other locales. Similarly, illicit drug use practices, such as mixing embalming fluid, PCP, and marijuana, are much more popular in some places than in others. Likewise, while methamphetamine is used across diverse social groups, it is associated with quite different meanings and practices when consumed among patrons in gay bars, long haul truck drivers, and members of outlaw biker gangs.

In contrast to indigenization processes in local-level drug adoption and use patterns, homogenization is particularly evident on the supply side of the drug use equation. Legal and illegal drug corporations, for example, use advanced communication and shipment technologies to spread their products around the world, rely on specialized branding and targeted packaging to make their products appealing to diverse consumer populations, and mobilize considerable amounts of capital to gain access to new markets worldwide. The *processes of homogenization and indigenization* are in dynamic tension in the global drug supply and demand chain.

Globalization and Inequality

Many of the drugs that reach the poorest sectors of American society are used to self-medicate overt and hidden injuries and daily indignities of social marginalization, discrimination, and poverty. For the poor, many of the wounds of subordination (e.g., the emotional costs of work devaluation, falling wages and benefits) are produced or enhanced by globalization. What sense can be made of this frequent connection between marginalization and poverty, on the one hand, and high rates of legal and illegal drug use, on the other? The primary thesis of this book is that *drugging the poor* helps to maintain a social order that is predicated on marked social disparity. In other words, poverty and social inequality are not the unfortunate but unintended consequences of the prevailing social order, they are integral to the system; they help sustain it. As Levy and Sidel explain:

> Social injustice often occurs when those who control access to opportunities and resources block the poor, the powerless and those otherwise deprived from gaining fair and equitable access to those opportunities and resources. Social injustice enables those in the upper class to receive a disproportionate share of wealth and other resources—"the good things in life"—while others may struggle to obtain the basic necessities of life. (2006:11)

How disproportionate is the share of the "good things in life" consumed by the wealthy? As aptly described by Project Censored, an information effort designed to identify important issues that are not covered by the corporate-owned mass media:

Since the late 1970s wealth inequality, while stabilizing or increasing slightly in other industrialized nations, has increased sharply and dramatically in the United States. While it is no secret that such a trend is taking place, it is rare to see a TV news program announce that the top 1 percent of the U.S. population now owns about a third of the wealth in the country. Discussion of this trend takes place, for the most part, behind closed doors. During the short boom of the late 1990s, conservative analysts asserted that, yes, the gap between rich and poor was growing, but that incomes for the poor were still increasing over previous levels. Today most economists, regardless of their political persuasion, agree that the data over the last 25 to 30 years is unequivocal. The top 5 percent is capturing an increasingly greater portion of the pie while the bottom 95 percent is clearly losing ground, and the highly touted American middle class is fast disappearing. (2004:1)

As globalization proceeds and the middle class shrinks, the number of people in poverty, near poverty, or at extreme risk of falling into poverty grows. Between the years 2001 and 2002, for example, the number of individuals below the federally defined poverty line increased from 11.7 to 12.1 percent of the U.S. population. By 2002, almost 35 million people were "officially poor" and millions more were not doing much better, including many working people who were struggling from paycheck to paycheck to keep their heads above rising water (U.S. Census Bureau 2002; Wolff 1995). The greatest increases in poverty during this period were among African Americans and Latinos, groups that are subject as well to ethnic discrimination and social marginalization. Indeed, minority poor are subject to "multiple marginalizations" (Vigil 2002), with poor men of color often being portrayed as "beggars and thieves," poor women as "welfare queens," and poor youth as "gangbangers."

Among the poorest of the poor are the homeless. As Muntaner and Greiger-Brown (2005:287) observe, "on any given night in the United States, more than 700,000 people are homeless, of whom 20 to 25 percent are mentally ill and 50 percent have a substance abuse disorder." Moreover, between 69 and 89 percent of the homeless smoke tobacco, more than triple the rate of the general population. The rate of alcohol dependence among the homeless may be as high as 60 percent. Illicit drug dependence among the homeless is four to six times that of the general population (Gelberg and Arangua 2006). As a result, "death rates and rates of disease are all higher among the homeless population, even in comparison to poor people with homes" (Baer et al. 2003:88).

For those on the bottom of the social hierarchy, social injustice is a fundamental life determinant:

Social inequality kills. It deprives individuals and communities of a healthy start in life, increases their burden of disability and disease, and brings early death. Poverty and discrimination, inadequate medical care, and violation of human rights all act as powerful social determinants of who lives and who dies, at what age, and with what degree of suffering. (Kreiger 2005:5)

Moreover, its impacts are multiple and they affect different segments of the impoverished population in somewhat different ways (Levy and Sidel 2006):

- For children in urban slums, educationally it often means fewer teachers, crowded classrooms, inadequate supplies, watered down curricula and resulting functional illiteracy, school drop out, and limited job skills.

- For teenagers and young adults from poor families, it commonly means lack of access to valued and decent-paying jobs, as well as long periods of unemployment, diminished job expectations, and the appeal of gangs and criminality.

- For adults who manage to find employment, it means limited opportunities for advancement, undependable employment, low income, exposure to on-the-job health and safety risks, and alienation in the work environment.

- For impoverished communities, it means substandard housing, exposure to toxins and physical hazards, disruptions in residential stability, exposure to high rates of crime, inadequate access to health care, and the presence of drug trafficking and other vice.

Social injustice, in short, is not merely a product of indifference and ignorance on the part of those who benefit from it, nor is it created and maintained by the moral, attitudinal, or behavior deficits of those who suffer from it. Rather, it is an arrangement that materially benefits some while harshly punishing others. The extent, nature, and causes of inequality in America are hidden, not just by the mass media and other mainstream social institutions, but by a set of hegemonic ideas about people and their personal responsibility for individual success and failure. Many Americans believe that poor people have no one to blame but themselves because they do not work hard; they do not plan for the future; they do not value education; they have too many children; they come from bad families that do not parent properly; they suffer from some other moral, social, or personal shortcomings, including the use of drugs. The role of drugs in maintaining inequality is not often addressed in public discussion of social disparities. Doing so is a primary purpose of this book.

Studies show that the abuse of drugs is fairly widespread in American society. In fact, a USA Today/HBO nationwide poll (Rubin 2006) of adults, conducted between April 27 and May 31, 2006, found that one in five people report that they have an immediate relative who at some point in their lives had been addicted to alcohol or other drugs. That amounts to approximately 40 million American adults with a spouse, parent, sibling, or child who has suffered from addiction. This problem cuts across social classes, including both the very poor and the very wealthy. This fact does not negate the importance of social class in assessing drug use. While even very wealthy people use illicit drugs and suffer addiction, they rarely are punished in the way poor people are when they are arrested for the possession of drugs.

Drug use among the rich has little enduring impact on society as a whole or on rich people as a social class. Drug treatment, not a prison cell, is the most common social response to drug abuse among individuals from the wealthier social classes. For them, drug abuse is seen as an expression of some personal misjudgment, defect, or bad experience rather than as a demeaning class or ethnic attribute. Furthermore, they enroll in drug treatment programs that, quite literally, only money can buy, such as a 90-day stay at the Betty Ford Center, which costs $21,000. These programs fully address the significant and complex psychosocial challenges that both contribute to and are a consequence of prolonged psychotropic drug use. In contrast, the treatment programs available to the poor are inadequate, underfunded, short-term, and narrowly focused. Access to them requires long waiting lists, cultural insensitivities, and judgmental providers. Furthermore, these programs suffer from a lack of social commitment to freeing the poor from drug dependency and addiction.

Why Focus on the Poor?

While drug use occurs in all strata in American society, the effects of drug use are not equally distributed. Drug use accounts for some of the morbidity and morality of the upper social classes—with alcoholism and tobacco-related illnesses taking the greatest toll; among the poor, however, it is a significant source of sickness, suffering, and death.

The dual market drugging of the poor is driven by several factors, including the high frequency of legal drug promotion in poor neighborhoods (e.g., billboards and sponsorship of community events by the alcohol and tobacco industries); the high concentration of outlets for the sale of legal drugs (e.g., liquor stores, bars, and clubs) in these neighborhoods; the routine use of the street corners and mass housing sites of low-income communities for the retail marketing of illegal (and legal) drugs; the existence of street "hot spots" in poorer neighborhoods in which drugs and sex are sold together in the same location; the social creation through social suffering of multiple motivations for mind/mood-altering drug use among the poor and oppressed; the consequent frequent pattern of drug mixing, polydrug use, and risky drug use in impoverished sectors of the population; and the unequal access to health care for drug-related illnesses and to drug treatment faced by the poor and uninsured. All of these contribute to the disproportionate toll of drugs on the poor.

As this discussion suggests, analysis of the dual drug industry necessitates an examination of socially and economically marginalized locations, such as inner-city neighborhoods, in terms of their use by drug capitalism as sites for licit and illicit drug marketing and consumption. It is of historic note that even prior to the era of alcohol prohibition, ethnic minority and low-income neighborhoods in the United States functioned as "the place where whites [from the suburbs] practiced their vices" (James and Johnson 1996:16).

This pattern has continued into the present, with suburban drug users regularly coming into inner-city neighborhoods to buy drugs and perhaps for other illicit pleasures as well, as revealed by point of purchase arrests by local police departments (Swift et al. 2001). Red light districts, commercial sex stroll areas, illicit drug copping sites, shooting galleries, crack houses, and similar exotic and erotic locations are concentrated in poor neighborhoods. Unlike those who are forced to live in lower-income areas, those who dwell in wealthier neighborhoods have the social power to block the emergence of illicit sales and public drug use locations close to home. The youth of poor families commonly grow up in marginalized social environments in which drugs of all kinds are plentiful. As Waldorf has observed with reference to heroin, it "is seemingly everywhere in Black and Puerto Rican ghettos and young people are aware of it from an early age" (1973:28).

Moreover, the lack of decent-paying jobs in the inner city helps to provide a willing workforce for the labor-intensive street sale of drugs in economically and socially marginalized neighborhoods. For the most part, there are comparatively few other readily accessible life options open to untrained youth and young adults in these areas. For them, the American dream rarely can be found in a prestigious job, material comfort, or social recognition in mainstream society; all of these are difficult to attain when the only options available are attending deteriorating schools that fail to teach and instead produce large numbers of school drop-outs who face discriminatory practices in hiring and confront an economy that no longer requires large numbers of unskilled laborers. Writing of young adults in the Spanish Harlem area of New York City, Philippe Bourgois queries:

> Why should these young men and women take the subway to work minimum wage jobs—or even double minimum wage jobs—in downtown offices when they can usually earn more, at least in the short run, by selling drugs on the street corner in front of their apartment or school yard? (2003:4)

Unlike socially respected jobs, drugs, and the kind of dreams (and nightmares) they offer, are widely available, dangerously alluring, and easily acquirable. The widespread presence of psychotropic drugs in poor neighborhoods, as well as lower-level involvement in drug sales, insures the likelihood of extensive use of drugs by the poor.

Dual Wars: For and Against Drugs

A critical piece of the story of the dual drug industry is shaped by the fact that the United States has been deeply involved in a war on illicit drugs, their producers, distributors, and consumers for over 40 years. This war has cost untold billions of dollars but has produced little in the way of sustained success beyond making the United States the country with the highest number of people (over 2 million) and highest percentage of its national population locked in prison, including astonishingly disproportionate numbers of impoverished African Americans, Latinos, Native Americans, and other ethnic minorities. Although there are 1.6 million drug-related arrests each year in the United States, the majority are for possession of drugs rather than for drug trafficking. Prisons increasingly serve as warehouses for the poor, while creating a labor force that can be put to work for extremely low wages, including for private companies that sign production contracts with prisons, while the support costs of inmate workers (e.g., food, housing, medical treatment) are picked up by tax payers (Singer 2004a). As Wacquant (2002) observes in his biting assessment of the contemporary system of incarceration:

> In the past few decades, the explosive growth of the incarcerated population has led to rampant prison overcrowding; the rapid rise in the proportion of inmates serving long sentences, the spread of ethnically-based gangs, and a flood of young convicts and drug offenders deeply rooted in the informal economy and oppositional culture of the street, have combined to undermine the older "inmate society" depicted in the classic prison research of the postwar decades. . . . The "Big House"—with its correctional ideal of melioristic treatment and community reintegration of inmates—gave way to a race-divided and violence-ridden "warehouse" geared solely to the physical sequestering of social rejects.

In that a majority of people in prison are drug-dependent, prisons serve a pivotal role in insuring the effectiveness of drugs in controlling the poor.

While the real profits of the illicit drug industry flow to wealthy individuals and the communities they live in, the frequent arrest of low-level drug dealers and users and the various tactics used to accomplish this goal contribute appreciably to the further *immiseration and control of the poor*. Ironically, however, drugs are available in prisons, usually smuggled in by guards as a way of supplementing their paychecks; syringes, by contrast, are often less available in such settings. Multiple-person use of syringes behind prison walls, a consequence of the limited supply of contraband syringes in the hands of inmates, is a common source of HIV and other infections, further contributing to ill health among the poor.

The actual flow of illicit drugs has been largely unaffected by the War on Drugs, except for brief periods of time (producing so-called "drug droughts") or with reference to specific drugs, and often only drugs from particular points of origin. During these drought periods, drug users simply turn to other illegal or legal drugs. An increasing percentage of the drugs that are used illicitly are produced by pharmaceutical companies located in the United States or are legally imported from pharmaceutical companies based in other countries. Like the alcohol and tobacco industries, the pharmaceutical industry has used its enormous profits to resist controls on its ability to make profits, while turning a blind eye to the regular diversion of various pharmaceuticals to illicit consumption, issues addressed in chapter 5.

Lost in the flood of public pronouncements that are issued each year by the president, Drug Enforcement Agency officials, and local police departments about the War on Drugs, is the simultaneous "War *for* Drugs" being waged by the alcohol, tobacco, and pharmacy industries. "The real pushers in terms of drugs," asserts Neil Boyd, a drug policy expert at Simon Fraser University, "are American alcohol and tobacco companies." Adds Boyd:

> I see this as a bizarre economic and cultural war of sorts in which the United States is trying to get its drugs disseminated worldwide even though they are more dangerous, and at the same it is trying to block through criminal means the distribution of drugs such as cannabis. (quoted in Martin 2001:1)

Tobacco, if used as directed by the manufacturers, is guaranteed to cause illness and death, and alcohol abuse is also a major cause of sickness and death in poor communities. Thus, it is fair to label these two products as "killer commodities." Their negative health impact, especially among the poor, is enhanced because they commonly are mixed, with each other and with illicit drugs like heroin, cocaine, methamphetamine, and marijuana. The immune system damage caused by psychotropic substances—as seen in the AIDS epidemic—as well as unequal access to health care add significantly to the toxic impact of licit and illicit drug use on the health of low-income populations.

The Health Effects of Psychotropic Drugs

Drug use among the poor is a significant factor in the unequal burden of disease in U.S. society (Sturm 2002). While many of the primary causes of death among low-income groups, including heart disease and cancer, have been linked to the use of tobacco and other drugs, the true extent of the contribution of drugs to morbidity and mortality among the poor has been made abundantly clear by the AIDS epidemic. AIDS was first detected among middle-class gay men in New York City and Los Angeles, but over the last several decades, as the role of injection and noninjection drug use became increasingly dominant sources of infection, AIDS has become disproportionately a disease of the poor. Thus, in a national assessment of the socioeconomic status of people living with AIDS involving almost 3,000 participants, Diaz and coworkers (1994) found that 77 percent of the men and 90 percent of the women were unemployed. Moreover, among women, 76 percent of white and 91 percent of Black female injection drug users in the study reported an annual household income of no more than $10,000. Additionally, among injection drug users in the sample, 35 percent of white men, 64 percent of Black men, 67 percent of Puerto Rican men, 29 percent of white women, and 63 percent of Black women had not completed 12 years of school.

Furthermore, AIDS is not the only drug-related issue of concern in assessing the health of the poor (Singer 2006a). Others include: (1) exposure to various infectious diseases besides AIDS, such as hepatitis C and soft tissue infection; (2) drug overdose, a common cause of death among drug users, which in recent years has become an even greater threat than HIV/AIDS; (3) brain damage as well as other mental and emotional health problems, including drug-related exacerbation of comorbid mental health disorders and posttraumatic stress; (4) damage to other organs of the body, such as the lungs and liver as a result of drug-related cancers and cirrhosis; (5) violence victimization through emotional abuse and outright assault; (6) exposure to harsh weather, especially hypothermia during winter; (7) burns and smoke inhalation as a result of the use of highly flammable liquids in the manufacture or consumption of drugs, but also accidentally starting and getting caught in building fires during drug use; (8) body trauma from drug-related vehicular and nonvehicular accidents, including as a pedestrian, as well as falls, cuts or other body trauma; (9) poisoning, from either drugs themselves or the adulterants used in preparing them for sale at higher profit; and (10) destruction of emotionally and physically supportive social relationships that allow people to cope with life's burdens and lower their risk of illness or ameliorate its outcome.

A significant feature of drug-related health problems among the poor is the pervasive tendency of multiple diseases to concentrate in poor populations, leading to various interactions among copresent threats to health, a phenomenon known as a *syndemic* (Singer and Clair 2003; Singer et al. 2006a). Disease concentration among the poor reflects their greater vulnerability due to multiple challenges to their basic health status, including inadequate nutrition, especially during the early years of life; high levels of stress due to overcrowding, living in unstable and threatening physical and social environments, stigmatization, and the internalization of social opprobrium, exposure to environmental toxins like lead in house paint, parasites such as cockroaches, and vermin like rats and mice, as well as inadequate preventive care and treatment. As a result, poor populations can become reservoirs of disease, with multiple life-threatening pathogens co-infecting the same individuals. For example, research among women prisoners found that those who reported HIV infection also tended to report with syphilis and genital herpes (Altice et al. 2005). Similarly, in a study of almost a thousand not-in-treatment injection drug users in Connecticut and Massachusetts, researchers found high rates of a range of major diseases, including HIV (25%), hepatitis B (23%), hepatitis C (32%), other sexually transmitted diseases (23%), and tuberculosis (8%) (Singer 2006b).

Under such conditions of multiple infections, diseases can interact through a variety of mechanisms, including gene assortment, immune system damage caused by a pathogen that allows opportunistic infection by another pathogenic species, chemical changes in the body caused by one disease that facilitates the spread of another disease, formation of lesions by one infection that promote the transmission of other infections, and other bodily damage caused by an infection or other health problem (e.g., a drop in blood platelets) that contributes to the spread of a second disease. Under such conditions, the overall burden of disease in a population and the toll it takes can rapidly increase. For example, infection with a sexually transmitted disease like gonorrhea has been found to increase a person's susceptibility for acquiring and transmitting HIV by two to five times (Nusbaum et al. 2004). Similarly, co-infection with HIV and Mycobacterium tuberculosis (MTb) increases the immunopathology of the human immunodeficiency virus, thereby accelerating the life-threatening progression of HIV disease (Ho 1996).

Several drug-related syndemics have been described among the poor; one has been termed "SAVA," and involves interactions between substance abuse, AIDS, and interpersonal and community violence (Romero-Daza et al. 2003; Singer 1996; Singer 2006c). In a SAVA syndemic, violence victimization, such as domestic and interpersonal violence, promotes involvement in risky behaviors, including drug use, which, in turn, increase the likelihood of HIV infection. Drug use, as well, can weaken the immune system, further facilitating the spread of disease. The end result is rapidly worsening health in a population. A second drug-related syndemic has been described by Marshall (2005:376): "In this syndemic, tobacco smoking interacts with obesity (brought on in part by a . . . diet high in fats, sugars, and salt), with binge beer drinking (which may also contribute to weight gain . . .), with less physical exercise . . . , and with heightened stress (instigated by crowded, noisy, and often unsanitary urban living conditions)." The consequence is high levels of morbidity and mortality from cardiovascular disease and stroke, cancer, and chronic respiratory diseases.

In short, rather than being separate and independent factors, poverty, poor neighborhoods, prisons, disease, and drugs constitute an intertwined complex. This book seeks to understand this complex by assessing it relationship to the global drug industry, and more broadly, to the encompassing capitalist world system.

CHAPTER 2

The Nature of Licit and Illicit Drug Capitalism

One Economy, Two Sectors

Psychotropic Complexities

The term *drug* is loaded with diverse meanings. As Courtwright (2001:2) observes, despite "all its baggage, the word has one great virtue, it is short. Indeed, one of the reasons its use persisted . . . was that headline writers needed something pithier than 'narcotic drug.'" Like many enduring terms, it has undergone various definitional changes over time. During the 19th century, it was primarily used to refer to medicines, and those who sold them were called druggists. Early in the 20th century, when some drugs began to be outlawed, the term drug came to be used frequently to label illicit substances, at which point druggists switched their name to pharmacists. Legal substances like tobacco, alcohol, coffee, and tea have tended not to be called drugs in everyday usage, although medicines still retain this tag. The implication of this labeling pattern was that the legal status of substances like tobacco and alcohol, and the resulting public use and acceptability, largely freed them of connection to illicit substances that had similar effects. This turn of events is ironic in light of the fact that drugs like cocaine, heroin, and marijuana were once legal, widely used across various social strata, and readily available at a range of outlets from druggists to newspaper offices, while alcohol was at one time the object of intense public derision and was temporarily banned by a constitutional amendment.

As mentioned in chapter 1, the social entities that produce different kinds of drugs also have come to wear differentiating labels in public discourse. Corporations produce legal drugs like Coors beer or Camel cigarettes. Cartels and "criminal enterprises" produce heroin, cocaine, and an array of other "scheduled drugs" (i.e., the Drug Enforcement Administration's schedule of substances that may or may not have medicinal value but are outlawed for nonmedical use).

Following from this division of drugs, individuals who use only tobacco or alcohol, to say nothing of caffeinated drinks, generally are fully embraced as citizens in good standing. At one time people with a dependence on alcohol could be arrested and incarcerated for public inebriation. Over time, however, alcoholism (which is almost never referred to as drug addiction) has won a degree of social acceptance as a genuine "illness" rather than as a punishable legal offense.

Tobacco use has lost a significant degree of social acceptance in recent years, and smoking is increasingly restricted in indoor and sometimes even outdoor public spaces, although the tobacco industry has vigorously fought these restrictions. Moreover, as the American Heart Association (2005) points out, a number of

> public officials like former Health and Human Services Secretary Louis Sullivan have . . . become outspoken on the tobacco issue. Sullivan characterized tobacco revenue as "blood money" and referred to sellers of cigarettes as "merchants of death." Interviewed during the 1992 Republican National Convention, Sullivan acknowledged that tobacco companies were among the convention sponsors. Sullivan also made specific reference to the strong presence of Philip Morris, whose senior vice president, Craig Fuller, was also the manager of the Republican Convention. "It's clear that they and the other tobacco companies are taking every opportunity to try to buy respectability."

Notably, as this case also makes clear, tobacco companies can participate in the public sponsorship of national political conventions and help to manage convention affairs, to say nothing of making large legal contributions to numerous political campaigns (e.g., just over $9 million in 2002, with 21 percent going to Democratic candidates and 79 percent to Republican candidates), clear indications that a fair degree of respectability is still maintained by Big Tobacco (Center for Responsive Politics 2005).

Among the illicit drugs, marijuana is the most commonly used and seen as the least threatening by several sectors of society, and many of its users are now well integrated into the mainstream. Some users, in fact, are involved in public campaigns for its legalization. Except where marijuana has been approved for medicinal use or where possession of small quantities is no longer targeted for legal action, sale, possession, and consumption are punishable in most places in the United States. Criminal justice efforts to interrupt marijuana production within the country's borders, interdict smuggling, and block sales of the drug remain strong and result in numerous arrests (Campbell 2002).

Other emergent drugs (some of which are not, at least initially, illegal) or drugs that have narrow appeal to particular subgroups in society and seem unlikely to gain wide appeal, have more ambiguous statuses. Many of the so-called club drugs (like Ecstasy), for example, have gained acceptance in certain contexts, including university campuses. Most club drugs have been scheduled by the DEA and have been the target of prevention campaigns by the National Institute on Drug Abuse and other entities. A number of widely sold pharmaceutical drugs, especially pain-killers and tranquilizers, also have complex statuses, because if medically prescribed their use is socially accepted, while nonmedical use, although widespread, is condemned, illegal, and punishable by the criminal justice system. In the case of other drugs, like steroids, use may be widespread in certain highly paid and socially valued professions, and their users may escape arrest and punishment.

Users of other illicit drugs, like heroin, cocaine, and methamphetamine, and especially those who sell these same socially demonized drugs, are subject to the highest levels of opprobrium and punishment, even though some of these drugs undergo waves of acceptance among sectors of mainstream society (e.g., the upper- and middle-class cocaine-use wave of the 1980s and the subsequent appearance of "heroin chic" clothing lines on Paris runways). For the most part, however, the media, government pronouncements, and the communications of other institutions regularly portray this group of illicit drugs as threatening to the social order; highly dangerous; entwined with various other criminal activities; linked to demonic forces, such as terrorism; and as being corruptors of vulnerable youth.

Discourse on Drugs

Flowing from the critical medical anthropological perspective, a purpose of this chapter is to shift the discussion of drugs beyond the dominant voice found in the official discourse. This is not easily done as the official discourse is ubiquitous and it is empowered; it is the voice of convention, the voice of authority, the voice of the law. It is reproduced across central social institutions from schools to places of employment and from sermons given in houses of worship to presidential speeches broadcast on television. It shapes the language we speak and the categories we learn and use to think about the world. It is, quite simply, embedded in our culture. As Geertz (1973) said of religion, the official discourse clothes certain conceptions with such an aura of factuality that they are experienced as physical reality. In the case of drugs, official discourse reflects a law enforcement perspective based on a "good guy/bad guy" imagery. Itty Abraham and William Van Schendel (2005:9) comment that in the official drug discourse:

> Many key words are reserved for the bad guys and their organizations—syndicates, cartels, gangs, triads, secret societies, mafias . . . and they all denote their special and separate status of being unauthorized, clandestine, underground. Such language constructs conceptual barriers between illicit bad-guy activities (trafficking, smuggling) and state-authorized good-guy activities (trade . . .) that obscure how these are often part of a single spectrum.

Going beyond official discourse means going beyond "the stultifying assumption that states always uphold the law" (Heyman and Smart 1999:1) or that laws are passed primarily to protect the public good

(Castro and Singer 2004). The related questions of why some drugs are legal and others illegal, or legal at one point in time but not at another, are important ones; the answers lie in an examination of complex social forces, ethnic prejudices, vested interests, and historic events and involve an assessment of how particular drugs come to be embroiled in tensions across gender, ethnic, and class boundaries. A full assessment of this sort is beyond the scope of this book, but it has been presented elsewhere (Musto 1987; Singer 2006a).

The dominant perspective on drugs emerged early in the 20th century when certain substances began to be banned, a process that was not easily accomplished, required multiple societal changes of diverse sort, and was fiercely resisted. Over time, however, the division came to seem natural and even traditional in the popular imagination, resulting in some drugs no longer even being called drugs in public discourse. Others became demon drugs, grave threats to social order, a means for those in power to "cultivate drug menaces as classic sociological 'moral panics' to divert attention from root causes in urban unrest" such as poverty and inequality (Gootenberg 2005:112).

Only in the later part of the 20th century did efforts begin to conceptually reconnect legal and illegal psychotropic substances under the common label of "drugs." This process was coincident with some loss in the public acceptability of both tobacco and alcohol, as seen in several historic court rulings against the tobacco industry, the imposition of restrictions on advertising for both the alcohol and tobacco industries, the legislation of mandatory warning labels on alcohol and tobacco products, the emergence of ever-widening legal limits on acceptable smoking contexts, and the development of grassroots community challenges to unfettered advertisement and promotion by the alcohol and tobacco industries. Nonetheless, it cannot be said that we have fully linked all psychotropic drugs together in popular understanding as representing a distinct and unified class of consumable substances that produce a specific set of experiential and/or physical effects.

The continued legal status of some drugs and the ongoing illegal position of others still cast them in very different lights in terms of how they are seen in society, the everyday experience of their use, and the nature of social control efforts directed at their production, distribution, and consumption. Packs of cigarettes may be required to carry warning labels about the role of tobacco in causing illness and death, but the War on Drugs is not being waged against Philip Morris. There are restrictions on the electronic advertising of alcohol products, but no public efforts have been launched by national officials to link the California wine industry to terrorism. Pharmaceutical companies, although the source of a significant proportion of drugs that are used illicitly, have not had their stocks banished from Wall Street, nor have their well-heeled boards of directors been placed behind prison bars.

Drug Economics

Similar differentiation into two camps—the formal sector and the informal sector—is found in the economics of drugs and other commodities. The formal sector refers to the official, socially legitimized and legal world of businesses and corporations, characterized by public accountability, payment of taxes, and government regulation. The formal sector of the economy, in fact, commonly is taken to be the whole of the economy. The informal sector, which is partially hidden and to varying degrees stigmatized, generates economic activity outside of the formal sector. If acknowledged at all, it is seen in some fashion as tainted, corrupt, and threatening to legitimate business enterprise and is often subject to severe restriction or punishment.

The earliest conception of the informal sector of the economy was developed by the United Nation's International Labor Organization (ILO) in 1972. The ILO defined economic informality as a

> way of doing things characterized by (1) ease of entry; (2) reliance on indigenous resources; (3) family ownership; (4) small-scale operations; (5) labor intensive and adaptive technology; (6) skills acquired outside of the formal sector; (7) unregulated and competitive markets. (World Bank 2005)

Since that time, a considerable literature and many alternative definitions of the informal sector have appeared. In 1999, the ILO refined its definition to cover three broad groups of informal sector actors: (1) owner-employers of small enterprises that employ only a few paid workers at most; (2) own-account workers who possess and operate one-person businesses, although they may have help from unpaid workers, commonly family members or apprentices; and (3) dependent workers who are either paid or unpaid, such as wage workers in micro enterprises, unpaid family workers, apprentices, contract labor, home workers, and paid domestic workers. Largely lost from this redefinition, which was driven by an effort to acknowledge the importance of the informal sector in the economies of most developing countries, were the larger-scale producers, transporters, and distributors of illicit goods like outlawed drugs.

In assessing the informal sector, economists have seen it as reflecting two economic strategies. The first involves survival activities among those who are denied access to employment in the formal sector, including taking temporary jobs or holding multiple part-time jobs; not included here, although it should be, is taking a low-paying job in the illicit drug industry. The second set of informal strategies involves unofficial earnings such as under-the-table payment for labor. These unofficial business practices commonly are conducted in violation of governmental regulation and taxation and hence are defined as criminal business activities. Importantly, however, close examination of the borderland between the formal and informal sectors of the economy reveal that definitively demarcating where the formal economy ends and the informal one begins can be difficult.

> Operationalizing the concept of informality for the purpose of measurement is not easy both because . . . [subcategories] of the informal sector overlap and because the border between the informal and the formal sector is blurry, . . . [Indeed] some formal market jobs or enterprises can be classified as informal if it is found that they have poor work protection or if the lifestyle and opportunities they entail are considered undesirable. [At the same time] if [a] street trader . . . registers her enterprise, the enterprise and the trader herself could be categorized as belonging to the formal sector if the profit is considered above the survival level. (World Bank 2005)

While it is recognized that there are "bad apples" in the formal economy, such as the Enrons of the world, significant involvement in criminal activity is said to be the exception not the rule in the formal economy. Instead, the top echelons of corporations in the formal sector produce candidates for the highest offices in the land. They are regarded as leaders and on this basis are selected to head charitable foundations; are made the trustees of universities; and constitute a pool of individuals who can be appointed to prestigious government positions, such as ambassadorships. Corporations in the formal sector, including those in the legal drug trade, are allowed to buy and rename public sports and entertainment facilities after themselves, are publicly honored for their generosity, are permitted to buy enormous blocks of time for advertising their products and themselves in the mass media, are sought out for partnerships by government bodies, and are otherwise accorded social praise, honor, and legitimacy. The tobacco industry even has successfully convinced "the courts, including the Supreme Court, that advertising of a product that causes addiction, disease and death is legal and protected by the First Amendment" (Kroop 2001) as "commercial speech."

The informal sector, by contrast, is the target of derision, mockery, condemnation, and often intensive law enforcement. Corporations involved in the illicit drug trade are condemned, vilified, and subject to declarations of "war." It is difficult to get a clear picture of what goes on in this sector because of what Gootenberg (2005:115) aptly labels "the cloud of passionate official rhetoric" that defines acceptable public discussion of illicit drugs. Nations, including most notably the United States, he emphasizes, "mystify drugs in order to fight them" (115–116). Mystification is needed in the War on Drugs because the differences between legal and illegal drugs, and the legal and illegal corporations that produce and distribute them, are too tenuous for straight talk, open debate, and the consideration of real social alternatives. Moreover, while the War on Drugs may not be winnable—indeed after 40 years it's still being waged—it serves other purposes that are, in the end, its real mission.

Social Legitimation

Why are such sharp differentiations made between legal and illegal drugs and the socioeconomic entities behind them? Is it because illegal drugs are far more harmful to individuals and society than legal ones? Is it because criminality is the inherent orientation of the producers of some drugs but not others? Is involvement in violence and corruption the feature that differentiates the illegal and legal drug industries? Is it because legal drug corporations accept that they have a public responsibility and hence engage in charitable and philanthropic programs, while the illicit drug cartels seek only to reap great profit at whatever cost to society?

As suggested in chapter 1, it is the argument of this book that all of these questions must be answered in the negative. First, while both legal and illegal drugs damage public health, the total accumulative harm caused by illegal drugs pales by comparison with that wrought by legal psychotropics. Second, engagement in criminal activity is not unique to the informal sector; illegality and corruption are quite common, indeed routine, in formal sector corporations. Still, because of the criminalization of some drugs, differences certainly do exist in the behaviors of corporations within the two sectors of drug capitalism, and these will be explored on subsequent pages. Third, like criminal activity, involvement in violence is not the distinguishing characteristic of the two halves of the dual drug industry, because violence is not peculiar to the informal economy. Although the illegal drug trade has a deserved reputation for being violent, this does not mean that legal corporations shun violence when it serves company interests. Finally, philanthropy can be found in both sectors of the dual drug industry, and it is generally driven by the same motivation: influencing public opinion. Again, however, because of legal restrictions, differences in public giving exist between the legal and illegal drug corporations.

It is the conclusion of CMA that the primary divide in the two sectors of drug capitalism is *social legitimation*. Despite their shared involvement in illegal activities, corruption, and violence, and their common efforts in philanthropy, legal drug companies are seen as socially acceptable (with the exception of the limited loss of face by the tobacco industry), while illegal companies are seen as a grave public threat.

White-Collar Crime

Like their illicit counterparts, legal corporations in and out of the drug industry routinely engage in a wide variety of illegal activities. This genre of criminality is known as white-collar crime. While the extent of white-collar criminal behavior has become somewhat more visible in recent years, its occurrence is hardly a recent development. In his classic book on this topic, called *White-Collar Crime*, originally given as a talk before the American Sociological Association in 1939, Edwin Sutherland (1985:210) asserted that the criminality of corporations was routine, "like that of professional thieves." Based on a study of 70 of the largest corporations in the United States at the time, he found that in the previous 20 years they had been convicted of an average of ten criminal violations each, suggesting that the total sum of corporate crime (which would include crimes that were never detected or were never prosecuted) was far greater.

The amount and damaging effects of corporate crime have reached new heights because laws and controls that once restricted the activities of corporations have been lifted by the government. The rationale for this deregulation is increased productivity and expanded employment activities. Moreover, the message was conveyed from the White House and Congress that corporations could be trusted to police themselves. Their lack of success in doing so long was hidden by the fact that lack of enforcement of the law "is common in such areas as price fixing, restraint of trade, tax evasion, environmental and consumer protection, child labor and minimum wages" (Parenti 1980:123). When corporate crimes do reach the front pages of local newspapers or headline the evening television news, individual corporate actors may be targeted for some degree of public opprobrium and possibly criminal prosecution; but not always, not usually.

In one of the largest scandals in the insurance industry, for example, the American International Group, Inc. (AIG) was alleged to have used various accounting tricks, such as fraudulent reinsurance contracts, to understate liabilities from claims and to hide losses. While no one was charged or arrested, AIG agreed to pay the government more than $1 billion to resolve the allegations (Westbrook 2006). AIG lost no stature as a criminal organization; business continued as usual. At about the same time, Prudential Financial, one of the largest U.S. life insurers, admitted that one of its units, called Prudential Securities, engaged in a scheme during 1999–2003 to defraud mutual funds and their shareholders of hundreds of millions of dollars. In the words of Deputy Attorney-General Paul McNulty, "Investors were dealt a bad hand by corporate conmen who stacked the deck against them" (Kirchgaessner 2006:39). Prudential Financial agreed to pay fines totaling $600 million, which the company had on hand in anticipation of the penalties the government would impose. On the stock market, the settlement—the largest so far in what has come to light as elaborate scandal across the industry—and all that it implied about the way business was done at Prudential, did not hurt the company; on the contrary, in financial circles it lifted a cloud of uncertainty and made company shares an appealing investment once more.

Even when corporate criminals are brought to court and found guilty, the penalties tend to be comparatively light relative to corporate budgets.

In fact, a low-level drug dealer is likely to serve more time than someone convicted of millions of dollars in securities fraud, illegal kickbacks, bribery, or embezzlement. In his book *Justice Denied*, Leonard Downie (1971) reports a classic case of a judge who on the same day imposed a small fine on a white stockbroker convicted of pocketing $20 million through illegal stock manipulations while sentencing an unemployed Black man to a year in prison for stealing a television set worth about $100 from a trucking company. Moreover, as the insurance company examples cited above suggest, the public critique of indicted corporate criminals is never accompanied by the fervor used to condemn illicit drug corporations, their leaders, or even their low-level functionaries and customers as notorious public enemies, evil threats to society, and immoral scoundrels who are beyond redemption. As journalist, television producer, and former drug addict Maia Szalavitz (1996) has written about drug prevention ads developed by the federal Partnership for a Drug-Free America (PDFA),

> In most of the . . . ads, addicts come across as stupid, shameful losers. One print ad has the subject saying, "I saw a dog and thought, if I was a dog, I wouldn't have a heroin habit. I wish I was a dog. . . . Several years ago, I was a part of a panel of ex-addicts asked to address the PDFA about better ways to reach those who use, but are not yet addicted. Each of us emphasized that addicts need hope and that we took drugs not just for pleasure, but because we were in pain. Many felt that the Partnership's previous ads demonized and demeaned us. . . . In fact, the PDFA considers stigmatizing addicts a big part of its mission. The studies included in its press packet show that what they saw as increased negative feelings towards drug users was a positive effect of their efforts.

Good Corporate Citizens. Those who focus on corporate crime are often startled by the ease with which major corporations are able to avoid loss of stature, privilege, or legitimacy when they are convicted of criminal activity. Russell Mokhiber (2005), a journalist who publishes the Corporate Crime Reporter, an informational website and weekly newsletter that identifies top corporate criminals, reports that "nine out the 30 companies that comprise the Dow Jones Industrial Index are convicted corporate criminals." Companies listed on the Dow Jones are considered highly successful and are generally depicted as "good corporate citizens," an appellation that would never be applied to illicit drug corporations. The public is often unaware of the extent of corporate crime among leading companies because the mass media traditionally have downplayed this issue and the government has tended to punish such behavior with negotiated fines that companies can easily pay with corporate profits. In this way, corporate crime is cleansed of defamation or enduring taint.

As a case in point, in 2005 the pharmaceutical company Eli Lilly agreed to plead guilty to a single misdemeanor count and to pay a fine of $36 million for its violation of the Food, Drug and Cosmetic Act in its promotional campaign for the anti-osteoporosis drug Evista (Corporate

Crime Reporter 2005). According to this law, a company must specify the medical purpose(s) of a new drug in its application for marketing approval to the FDA. Once a drug is approved by the FDA, it legally can only be marketed for the use(s) specified in the application. Promotion for what is called "off-label" uses is outlawed. In the case of Evista, Lilly was disappointed with sales during the first year after the drug was released in the market; it brought in only about a fourth of the projected annual sales of $400 million. To make up for the loss in expected income, Lilly decided to widen the market for their drug by promoting it for several unapproved uses.

Although application by Lilly to the FDA to include these new uses was rejected, the company began pushing use of the drug in the prevention of breast cancer and cardiovascular disease. The consequences of such an action are not trivial in that doctors, assuming that the drug is effective in cancer and heart disease prevention, may prescribe it instead of drugs that have proven in clinical trials to have value in these areas. In its expanded promotion efforts, Lilly used a variety of strategies, including training sales representatives how to get physicians to ask about other uses of Evista; sending unsolicited medical letters to physicians promoting unapproved uses of the drug; distributing an "Evista Best Practices" videotape that states "Evista truly is the best drug for the prevention of all these diseases," referring to osteoporosis, breast cancer, and cardiovascular disease; and distributing a medical reprint highlighting findings about the various benefits of Evista that was written by company employees and paid consultants while hiding a line in the reprint that acknowledged that the effectiveness of the drug in reducing cancer risk or cardiovascular disease had not been established.

Courting Favor.   Notably, the courts aid in the cover-up of corporate crime and the glare of adverse publicity its exposure could create by sometimes supersealing criminal cases brought against corporations. In September 2003, for example, Essex County, New Jersey, Superior Court Judge Theodore Winard sealed a court decision that blocked news organizations from having access to documents and proceedings in a fraud suit brought by several former employees against a major insurance company. The judge even ordered the media lawyers not to show his opinion to their clients (Gottlieb 2003). The impression created by such protection is that corporations have a right to be shielded from public awareness of their criminal activities. Corporate reputations, in short, are given priority over public awareness. At the same time, such behavior implies that the public is not harmed by corporate crime, a notion that is highly questionable. In fact, corporate crime is probably a major source of lost income for the average citizen, a primary force damaging the environment and people's quality of life, a threat to workers' health and health benefits, and a significant reason dangerous commodities reach the market. As Mokhiber (2005) argues, even repeat corporate offenders rarely are subjected to extensive criticism.

> Few Americans realize that when they buy Exxon stock, or when they fill up at an Exxon gas station, they are in fact supporting a criminal recidivist corporation. And few Americans realize that when they take a ride on a cruise ship owned by Royal Caribbean Cruise Lines, they are riding on a ship owned by a criminal recidivist corporation. Six corporations that made the list of the Top 100 Corporate Criminals were criminal recidivist companies during the 1990s. In addition to Exxon and Royal Caribbean, Rockwell International, Warner-Lambert, Teledyne, and United Technologies each pled guilty to more than one crime during the 1990s.

The Bad Apple.   Enron, no doubt the poster child of contemporary criminal corporations, prior to its implosion in 2001 had been named "America's Most Innovative Company" for six consecutive years by *Fortune* magazine. Moreover, the company was so entwined with government leaders, through campaign donations and personal relations, that "Attorney General John Ashcroft and virtually the entire legal staff of the United States attorney's office in Houston [were] disqualified from the Enron criminal investigation" (Johnston 2002:C7). Ashcroft, for example, had received substantial donations from Enron and its executives for his failed campaign to be elected to the U.S. Senate in 2000. Additionally, as Jeffrey Reiman and Paul Leighton (2003a) suggest, the Justice Department at the time that Enron's crimes began making media headlines did not focus on the case because it had "other priorities," such as Operation Pipedream, an investigation that eventually led to the roundup of about 50 people for conspiring to sell drug paraphernalia over the Internet. In announcing these indictments, Ashcroft personally condemned those involved for using the Internet, which he stressed meant that they had access to private homes and families around the country. The impact of large-scale corporate crime on families is rarely a topic of public discussion, however.

In the case of Enron, the Powers Committee, which was composed of Enron board members, concluded that high-level Enron executives had a history of hiding Enron's considerable losses and liabilities, while personally earning tens of millions of dollars in fees. Specifically, the committee found "a systematic and pervasive attempt by Enron's Management to misrepresent the Company's financial condition" and that the Enron executives involved received "tens of millions of dollars they should never have received" (Reiman and Leighton 2003b:248). Included in Enron's list of criminal behavior was: (1) the intentional manipulation of California power crisis for financial gain; (2) entering into financial transactions despite clear-cut conflicts of interest; (3) engaging in fraudulent transactions; and (4) attempting to punish those who questioned the appropriateness of the company's business transactions and practices. As the company's failures, which led eventually to bankruptcy, began to mount, Enron executives sold off over $1 billion worth of their Enron stock. As they were doing so, Enron's leaders consistently urged employees to buy company stock while blocking them from selling any of their Enron shares on the grounds that "administrative changes" were being made to the company's employee stock plan. During this period, when Enron stock was losing 28 percent of its value, the CEO, Ken Lay, received $19 million in cash advances from the company on the basis of his alleged stellar performance.

With Enron's demise, thousands of its employees lost their jobs, their life savings, the college funds for their children, and their pensions. The fallout from Enron's "life of corporate crime" is far broader and includes grievous damage to many communities that invested in the company, loss to holders of Enron's "blue chip" (i.e., highly valued) stock, and the devastation of many other companies that were financially involved with Enron (Eichenwald 2005). Enron was but the tip of corporate criminality exposed in recent years; other major corporate criminals have included WorldCom, Tyco, Equities Funding Corporation, Global Crossing, among many others. Following in their dark shadow have been a series of exposures of involvement by many companies in insider trading, pension fund crimes, consumer frauds, price fixing, bribery, environmental crimes, securities fraud, and other significant corporate violations of the law. These cases are jarring, precisely because they contradict established conceptions about corporations as social models of efficiency, legality, and productivity. For example, opinion polls commonly list accounting as one of the most honest and respected professions, and yet accounting fraud is usually at the core of corporate crime, as was certainly the case with Enron (Salinger 2004).

Get Out of Jail Free.   In 2000, two workers (who were later joined by five others) at the General Electric plant in Madisonville, Kentucky, filed a lawsuit against their employer claiming the company sold defective turbine parts to the government. The parts were assembled into jet engines in U.S. military jets, helicopters, and ships or sold as spare parts to the military. In their suit, the workers claim that General Electric was well aware of the fact that the blades in the turbines were defective but covered this up and sold them to the government. Denying any fault, General Electric settled with the workers for $11.5 million (Associated Press 2006b). The government took no legal action against General Electric or against any decision makers in the company who approved the fraudulent and potentially highly dangerous action by the company. General Electric suffered no loss of reputation, the story received minimal news coverage, and the company continued to do billions of dollars of business with the government.

About the same time that General Electric was settling with its whistle-blowing employees in Kentucky, another group of whistle-blowers exposed a fraudulent effort by two former Pentagon officials, acting Secretary of the Navy Hansford Johnson and acting Navy Undersecretary Douglas Combs, to contract with a company that had been suspended for two years from receiving government contracts because of having a history of submitting millions of dollars in fake invoices. The company involved in this case is known as Custer Battles LLC, after its founders Scott Custer and Mike Battles, army veterans with strong Washington connections.

The company, whose motto is "turning risk into opportunity," previously lost a civil suit filed under the False Claims Act for $10 million brought by a former employee who contended that Custer Battles created phony offshore companies that charged the Provisional Authority—the entity that ran Iraq after the U.S. invasion in 2003—at least $50 million for imaginary services. This led to the two-year ban on Custer Battles receiving new government contracts beginning in 2004. The company is also under investigation because on two known occasions its security guards in Iraq opened fire on Iraqi civilians and soldiers.

To get around the ban and hide its involvement in swindling the government, Custer Battles created several new entities, including Emergent Business Services and Tar Heel Training, both headed by Rob Roy Trumble, a former operating officer at Custer Battles. Offices for both "companies" were located in the Rhode Island headquarters of Custer Battles. These two front organizations continued to earn millions of dollars doing contracting work (e.g., arranging travel and administering benefits) in Iraq despite the ban (Hastings 2006). Custer Battles also worked closely with Windmill International Ltd., a contracting firm set up by former Navy officials Johnson and Combs, individuals with a history of working closely with contractors in Iraq. The business address of Windmill is the home of Combs, its president. It is also the official address of Windmill director Michael Ussery, a former State Department official and former U.S. ambassador to Morocco, suggesting that the company exists only on paper and was set up to provide a front for Custer Battles. Again whistle-blowers filed suit against the company under the False Claims Act, which could result in another monetary settlement but, because it is a civil suit, will not lead to prison time for any of the conspirators. Custer Battles has countersued the whistle-blowers—who are affiliated with another "war for hire" company—claiming they, not Custer Battles, defrauded the government.

From the perspective of corporations, settlement of such lawsuits are just part of the cost of doing (fraudulent) business. Having connections in high places and a willingness to engage in "unethical competitive practices" appear to be valued strategies for success in global capitalism.

The Price of Influence.   One of the common crimes of illegal drug corporations is bribery; payoffs occur up and down the line from border guards to country presidents, from the cop on the beat to prison officials. Without doubt, bribery is the fiscal lubrication of the unceasing flow of illicit substances. Bribery is far from unknown among legal corporations as well. In the world of contract bidding, for example (for lucrative contracts by private corporations), it appears to be all but customary. The Center for Corporate Policy (2005), for example, reports that mammoth multinational corporations like Xerox, IBM, and Monsanto have been involved in major bribery cases in recent years. Additionally, unlike illegal corporations, mainstream companies can hire well-connected lobbyists to "grease the wheels" in their favor. Exemplary, is the case of former Attorney General John Ashcroft.

Shortly after leaving government, Ashcroft landed a number of sizeable lobbying contracts from companies seeking to sell homeland securities technology and software to the government, including in some cases sales that could come in under the fast-paced noncompetitive bidding system Ashcroft himself created while heading the government's homeland security initiative. Companies such as Oracle Corp., one of the world's largest software companies, ChoicePoint, a company that sells credit reports to federal agencies, and LTU Technologies, Inc., a maker of technology for the analysis of video, all hired Ashcroft not long after he left the government to help them get lucrative homeland security contracts. Ashcroft's actions are not technically illegal, although they might be considered inappropriate. As Charles Tieger, former deputy general counsel to the House of Representatives noted, "The attorney general is very much supposed to embody the pure rule of law—like the statue of 'Blind Justice'—and he's not expected afterward to cloak, with the mantle of his former office, a bunch of greedy interests" (Zajac 2006:9).

When policies that will have a major impact on profits are at stake, corporate lobbying can be both intense and costly. In 2003, when Congress enacted a new Medicare law to provide prescription drug coverage, the profit opportunities for the insurance and pharmaceutical industries were immense and they hired almost 1,000 different lobbying firms and spent over $140 million on lobbying. The Pharmaceutical Research and Manufacturers of America, for example, paid over one million to two lobbying companies. During this period, insurance and pharmaceutical giants also spent $30 million on campaign contributions to key congressmen and senators, which could be viewed as a form of legal bribery. The end result was a bill that thrilled the pharmaceutical companies, and within a year their profits jumped by $182 billion. The losers from the view of the citizen health action group Public Citizen (2004) were seniors, those who are supposed to benefit from Medicare.

As these examples suggest—and they are but a small sampling of what is a frighteningly long list of known corporate crimes—the great barriers that we assume divide the social world of wealth and respectability from the netherworld of corruption and criminality often are a chimera. Socially manufactured images and carefully crafted and mobilized words protect those who commit crime in the high-rise suites from the opprobrium suffered by those whose crimes are committed on the black-top streets. The issue is not that wealthy individuals or multibillion-dollar corporations *sometimes* commit crimes. Rather, the point is that criminal acts are common, indeed, regular and built into normal corporate operating procedures and upper-class ways of life. While some individuals engaged in so-called white-collar crime are occasionally caught, and some, like lifestyle and homemaking celebrity Martha Stewart, indeed, go to prison, wealthy criminals and law-breaking corporations generally do not lose social approval, public recognition, or their wealth. At best, those who are caught, assuming their names are ever known, are seen as the "bad apples" in an otherwise wholesome barrel. As the examples presented above suggest, involvement in crime is not the real difference between entities in the above- and belowground sectors of the economy, including the producers and distributors of legal drugs and those involved in making and marketing their illegal counterparts.

Violence, Crime, and the Dual Drug Industry

Violence is another issue that is raised to differentiate the above- and belowground sectors of drug capitalism. Without doubt, the world of illicit drug trafficking can be extremely violent. Like the illegal drug industry itself, the pattern is global. Exemplary of the heinous violence that surrounds the illicit drug trade, toward the end of 2005, Peter Philips, national security minister of Jamaica, announced that over 1,400 people had been killed during the year in that country, which has a total population of only 2.7 million. This was not a unique year, either, as there had been over 1,400 homicide deaths on the island-nation the previous year as well (as contrasted with 900 in the year 2000). Much of the increase in violence, Philips announced, was the result of turf wars over drugs and drug profits among rival gangs (*USA Today* 2005).

The Ballad of Drugs and Violence. Like all corporate heads, the CEOs of illicit drug corporations face a variety of challenges on the road to success. They must recruit and control a workforce, develop both sites and methods to systematically produce commodities for sale, research new or in someway updated products and less-expensive production methods, identify potential new markets for their goods, insure the delivery of their products to the market, advertise their wares, and handle the flow of payments from consumers. Functioning in a subterranean world of illegality, the day-to-day operating procedures adopted by illicit drug corporations tend to be a mix of standard business practices (e.g., developing workforce supervision and quality control procedures, implementing computer-based accounting systems, and purchasing transport vehicles on the open market) and a range of additional practices that in and of themselves are illegal, such as bribery, smuggling, and the use of intimidation and physical violence. Indeed, part of the public reputation of illicit drug corporations is that they are cutthroat, corrupting, and highly dangerous to the health and well-being of everyone around them. While such corporations engage in many activities that are not violent, they certainly can live up to this reputation, as seen, for example, in the illicit cocaine corporations of Medellín, Colombia.

While violence was long part of the illicit cocaine scene in Colombia, during the 1980s and early 1990s the use of violence to achieve the aims of the illicit drug corporations of Medellín reached a pinnacle. During this period, illicit drug corporations were under increasing pressure from the Colombian government and the United States as a result of the War on Drugs. To undermine the legal attack launched against them, the cocaine corporations sought to intimidate judges and other sectors of the criminal justice system and society at large.

During these years, almost 500 police and 40 judges were killed, leading to a strike by judicial employees to protest the failure of the government to protect them. The illicit drug corporations also were implicated in the murder of a minister of justice, a leader of the Patriotic Union political party, the governor of the state of Antioquia, the attorney general of Colombia, and the leading Liberal Party candidate for the 1990 presidential election. Additionally, numerous car bombs were detonated resulting in the deaths of over 500 people, mostly civilians. In Bogotá, the façade of the Department of Administrative Security headquarters was blown off, killing 100 people. Bombs also were placed in banks, hotels, the offices of political parties, and in commercial centers. In one case, over a hundred passengers were killed by a bomb loaded aboard an Avianca flight from Bogotá to Cali. In the end, this campaign of violence achieved some of the immediate goals of the cocaine corporations, such as defeat of the Colombian-U.S. extradition treaty (which would have permitted the extradition of illicit drug traffickers from Colombia to the United States for prosecution), but it also turned public opinion sharply against them and thereby emboldened government efforts to curtail the Medellín-based drug corporations.

The most vicious and intense violence exhibited by illicit drug corporations is usually reserved for competitors, especially during periods when a drug market has been disrupted in some fashion. A typical case occurred along the U.S.-Mexican border in 2003 when a highly lucrative drug trade was thrown into disarray after Mexican police arrested the leader of the so-called "Gulf Cartel." Seeing an opening, a rival illicit drug corporation, the "Sinaloa Cartel" sent a representative to grab the cocaine and methamphetamine drug smuggling routes in the vicinity of Nuevo Laredo, Mexico. In defense of their "turf" the Gulf Cartel called on Los Zetas, a group of Mexican special forces officers who had deserted the military to serve as muscle in the drug trade. An all-out drug war erupted across Mexico that left about 1,000 people dead (Thomas 2005).

Violence in illicit drug commerce does not reside only at the top of the industry pyramid. At the street level, where illicit drugs are diluted, packaged, and sold to user-customers in $5, $10, and $20 deals, violence also is a routine part of doing business. The nature and extent of the violence at this level is seen, for example, in the life and activities of Frankie Estrada, who grew up in the working-class town of Bridgeport, Connecticut. By age 12, Estrada was smoking marijuana with his friends and had moved on to cocaine by 16; he soon began selling both of these illicit mind-altering substances on the gritty streets of Bridgeport. Estrada's father, who lived in New York, also was a drug user, and he, too, had become involved in the drug trade. Soon he became the supplier for his son's incipient drug business. Then, as often happens in the world of illicit commerce, even among family members, a cocaine deal went south, sending Estrada to prison, while his father pocketed $17,000 he had been given to pay for the next drug delivery to his son.

Undaunted, when Estrada got out of prison in 1995, he found another drug supplier, recruited employees, and got back into the game. Before long, he re-emerged as a major drug distributor in the sprawling, crumbling and eventually infamous P. T. Barnum housing project—a place named, ironically, after the circus entrepreneur who coined the phase "There is a sucker born every minute." Estrada had moved into the squalid housing project with his mother when he was 17 and he had come to know it well inside and out, including the illicit desires of its residents.

Supplying the considerable demand for psychotropic drugs among project dwellers required "marathon 'bagging sessions'—packaging up to half a million dollars of heroin at a time into $10 bags" for street distribution to the impoverished, self-medicating residents of Barnum (Tuohy 2005a:16)—but it paid off in an enormous windfall of profits. The drugs came from contacts in Colombia via intermediaries in New York City who would send "mules" from South America (individuals who for a fee had swallowed from 80 to 100 balloon-covered packages of heroin or cocaine) to bring Estrada the drugs he had ordered. When the mules arrived, Estrada would drive to the airport to pick up them up and wait with them until they had passed his precious cargo through their systems. To launder his drug profits, Estrada purchased a small grocery store in the projects.

Over the years, Estrada's meteoric rise in illicit drug capitalism was marked by

> moving kilos of heroin [which at the time could be purchased retail for $80,000 and would bring in $300,000 in street sales] and ordering the killings or "beat downs" of rival drug dealers. If their drugs were better quality, he stole their stashes and marketed them as his own. He stockpiled an arsenal of assault weapons and maintained a cluster of "stash houses" to store his drugs, cash and weapons. (Tuohy 2005a:1)

Estrada used the guns to arm his employees and protect them from "stick up boys" (those who make their living robbing drug dealers at gun point) while they peddled drugs at several locations around the housing complex; drugs also were sold by Estrada's crews inside a local prison with the help of corrupt prison guards. As Estrada testified during the murder trial of one of his associates,

> Stick-up boys and drug dealers don't mix. . . . They're out to steal money and I'm out to make money. Drug dealers are easy targets of the stick-up boys; drug dealers don't call the police. (quoted in Tuohy 2005a:16)

The guns, according to Estrada, were used "to shoot people, hurt people, protect the block [from competitors]" (quoted in Tuohy 2005b:B1). However, he matter-of-factly added during his court testimony, "I didn't kill everybody who did something [bad] to me, or there'd be a lot less people out there. . . . If somebody needed to be killed, they would be killed" (quoted in Tuohy 2005a:1). Needless to say, in this instance and many similar ones involving the sale of illicit drugs in communities, "the line between protection and predation [is] always thin" (Murray 1993:181).

When two former employees robbed Estrada's sister's apartment—a place he used to store drugs—and in the process both shot one of Estrada's associates in the head and expressed their disrespect for Estrada by throwing his sister and mother out of a second-story window, Estrada, who carried the street name Terminator, retaliated. He ordered his enforcers to hunt down the culprits, especially a man known on the street as Junior, who was believed to have planned the raid. As he testified on the witness stand, "I ordered Sam Colon to kill him. . . . He shot him. He killed him. I gave him the gun" (quoted in Tuohy 2005b:B1). Why did Colon obey? According to Estrada, "I was calling the shots. I'm the No. 1. I was running everything." Also in his employment were young men like Billie Gomez who, during his own testimony, told the court that he had acquired the nickname "Billie the Kid" because "I like to shoot at people" (Mayko 2005:1).

Convicted of murder and 14 racketeering-related charges, Estrada also testified about a string of other violent acts he ordered "to protect the block." When a rival in the drug trade, Ty Holman, burned several cars belonging to Estrada and his "crew," Estrada planned a revenge attack on Holman as he exited a local club where he had gone to celebrate his birthday. Although Holman escaped, one of his associates was killed in the spray of bullets fired at them. As she listened to Estrada's speak to the court, reporter Lynne Tuohy (2005b:B1) noted that "It was nearly impossible to keep track of the number of shootings Estrada had directed that were described in just the first hour of his testimony."

In sum, it is apparent that the world of illicit drugs is violence-heavy (although, the actual extent and regularity of violence is often overplayed because it confirms popular expectations, attracts media attention, and supports the need to keep fighting and funding the War on Drugs). But is violence a unique attribute of illicit drug capitalism? Is it the feature that effectively distinguishes illegal corporations from the aboveground companies whose names adorn football stadiums, towering buildings, and golf tournaments? There is abundant evidence to suggest that while violence is commonly used by illicit drug corporations to achieve their aims, this approach to having your way is not limited to this sector of the capitalist economy and is enacted as needed by legal corporations in and beyond the drug trade.

The Mansions of Violence.   Historically, one need look no further than the tobacco trade to find a deep legacy of unconscionable violence, as well as of criminality. The organized cultivation of tobacco as a commodity in the New World began with the transatlantic violence of slavery, a system of kidnapping and labor extraction inflicted on an estimated 12–13 million Africans between the early 1400s and the late 1800s. The entanglement of tobacco and slavery began in the Portuguese colony of Brazil in the mid-16th century in what is today the state of Bahia (Horton and Horton 2004). While Brazilian tobacco was not of high quality and its sale was banned in Europe, Portuguese merchants found important uses for it in fueling the slave trade. Rolls of tobacco were soaked in molasses (from colonial sugar production) and used as

> a trade item with West African slave dealers. As the habit of tobacco use became established among African rulers, it became associated with social rank: men of importance had ornamental pipes and attendants to carry the pipes. In some regions of Africa (such as the interior of Cameroon), tobacco became legal currency. Tobacco theft became a felony punishable by enslavement. By the beginning of the 1600s, tobacco had become more profitable to Brazilians than sugar because of its role in the slave trade. (West 2004)

During this era, a human being could be purchased for six or seven roles of molasses-sweetened tobacco weighing a little less than 500 pounds. Between 1640 and 1870, it is estimated that two to five million slaves, including men, women, and children, were brutally ripped from their families and communities, herded like cattle onto waiting ships, transported under treacherous conditions across the seas, and forcibly landed in Brazil to work and die in colonial production. Traders from other lands and colonies saw the opportunity to reap profit from slaves and tobacco, people we would today call venture capitalists, and rushed into the business.

In 1721, British trader Humphrey Morice, for example, enlisted Captain William Clinch of the *Judith* to sail his ship to the African slave coast and trade "tobacco, guns, Sringe, corrall, Amber, Pipes [for smoking tobacco], gunpowder, spirits and beans" for slaves (West 2004). Notably, tobacco and a pipe to smoke it with, as well as rum and brandy, were given to slaves to keep them as sedated as possible during their grueling 21–90 day trip (in chains) from Africa to the colonies, a segment of the slave trade known as the Middle Passage. Notably, if only one-quarter of the African captives died during the Middle Passage, ship owners and traders considered the voyage a success. While the exact number of Africans who died in route and were dumped into the ocean is unknown, it is estimated to be in the millions. Upon arrival in the New World, "tobacco smoke also was used to fumigate the decks of slave ships once the slaves had been removed" (West 2004).

In North America, the tobacco-slavery complex began with the English settlement of Jamestown in the Virginia Colony. John Rolfe, who saved the colony from ruin, planted tobacco (using a variety developed in Spain) and found that it grew well in Virginia's hot lowlands. Other colonists followed Rolfe's lead and soon the Virginia Colony was shipping tobacco back to England, where it sold for three shillings a pound. Before long, dozens of tobacco plantations had been planted, fueling territorial expansion of the colony and threatening the peace with the neighboring indigenous peoples, including the family of Rolfe's wife, Pocahontas. Additionally, the tobacco economy created a serious labor shortage, which pushed the colonists to implement a system of indentured servitude, a strategy that attracted many young boys from the poorest classes of England to the Americas. Native Americans also were pressured to work the tobacco fields, but without much success.

The first Africans, twenty people taken from a slave vessel, arrived at Jamestown in 1619 and were sold to settlers as indentured bondsmen rather than as outright slaves. By the 1660s, however, Virginia's need for labor in the tobacco fields exceeded the supply of indentured servants from any source.

> By 1689, British traders had carried 90,000 slaves from Africa to the New World, including several thousand to the Tobacco Coast (the Chesapeake colonies of Virginia, Maryland, and North Carolina). . . . Despite the preference for Brazilian tobacco in most slave trading regions, Virginia tobacco became the preferred tobacco in the Senegambia area; the product of Chesapeake slaves' labor was used to enslave yet more Africans in the vicious circle that was the slave trade. Between 1750 and 1860, black slaves accounted for 40 percent of Virginia's population on average. A census of eight Tidewater-Piedmont counties in 1782–1783 Virginia recorded 15 citizens who held over 100 slaves. . . . In areas where the tobacco plantation system was less significant, the average slaveholder decreased below an average holding of eight slaves. . . . To protect their increasingly costly investment in slaves, Virginia's colonial government passed a series of acts that created a system of hereditary, perpetual slavery. (West 2004)

Those who profited from this system of violence were the wealthiest and most respected citizens of the colonies and, later, of the new United States. They included some of the original owners of the elegant mansions of Newport, Rhode Island, a point not stressed to the awed tourists who flock to New England to tour the palatial buildings each summer. The DeWolf family, for example, "one of the wealthiest in New England in the 18th century, made its fortune from the business of slavery" (Taylor 2006). Patriarch James DeWolf, in fact, was "reputed to be the richest man in America" during this era (Farrow et al. 2005:101). Ships owned by the DeWolf family carried an estimated 11,000 slaves to the Americas. Despite their social standing, when the importation of slaves was outlawed in 1807, the DeWolfs readily turned to illegal smuggling to keep the profits on human misery flowing.

At least one segment of the alcohol industry also has its roots in the slave trade. Rum production, which depends on sugar cane, developed as part and parcel of the slave trade, and many of the same players involved in tobacco were also caught up in the rum trade.

> At slave depots on the African coast, Rhode Island vessels were known and welcomed as "rum-men." When the Newport trade first reached a peak just after the Revolution, its vessels were carrying 200,000 gallons of rum a year to Africa, where ship captains bartered for slaves by the barrel. An African man in his prime could be bought for about 150 gallons. . . . Two dozen distilleries operated in Newport alone. (Farrow et al. 2005:98)

The wealthy merchants and sea captains who flocked to Newport and built their summer mansions there also founded the Fellowship Club, a charitable organization that had rules of proper conduct banning cursing, gambling, and drunkenness. The horrors they helped finance on the African coast, during the Middle Passage, and on the tobacco, sugar, and other plantations where slaves toiled to make profit for others were well hidden by the grace and style that typified upper-class life in Newport and elsewhere. As Harriet Beecher Stowe (1879) said of them, "The Northern slaveholder traded in men and women whom he never saw, and whose separations, tears, and miseries, he determined not to hear."

In sum, the legal drug industry in America was born and raised in violence. Moreover, the violence of legal corporations did not end with slavery. In both historic and modern times, violence has regularly been used by "captains of industry," for example, to regularly break workers' strikes and their unions. This usually has taken one of three forms: the use of hired thugs to intimidate, injure, or kill workers and their supporters; the use of state violence (by way of the police, state militias, the national guard, or even the national armed forces); or some blend of the two approaches. The ability to use these mechanisms is rooted in the social legitimacy accorded legal corporations, the special privileges that corporate wealth can finance, and the close connections that tend to abide between legal corporations and the state. All of these are evident in an examination of some of the classic struggles of the American labor movement.

We Never Sleep.   On its website (Pinkerton 2006), the Pinkerton company (now, as a result of mergers, called Security Services USA, Inc.)—a company whose original logo, an eye adorned with the slogan "We Never Sleep," inspired the term "private eye"—describes its history in the following way:

> Pinkerton's history dates back to 1850 in Chicago, when Allan Pinkerton, the original "private eye," founded Pinkerton's National Detective Agency. Pinkerton achieved national renown in 1861 when he uncovered and foiled an assassination plot on the life of Abraham Lincoln. During the Civil War, Pinkerton organized America's first secret service. His pursuits of Jesse James, the Younger and Dalton gangs and his longstanding pursuit of the Wild Bunch brought extraordinary visibility to his agency. Pinkerton's tradition of excellence continues with the experience you can trust, and the integrity you can rely on as a respected leader in the security consulting and investigation industry. Pinkerton offers corporations comprehensive security services, a consultative approach to identifying risks and the professional expertise to partner in effective solutions.

Missing from this self-congratulatory account of the corporation's history is the role of the company in strike breaking. This apparently forgotten dark side of Pinkerton's history coalesced in the period after the Civil War.

In the antebellum years, struggles between workers and industrial corporations were intense. The character of this conflict is seen in what has been called the Great Railroad Strike of 1877. In the period prior to the strike, the American economy had fallen into a shambles. Workers were being fired, and those who managed to hang onto their jobs saw their wages slashed. As Richard Boyer and Herbert Morais (1955:127) describe in their book *Labor's Untold Story*, "Weekly the layoffs, wage cuts, strikes, evictions, breadlines and hunger increased." By the cold winter of 1873–74, tens of thousands of unemployed workers and their families were facing starvation and tempers were raw. Then in June of 1877, the Pennsylvania Railroad, the nation's largest railroad corporation, which had already cut its worker's salaries by 10 percent, slashed wages by another 10 percent. A month later, the company announced that all east-bound trains leaving Pittsburgh would be doubled in length but the size of the onboard work crews would remain the same, thereby doubling their workload as wages were being cut.

Outraged workers blocked the movement of trains leaving Pittsburgh. The strike spread to other cities where railroad workers were also seeing their income shrink as the demands put upon them by the wealthy railroad corporations spiraled. State militias and police were used to try and break the strikes, and Pinkerton agents were brought in as well. These efforts failed to diminish the workers' resolve. Finally, the troops opened fire on the crowd of strikers, emptying their rifles into the stunned rows of men, women, and children who faced them. Twenty strikers and family members were killed, including several children; another 29 were wounded. Newspaper writers vented their horror at the cold-blooded shooting and provided detailed descriptions of the dead and dying.

On July 21, President Hayes, who was beholden to the railroad companies and their ability to wield power in Congress, issued a proclamation demanding that strikers disperse within 24 hours. The next day, the governor of Pennsylvania ordered state troops to join the fight against the struggling strikers. Subsequent clashes between the troops and workers in Reading, Pennsylvania, added to the body count.

As this glimpse at the early struggles of the labor movement suggests, legal corporations have been able to call on state forces of legalized violence to achieve their goals. While God may not be on the side of legal corporations, the law generally is.

> Far from being a neutral instrument, the law belongs to those who write it and use it—primarily those who control the resources of society. It is no accident that in most conflicts between the propertied and the propertyless, the law intervenes on the side of the former. . . . The protection of property is deemed tantamount to the protection of society itself. (Parenti 1980:121)

In other words, a significant benefit of social legitimacy is the ability to enlist the law and the enforcers of the law (police, prosecutors, the courts), including the power of state institutions to invoke violence, to achieve corporate goals. Illicit drug corporations, by contrast, usually cannot call on state power for this end (although this hasn't stopped them from using bribes, intimidation, and violence to try and achieve the same capacity so coveted by legal corporations).

Buying War.   A notable contemporary expression of the use of violence by legal corporations is the mobilization of paramilitary forces to gain access to oil or mineral resources and to create a cordon sanitaire around processing facilities. In the Republic of Sudan, for example, large stretches of oil-rich land have been cleansed of their indigenous inhabitants, primarily the Nuer and Dinka peoples, by violent attacks launched by paramilitary forces.

Christian Aid asserts that foreign oil companies in Sudan are complicit in human rights violations by using militias to provide security around the oil fields, by building roads and air strips that are used to move troops to further cleanse the land of its people, by knowingly paying the government revenues from oil production and exports that are used to wage war, and by their very presence in the country lending credibility and legitimacy to forces that have unleashed a reign of terror:

> In April 1999, Lundin Oil of Sweden drilled an exploratory well at Thar Jath,10 miles from the Nile, and reported finding as many as 300 million barrels of "excellent" reservoir quality oil. A month later, according to Human Rights Watch, the government moved troops to Thar Jath and adjacent areas, displacing tens of thousands of people. . . . In early March 2001

Lundin announced that it had struck oil at Thar Jath, a source of an esti-mated 4,260 barrels a day. "This is a significant and exciting event for Lun-din Oil," said company president Ian Lundin. (Christian Aid 2001)

Not mentioned in the Lundin announcement were the government heli-copters that flew over the Thar Jath area dropping bombs and shooting at any people seen below, the thousands of people who were driven from their villages, the villages that were burned to the ground, the government allied militias that "rounded up the elderly... and burned them alive," and the transformation of Thar Jath into a depopulated government-con-trolled security zone around Lundin oil facilities (Christian Aid 2001).

In short, while the armies do not belong to the oil companies, the violence they employ serves corporate ends, and the consequences for the victims are no less brutal, socially destructive, or smaller in scale than what is seen among illicit drug companies. The difference: while violence and criminal activities of illegal drug corporations are discussed regularly in the mass media and by government spokespersons, and reproduced in movies and television programming, leading to wide-spread awareness in the general public about such behavior, the crimes and cruelties of legal corporations, while not completely erased, are obscured and made to seem the exception rather than the rule.

Unnatural Disaster. Corporate violence includes failing to provide safe working conditions for employees. Tragic "accidents" have taken workers' lives, as seen in the internationally lamented 1984 explosion at the Union Carbide Corporation plant in Bhopal, India, that released over 25 tons of lethal gases immediately killing more than 3,000 people and injuring 200,000 others. Ultimately, as many as 20,000 people died as a result of the explosion. In the case of Bhopal, the accident followed a series of cost-cutting measures that left the safety system designed to contain leaks inoperative and the siren that was intended to warn the surrounding community shut down. In its public statement on the trag-edy, Union Carbide (2005), which since 2001 has become a component of the Dow Chemical Company, downplayed its role and responsibility by pointing the finger at its Indian subsidiary:

> The Bhopal plant was owned and operated by Union Carbide India, Limited (UCIL), an Indian company in which Union Carbide Corporation held just over half the stock. The other stockholders included Indian financial insti-tutions and thousands of private investors in India. The plant was designed, built and managed by UCIL using Indian consultants and workers. In 1994, Union Carbide sold its half interest in UCIL to MacLeod Russell (India) Limited of Calcutta. . . . As a result of the sale of its shares in UCIL, Union Carbide retained no interest in—or liability for—the Bhopal site.

Such patterns did not end with Bhopal. The year 2006 began for mine workers and their families in West Virginia with word that an explosion at the Sago Mine, owned by the International Coal Group, had trapped 13 miners 260 feet belowground. Despite early reports that the miners had survived the explosion—reports that the company admitted it did not refute even though it was aware they were wrong—all but one of the miners died in the mine.

In the case of the Sago Mine, the history of safety violations is telling. The mine had been cited 208 times for safety violations in the year 2005 alone according to the U.S. Department of Labor. Of these violations, 96 were considered "significant and substantial" by federal inspectors (Warrick 2006:A4). West Virginia state inspectors at Sago Mine also had issued 144 citations for unsafe conditions in 2005. Prior to the explosion, the mine had been the site of 42 worker injuries since 2000. In 2004, the mine's injury rate per hours worked was three times the national average for mines of its type. The company that owns Sago announced after the disaster that it had no plans to close the mine.

Donning the Mask of Philanthropy

In 1964, the Beatles had a hit song, "Can't Buy Me Love." While love may be hard to come by with an exchange of cash, social respectability and a positive public image may be acquirable. In the year 2004, for example, the Bentonville, Arkansas-based, discount retailer Wal-Mart Stores Inc., donated just under $200 million (almost all of it locally in the United States), or about 1 percent of its earnings for 2003 according to Forbes.com (Moyer 2005), to philanthropic causes.

This largesse comes at time when Wal-Mart has been in the news frequently for negative reasons. Despite its tremendous size and considerable power, Wal-Mart keeps running afoul of the law. Indeed, some have argued, it is through its cutthroat approach to profit making, which tramples employees, competitors, suppliers, and the environment, that Wal-Mart has achieved its colossal size. In December of 2005, for example, Wal-Mart lost a $172 million class action suit in California to a group of employees who claimed that the company had violated a law that requires employees to receive a 30-minute meal break after they have worked for six hours. In fact, in recent years Wal-Mart has been accused of numerous workplace violations against its employees around the country. For example, in 2002, Wal-Mart was sued in Texas for underpaying its workers. Notes *New York Times* reporter Steven Greenhouse (2002:1):

> In a recently certified class action suit in Texas on behalf of more than 200,000 current and former Wal-Mart workers, statisticians estimate that the company underpaid its Texas workers by $150 million over four years by not paying them for the many times they worked during their daily 15-minute breaks. That $150 million estimate does not include other types of unpaid work. The statisticians, who analyzed time records from 12 Wal-Mart stores, found that the Texas employees averaged at least one hour of unpaid work each week from working through breaks.

In California, a class action lawsuit has charged that Wal-Mart eliminated thousands of hours of time worked from employees' payroll
records. The time shaving was achieved by deleting overtime hours and
by penalizing employees who forgot to punch back in at the time clock
after their meal breaks, even though they did return to work. One of the
plaintiffs, Jessica Grant, told reporters that despite the many ads Wal-
Mart has placed in newspapers around the country defending its reputation, the company "is not the best place to work" (*Bay City News* 2005).

In its home state of Arkansas, according to the *Arizona Democrat Gazette*
(Baskin 2005), almost 4,000 Wal-Mart employees, about 8 percent of its
workforce in the state, have had to go on public assistance because their
wages are so low and health insurance is unaffordable. The pattern has
been reported for Wal-Mart workers from California to Connecticut, with
the result being that taxpayers often pay the health insurance benefits of
Wal-Mart employees and their families. The corporation is also under
investigation by the government over its handling and transport of merchandise that is classified as hazardous waste, such as damaged aerosol
paint cans (Forbes.com 2005). Further, a recent study by researchers at the
University of California, Berkeley's Labor Center (Dube 2005), found that
Wal-Mart's low wages generally "drives down wages in urban areas" with
annual losses of almost $5 billion to working-class salaries. As a result of
its practices, Wal-Mart has gained a reputation as a global corporate bully, a
company that "does not hesitate to use its power, magnifying the Darwin-
ian forces already at work in modern global capitalism" (Fishman 2003:68).

Ironically, despite being a for-profit corporation, Wal-Mart has been
called a "welfare queen" because of the company's extensive reliance on
government subsidies (sometimes called "welfare for the rich"). A study
by the group Good Jobs First (Mattera and Purington 2004), funded by
the United Food and Commercial Workers International Union, concluded that Wal-Mart achieved its growth into the world's largest corporation by relying heavily on government handouts in the amount of $1
billion. According to Philip Mattera, codirector of the study, "Wal-Mart
presents itself as an entrepreneurial success story, yet it has made extensive use of tax breaks, free land, cash grants and other forms of public
assistance" (quoted in Oligopoly Watch 2004). The study also found that
Wal-Mart received more in subsidies from state and local governments
than any other U.S. corporation, including far more than were received
by locally based companies that compete with Wal-Mart for customers,
adding fuel to the fire among the growing ranks of labor, environmental,
community, and small business critics of Wal-Mart.

One way Wal-Mart has responded to its sullied reputation is through
its "good works" and through funding a group inaccurately named Working Families for Wal-Mart, a high-powered team of public relations and
political specialists organized to defend the company from its critics by,
in part, playing up Wal-Mart's charitable donations (Edwards 2005).

Similarly, over the years, legal drug companies have been quite active in charitable giving. In 2005, for example, it came to light that the pharmaceutical corporation Eli Lilly was among the corporate donors to Republican Senate Majority Leader Bill Frist's AIDS charity called World of Hope, Inc. The charity has been under public scrutiny since it was revealed by belatedly filed tax returns that Frist paid out almost a half-million dollars from the charity in consulting fees to members of his conservative political inner circle. Eli Lilly's contributions to the charity, which tends to fund faith-based programs, also have been questioned because the company has frequent business before Congress (Katz and Solomon 2005).

Revelations of this sort have raised public skepticism about corporate giving. A *Wall Street Journal* article warning business readers about the perils of corporate giving (Alsop 2002), for example, notes the findings of a survey by the Reputation Institute, part of the New York market-research company Harris Interactive, Inc.; over 20,000 respondents affirmed public discomfort with aspects of corporate giving. The study found that "many people have scoffed at the lavish Philip Morris Co.'s $250 million ad campaign touting its charitable activities. For one thing, they believe the company should have spent its 'corporate outreach' budget on more philanthropy rather than publicity." Part of Philip Morris' philanthropic spending has been on anti–domestic violence programs. The company, however has spent more money on publicizing its "good works" in this area than it has spent on the actual social programs it sponsors, a pattern "which strongly suggests that image is more important than charity" (Smith and Malone 2003:555) to the company. "Some [survey participants] also view it—and a planned [corporate] name change to Altria Group—as a smoke screen to divert attention from its cigarette business" (Alsop 2002). As Smith and Malone (2005) comment:

> For more than a decade, Philip Morris planned this renaming and restructuring in order to distance itself from the ever-increasing liability of selling tobacco, a product that kills more than a third of its long-term users. As part of this strategy, Philip Morris hopes to be perceived as an outstanding corporate citizen by increasing its philanthropy under the name of Altria.

Illicit Drug Philanthropy

Notably, legal corporations like Wal-Mart, Eli Lilly, and Altria/Philip Morris are not alone in seeking to shape their public image through philanthropic giving. Illicit corporations also engage in the practice. Clawson and Lee (1998:48) report that illicit cocaine corporations in Colombia have sponsored "some high-profile civic programs, including the donation of several hundred new housing units to poor slum dwellers and construction of some eighty illuminated sports arenas in Medellín and surrounding communities." A legal business owned by one of Medellín's illicit cocaine corporations was the newspaper *Medellín Cívico*. In the paper, the CEO of one of the largest illicit drug corporations, Pablo Escobar, was applauded for his generosity and public-spiritedness, which was contrasted "with the indifference of local [licit] businesses and the selfishness of the Colombian political establishment" (Clawson and Lee 1998:48). The latter was accused in the paper of having done nothing for the welfare of the people. Another article in the paper itemized the good deeds of local illicit drug corporations:

> Fifty thousand trees planted in fifty barrios of Medellín . . . schools built with plenty of space, with an eye to beauty and pedagogical function. Broken sewers repaired to protect residents from contaminated water and from epidemics—[sewers that were] a health hazard that the government has ignored for years. Basketball courts, skating rinks, multi-sports arenas . . . thousands of bricks to expand the houses of poor families, to finish buildings, churches, and wings of schools. Illumination of barrios trapped in darkness because of indifferent bureaucrats or politicians who do not keep their promises. (quoted in Clawson and Lee 1999:49)

At the local level, in the impoverished communities from which so-called drug lords often emerge, public giving by those in the illicit drug trade also is common (E. Arias 2006). When Rio de Janeiro police bullets brought down 28-year-old Erismar Moreira, the city's most-wanted criminal and the flamboyant and colorful leader of the Amigos dos Amigos (Friends of the Friends) illicit drug corporation, city officials cheered; justice had been served, a multimillion-dollar drug gang had been beheaded (Chang 2005). In the hillside *favela* (squatter community) of Rochina, which Amigos seized control of from a rival group in 2004, however, black banners were hung over the main street and the initials of Moreira's street name were spray painted on surrounding walls.

During his time as a drug entrepreneur, Moreira actively courted the sympathies of Rochina's impoverished residents, using drug profits to fund soccer fields and sponsor lavish community parties. His gang, which operates relatively openly, carbines in hand, on the narrow and heavily congested and crowded streets and hidden passageways of Rochina, is credited with building the water tower that helps insure the steady flow of water to the community. The city government of Rio, by contrast, has only offered partial recognition and municipal services to the people of Rochina. Young people from the community with few prospects for upward social mobility were inspired by Moreira's flashy rags-to-riches career in illicit drug commerce. For them there were few comparable meaningful role models from "the asphalt" (as Rochina's residents call the wealthier, lowland areas of the city below their favela).

A visit to Rochina in 2006 by the author revealed that little had changed since Moreira's death. Despite poverty, the community is almost completely free of petty crime (and, as a result, has become an increasingly appealing place to live for the middle class); Amigos does not allow behavior that might attract the police and disrupt the gang's profitable drug operations (and the willingness of their many customers from the asphalt to drive up into the favela to buy drugs).

Similar local philanthropy has been described for Tony, a low-level drug dealer and addict from a small city in Connecticut (Singer 2006b). Tony and his fellow gang members used profits from their drug business as well as from shoplifting at local supermarkets to support free-wheeling summer barbeque parties for residents of the housing project in which they had grown up together. Like Moreira, Tony and his associates viewed their involvement in violence as merely protecting their community from rivals.

While illicit drug corporations probably would not consider attempting to use general community giving to bolster their status in the United States, since the government would swiftly step in to block any such effort, it is clear that when possible they, too, are quite willing to use philanthropy to portray themselves as caring, public-spirited, and generous members of the business community.

Critical Junctures: Where the Twain Meet

In the 2001 Annual Lecture to the International Institute for Asian Studies in Leiden, Netherlands, Chris Patten (2001) observed:

> More than 100 years ago, in *The Ballad of East and West*, the British poet Kipling wrote a line of verse which would subsequently enter the English language almost as a cliché: "Oh, East is East, and West is West, and never the twain shall meet." Much has changed since then. . . . But the biggest change of all, the change that has and is touching more lives than even the world wars did, is the phenomenon known as globalisation. Of course, there is nothing new about globalisation. A century ago, when there was no such thing as passports, or visas, or work permits, the world witnessed an enormous expansion in both trade and the movement of people and money. . . . What is new about this "second wave" of globalisation is not the ideas which underpin it. After all, belief in free trade, open markets, private ownership, property rights, and capitalism were hallmarks of the first wave. The difference this time is its scope. . . . Not only is globalisation now reaching into a vastly greater number of countries, it is also reaching into vastly greater areas of our lives.

As a result, the twain have met, or more precisely, meet daily in many ways and places. Today global capitalism is a fluid mode of production. It is flexible, mobile, and penetrative. Moreover, it facilely dodges hindrances and barriers like fast flowing water. It can adapt to diverse local conditions and on-the-ground social and economic configurations, while absorbing and retooling new social arenas to fit its needs. As a result, things are not always as they appear: social relations are transformed into labor-control mechanisms and marketing niches, traditional goods are commoditized, commodities are fetishized, national boundaries are vaporized, and legal systems transcended. Such is the nature as well in that sector of global capitalism that is here termed "drug capitalism." While ostensibly the sinister drug cartels and criminal gangs of illicit drug traffickers, on the one hand, and public corporations that make and sell legal commodities, on the other, are disconnected, the intersections between them, in fact, are numerous and diverse, including

> mainstream companies investing in the illicit drug trade for quick profit, respectable banks and other financial institutions laundering illicit drug profits, drug profits being reinvested in legal corporations, pharmaceuticals boosting production to meet the illicit demand, physicians profiting from aggressively prescribing psychotropic pharmaceuticals, transportation and delivery companies transporting illicit drugs to the marketplace, and restaurateurs and shopkeepers buying and re-selling "hot" merchandise pilfered by drug addicts from other stores. (Singer 2006b:150)

Money laundering is one of the better publicized and key points of contact between illicit drug capitalism and the wider capitalist economy. Each year, illicit drug corporations successfully "alchemize uncounted billions in ill-gotten gains into legitimate assets" (Porter 1991). In fact, the U.S. State Department (2001) reports that worldwide the laundering of "dirty money" (from the sale of drugs and other illicit commodities as well as an array of other illegal activities) may be a trillion-dollar-a-year business (or about 2 to 5 percent of the world's gross domestic product), with $2 million in laundered cash flowing through the U.S. economy each day. While the practice is quite old, the term *money laundering* is fairly new, dating to the Watergate scandal during the Nixon administration. The practice was not officially outlawed until the mid-1980s.

According to Paul Bauer, an economic adviser to the Federal Reserve Bank of Cleveland, and Rhoda Ullmann, a research assistant at the bank, money laundering tends to involve a three-step process: placement, layering, and integration (Bauer and Ullmann 2001). During the first step, placement, the objective is to disguise the illicit origins of ill-gotten gain. For example, the sale of illicit street drugs produces an accumulation of a large volume of small-denomination bills, including one-dollar and five-dollar bills that impoverished drug users spend for each individual bag, vial, or stick of their drug of choice. Converting this bulky weight of bills into more easily transported larger denominations, cashier's checks, or some other form of easily negotiable monetary instrument often entails the use of cash-intensive businesses that regularly take in numerous small bills and even coins, such as vending machine companies, restaurants, hotels, casinos, and car washes, as fronts. For example, in the two-year period after the U.S. Treasury issued a ruling that casinos must report all suspicious activities in their operations, the American Gaming Association, a member organization of the commercial casino industry in the United States, reported approximately 5,000 such incidents, about 15 percent of which involved large cash transactions but a limited amount of actual gambling activity, which is suggestive of a money laundering effort. During the same period, about half of the suspicious transactions reported by U.S. banks were believed to have been money laundering schemes (Fahrenkopf 2004).

The second step, layering, uses a series of complex financial transactions to hide the trail that links converted funds back to criminal activity. One layering strategy is to set up several "shell companies" in a foreign country that maintains tough bank secrecy laws, or, conversely, in countries with weak enforcement of money laundering statues. Importantly, many U.S. banks maintain correspondent relationships with foreign banks—sometimes with dozens or even hundreds of such entities—some of which, upon investigation, turn out themselves to be shell companies with little in the way of banking structures and staff. Others have banking licenses that limit their operation to clients from outside of their licensing jurisdiction and operate primarily to reap profits by moving money for a fee. Moreover, offshore banks have their own correspondent relationships with other offshore banks, further complicating the money trail. With the press of a few keys on a computer keyboard, tainted funds can be electronically moved, easily and instantly, back and forth among the accounts of several shell companies or shell banks, and even into U.S. banks connected to offshore banks, thereby obscuring their ultimate origin.

Sometimes, however, the trail is not successfully hidden and banks get caught being deeply involved in money laundering. According to Robert Morgenthau, Manhattan district attorney, "There's a lot of money going through New York—$19 billion—where people don't know the source" (quoted in Freifeld 2006:E3). Much of the money passing through New York–based financial institutions was wired from Brazil. Over the last several years, Morgenthau reported that 34 people and 16 Virgin Island companies linked to Brazil have been indicted for laundering-related illegal money remittance in Manhattan through Valley National Bank. Additionally, in September 2006, Bank of America, the second-largest U.S. bank, agreed to pay a fine of over $7 million to settle a money laundering probe initiated by Morgenthau's office. In 2005, Israel Discount Bank, Israel's third largest money lender, paid a settlement of $25 million stemming from its money transfers from Brazil. In 2004, Hudson United Bancorp settled a money laundering investigation of its lower Manhattan branch by paying a $5 million fine. By paying these fines, the banks under investigation are able to protect themselves both from further legal inquiry and from prosecution, a legal benefit that illicit drug corporations would no doubt also love to have.

Another layering strategy involves

> buying big-ticket items—securities, cars, planes, travel tickets—that are often registered in a friend's name to further distance the criminal from the funds. Casinos are sometimes used because they readily take cash. Once converted into chips, the funds appear to be winnings, redeemable by a check drawn on the casino's bank. (Bauer and Ullmann 2001:1)

Internet-based payment systems also allow rapid electronic transactions, and some offer users a high level of anonymity. The "reverse flip" is another layering scheme. In this strategy, the money launderer enters into a secret contract with someone selling real estate or another expensive item. The seller agrees to accept a price that is well below the market value of the item for sale and receives the difference up to or even above the asking price under the table. The launderer then flips or resells the item at its true market value, thereby converting a large amount of dirty money into clean money, while the seller reaps tax benefits.

The final step in the laundering process is the integration of dirty and clean money. Again, several alternative methods are in play. In one of these, called "loan-backs," the profits of illicit activity are put into an off-shore account, and the funds are then loaned back to their owner of the account. Alternately, integration may involve an approach known as "double-invoicing" in which the offshore financial company maintains two sets of books. Then "to move 'clean' funds into the United States, a U.S. entity overcharges for some good or service. To move funds out (say, to avoid taxes), the U.S. entity is overcharged" (Bauer and Ullmann 2001:1). Laundered funds often are then moved into legal activities, such as investment in mainstream companies, purchase of real estate, or acquisition of luxury items for personal use. Integration also occurs through legal companies owned and operated by criminal organizations. The Bufalinas, a Mafia family based in Pennsylvania with a wide range of criminal enterprises in parts of New Jersey and New York as well, for example, are believed to have used solid waste management and transportation companies owned by the family to launder proceeds from the sale of illicit drugs and from loan sharking, bookmaking, and securities fraud schemes. Illicit cash, in this instance, was recorded on company books as legitimate income from work that never occurred or as income from real work but at an inflated rate (Anastasia 1998).

Like capitalism itself, money laundering is a fast-paced, metamorphic activity, changing its approaches and guises over time and place. Since the late 1980s, changing patterns of money laundering have been tracked by a newsletter called the Money Laundering Alert. The Alert is published by Charles Intriago, a former assistant U.S. attorney in Florida and legal advisor to a congressional subcommittee. Intriago reports, for example, on a well-known case from 1998 in which 22 bank officials representing 12 different banks in Mexico were caught in a scheme to transfer dirty money into U.S. accounts and withdraw it as "clean" money ready for shipment to illicit drug companies based in Mexico and Colombia. Notably,

> money-laundering has increasingly worked its way into Main Street, USA. In some cases, for instance, the launderers divide their money into bundles of less than $10,000—the lowest limit on cash deposits or purchases that must be reported to the IRS—and parcel them out to "Smurfs," named for those industrious little blue cartoon characters, who in turn deposit them in hundreds of banks throughout the country. With growing frequency, launderers have also been doing their washing through small businesses, such as real estate companies, car dealerships, jewelers, art galleries—anywhere they can find someone willing to sell something expensive that will hold or increase its value and who will agree to take payment in cash. (Porter 1991:1)

Large corporations other than banks, including legal drug manufacturers, are involved in money laundering as well. In 1995, distributors for Philip Morris were indicted for laundering $40 million in what the government called a "black market peso" operation involving purchase of Philip Morris products for sale in Colombia. Five years later when Philip Morris was sued by a group of Colombian tax collectors who accused the company of involvement in cigarette smuggling and drug money laundering, the company, without admitting to wrongdoing in the past, agreed to prevent its products from entering the black market or being used in money laundering (Zill and Bergman 2001). The company, of course, did not agree to stop producing and internationally distributing tobacco, although it is a drug that is responsible for more illness and death around the world and in the United States than any of the illicit substances discussed in this book. There is little likelihood any time soon, however, that Philip Morris will suffer criminal penalties or be fully demonized for peddling tobacco.

Philip Morris' stance in this instance exemplifies an attitude known as "willful blindness" in the lexicon of money laundering law enforcement officers. According to former IRS investigator Michael McDonald, despite their public denials, many companies are aware that what they are doing is illegal:

> Law enforcement and these companies are on a collision course right now because there's a legal principle called Willful Blindness, which means if you totally disregard all the facts and circumstances that would lead you to believe and know that this is illegal money, that's the same as knowing it's illegal money.... So what's the responsibility of these companies when they know they're getting paid with black market dollars? Most of these companies know that they're getting paid with money that comes from the black market. And the black market is fueled by the drug trade. (quoted in Zill and Bergman 2001)

Adds Greg Passic, a veteran DEA official, "What are we going to do? We've got the Fortune 500 involved in our drug money laundering process" (quoted in Zill and Bergman 2001).

Many small companies also have been implicated in money laundering. The Drug Enforcement Administration (2005:1), for example, notes with reference to the state of New Jersey:

> Local money launders have turned to loosely organized money service businesses such as international money remitters to move huge sums of cash out of the country undetected. Despite increased regulation in this area, the DEA-Newark experience has been that these businesses, which are often small and individually owned or managed, largely ignore suspicious transactions that are clearly indicative of money laundering. Moreover, overwhelming evidence exists that many of these businesses are fully aware of the illegal source of their clients' funds and are complicit in their laundering activities. . . . Additionally, the state's close proximity to New York offers traffickers more financial alternatives to transfer money to source countries. Atlantic City casinos allow money launders to convert cash into casino chips and also write checks on casino bank accounts.

There are many other direct points of contact between illicit drug capitalism and legal corporations, including the legal drug manufacturers. One of them is the profitable overproduction of pharmaceuticals resulting in a surplus that is diverted for nonmedical use as discussed in chapter 5. While pharmaceutical companies deny this occurs, and claim that they have protections in place to avert it, critics have questioned the credibility of these assertions.

This chapter has argued that the high and low roads of drug capitalism, one legal and the other not, run closely parallel as well as meet at critical junctures. Rather than being separate and different, they are at times connected and even more often mirror each other in critical attributes.

CHAPTER 3

Big Tobacco
An Aboveground Drug Industry

Birth of the Tobacco Corporation

The emergence of the modern tobacco corporation can be traced to the voyage of Christopher Columbus and to what was to him, to his crew, and to all Europeans a brand New World. To whatever degree he was motivated in his difficult cross-ocean journey, Columbus also embraced crass pecuniary aims and considerable personal ambition; he hoped to return to Europe with gold, spices, and other material wealth. Instead, Columbus returned to Europe with a few small gold ornaments of nominal value; a handful of the indigenous people from the distant land he had visited; and some dried, yellowish, strangely aromatic leaves of a cultivated plant that the indigenes called *tabaco*. He introduced "tobacco" as a medicinal drug, and it was at first cultivated in Europe for this purpose. Pipe smoking caught on through the initiation of Sir Walter Raleigh, an influential court figure in England in the mid-16th century. By 1600, smoking was a common practice of working people in the port cities of England and Ireland, and by the end of the 17th century, tobacco was legal and widely used throughout Europe.

Britain, in particular, pushed for legalization because, as noted in chapter 2, the soil of its Virginia colony proved to be an especially good medium for tobacco growth. Dried tobacco was lightweight and could be shipped across the ocean at comparatively low cost. The high demand for tobacco in England and the rest of Europe meant that the new commodity would attain a highly profitable sales volume. In due course, tobacco was legalized across the European continent. Tobacco taught the elite of Britain an important lesson that it would apply later upon gaining colonial control of opium production in India: trade in psychotropic commodities can be the source of great wealth. It was a lesson many others would learn in time as well.

A critical step in the birth of Big Tobacco was the transition from independent planter, to cottage factory, to corporation. Success of the initial tobacco plantations in Jamestown led to planters throughout the

Tidewater region of Virginia taking up the crop. As a result of their burgeoning harvests, Fredericksburg, Virginia, emerged as a center of transatlantic tobacco commerce. Some tobacco planters grew particularly wealthy, purchased large numbers of slaves to work their growing land holdings, and built many warehouses to dry their tobacco leaves prior to shipment to England. From these beginnings, small cottage industries began to emerge.

> Virginians began to process tobacco into snuff in small factories during the 1730s. By 1860, there were at least 348 factories in Virginia and North Carolina, almost all of them producing chewing tobacco. Nearly 13,000 Virginia slaves worked in the tobacco factories of Richmond, Petersburg, and Lynchburg. About half of these slaves were seasonal workers hired out by the planters in the spring and fall to small, local factories. The mostly male factory workers would stem, cut, and shape the tobacco into plugs and twists. (West 2004)

These were packed into barrels for shipment to England and from there to many parts of the world. Tobacco cultivation spread throughout what came to be called the Tobacco Coast colonies of the Chesapeake, a region that, just before independence, accounted for over half of the imports coming into England. As tobacco depleted the soils of the Chesapeake region, cultivation of the leaf crop moved westward across Virginia and passed the Appalachians to Kentucky.

In 1847, a London tobacconist named Philip Morris opened a shop on Bond Street. By 1860, the establishment was selling hand-rolled cigarettes. At the time, cigarettes were specialty items that cost a penny apiece and were considered secondary to pipe smoking and other tobacco-consumption methods. When Philip died, his brother Leopold took over and the successful company went public in 1881. In 1902, the company was incorporated in New York, and in 1919 it was incorporated in the traditional tobacco state of Virginia under the name of Philip Morris & Co., Ltd., Inc. During this same era, J. E. Liggett and Brothers was incorporated in St. Louis, and R. J. Reynolds Tobacco Company was founded by Richard Joshua Reynolds as a chewing tobacco manufacturer in Winston (later Winston-Salem), North Carolina. The automated cigarette-rolling machine did not appear until 1883. An invention of 18-year-old James Bonsack, it revolutionized cigarette production and transformed the tobacco industry.

The substance modern tobacco companies fill their cigarette papers with today is far different from the strange yellow leaf Columbus took back to Europe. Known as bright-leaf tobacco, it has been specially bred to be mild enough to be inhaled deeply, and its nicotine cannot readily be absorbed through the mucus lining of the lips and inner cheeks but must be smoked and absorbed by the bronchi of the lungs to reach the bloodstream. Modern cigarettes are treated with ammonia to produce high doses of free-base nicotine and are designed to produce smoke particles of small and uniform size that can carry nicotine deep into the respiratory system. Moreover, very recent research suggests that nicotine-induced neuromolecular changes in the nerve-cell membranes of the brain could change developmentally controlled "hardwiring" that is established during the period from adolescence to young-adulthood. These brain changes among youthful smokers may contribute to the long-term addictive potential of nicotine (Pettegrew et al. 2006). With their highly addictive properties and backing from aggressive marketing, prepackaged cigarettes have developed into a global commodity.

Just as the cigarette has radically changed, so, too, has its manufacturer. From a small cottage industry a giant was born; small tobacco became Big Tobacco, and, as a result, everything from the way tobacco was grown to the consequences of its consumption changed as well. As Bill Moyers (2002), host of the *NOW* program on PBS has stated, "By Big Tobacco, we mean companies so huge, their revenues dwarf the gross national product of some countries; companies so powerful they can become a law unto themselves."

Our examination of the development of the tobacco industry and assessment of the role of tobacco in drugging the poor is framed by an exploration of the worldview of legal drug capitalism, the social performance of the tobacco industry in light of this understanding of reality, and an alternative, critical view of industry behavior. This strategy is informed by a lesson learned from the provocative writings of Nobel Prize–winning author Toni Morrison (1993:xi):

> For the kind of insight that invites reflection, language must be critiqued. Frustrating language, devious calls to arms, and ancient inflammatory codes are deployed to do their weary work of obfuscation, short circuiting, evasion and distortion.

Seeing like a Legal Drug Corporation

In his widely celebrated book, *Seeing like a State*, James Scott (1998) argues that nations develop and maintain particular "optical models" of what the world looks like to them—their constructed image of reality as it is and as it should be. Such models tend to be very simplified and orderly compared to the complex, messy, and even contradictory places that comprise understandings of the world constructed by nonstate observers, such as fiction writers, journalists, and social scientists. Nations use their models of the world as the basis for nation-building and governance. State functionaries impose their simplified visual "realities" on the locally diverse physical and social configurations that comprise the nation by requiring and enforcing standardized operating procedures, uniform rules, and inflexible organizational grids. To implement all of this, the state apparatus employs its authority to influence and power to coerce.

As one example of seeing like a state, Scott cites the planning of Brazil's new capital during the 1950s. In laying out Brasilia in what until then had been a heavily forested district, government-sponsored designers imposed spatial segregation onto urban functions, such as public administration, housing, commerce and banking, and recreation. The result, although quite imposing, and even, in places, breathtaking, is ill-fit for human use, as exemplified by the vast Plaza of the Three Powers and the flanking Esplanade of the Ministries, the federal administrative center of the capital. Observes Scott (1998:121), the plaza

> is of such a scale as to dwarf even a military parade. . . . If one were to arrange to meet a friend there, it would be rather like trying to meet someone in the middle of the Gobi desert. And if one did meet up with one's friend, there would be nothing to do. . . . This plaza is a symbolic center for the state; the only activity that goes on around it is the work of the ministries.

The larger point Scott makes in his book about social activities harkens back to the discussion in chapter 2 about the relationship between formal and informal economies, namely a relationship that is much more intertwined and interdependent than is commonly recognized, and especially rarely so by the state which treats them extremely differently:

> By themselves, the simplified rules [of state planning] can never generate a functioning community, city, or economy. Formal order, to be more explicit, is always to some degree parasitic on informal processes, which the formal scheme does not recognize, without which it could not exist, and which it alone cannot create or maintain. (Scott 1998: 310)

Interestingly, James Ferguson has taken Scott's political optics model and applied it to global capitalism, specifically to corporate mineral resource extraction in Africa, in a paper called "Seeing Like an Oil Company." It is Ferguson's (2005:378) contention that a sharp contrast exists between the homogenizing state optics that Scott asserted for the developmental state and the "rather different way of seeing proper to the contemporary global oil company." While states in Scott's analysis see the world as a set of orderly homogenized grids, increasingly oil companies, according to Ferguson, see the world as a number of small mineral rich enclaves that are isolated from the surrounding country but closely linked to the corporation.

In this vision, weak governments are not a problem for oil companies and perhaps they are preferred. Even social unrest is not a threat, as private armies can be hired to secure and control mineral-rich "islands" in the sea of social resistance. The same is true of infrastructure and labor: companies can build their own facilities, lay out roads, erect housing, and import labor, "bypass[ing] the nation-state frame altogether" (Ferguson 2005:379). In this way of seeing the world, an image emerges in which governments and countries fade into the background, and a series of exploitable resource patches stand in bold relief in the foreground. In the world as seen by an oil company, it is only these patches that matter.

Reaching Out to the World

What then does the world look like from the vantage of a legal drug company; what are the "optics" of this kind of corporation? Moreover, because it is possible to listen to (or read) the words of legal drug company spokespersons, how do such companies talk about the world? The starting point for answering these questions is to follow Ferguson's lead and to ask another question: what is important to a legal drug company, in this case, a tobacco company? The answer is fairly straightforward: on the one hand, it is the points of production (around the world), including both the fields where tobacco is grown, harvested, and dried, a domain referred to in the industry as "the farming community," as well as the factories where it is processed into cigarettes or other tobacco products, all of which constitute a part of the world known in the tobacco industry as "the supply chain." It is estimated that over 30 million people worldwide are involved in tobacco farming on either a full- or part-time basis. On the other hand, tobacco companies are vitally concerned with the various markets in which great profit is made and through which tobacco products find their way into the hands (and bodies) of various population segments or market niches, such as Hispanics, youth, and women, within the United States and worldwide.

As expressed by the British American Tobacco company (BAT), which ships its products to 180 countries around the globe, their tobacco enterprises extend "from seed to smoke" (British American Tobacco 2006a). Another somewhat different tobacco industry giant (and hence one with a somewhat different view of the world), the Universal Corporation (2006), describes its complex chain of activities:

> Universal's tobacco business includes selecting, buying, shipping, processing, packing, storing, and financing of leaf tobacco in tobacco growing countries for sale to, or for the account of, manufacturers of tobacco products throughout the world. Universal does not manufacture cigarettes or other consumer products. Most of the Company's tobacco revenues are derived from sales of processed tobacco and from fees and commissions for specific services.

Based on self-descriptions of this sort, on one level, the world in the eyes of a tobacco corporation resembles a complex web emanating from a nucleus. The nucleus is a company's administrative headquarters (as well as dispersed branch management sites). On one side of the nucleus there are lines (of transport and communication) stretching to many places of tobacco production (within the U.S. and globally) and on the other side, lines reach out to the industry's diverse markets, which, at the level of individual retail outlets, also constitute important product promotional sites. Of course, other critical tentacles in a tobacco company's web-like complex extend to other entities, including company laboratories, where new ways to increase the nicotine level of cigarettes, for example, are investigated; advertising agencies that are contracted to use creative imagery and messaging to convince people to smoke a deadly product; government offices and the courts, especially in light of the enormous lawsuits that have been brought against the tobacco industry in recent years; machine companies that produce farming and processing equipment; and the insurance industry.

Conquering the World and Defending Interests

How do tobacco companies view their relations with the regions and locations engaged by its many appendages? The answer to this question can be found in the recorded speeches made to various audiences by tobacco industry leaders. For example, some tobacco companies, like BAT and Philip Morris, maintain accessible archives on their websites of talks given to shareholders or at assorted industry meetings and conferences.

In these speeches, war appears as a general framing device in the worldview of the tobacco industry. In the case of BAT, the use of war images began early in the company's history. As Martin Broughton (2002), former head of BAT's Board of Directors, explained at an annual stockholders meeting in 2002:

> Your business has come a long way since that extraordinary US entrepreneur, Buck Duke, arrived in the UK just over a century ago, with the technology that would enable mass cigarette production, with the all-powerful American Tobacco Company in his control and a plan to corner the UK market. With the immortal words: "Hello boys, I'm Duke from New York, come to buy your business," he triggered the trade war with Imperial Tobacco that was settled in 1902 with the birth of a new joint venture—British American Tobacco—that has today grown to be bigger than both its parents.

Almost a hundred years after Duke's consequential arrival in England, war-like imagery in industry discourse grew to be particularly sharp and frequent. "War" was ignited by public health pronouncements about the dangers of smoking that included linking smoking with lung cancer, and the mounting legal efforts against the tobacco industry for selling products it knew to be addictive and dangerous. In a July 17, 1963, memo, Addison Yeaman, general counsel for the Brown & Williamson Tobacco Company, discussed the damaging effects of the Surgeon General's Report on the dangers of smoking:

> Thus to accept its responsibility [to conduct research in the hopes of proving that tobacco consumption is not dangerous] would, I suggest, free the industry to take a much more aggressive posture to meet attack. It would in particular free the industry to attack the Surgeon General's Report itself by

pointing out its gaps and omissions, its reliance on statistics, its lack of clin-ical evidence, etc., etc. . . . The issuance of the Surgeon General's Report will, in my opinion, insure the success of that defense as to causes of action aris-ing in the future if the industry can [also] steel itself to issuing a warning. I have no wish to be tarred and feathered, but I would suggest the industry might serve itself on several fronts if it voluntarily adopted a package legend such as "excessive use of this product may be injurious to health of suscepti-ble persons. . . ." The point is: On this new terrain, permitting strong offen-sive action, *we get there fastest with the mostest.* (FRONTLINE 2006)

One area of particular importance to a global company is "conquer-ing" the international domain. Philip Morris International, for example, has 50 tobacco products factories around the world and sells the com-modities they produce in over 160 national markets. From the perspec-tive of Western tobacco companies, it appears that foreign tobacco markets are viewed as being potentially dangerous places, from a fiscal perspective. In a speech to shareholders on April 27, 2006, Jan du Plessis (2006), chairman of the board of BAT noted that in accessing foreign markets the company should expect to encounter "rough waters . . . from time to time, such as sudden hikes in excise duties or price wars in cer-tain countries." But, like an army, as the company enters a new market (or "front" in the words of one executive), it should seek to first "estab-lish a foothold" and then "power ahead," "together under one banner" as former chairman of the board of BAT, Martin Broughton, emphasized in his annual board presentations (2002, 2004).

War-like imagery also is invoked in talk about intentions to "protect fundamental business interests" from the assaults of antismoking and regulatory bodies, which often are described as "external forces." In his retirement speech, Martin Broughton (2004) told BAT shareholders that some health policy makers in Europe "show signs of having been 'cap-tured' by narrowly based, vociferous anti-tobacco activists." In similar dramatic language, Michael Prideau (2004), director, corporate and regu-latory affairs at BAT, talked of the company having to battle back against the "full force of the 'Decade of Demonisation' in the United States." Part of this battle involves rallying the troops, namely organizing smok-ers to defend their "right to smoke." Prideau (2004) reported:

In Canada, where 5 million tobacco consumers have so often been side-lined and ignored in regulation, our company is helping to enable a new online smokers' association, My Choice, where consumers as citizens and taxpayers can start building their voice.

Tobacco companies do not see the contradiction in selling addictive products known to damage the larynx or "speech box" that produces the human voice and then helping its customers to build "their voice" to defend their right to engage in their addiction in public, and thereby help sustain company profits.

Ironically, when addressing the issue of "counterfeiting," the term used by the industry to refer to illegal production and sale of tobacco by illegal operators, in addition to the frequent use of "fighting words"—as illicit tobacco is seen as an evil that must be "combated" forcefully through the building of "alliances" and the "seizing and destroying" of cigarette counterfeiting machinery—tobacco companies also employ medical language, referring to the growing global pattern of illicit tobacco sales as a "social epidemic" that could "escalate out of control" (Broughton 2002; Philip Morris International Management 2006). Indeed from the perspective of the tobacco companies, "No branded goods are safe, or country immune" from this spreading epidemic (Broughton 2002). Tobacco companies, which are sustaining huge loses as a result of illegal tobacco sales, are frustrated by the fact that governments do not take this illegal intrusion as seriously as they do the illicit drug trade or the counterfeiting of money:

> As increasing public resources are rightly focused on hard drugs and money laundering, so counterfeiting has become an attractive soft option for criminals. It is often as profitable as traditional criminal activities, but without the high risks, severe penalties and social stigma. . . . The laws of most countries distinguish between faking public property like banknotes, and faking private property—like brands. The penalties are much tougher for copying banknotes, even though, unlike fake brands, fake money doesn't cause injury. Society deters the counterfeit of banknotes, and easy though it is to do, there is little of it around. . . . As things stand, almost nobody is going to jail for counterfeiting. Our laws are not set up to throw white-collar criminals into overcrowded prisons. (Broughton 2004)

Ignoring their own history, with reference to illicit tobacco production and smuggling and their own involvement in other white-collar crime, the tobacco companies plaintively ask: "Is it appropriate that raw material producers can hide behind a real or feigned lack of knowledge?" (Broughton 2004). While it does not yet appear that the tobacco companies have imagined a way to link tobacco counterfeiting to terrorism, should such a connection, however thin, ever present itself, there is little doubt that it would be seized upon with vigor.

Weapons of the Wealthy

In the aftermath of the settlements of major lawsuits against the tobacco industry, war imagery has been fading (except with reference to certain topics), while the language of compromise, constructive engagement, reconciliation, collaboration, societal alignment, and social responsibility have pushed to the forefront. A brief consideration of the lawsuits that have been filed in recent years against the tobacco industry and the outcomes of these suits will help to clarify the changes in the public face of the tobacco industry. In an early individual suit, Rose

Cipollone, a smoker dying from lung cancer, sued Liggett Group in 1986, charging the company failed to warn her about the grave dangers of its tobacco products. Cipollone initially was awarded a $400,000 judgment against Liggett, but this was overturned by another court. After two arguments before the Supreme Court, and Rose's death from lung cancer, the Cipollone family, unable to afford the cost of the continued battle against a giant tobacco company, was forced to drop the suit, providing a lesson for Big Tobacco in how to defeat individual suits. At this point in time (1992), "the tobacco industry was an impenetrable fortress. The industry admitted nothing, denied everything, and successfully defended nearly every lawsuit filed against it" (Luka 1999:1). In significant ways, this soon changed.

Of special note in this regard are the settlements Big Tobacco made with the states that sued because of the enormous costs they faced treating smoking-related cancer cases, especially The Master Settlement Agreement of 1998. In defending themselves against these suits, the tobacco industry leaned heavily on American cultural values, especially the bedrock belief that an individual has agency and can make his/her own decisions; further, the responsibility to make good decisions lies with the individual and hence it is the individual who must bear the consequences of poor decisions. It was the stance of the tobacco industry that it never forced anyone to smoke; smokers made that decision on their own.

Attorneys for the plaintiffs countered that: (1) the massive tobacco advertising enterprise was designed to defraud and mislead people about the risks of smoking, even though those risks were well-known to the tobacco companies; (2) the decision to continue smoking is driven not only by a freely engaged decision but by the fact that cigarettes, because of nicotine, are highly addictive and that tobacco companies, although denying it, intentionally manipulated the nicotine levels of tobacco products to insure that its customers were addicted; and (3) tobacco companies target nonsmoking youth, a social group that society does not accord the right to make its own decisions, in an effort to continually win new generations of addicted smokers. Relying on internal documents subpoenaed from the files of tobacco companies, the plaintiffs made their case, and strongly so; as a result the tobacco companies agreed to a settlement.

While 46 states joined together in a joint settlement for a total sum of $206 billion to be paid over 25 years, four states reached their own settlements with the industry for an additional $40 billion. Beyond the payments to the states, tobacco companies agreed to spend almost $2 billion to study smoking among youth and to pay for antismoking educational efforts. Moreover, they agreed to accept restrictions on marketing, especially with regard to advertisements that target children, such as using cartoon characters in ads, advertising on billboards, and putting cigarette brand names on promotional shirts, hats, and other merchandise. The settlement received mixed reactions among antismoking advocates, with some seeing it as an important step in the right direction and others complaining that the bottom line was significantly less than a broader agreement for a payment of $368.5 billion that had been reached in 1997 but did not win congressional approval.

In another case, in Florida, plaintiffs in a class action suit against the five biggest tobacco manufacturers were initially awarded $145 billion in punitive damages because the companies were found to have negligently misled the public about the health risks and addictive nature of cigarettes. In the trial, which lasted for two years, seven jurors deliberated for less than five hours before reaching their verdict, which would have cost Philip Morris $74 billion, Reynolds $36 billion, Brown & Williamson $17.5 billion, Lorillard $16.25 billion, and Liggett $790 million. On July 6, 2006, however, the Florida Supreme Court overturned the punitive damages awarded by the jurors, claiming that while it was true the tobacco companies were negligent, the award was excessive, and that a class action suit by thousands of Floridian smokers made ill by tobacco should not have been allowed to go forward. Each smoker, the supreme court justices ruled, must file on his/her own, and thus the Florida Supreme Court upheld awards of $2–$4 million to several individuals (Kellestad 2006). The ruling was music to the ears of Big Tobacco, as tobacco companies, with their deep pockets, have developed a strong track record of beating individual lawsuits. In response to the court ruling, tobacco company stock shot up on the New York Stock Exchange.

In asking how tobacco companies see the world, it is also appropriate to ask as well how they don't see the world; that is, are there features of the world seen by others that they don't see? Although tobacco companies now publicly admit that tobacco use can be dangerous, one feature of the world that they do not appear to fully see is that one billion people in the world are expected to die of tobacco-related illnesses during the 21st century if current trends continue, according to the World Health Organization (Associated Press 2006a). Perhaps this is just too big a number to see.

Smoke, Mirrors, and the Tobacco Industry

From the perspective of the legal drug industry as described above, there are several central tenets that define tobacco industry reality, including:

- Tobacco is a vital part of the U.S. and world economies, supporting the livelihood of millions of workers and providing billions of dollars to governments through taxation.

- Undue government regulation harms the tobacco industry and must be controlled by tobacco companies "demanding an active role in shaping the regulatory environment" in which they operate (Davies 2003).

- The advertisement of tobacco products—what has been called "commercial speech" in cases before the Supreme Court—is protected by the free speech and free press clauses of the First Amendment to the U.S. Constitution.
- Smokers, be they adults or children, are responsible for their own actions; no one is forced to use tobacco products.
- Adolescents who smoke are breaking the law and should be punished; the tobacco industry is not responsible for the choices children make.
- The rights of adults to choose to smoke must be protected.
- It is not clear that environmental or secondhand smoke is harmful to nonsmokers, hence banning smoking in public places is inappropriate.
- Smokers have rights that must be protected.

These tenets comprise what Kroop (2001) has called "the topsy-turvy world of tobacco, where wrong is right, and bad is good." All of these tenets, as well as the attitude noted earlier that governments have a mandate to crack down on illicit tobacco sales, stem from and reflect the legal status of tobacco companies. The tobacco industry sees laws and law enforcement as resources that can be called upon to promote and protect it. When necessary, however, to strengthen the bottom line, laws can be subverted in various ways.

Using the Legal Advantage

Advertising.   Were an illicit cocaine company to attempt to buy advertising space in the New York Times or the Peoria Journal Star or any other mainstream U.S. newspaper, disclaiming that regular cocaine use was harmful, the First Amendment to the U.S. Constitution notwithstanding, the advertisement would not be accepted and the attempt, if taken seriously, would probably quickly be reported to the local police or other law enforcement agency. In the decades leading up to 1914, before cocaine was made illegal, however, the manufacturers of various elixirs, tonics, and patent remedies that contained heavy doses of the drug—or of heroin and marijuana—not only frequently advertised their products, such drug ads were a mainstay of early newspaper advertisement. These ads proclaimed the innumerable health benefits of what are now illegal substances, for men, women, and children alike. Furthermore, the flowering poppy, the source of opium, was freely and widely grown in the United States, and food markets, general stores, and pharmacies stocked and sold opiates. A survey conducted in the late mid-1880s in Iowa, which at the time had a population of under two million, found 3,000 stores in the state where opiates were on sale, and this did not include the physicians who dispensed opiate-based drugs directly to patients (Brecher 1972). As the federal government began to criminalize the use of the opiates, cocaine, and other psychotropic commodities, colorful posters and newspaper ads for these products quickly disappeared.

One of the great benefits of tobacco being legal is the ability of Big Tobacco to publicly advertise its products (even if this capacity has been constrained in recent years) as well as to communicate through advertisement with consumers, policy makers, and other valued audiences. When television programs first began to appear in an increasing number of U.S. homes during the 1950s, tobacco companies quickly saw the advertising potential and began to sponsor programs on the new, but increasingly popular media. The program *Your Hit Parade*, one of the first successful TV programs with a seven-year run beginning in 1950, was sponsored by Lucky Strike. One of the early TV ads produced to promote this cigarette brand, called "Be Happy, Go Lucky," won *TV Guide*'s commercial of the year award. In the ad, a group of cheerleaders sing the rhyme: "Yes, Luckies get our loudest cheer on campus and on dates. With college gals and college guys a Lucky really rates" (quoted in Borio 2003). The targeting of young potential smokers, as well as the subtle connection of smoking, sex, and fun, became foundations of subsequent tobacco promotional efforts. In 1951, the long popular *I Love Lucy* show began with Philip Morris as a sponsor. In the opening credits, stick figures of Lucy and Desi Arnaz are shown climbing up a giant pack of Philip Morris cigarettes. Sponsorship by a tobacco company also led to Lucy and Desi being shown smoking during the program's introduction and throughout individual shows, as well as the appearance of the "Call for Philip Moooriiiiuuss" kid shown during commercial transitions. The goal was to interweave smoking throughout all parts of the program with the intention—largely achieved for many years—of making cigarette smoking normative for all sectors of society.

Discrediting Science.   Being legal has also afforded the tobacco industry the ability to publicly oppose any threats to its bottom line. For example, when the first independent studies showed tobacco to be carcinogenic, the industry launched a sustained public effort to counter these findings. The public health case against tobacco began to build in 1950 when the *Journal of the American Medical Association* (which banned cigarette ads three years later) published several case control studies linking lung cancer and smoking (Levin et al. 1950; Wynder and Graham 1950). Ernest Wynder and Evarts Graham (1950), for example, reporting on a review of 684 patients with lung cancer, found that 96.5 percent were at least moderately heavy to heavy smokers. Morton Levin, an infectious disease epidemiologist on the staff of Roswell Park Memorial Institute in Buffalo, began studying cancer with the idea that it might be caused by viruses. As part of his investigation of this link, he added a number of new questions to the standard intake form of the institute, including a question about smoking. A subsequent study of patients with lung cancer in comparison with three control groups revealed the relationship of lung cancer to being a smoker. Levin and his colleague wrote up their findings and submitted them to the *Journal of the American Medical Association*, where they quickly ran into problems. As Armenian and Szklo comment:

> The journal was hesitant to publish the report because the Editor was not certain of the scientific value of the research approach used. However, shortly after the receipt of the Levin et al. paper, Wynder and Graham submitted a paper to the same journal reporting essentially the same results from a case-control study! The second author, Evarts Graham, was a surgeon with an international reputation as an innovator. It was therefore difficult for the Editor to dismiss the Wynder and Graham paper. Hence, both papers were published in the same issue of the *Journal of the American Medical Association*. (1996:648)

The medical and scientific communities initially were quite resistant to accepting the fact that smoking causes cancer, in no small part because a high percentage of doctors and scientists, including Evarts Graham (who quit smoking in 1951 but died of lung cancer in 1957), were smokers. As Doll (1998:131) later commented "the ubiquity of the habit . . . had dulled the collective sense that tobacco might be a major threat to health." Seizing on this fact, tobacco companies ran ads claiming that most physicians preferred their respective brands. As Gardner and Brandt (2006) point out, the use of reassuring images of doctors (always white, male, and middle aged) in cigarette advertisements in 1930–1953 reflected the tobacco companies' response to the first rumblings of public concern about potential risks of smoking. Wynder, who was a medical student when he began his study, went on to publish 750 peer-reviewed papers (Thun 2005). When his coauthor, Graham, read the final draft of their paper, he told Wynder (1998:737):

> You are going to have many difficulties. The smokers will not like your message. The tobacco interests will be vigorously opposed. The media and the government will be loath to support these findings. But you have one factor in your favour. What you have going for you is that you are right.

Soon after these two papers appeared, Doll and Hill (1950) (both of whom were smokers when they began their research) published a parallel study in the *British Medical Journal* (which stopped carrying cigarette ads in 1958). They reported that heavy smokers were fifty times more likely than nonsmokers to develop lung cancer. Slowly the tide was beginning to turn.

At the popular level, George Seldes, a noted foreign correspondent during the 1920s and later an author of several books on the impact of big corporations on the media, began publishing a critical newsletter in 1940 called *In Fact: An Antidote to Falsehood in the Daily Press*. In January of 1941, Seldes published the first of an eventual 50 pieces outlining the dangers of tobacco use. The article reported on the findings of Dr. Raymond Pearl of Johns Hopkins University indicating the contribution of smoking to shortening tobacco users' lifespans. Seldes published the piece because he recognized, correctly, that the mainstream media, particularly the largest daily newspapers around the country, fearful of losing tobacco advertising, would avoid writing about Pearl's findings even though a story about the study was carried on the AP wire.

Eleven years later, in 1952, *Reader's Digest*, the largest selling U.S. magazine at the time, and one that could not easily be threatened by the tobacco industry because it carried no advertising, republished an article from the *Christian Herald* by Roy Norr (1952) entitled "Cancer by the Carton." This was the first in a series of articles on the many health risks of smoking in the widely read magazine. Norr (1952:7) began his article by arguing that the risks of smoking were being "kept from public notice," which subsequently proved to precisely the case.

In 1957, a *Reader's Digest* article also drew attention to the fact that levels of tar and nicotine in filtered cigarettes had been regularly increasing. When the public relations director at American Tobacco noticed articles critical of smoking in *Reader's Digest* he contacted Batten, Barton, Durstine, and Osborn (BBDO), the advertising agency used by both the magazine and American Tobacco. BBDO was told in no uncertain terms that either it dropped *Reader's Digest* as a client or loose $30 million a year in business from American Tobacco. The magazine was dropped as a client. The cat—which would ultimately grow into a lion—was beginning to creep further out of the bag, but not without meeting intense opposition. From this point on, the cancer/tobacco link would grow steadily clearer, strident industry efforts notwithstanding.

In response to all the bad news from the world of science, the head of major tobacco companies, including American Tobacco, R. J. Reynolds, Philip Morris, U.S. Tobacco, Lorillard, and Brown & Williamson, banned together to form the Tobacco Institute Research Committee or TIRC (which was renamed The Council for Tobacco Research in 1964). The TIRC soon hired a public relations firm to launch a vigorous campaign designed to undercut the threat to profits inherent in the public linking of cancer with smoking. One of the first actions taken by the public relations company was to run a full-page ad in more than 400 newspapers around the country. Entitled "A Frank Statement to Cigarette Smokers," the ad boldly if disingenuously proclaimed:

> Distinguished authorities point out: That medical research of recent years indicates many possible causes of lung cancer. That there is no agreement among the authorities regarding what the cause is. That there is no proof that cigarette smoking is one of the causes. That statistics purporting to link cigarette smoking with the disease could apply with equal force to any one of many other aspects of modern life. Indeed the validity of the statistics themselves is questioned by numerous scientists. We accept an interest in people's health as a basic responsibility, paramount to every other con-

sideration in our business. We believe the products we make are not injurious to health. We always have and always will cooperate closely with those whose task it is to safeguard the public health. For more than 300 years tobacco has given solace, relaxation, and enjoyment to mankind. At one time or another during those years critics have held it responsible for practically every disease of the human body. One by one these charges have been abandoned for lack of evidence. (quoted in Borio 2003)

With this inauguration, TIRC's mission became that of refuting, discrediting, and otherwise attacking and neutralizing scientific findings on the multiple risks of tobacco consumption. So began a decades-long initiative by the tobacco companies to publicly claim as fact what they privately knew was false. Larry White (1988) points out in his book, *Merchants of Death: The Tobacco Industry*, the American Cancer Society responded to the TIRC and the tobacco companies in 1954 by announcing that there was essential agreement among cancer researchers, surgeons, and pathologists that smoking was a very likely cause of lung cancer. The *New York Times* reported this announcement, but sought out the TIRC's reaction. Timothy Hartnett, the TIRC's chairman was quoted in the *Times* article as calling the American Cancer Society's poll of scientists and doctors "biased, unscientific and filled with shortcomings."

More recently, in 1981, Takeshi Hirayama (1981), the chief of epidemiology at the Research Institute at Tokyo's National Cancer Center, published his findings based on a 14-year study of nonsmoking wives of smoking and nonsmoking husbands to assess their relative risk for developing lung cancer. The study had three key findings. First, wives who were married to ex-smoking or current smoking husbands who smoked up 14 cigarettes per day had a 40 percent higher rate of lung cancer than wives whose husbands did not smoke. Second, wives whose current smoking husbands smoked a pack or more each day had a 90 percent higher rate of lung cancer. Finally, nonsmokers who lived with smokers developed lung cancer between one-third and one-half as often as did the smokers. These findings addressed a particularly contentious issue: is smoking harmful to nonsmokers exposed to secondhand smoke? Hirayama's findings, which have been supported by subsequent research (Ong and Glantz 2000), is today credited with bringing the issue of secondhand smoking into public discourse. Concluded Hirayama:

> The fact that there was a statistically significant relation . . . between the amount the husbands smoked and the mortality of their non-smoking wives from lung cancer suggests that these findings were not the result of chance. (1981:942)

The tobacco industry is particularly sensitive to findings like these because they fuel public and policy maker interest in bans on smoking in public locations. As a result, the tobacco industry, taking full advantage of its legal status, launched a multimillion-dollar advertising campaign, including costly full-page ads in hundreds of newspapers around the country, to discredit Hirayama's findings (Glantz 1983). The campaign against Hirayama also was carried out in other countries around the world. For the ad, the industry hired its own epidemiologist, Nathan Mantel, to pen a criticism of Hirayama's finding (which the *British Medical Journal*, in an unusual move that reveals the tobacco industry's ability to have its influential voice heard, included in a follow-up discussion nine months after the original article appeared). Hirayama, up for the challenge, effectively refuted Mantel in his own contribution to the follow-up discussion.

In Australia, the Federation of Consumer Organizations sued a number of tobacco companies and won its case on the grounds that the advertisements critical of Hirayama were false and misleading. Ironically, rather than stymie secondhand smoking research, the controversy attracted the interest of other epidemiologists who carried out their own studies on secondhand smoking. Findings of these researchers, on the whole, not only supported Hirayama, they led to reports by both the U.S. Surgeon General and the National Academy of Sciences on the significant public health risks of exposure to secondhand smoke. All the while, the industry had a little secret that was unknown to the *British Medical Journal*, the newspapers that ran industry attacks on Hirayama's work, the U.S. Surgeon General, the National Academy of Sciences, or the general public: its own scientists believed that Hirayama was right, as documented in internal industry memos. As stated in one such document (Wells and Pepples 1981), "Hirayama is a good scientist and his non-smoking wives publication was correct."

Product Placement.   An additional advantage of making and marketing a legal product is the ability of the tobacco industry to engage in a practice known as "product placement," which involves a form of subtle indirect advertising through the display of products and product labels in movies, blended into the flow of dramatic events. A noteworthy example of the tobacco commodification of a movie is *Superman II*, a film clearly targeted to young audiences that for years has been reshown on TV. In the movie, there are over 20 exposures of the Marlboro logo, for which Philip Morris is believed to have paid over $40,000. Moreover, although the character Lois Lane never smoked in the comic book on which the movie is based, she chain-smokes her way through the second Superman movie, and in the final climatic scene Superman fights it out with his enemies in an urban landscape replete with Marlboro billboards. *Superman II* does not stand alone; many other movies from this era, most with strong appeal to children, included smoking scenes, such as *Beverly Hills Cop*, *Crocodile Dundee*, *Batteries Not Included*, and *Who Framed Roger Rabbit?* Research has shown that while the percentage of Americans who smoke was falling, the reverse was happening on the big screen. There was a doubling in the number of young adults shown smoking in movies, from 21 percent in the 1960s to 45 percent by the 1980s. At a time when only 19 percent of wealthy Americans reported smoking, 57 percent of the characters portrayed as wealthy individuals in movies were puffing in front of the camera (Action on Smoking and Health 1996).

Besieging the Capitol.   Another way in which the tobacco industry is able to use its legal status to good advantage is in lobbying politicians for favorable policy development and enforcement. In 1998, for example, a number of public health groups began pushing for the passage of a national tobacco bill that would have imposed significant restrictions on the industry, as well as a $1.10 per pack price increase over a five-year period. To oppose this legislation, the tobacco industry spent $43 million more on lobbying than it had during the same time period the year before, which amounted to 23 percent more for the six-month period of intensive lobbying than for the entire previous year (Torry 1998). A large chunk of this extra money went into hiring several high-priced lobbying firms. According to the public activist group Public Citizen, the industry "besieged the Capitol with 192 lobbyists," about "one for every three members of Congress" (quoted in Torry 1998:A10). Additional sums were used for campaign contributions and for a massive advertising effort. The team enlisted the help of well-connected Washington figures, including former Senate majority leader Howard Baker Jr. (R-Tennessee), and numerous former congressional office staffers. With such a well-funded, well-connected, and carefully crafted campaign, it is not surprising that the bill went down to defeat.

Scott Williams, a spokesman for the tobacco industry, defended the effort saying that "the industry was facing possibly the largest excise tax increase on a consumer product in the history of the country. If the public health community faced a threat of equal magnitude, it would make every effort to exercise its right to communicate its views with the government and the public." The inability of the public health community to bankroll an effort of this magnitude escaped Williams' attention.

Subverting the Law

Being Vicious in Mauritius.   When deemed necessary, tobacco companies are not adverse to bending or outright breaking the law. A case in point can be found on the island nation of Mauritius, which lies in the Indian Ocean east of Madagascar. Formerly a colony of first the Dutch, then the French, and finally the British, the country has been independent since 1968. Like many islands, it is touted by the local tourist industry as an escape from the everyday world, a place of contrasting colors and tastes, a quiet oasis of peace and tranquility, a melting pot of cultural traditions where the past and the present blend together smoothly. Wafting through the air of this seemingly pristine island, however, is the carcinogenic smoke of many cigarettes held in the hands of islanders and tourists alike. At a time of growing global concern about the long-term costs of smoking, in 1999 the government of Mauritius joined the swelling ranks of countries that have begun to put the brakes on the aggressive promotion of tobacco consumption by modifying the nation's Public Health Act to ban tobacco advertising and specifying:

> No person involved in the production, marketing, distribution or sale of any tobacco product shall offer, or agree to provide, any form of sponsorship to any other person in relation to a tobacco product or trade name or brand associated with a tobacco product. (quoted in LeClézio 2002)

According to the Mauritian antismoking group, ViSa, BAT, which has included Mauritius as a market since 1926, responded to the amended law and ban on tobacco company sponsorships by:

- donating libraries to poorer villages, with the support of national government officials, and promoting the opening of these libraries and other resources through media photographs and reports;
- donating prenatal and orthopedic wards to Mauritian public hospitals;
- sponsoring a national art gallery;
- building a home for elderly people;
- advertising smoking products through the use of help-wanted notices in local newspapers;
- using youth smoking-prevention programs at point of purchase sites to draw customer attention to cigarette displays;
- giving away T-shirts displaying the company's logo to all walkers at the annual Day of the Blind fundraiser;
- instituting the competitive BAT Undergraduate Scholarship program and organizing free training opportunities for students at BAT Mauritius;
- developing youth smoking-prevention materials that portray tobacco products as an adult reward, thereby making use of them a marker of grown-up status;
- selling Lucky Strike cigarettes with higher tar and nicotine levels in Mauritius than those sold in the United States (LeClézio 2002).

Not only was BAT not prosecuted for violating Mauritius' Public Health Act, but ironically, the Mauritius Ministry of Health and Ministry of Labour awarded BAT the first prize in the National Occupational Health and Safety competition in 2001. As this example suggests, the tobacco industry has long known that passing laws is one thing, but enforcing them is another. In resource-poor and developing countries, in particular, tobacco profits can be used to gain a considerable amount of influence.

The Smoke Screen.   The illegal activities of the tobacco industry are far older and of far greater significance than what has occurred in Mauritius. As a result of the lawsuits in the United States that led to the tobacco settlement of 1998, numerous industry documents have come to light that suggest that tobacco industry lawyers carefully controlled the release of scientific research in a planned effort to hide findings that were damaging to the industry. Put simply, the tobacco companies covered up evidence in their possession that showed smoking is addictive and causes an array of diseases, including various deadly cancers. As part of the cover-up, tobacco companies manipulated attorney–client privilege rules to hide damning evidence from public awareness. As summarized by the U.S. Justice Department, the tobacco companies should not be allowed to retain the untold billions of dollars "they acquired through their unlawful conduct" (Reno 1999).

Statements of this sort are supported by considerable evidence that by the mid-1950s (and probably years before that), the tobacco industry was well aware of the link between smoking and cancer, an association they continued to deny publicly for decades afterward (Kessler 1994). In his book, *Ashes to Ashes*, for example, Richard Kluger (1996:165) cites the minutes of a meeting held at the Liggett Tobacco Company on March 29, 1954, in which a company scientist is quoted as saying "if we can eliminate or reduce the carcinogenic agent in smoke we will have made real progress." Similarly, a Philip Morris company document from the early 1960s states that "carcinogens are found in practically every class of compounds in smoke" (Wakeham 1961). Similarly, on April 3, 1970, the general manager for research of the British tobacco company Gallagher Limited wrote a memo summarizing the results of a study done on the consequences of exposure to tobacco smoke among dogs. The memo states:

> One of the striking features of the Auerbach experiment was that practically every dog which smoked suffered significantly from the effects of the smoke, either in terms of severe irritation and bronchitis, pre-cancerous changes or cancer. This, of course, is a much more extreme situation than in human beings where only one in ten heavy smokers get lung cancer and one in five suffer from some form of respiratory infection, often described as mild bronchitis. . . . However, in spite of the qualifications, . . . we believe that the Auerbach work proves beyond reasonable doubt that fresh whole cigarette smoke is carcinogenic to dog lungs and therefore it is highly likely that it is carcinogenic to human lungs. (FRONTLINE 2006)

During this era, the tobacco companies were publicly denying that cigarettes were dangerous. At the same time, armed with knowledge about how deadly tobacco was, tobacco company scientists were aggressively (although ultimately unsuccessfully) attempting to develop a safe cigarette. Had the industry been able to produce a safe cigarette, they were well aware that it would cause significant public relations problems because of their continual denial of the risks of smoking. As a British American Tobacco Company (1962) document notes:

> When the health question was first raised we had to start by denying it at the PR level. But by continuing that policy we had got ourselves into a corner and left no room to manoeuvre. In other words if we did get a breakthrough and were able to improve our product we should have to [do an] about-face, and this was practically impossible at the PR level.

The tobacco companies were in a bind, knowing the value of inventing a safe cigarette (a dream they have not abandoned to this day), yet realizing that announcing the launch of such a product would expose their long history of lies.

Reassuring the Consumer.   As public awareness of the potential risks of smoking increased over the years, the industry entered into a period of internecine warfare, with each company using its advertising budget to assert that its products were safer than those of other companies. Noted one industry document: "All work in this area should be directed towards providing consumer reassurance about cigarettes and the smoking habit. This can be provided in different ways, e.g. by claiming low deliveries [of tar], by the perception of low deliveries and by the perception of 'mildness'" (Short 1977). The cigarette filter was one of the mechanisms used by the tobacco industry to try and calm the nerves of an increasingly informed and worried public. In 1952, the tobacco company P. Lorillard excitedly launched Kent cigarettes with what it called a protective "Micronite filter" on the end. At a press conference held at the Waldorf-Astoria Hotel in New York, Lorillard representatives exuberantly claimed that this filter provided "the greatest health protection in cigarette history." In an ad placed in the very popular *Life Magazine*, Lorillard emphasized that "Kent and only Kent has the Micronite Filter, made of a pure, dust-free, completely harmless material that is not only effective but so safe that it actually is used to help filter the air in operating rooms of leading hospitals." In other ads, the company boasted that "No other cigarette approaches such a degree of health protection and taste satisfaction" (ads quoted in Borio 2003).

Lorillard, however, failed to tell the public that the company that supplied the materials for the "Micronite Filter," the Massachusetts-based manufacturer Hollingsworth and Vose, insisted on a 100 percent indemnity agreement signed by Lorillard. The agreement required Lorillard to pay any legal costs or damages stemming from lawsuits over the filter's health effects. Hollingsworth and Vose wanted this protection because the material they supplied to Lorillard for the filters was asbestos. As early as the 1930s and 1940s, epidemiological studies in both Britain and the United States had identified the health hazards of exposure to asbestos, including cancer and pulmonary problems associated with asbestosis, a disease caused by asbestos fibers invading the body through inhalation or ingestion (Gottlieb 1989). The initially lauded "Micronite Filter" was removed from Kent cigarettes in 1956.

All along, the industry was well aware that the filters they put on cigarettes provided no protection from the many harmful chemicals given off during smoking. A document, for example, from a tobacco industry lawyer noted, "In most cases . . . the smoker of a filter cigarette was getting as much or more nicotine and tar as he would have gotten from a regular cigarette" (Pepples 1976/1996). Catching wind of the possible duplicity inherent in advertising filtered cigarettes as healthy, in the mid-1950s the Legal and Monetary Affairs Subcommittee of the House Government Operations Committee, under Congressman John Blatnik of Minnesota, held hearings to determine if the Federal Trade Commission should regulate tobacco company advertising claims about filtered cigarettes. The report issued by the subcommittee concluded: "The cigarette manufacturers have deceived the American public through their advertising of cigarettes" (quoted in Borio 2003). Not long after the report was issued, Blatnik was stripped of his subcommittee chairmanship and the subcommittee was disbanded.

Similarly, cigarettes from this period that regularly were advertised as being low in tar were known to be no safer than other cigarettes. As a memo from a British American Tobacco Company (1979) scientist revealed, the industry was aware that "the effect of switching to low tar cigarettes may be to increase, not decrease, the risks of smoking." From the industry's sales and marketing perspective, however, effective advertisement could be used to convince people that low-tar cigarettes were safer. A Brown & Williamson Tobacco Company (1982) document, for example, notes:

> B&W will undertake activities designed to generate statements by public health opinion leaders which will indicate tolerance for smoking and improve the consumer's perception of ultra low "tar" cigarettes (5 mg or less). The first step will be the identification of attractive scientists not previously involved in the low delivery controversy who would produce studies re-emphasizing the lower delivery, less risk concept.

Throughout the years, the tobacco industry has been committed to insuring that the nicotine levels in tobacco products remained adequate to insure addiction. Thus, an internal document from the British American Tobacco Company (1959) from the late 1950s states, "Reducing the nicotine per cigarette might end in destroying the nicotine habit in a large number of consumers and prevent it ever being acquired by new smokers." Indeed, among tobacco industry executives, as documented in an internal memorandum written by the director of research at Philip Morris in 1972, the cigarette was seen as an ideal nicotine delivery system for addicted users:

> Think of the cigarette pack as a storage container for a day's supply of nicotine. . . . Think of the cigarette as a dispenser for a dose unit of

nicotine. . . . Think of a puff of smoke as the vehicle for nicotine. . . . Smoke is beyond question the most optimized vehicle of nicotine and the cigarette the most optimized dispenser of smoke. (Kessler 1994)

The general pattern of deception—commonly involving a cover-up by the tobacco industry of what it knew about the risks of smoking—is seen as well in other efforts to keep in-house research findings under wraps. A review of documents produced over the years by the British American Tobacco Company by Hammond and colleagues, for example, found a pattern suggesting "a product strategy intended to exploit the limitations of the testing protocols and to intentionally conceal from consumers and regulators the potential toxicity of BAT products revealed by BAT's own research" (2006:781). Not long after the study by Hammond and coauthors was published in *Lancet*, U.S. District Judge Gladys Kessler issued a 1,742–page ruling that affirmed that the largest tobacco companies "have marketed and sold their lethal product with zeal, with deception, with single-minded focus on their financial success, and without regard for the human tragedy or social costs that success exacted" (quoted in D. Arias 2006:20). As part of her ruling, Judge Kessler ordered tobacco companies to stop using terms like "light" and "low tar" to describe their products. Notably, within two weeks of this ruling, several tobacco companies filed a motion with Judge Kessler that requested they be allowed to use the terms "light" and "low tar" in overseas cigarette advertising.

Targeting Youth.   Tobacco companies also long denied (and, in the post-settlement era, deny again) that they target nonsmoking youth with their advertisement efforts. Moreover, they asserted to the media, in testimony before Congress, and at their own annual shareholders' meetings that they really do not need young people to start smoking to sustain and even expand their respective businesses, in that their vast advertising and promotional campaigns target existing smokers who happen to be using the brands of other tobacco companies. The tricky question of how all tobacco companies can sustain a profit and even grow by swaying the customers of competitors' brands is generally left unanswered. On this point industry spokespersons realized it was best to never speak as an industry.

Not surprisingly, the internal memos of industry companies contradict the public pronouncements of industry executives about marketing to children. One such memo, titled "Young Smokers—Prevalence, Trends, Implications, and Related Demographic Trends," a Philip Morris company correspondence written in 1981, details the dual problem of the dropping U.S. birthrate and the shrinking number of youth who smoke (as well as the rising number of people in the age group 45–54, most likely to quit smoking) (Daniel, et al. 1981). The document, which when he was shown it at the Minnesota Medicaid Trial prompted Philip Morris CEO Geoffrey Bible to say he was "shocked" by its contents, reveals just how concerned industry leaders were about the fact that existing trends suggested a significant decline in young smokers.

To counter declines in the number of youth who take up smoking, tobacco companies initiated various programs. One program, designed to increase the number of Marlboro smokers, included several components, such as:

- a campaign targeted to spring and summer youth-oriented resort areas in several states in which the company's "sales force promotes the brand heavily at POS [points of sale, i.e., stores that sell cigarettes]. Marlboro T-shirts, visors, etc., are given away at the beach, bars, and other hang outs. *No publicity nor outside visibility is desired*"; and

- a summer program in which sampler packs of cigarettes are distributed at "beaches, shopping centers, and other markets of opportunity. This program maintains a pressure on the marketplace" (FRONTLINE 2006, emphasis added).

Not surprisingly, the industry was wary about attracting too much public attention to its efforts to reach large gatherings of young people with promotional material giveaways and free packs of cigarettes, as someone might get the impression that the real goal of such efforts was to get nonsmoking youth to light up. Similar strategies are used by tobacco companies around the world to circumvent national laws and gain new waves of youthful smokers (Global Partnerships for Tobacco Control 2002). These strategies are used

- in Togo, where youth numerically dominate the population and soccer is king, tobacco products are linked through advertisement to music and soccer; such "[a]dvertising and marketing continues to be conducted aggressively and in contempt of existing laws" (Agbavon 2001);

- in the Czech Republic, where Lucky Strike sponsors youth concerts advertised as being for "Lucky People" and Marlboro sponsors "Ultimate Clubbing" concerts featuring U.S. bands to "Light up the Night";

- in Uruguay, where Philip Morris carries out a promotional campaign entitled "Yo tengo poder" ("I have the power") that was specifically directed to children in public schools; and

- in Jordan, where girls dressed in red visit restaurants and give away free cigarettes, 10 packs of Marlboros per person, to smokers and nonsmokers alike.

Similar youth-oriented strategies are used by tobacco companies in many other countries, suggesting a global program for the development of a new generation of addicted smokers. As Jeremy Seabrook (1999) painfully observes, "It is an epic irony that tobacco, a product of Empire, should now be pushed most vigorously by colonising tobacco companies to those who have supposedly freed themselves from the colonial yoke."

But what of the United States? In the shadow of the Master Settlement Agreement between the states and the tobacco industry are tobacco companies still attempting to market their products to youth? Are they in violation of the settlement agreements about advertising and promoting tobacco use among those under 18 years of age?

According to Jeffrey Arnett (2005), tobacco company "talk is cheap." Arnett conducted two post-tobacco settlement studies with adolescents and adults concerning their perceptions of the ages of the models used in new cigarette ads as well as whether the ads portrayed smoking as essential to sexual attraction or success, issues of concern to youth. Findings indicate that for many of the ads, particularly those for brands that are most popular among younger smokers, a majority of the participants assumed the models to be less than 25 years old and a majority also perceived that many of the ads depicted smoking as fundamental for sexual attraction and life success. Concludes Arnett, "Despite their public pledge, the tobacco companies routinely violate a variety of aspects of the Cigarette Advertising and Promotion Code" (2005:419).

Several additional studies have found that immediately following the tobacco settlement the producers of several major brands of cigarettes and smokeless tobacco increased their advertising in magazines that are popular among adolescent readers, such as *Sports Illustrated* and *Rolling Stone*. In June 2002, as a result of a lawsuit initiated by California Attorney General Bill Lockyer, R. J. Reynolds was fined $20 million by a California court for continuing to advertise in youth-oriented magazines sold in the state. The court also ordered R. J. Reynolds to take all "reasonable" steps to stop advertising aimed at underage youth. While some tobacco companies subsequently stopped or at least reduced their advertising in youth-oriented magazines, their compliance seems to be closely tied to the willingness of state attorneys general to take legal action, something that is unlikely, given regional politics, in many states (Myers 2002a).

Additionally, since the tobacco settlement there has been a growing emphasis on advertising smokeless tobacco in youth markets. The Massachusetts Department of Public Health (2002) found that in 2001, three years after the settlement, the United States Smokeless Tobacco Company (USST), the country's largest smokeless tobacco manufacturer and the only smokeless tobacco producer that was part of the tobacco settlement, spent over $9 million advertising its products in magazines that had a significant number of adolescent readers. The average annual level of spending on advertisements placed in youth-oriented magazines by USST increased from $5 million in the years immediately before the settlement to $6 million during 1999–2001. Almost half of USST advertising during this period was in youth-oriented magazines (Myers 2002b).

Overall, according to the Federal Trade Commission, since the tobacco settlement, tobacco companies have elevated their cigarette advertising expenditures by 125 percent to a record level of over $15 billion per year. This translates to over $41 million a day (Campaign for Tobacco-Free Kids 2005). Much of this advertising money is still targeted to children and young adults. Brown & Williamson, for example, began advertising its Kool brand of cigarettes with hip-hop images and music. In response, three states, New York, Maryland, and Illinois, sued the company arguing that its "Kool Mixx" promotional campaign—which was billed as a celebration of hip-hop music and culture—violated the 1998 settlement concerning advertisement to youth. Recognizing it would lose the suit, R. J. Reynolds, which by that point had acquired Brown & Williamson, agreed to pay $1.46 million to the three states to pay for youth smoking prevention programs. According to Illinois Attorney General Lisa Madigan (2004), a participant in the suit, "The tobacco industry has been creative when it comes to trying to lure our children into a lifetime of addiction. Since the Master Settlement Agreement was reached in 1998, companies have tried to get around the prohibition on marketing to youth." Undaunted by the new settlement, the industry looked for new ways to target youth, including new products such as candy-flavored cigarettes.

Throughout the years, the tobacco industry, while spending untold billions of dollars on advertising, has maintained that it is impossible for advertisements to induce people to smoke and that in fact parents are the primary influence on youth smoking (and, hence, following the logic of responsibility in U.S. culture, parents are the real culprits in young people taking up a deadly habit). To investigate an aspect of this issue, Pierce and colleagues (2002) conducted a longitudinal study of the impact of tobacco advertising on the initiation of smoking among teenagers with more- and less-authoritative parents. They found that about 40 percent of adolescent smoking in families with more authoritative parents was attributable to the tobacco industry advertisements and promotions. This percentage is about five times greater than that found in families with less-authoritative patents. On this basis, these researchers conclude, "The promotion of smoking by the tobacco industry appears to undermine the capability of authoritative parenting to prevent adolescents from starting to smoke" (Pierce et al. 2002:73). They go on to note:

> At the time of [our] baseline survey (1996), the Joe Camel [advertisement] campaign was still very active, and it was differentially favored by young adolescents. . . . The marketing approach of this campaign is outlined in previously secret tobacco-industry documents. . . . The goal was to associate the brand with themes of "independence, coolness, fun, imagination, sex, reality-based success (such as a date, a good party), fantasy-based success, excitement (living to the limit, or at least imagining so), taking risks and living on the edge." Adolescents with more-authoritative parents (com-

pared to those with less-authoritative parents) have more limits regarding their time out and receive more monitoring from their parents. It is possible that the message themes of the Joe Camel campaign were, therefore, more novel, salient, and relevant to these adolescents. Models of persuasive communication specify these message themes as essential to maximizing the persuasive power of marketing messages. (Pierce et al. 2002:79)

In light of the impact of the tobacco industry on the lives of children worldwide, Mark Nichter and Elizabeth Cartwright (1991) have questioned whether all of the global public health efforts that have been carried out to insure child survival (e.g., mass immunization, oral rehydration campaigns to combat diarrheal disease) may be undone by the War for Drugs fought by the tobacco industry. Are we, they question, "saving the children for the tobacco industry?"

Laundering Section 107(B). In the aftermath of the 9/11 terrorist attack in New York City, the federal government proposed legislation that would eventually be passed as the Patriot Act. Part of this effort to increase the powers of the federal government focused on the financing of terrorism—an issue that would later become a major controversy—and involved imposing stronger controls on money laundering, forcing financial institutions to be more transparent about their activities and allowing greater leeway in tracking international movement of money by criminal organizations. As the government was shaping the new regulations, one section of the proposed new law, Section 107(B), which had originally been requested by the Justice Department, was cut out and did not appear as part of the Patriot Act. This section would have broadened the definition of money laundering to include "fraud or any scheme to defraud against a foreign government or foreign government entity, if such conduct would constitute a violation of this title if it were committed in interstate commerce in the United States" (quoted in Shapiro 2002). The section was dropped in response to direct lobbying by the tobacco industry, fearful that it might be imposed against tobacco companies that are accused by foreign governments of smuggling cigarettes into their respective countries. As noted in chapter 2, this had already occurred in the case of Philip Morris in Colombia. In fact,

> at the time, the tobacco companies were facing legal assaults on several fronts. On the docket at the U.S. federal courthouse in New York City were two cases being argued in parallel: Twenty-two Colombian states and the city of Bogotá, and ten European governments—including France, Germany, Italy, Spain and Greece—had accused Philip Morris, R. J. Reynolds and British American Tobacco of defrauding their governments of hundreds of millions of dollars in tax revenues and of taking the illicit profits back to the United States, which would constitute money laundering. In Colombia, as in Europe, the bulk of cigarette taxes are used to fund education and health programs, many of which deal with the health effects of smoking. (Shapiro 2002)

At first, the tobacco companies tried to get the White House to insert language into antiterrorist legislation that would specifically block any court in the United States from supporting a "claim for monetary damages for the nonpayment of taxes or duties under the revenue laws of a foreign state." The White House was more than willing to be of help. Notes Maud Beelman (2001), "Known in legislative parlance as a 'rule of construction,' the administration-backed measure was added to the Financial Anti-Terrorism Act of 2001 late on Oct. 16, on the eve of its passage in the Republican-controlled House of Representatives." Democrats balked, however, and the measure didn't pass.

The tobacco companies then tried a different tactic. Because the cases against them by foreign countries were filed in 2000, the new strategy of tobacco company lawyers was to argue that they should be dismissed because existing laws stated that U.S. courts have no jurisdiction in the collection of foreign taxes. If it became law, Section 107(B) would have changed the legal standard and left the tobacco companies vulnerable to U.S. prosecution for illegal activities abroad. Notes Shapiro (2002), "According to a Congressional source close to the negotiations, Representative Oxley [Michael Oxley of Ohio, chairman of the House Financial Services Committee] removed the provision from the bill at the behest of the White House and the GOP whip Tom DeLay under pressure from big tobacco."

Notably, both DeLay and Oxley were big recipients of tobacco industry donations. DeLay subsequently had to step down from his position when he was indicted by a Texas grand jury on a charge of criminally conspiring with two political associates to use illegal corporate contributions to help the Republican Party win control of the state legislature. Oxley's ties to Big Tobacco were revealed in 2000 when he hosted a party at the 2000 Republican convention that was paid for by Philip Morris (Shapiro 2002). Oxley was later found to be one of the top beneficiaries of corporate funded travel. Congressional acceptance of corporate travel offers has been criticized since disgraced lobbyist and Tom DeLay associate, Jack Abramoff, pled guilty in January 2006 to conspiring to bribe public officials, in part with sumptuous overseas excursions. To insure that he made his court date in Houston, DeLay flew from Washington, D.C., aboard a corporate jet owned by R. J. Reynolds. The company also donated $17,000 to DeLay's legal defense fund (J. Smith 2005).

Smugglers' Paradise.   Analyses of smuggling by tobacco companies suggest that it was motivated, in part, by a desire to

> make inroads into closed or restricted markets with a low-cost cigarette that can compete with local brands. . . . By doing this, the tobacco company gains market share and actually weakens the local producers. According to government investigators, tobacco companies often use the smuggling problem as a bargaining chip to convince governments to lower tariffs (de Granados 2002).

According to a long-time cigarette smuggler interviewed by the Center for Public Integrity, "It's very clear to me that tobacco companies knew more about smuggling and how it worked and how to improve it than any smugglers on Earth" (quoted in Center for Public Integrity 2001). Moreover, there is considerable evidence that these smuggling activities put tobacco companies in direct collaboration with underground criminal groups who move large quantities of cigarettes across national boundaries. This connection came to light during the investigation of cigarette smuggling into Hong Kong and Canada. Although tobacco manufacturers routinely blame international smuggling of their products on organized crime,

> a year-long investigation by the Center for Public Integrity shows that tobacco company officials at BAT, Philip Morris and R. J. Reynolds have worked closely with companies and individuals directly connected to organized crime in Hong Kong, Canada, Colombia, Italy and the United States. In fact, one Italian government report obtained by the Center states that Philip Morris and R. J. Reynolds licensed agents in Switzerland were high-level criminals who ran a vast smuggling operation into Italy in the 1980s that was directly linked to the Sicilian Mafia. Corporate documents, court records and internal government reports, some going back to the 1970s, also show that BAT, Philip Morris and R. J. Reynolds have orchestrated smuggling networks variously in Canada, Colombia, China, Southeast Asia, Europe, the Middle East, Africa and the United States as a major part of their marketing strategy to increase profits. (Center for Public Integrity 2001)

These shady activities have led, in fact, to direct links between illicit narcotic smuggling and illicit tobacco smuggling, as well as to the deaths of several individuals. According to Douglas Tweddle, the former director for Compliance and Facilitation of the Brussels-based World Customs Organization, an independent intergovernmental body concerned with international custom laws, "Organized criminals, who have traditionally been involved in smuggling illicit narcotics, are suddenly realizing that tobacco is a good thing to get into, as you make just as much money, and it's perhaps not quite as anti-social" (quoted in Center for Public Integrity 2001).

As investigations of Big Tobacco in various countries came to light, however, the European Union filed suit in the United States against the tobacco companies, accusing them of aiding and abetting smuggling, involvement in organized crime, defrauding state treasuries of billions of tax dollars, laundering drug money, and committing both wire and mail fraud. In response, tobacco industry lobbyists moved into action, working the corridors to derail the court case against them. As Congressman Waxman stated on Bill Moyers' (2002) televised *NOW* program, "The tobacco companies are famous in the Congress for working behind the scenes, often without people being aware of what they are doing." In the end, elimination of Section 107(B) from the Patriot Act resulted in the

U.S. courts dismissing the charges against Big Tobacco, a common pattern when big corporations break the law.

In light of this discussion, it is evident that a pattern of "breaking the law" is not a meaningful distinction between legal tobacco companies and illegal heroin or cocaine corporations. Instead, it appears that it is primarily the ability to take advantage of their legal status to promote their products, increase sales, and protect themselves from the laws that separate legal and illegal drug companies. Being legal, Big Tobacco does not have to resort to direct violence to protect itself or to advance its interests. Rather than killing opponents, the tobacco industry has been quick to use its considerable war chest to sustain prolonged legal battles as a means of contending with and defeating those that sue the industry. When faced with damning truths, rather than overtly silencing truth tellers, Big Tobacco, as summarized by Borowski (2004), "has relied on obfuscation, bogus science and deep-pocketed PR campaigns." Legality, in short, has served Big Tobacco well as a license for deception, coercion, and manipulation. The greatest violence of the tobacco industry is found in the effects of its product on the human body. In this, its contribution to morbidity and mortality as well as human misery is unparalleled.

Secondhand Smoke's Contributions to Illness

In the words of Richard Carmona, the surgeon general of the United States, "the debate is over. The science is clear. Secondhand smoke is not a mere annoyance but a serious health hazard" (quoted in Szabo 2006:4a). Current estimates are that exposure to secondhand smoke causes 3,000 lung cancer deaths and 62,000 deaths from coronary heart disease in adults who do not smoke each year in the United States alone (Singer 2004b). Research by Miner and Crutcher (2002) in the state of Oklahoma, for example, found that for every eight people who die from smoking, one dies from secondhand exposure to environmental tobacco smoke. For the state of Oklahoma, this amounts to approximately 750 nonsmokers dying from tobacco smoke each year.

In a 700-page report issued in 2006, the surgeon general cited a massive amount of conclusive scientific evidence that supports the banning of smoking in public places, including bars, restaurants, and all places of business. The report maintains that nonsmokers exposed to secondhand smoke have a 30 percent greater chance of developing heart disease and cancer than those who are not exposed. Contrary to tobacco-industry-funded studies, the report also shows that smoke-free laws do not hurt businesses like bars and restaurants. Indeed, the report criticizes the tobacco industry for funding biased studies designed to undermine rigorous, peer-reviewed research on the economic effects of smoking bans. R.

J. Reynolds Tobacco spokesman, David Howard, responded to the surgeon general's report by asserting, "Adults should be able to patronize establishments that permit smoking if they choose to do so" (quoted in Szabo 2006:4a). And what of the health of workers like bartenders and servers, jobs that have some of the highest exposure to secondhand smoke? According to Howard, "People who don't want to work around it don't have to work at that establishment." In other words, from the industry perspective, employers should be given the power to place their employees at grave risk and workers should be forced to choose between livelihoods and disease.

Cigarettes and cigars have serious toxic effects on nonsmokers who are exposed to secondhand smoke not only in public places, but they also take a significant toll on people who live with and around smokers, such as the children or parents who smoke. Research on general populations suggests that both mothers and fathers make substantial contributions to children's immediate exposure to tobacco smoke and, further, that the number of household smokers, knowledge of secondhand smoke, and attitudes toward smoking may be important determinants of child exposure to tobacco toxins. Among children, secondhand smoke exposure is associated with sudden infant death syndrome (SIDS), chronic middle-ear infections, and respiratory infections such as asthma (National Cancer Institute 1999). In fact, parental smoking inside the home has been found to be associated with the number and frequency of health-related complaints among children (Lee, Gaynor and Trapido 2003). Secondhand smoke is especially noteworthy as a contributor to asthma in children, a disease that is disproportionately common among low-income African American and Latino families.

Available correlational studies linking secondhand smoke to disease are supported by laboratory research. Bio-marker research, for example, affirms that children exposed to tobacco smoke in their homes do in fact absorb the chemical components of tobacco smoke into their bodies. Research by Thaqi and coworkers (2005) found that nonsmoking children who were exposed to parental tobacco smoke had significantly higher rates of the toxic tobacco smoke components like nicotine and cotinine in their urine than children who were not exposed to environmental tobacco smoke. Further, these researchers found that there were increased rates of these bio-markers with numbers of cigarettes being smoked in the child's household. Maternal smoking showed a stronger effect on nicotine and cotinine levels in children than did paternal smoking, presumably because of the longer daily duration of contact with mothers over fathers on average. Additionally, research by Mannino et al. (2003) found elevated levels of lead among the children of smokers in a nationally representative sample of over 5,500 U.S. children, age 4–16 years.

Nichter and Cartwright (1991) argue that beyond direct exposure to tobacco fumes, secondhand smoke damages the health of families in two additional ways: it leads to or complicates chronic illness, thereby reducing the ability of adults to care for and socialize children; and it diverts scarce household resources from healthier items, such as nutritious diets. In that smoking is more prevalent in low-income households compared to middle- and upper-class households, the poor suffer a double hit—both primary and secondhand exposure to the smoke. Existing evidence indicates that the size of this double hit is significant.

After decades of denial, as a result of the Master Settlement Agreement of 1998, tobacco companies publicly admitted that smoking is dangerous and that nicotine is addictive. There has been a notable shift in the public pronouncements of tobacco companies, although they have not conceded fully that secondary smoke also is dangerous and deny marketing products to nonsmoking youth. On their website, for example, Philip Morris (2006a) proclaims:

> Philip Morris USA agrees with the overwhelming medical and scientific consensus that cigarette smoking causes lung cancer, heart disease, emphysema and other serious diseases in smokers. Smokers are far more likely to develop serious diseases, like lung cancer, than non-smokers. There is no safe cigarette. . . . Philip Morris USA agrees with the overwhelming medical and scientific consensus that cigarette smoking is addictive. . . . Smokers should not assume that lower-yielding brands are safe or safer than full-flavor brands. . . . Public health officials have concluded that secondhand smoke from cigarettes causes disease, including lung cancer and heart disease, in non-smoking adults, as well as causes conditions in children such as asthma, respiratory infections, cough, wheeze, otitis media (middle ear infection) and Sudden Infant Death Syndrome.

Notably, when it comes to the issue of secondhand smoke, which is estimated to impact over 125 million people in the United States each year, the prefix "Philip Morris agrees" is not used. As to how best to deal with the issue of secondhand smoke, Philip Morris (2006b) reverts to the language of agency and choice:

> In many indoor public places, reasonable ways exist to respect the comfort and choices of both non-smoking and smoking adults. We believe that business owners—particularly owners of restaurants and bars—are most familiar with how to accommodate the needs of their patrons and should be awarded the opportunity and flexibility to determine the smoking policy for their establishment. The public can then choose whether or not to frequent places where smoking is permitted.

On the issue of secondhand smoke, or what is also called Environmental Tobacco Smoke (ETS), another tobacco giant, British American Tobacco (2006b), avows:

> Some public health lobbyists who call for draconian bans argue that ETS is dangerous, causing chronic diseases such as lung cancer and heart disease in

non-smokers. The science on ETS and these types of chronic diseases is in our view not definitive and at most suggests that if there is a risk from ETS exposure, it is too small to measure with any certainty. . . . British American Tobacco's Chairman has criticised as "intolerant and paternalistic" the campaign to ban smoking in all enclosed public places in England and Wales.

As these statements suggest, tobacco companies do not admit to the risks of secondhand smoke or support outlawing public smoking in some contexts, perhaps because to the tobacco industry it's a slippery slope that could lead policy makers to consider banning all smoking—as they do the use of other harmful commodities like heroin or cocaine. Rather, the tobacco industry insists on "balance," making sure "all stakeholders" (including smokers) be consulted in developing policy, while minimizing "the risk of 'regulatory capture'" (i.e. regulations that only reflect the views and objectives of particular interest groups) (British American Tobacco 2006b).

Tobacco For the Poor

Smoking and its consequences are not evenly distributed in society. Smoking consistently has been found to be more prevalent among people with lower socioeconomic status and lower education (Delpesheh, Kelley and Babin 2006; Thaqi et al. 2005).

> The disproportionate number of smokers in lower social classes has contributed to the increased health inequalities between rich and poor. People in poorer social classes are more likely to die early due to a variety of factors. Among men, the dominant factor is smoking, which accounts for *over half* of the difference in risk of premature death between the social classes. . . . Analyses of smoking by lower income groups can be categorised by: manual or nonmanual occupations; social class; deprivation levels. It is notable that the gradient between smokers and non-smokers becomes steeper when more determinants of disadvantage are taken into account. (Richardson 2001:4)

In short, not only are the poor more likely to smoke than the non-poor, the greater the disadvantage faced by the poor (indicated by employment status, type of occupation, level of education, car ownership, living in crowded housing, residential stability, and living in a single-parent family), the higher the level of smoking and the greater the health consequences, both in terms of life expectancy and health status. Moreover, the gap between wealthier and poorer social classes in terms of prevalence of smoking has been widening in recent years. As Jarvis and Wardle (1999) found in their study of social class and smoking in Britain, the overall risk of dying among middle-aged men who are from wealthier classes was 36 percent in 1970–1972, of which about 33 percent was attributed to the toxic effects of smoking. Twenty-five years later, the overall risk of dying among wealthier middle-aged men declined to 21 percent, with only about 4 percent being attributed smoking. By contrast, among poorer men, the overall risk of dying among middle-aged men was 47 percent in 1970–1972, of which 25 percent was attributable to smoking. Among poorer men, the risk of death had fallen slightly to 43 percent, with 19 percent accounted for by smoking. *By 1996, two-thirds of the difference in the mortality rate of rich and poor men was found to be caused by smoking.*

Why might these dramatic differences in the prevalence and consequence of smoking exist across social classes, and why has the gap widened in the impact of smoking on wealthier and poorer men? In finding the answers, two other questions must be explored: (1) Why do people smoke? (2) Are the poor being targeted by Big Tobacco as an important source of tobacco industry revenue at a time when the middle and upper classes are curtailing their smoking habits?

Why Do People Smoke?

Most smokers report that one of the reasons they smoke is to handle stress. The role smoking plays in coping with stress stems from the effect nicotine has on the brain. Like a number of other substances, nicotine triggers the release of neurotransmitter chemicals in areas of the brain involved in pain and anxiety reduction and increased feelings of pleasure (National Cancer Institute 2005). Further, stopping smoking is itself experienced as a highly stressful event. The brains of smokers become habituated to the presence of nicotine and drops in the level of nicotine (caused by not smoking) produces feelings of nervousness and craving, which are the first physiological signs of nicotine withdrawal. For smokers, the learned response to the experience of stress is to light up a cigarette, sending the smoker into a cyclical pattern that insures continued smoking, a pattern that has been identified in a review of studies on adult smokers, novice adolescent smokers, and smoking cessation efforts (Parrott 1999).

In fact, tobacco companies have known for some time that the experience of stress leads to increased smoking, and they have used this fact in selling tobacco products, as indicated by an internal R. J. Reynolds document that recognizes the role of stress in smoking among young people:

> For young adults who smoke, the use of cigarettes is seen as a mechanism to help ease the stress of transition from teen years to adulthood. The psychological role smoking plays for these young adults can be compared and contrasted with its use for teens and also for adults. (Business Information Analysis Corporation 1985)

Paradoxically, higher rates of smoking among the poor may well reflect efforts to cope with stress caused by a threatening and unsupportive social environment, a life experience found disproportionately among the poor. The issue of elevated levels of smoking among the poor does not appear to be caused by a lack of motivation to quit. In response to the question: "would you like to give up smoking altogether?" the poor are just as likely as the nonpoor to say that they would like to stop smoking (Richardson 2001). Once addicted to nicotine, it is difficult for most people, whether rich or poor, to quit smoking. It is estimated, for example, that only about one in 100 people succeeds in quitting on his/her own without the aid of a cessation program. For those whose lives are particularly stressful, like many people who are poor, trying to quit may, in turn, be particularly difficult, and, given high rates of lack of health insurance among the poor, organized cessation intervention is likely to be more difficult to access than is the case with middle- and upper-income individuals (Jarvis and Wardle 1999).

Poverty may also work against the ability to stop smoking in that success in cessation efforts may be tied to optimism about the future. Interviews with inner-city young adults through project PHRESH (Singer et al. 2006b), however, suggests that hope for a better tomorrow is comparatively limited among many individuals from low-income families. Studies of smoking during adolescence by Judith Brook and her colleagues further suggest that smoking itself may be a factor in these attitudes. These researchers have found that "a history smoking in adolescence may be associated with depressive mood throughout adolescence and young adulthood and ultimately lead to an increase in depressive mood in adulthood" (Brook et al. 2004:164). In research focused on inner-city African American and Puerto Rican youth, these researchers also found a significant relationship between smoking during adolescence and problems or dysfunctional behaviors in young adulthood that jeopardize stability in relationships and job functioning (Brook et al. 2005).

Are the Poor Being Targeted by Big Tobacco?

On July 11, 2001, the Associated Press carried a story entitled "Tobacco Advertising Linked to Health Problems in Poor Neighborhoods." This linkage was suggested by a study that had just been published in *The New England Journal of Medicine* by Ana Roux and coworkers (2001) from Columbia University. Roux's study examined a sample of over 13,000 participants between the ages of 45 and 64 years, drawn from four sites dispersed across the United States: Forsyth County, North Carolina; Jackson, Mississippi; the northwestern suburbs of Minneapolis; and Washington County, Maryland. During a tracking period of 9.1 years, the researchers recorded 615 coronary events among study participants. In assessing the distribution of these heart attacks and related heart problems, the researchers found that, after controlling for income, education, and occupation, residents of poor neighborhoods had a higher risk of disease than those of middle-class neighborhoods. Hazard ratios for heart disease among low-income persons living in the poorest neighborhoods were from 2.5 (among African Americans) to 3.1 (among whites) greater than their counterparts living in wealthier neighborhoods. Where you live, these researchers concluded, was critical to the rate of heart problems. One factor differentiating neighborhoods, the researchers pointed out, was the level of tobacco advertising. While rare in wealthy neighborhoods, billboards and other tobacco advertisements and other promotion was found to be widespread in poor neighborhoods.

In another study, Douglas Luke and coworkers (2000) counted billboards in the greater St. Louis metropolitan region. In all, these researchers examined over 1,200 billboards that contained advertising. They found that 20 percent of these billboards advertised tobacco products, which was more than for any other commodity. Billboards advertising tobacco were found in all parts of St. Louis except in the wealthiest neighborhoods. Tobacco-specific advertising, however, was more likely to be found in low-income areas and areas with the highest percentage of African American residents. Images of African Americans on tobacco billboards were primarily concentrated in areas with the densest African American population. Notably, almost three-quarters of the billboards were within 2,000 feet of a public school. The researchers concluded that the "geographic distribution of tobacco billboards, as well as the types of images found on these billboards, is consistent with the hypothesis that tobacco companies are targeting poor and minority communities with their advertising" (Luke et al. 2000:16). Similarly, a study conducted in Los Angeles found that the highest density of billboards advertising tobacco products was in African American neighborhoods and the lowest was in white neighborhoods (Stoddard et al. 1997). The same was true during the time of the Stoddard study of magazine advertising. A study of magazine advertisements for cigarettes by Cummings and coworkers (1997), for example, found that three major African American publications—*Ebony*, *Jet*, and *Essence*—had 12 percent more cigarette advertisements than publications like *Newsweek*, *Time*, *People*, and *Mademoiselle*.

One route taken by the tobacco industry has been to develop cigarette brands that are targeted to specific segments of the population (Pollay et al. 1992). One of the primary groups marked for menthol cigarette advertisement, for example, has been the African American population. As Charyn Robinson and Robert Sutton indicate:

> The tobacco industry has performed its most blatant targeting for menthol cigarettes over the years in Black communities, with billboards located throughout urban communities, financial support of Black organizations, segmented advertising in various media, and flashy product introductions of so-called "Black" cigarettes such as Uptown and X. (2004:S83)

Before the 1960s, the relative percentage of menthol and nonmenthol smokers in the African American community paralleled patterns in the white population. By the year 2000, three-fourths of African American smokers were using menthol cigarette brands like Kool, Salem, and Newport. This is especially the case among younger smokers in the African American population (Hymowitz et al. 1995). In their analysis of the advertisements for menthol cigarettes, Robinson and Sutton (2004) identified four themes

- Healthy/medicinal
- Fresh/refreshing/cool/clean/crisp
- Ethnic awareness
- Youthfulness, pleasure, playfulness, and fun

Playing on public awareness of menthol as an ingredient in cough and cold medications, early advertisement of menthol cigarettes implied or outright indicated that menthol cigarettes had medicinal qualities including soothing a rough throat. Later, the emphasis on health was replaced with reference to the refreshing qualities of menthol cigarettes. Beginning in the 1960s, ethnic awareness was mobilized by the tobacco companies to sell their products.

> Brown & Williamson took a proactive stance in marketing to Blacks. Whereas their Kool advertisements in White-oriented media continued with the standard fare of waterfalls, country streams, and romantic couples, advertisements for Kool cigarettes in Black-oriented media featured darker-skinned models, slang terms associated with the Black experience (e.g., "groovy," "baby," and "soul"), and more masculine imagery. (Robinson and Sutton 2004:87)

By 1969, Kool was the top-selling cigarette brand among African Americans.

Notably, recent research shows that while the health risk of menthol and regular cigarettes are the same, menthol smokers may have a harder time quitting cigarette smoking. In a longitudinal study of over 1,500 smokers, Mark Pletcher and coworkers (2006) found that among people who were smoking in 1985, compared to regular cigarette smokers, menthol smokers were more likely to still be smoking by the year 2000. More recently, the industry has begun promoting flavored cigars and cigars made with pipe tobacco to poor youth (Page and Evans 2003).

Similar patterns can be seen with reference to the Latino community, which, like the African American population is disproportionately impoverished. The cigarette brands called Dorado and Rio, for example, were introduced specifically to capture larger numbers of Latino smokers, as reflected not only in the names of these brands but in the advertising done for them.

The tobacco settlement imposed some important restrictions on tobacco advertising in the U.S., as did parallel efforts in Western European countries. Elsewhere in the world, especially in resource-poor nations, it has tended to be business as usual, if not more intensive than usual, in advertising tobacco products to the poor. Under the banner of protecting "free trade," political lobbying by the U.S. and England have targeted efforts to impose bans or limits on tobacco advertising in developing countries.

In New Zealand a study by researchers at Otago University found that smoking has become an increasingly important factor in explaining the growing gap in death rates between those with only a high school education and those going on to further study, a proxy measure of social class status. In the period between the early 1980s and the late 1990s, the portion of the gap that was caused by smoking increased from 16 to 21 percent. The study found that about half of New Zealanders who start smoking die of tobacco-related diseases, and increasingly they are drawn from lower-income groups. The reason, according to Becky Freeman, director of the antismoking group Action on Smoking and Health, is because the tobacco industry consistently targets lower socioeconomic groups in its advertisement and promotional efforts (NZPA 2005). In this way, Big Tobacco contributes to the maintenance of social inequity.

CHAPTER 4

Big Alcohol
An Aboveground Drug Industry

> Drinking is a curse. It makes you shoot at your landlord and it makes you miss him.
>
> —Irish Proverb

Does Big Alcohol Exist?

Like tobacco, alcohol is very big business. The total consumer expenditure for alcoholic beverages in the U.S. in 2001 was $128.5 billion. Notably, as Susan Foster and coworkers (2006) found in their appraisal of several national databases on alcohol consumption, the combined value of illegal underage drinking and adult pathological drinking in 2001 was almost $50 billion, or about 40 percent of total consumer expenditures for alcohol. Other assessments suggest the amount is far greater than $50 billion and may come close to half of all consumer expenditures for alcohol. In other words, population segments that alcohol manufacturers claim are not their intended consumer audiences constitute a significant arena of alcohol commerce and consequence.

Still, there are those who deny the existence of a "Big Alcohol," let alone a unified alcohol industry. According to William DeJong, director of the Higher Education Center for Alcohol and Other Drug Prevention:

> And what exactly is the "alcohol industry"? By applying this phrase, prevention experts are trying to tap into the public's general suspicion of profit-making big business. Harking back to the trust-busting days of the early 1900s, some advocates have even started throwing around the epithet "Big Alcohol." (2004:3)

What's the problem with the use of these terms? According to DeJong: "Using these catchall terms obscures important differences between producers, distributors, and vendors. It also masks differences between beer and distilled spirits producers, who are frequently at odds over industry-related public policy" (2004:3). There is, as well, another reason to avoid such terminology in DeJong's view: "these terms delegitimize efforts to find common ground between prevention advocates and certain elements of the industry" (2004:3). This assumes, of course, that those concerned with limiting the health and social consequences of problem drinking believe that there is common ground to be found that furthers the cause of public health and not the alcohol industry's narrow pecuniary mission.

Independent Voices or Hired Hands?

Some people hardly agree with DeJong, or even go him one better. One fellow thinker is Radley Balko (2003), a policy analyst for the Cato Institute, who warns that a

> well-funded movement of neoprohibitionists is afoot, with advocates in media, academia, and government. The movement sponsors a variety of research organizations, which publish dozens of studies each year alleging the corruptive effects of alcohol. . . . Taken together, the well-organized efforts of activists, law enforcement, and policymakers portend an approaching "back-door prohibition"—an effort to curb what some of them call the "environment of alcoholism"—instead of holding individual drinkers responsible for their actions. Policymakers should be wary of attempts to restrict choice when it comes to alcohol.

Another backer of Dejong is David Hanson, host of the website "Alcohol Problems and Solutions." In Hanson's (2005a) view, "The so-called alcohol industry is highly fragmented, has many conflicting interests, and is unable to speak with one voice." Hanson (2005a), who quotes DeJong and reproduces his argument against using terms like "alcohol industry" and "Big Alcohol," further asserts that rather than a threat to public health, "producers, distributors and retailers have for many decades demonstrated a strong and continuing commitment to reducing alcohol problems." Instead of a consolidated alcohol industry, what actually exists in Hanson's view (2005b) is, in fact, an "enormous and well-funded anti-alcohol industry," composed of organizations like the Robert Wood Johnson Foundation, the American Medical Association's Office on Alcohol and Other Drug Abuse, the Center for Substance Abuse Prevention, and Mothers against Drug Driving. Organizations like these, Hanson argues, are "neoprohibitionists" who try to equate alcohol with illicit drugs by substituting useful terms like *alcohol and drug use* with problematic terms like *alcohol and other drug use* in their publications, educational literature, and public pronouncements. It is wrong, asserts Hanson, to link alcohol, which is produced and distributed by responsible companies that are concerned about their communities and work hard to insure moderate levels of consumption, and illicit drugs, which are produced by criminal organizations that have none of these social concerns. In short, Hanson believes it is neoprohibitionist organizations that are dangerous to the public, not the alcohol industry. A similar view is expressed by Dan Mindus of the Center for Consumer Freedom (2003), who sees the Robert Wood Johnson Foundation as the ringleader of the so-called neoprohibition movement.

Laboratory research involving scanning the human brain during exposure to substances like alcohol, cocaine, and heroin, however, underscores why calling alcohol (as well as tobacco) a drug is perfectly justified: alcohol exposure produces the same patterns of damaging effects on the brain as various illegal substances. Consequently, the term ATOD (alcohol, tobacco, and other drugs) has become widespread in public health and medicine. Substances included under the ATOD rubric have been shown objectively to restructure neurotransmitters in the brain, leading to chemical dependency and addiction. Whether legal or not, in terms of their physical, emotional, and behavioral effects, alcohol, tobacco, and other drugs constitute a distinct class of neuro-active chemicals.

Drinking From Rose-Colored Glasses

A fuller perusal of Hanson's fairly extensive website, in fact, shows that he consistently takes a pro-industry stance and paints a somewhat rosy picture of alcohol-related problems. Thus, he argues:

- alcohol advertising doesn't increase consumption;
- there is no evidence of targeting underage drinkers with alcohol advertisement;
- moderate consumption of alcohol during pregnancy appears to be safe;
- the tougher the controls over alcohol availability, the greater the alcohol abuse;
- warning labels on alcohol containers have virtually no impact on drinking;
- increasing taxation on alcohol will not impact level of abuse;
- stop stigmatizing alcohol as a "dirty drug";
- permit parents to serve alcohol to their offspring of any age, not only in the home, but in restaurants, parks and other locations, under their direct supervision; and
- integrity seems to be a continuing problem for Mothers Against Drunk Driving (MADD) (Hanson 2005b).

Hanson (2005a) asserts that he has reached these conclusions through independent analysis of the facts, adding, that because he "does not require outside research funding," and he "is free to draw whatever conclusions logic dictates without regard to whomever might be either pleased or offended." In fact, however, support to establish his website came from the Distilled Spirits Council of the United States, Inc. (DISCUS), the national trade association of producers and marketers of distilled spirits, a $95 billion-a-year sector of the larger alcohol industry. This type of deceit, already seen in the previous chapter in the case of Big Tobacco, is found as well in the behavior of Big Alcohol companies and organizations.

Similarly, the Center for Consumer Freedom, an active voice critiquing efforts to connect the alcohol industry to significant levels of health problems, is not really a consumer group but is supported by restaurants, food companies, and other industry sources and linked individuals.

United We Stand

Importantly, while intra-industry conflicts exist (as they do in the tobacco industry), it is through trade organizations like DISCUS and ABL (American Beverage Licensees, the association of beer, wine, and spirit retailers), that the dominant sectors of the alcohol industry reach broad consensus and effectively speak with one main voice and act with one central purpose (e.g., to impact policy). In 2005, for example, DISCUS took credit for blocking 32 of 34 legislative efforts across the country to increase taxes on alcohol (*Night Club and Bar Magazine* 2006).

At the same time, multiple alcohol corporations donate millions of dollars to support organizations like The Century Council, the pro-industry alternative to MADD, and other independent prevention organizations. The Century Council has initiated projects, such as the distribution of a video on underage drinking in conjunction with Boys and Girls Clubs of America, with public support from over 35 members of the U.S. Congress. An assessment by the American Medical Association, however, found that industry-generated prevention materials

> offer a consistent theme: Environmental strategies [like decreasing the number of alcohol outlets in an area, limiting advertising, increasing alcohol taxation] do not work and the individual drinker (or the underage individual with his or her parent) bears the sole responsibility for any problems that occur. The individuals the industry seeks to blame for problems with its products are also their best customers, and the industry's marketing budgets, which dwarf its expenditures on educational programs, are tailored to reinforce and encourage heavy drinking behavior. Perhaps most deceptive is the industry's claim that its educational and public awareness programs targeting individual behavior are effective in reducing alcohol problems and are largely responsible for gains that have been made in the last 15 years. Evaluation research provides no support for this view. (2002:8–9)

Alcohol industry prevention materials, in fact, are a sophisticated marketing device; their messages are often ambiguous and contain individual behavioral strategies that are not easy to follow once someone is under the influence of alcohol (e.g., "think when you drink," "know when to say when"), the company logo rather than the message is what is most remembered by those exposed to these materials, and an embedded theme is the normalization of drinking. As affirmed by DISCUS President Peter Cressy (2000), his organization works "to ensure cultural acceptance of alcohol beverages by 'normalizing' them in the minds of consumers as a healthy part of a normal lifestyle." Such acceptance, asserts Cressy, is the key to enhancing industry sales, and hence the importance to the industry of its collective endeavors in the realm of prevention.

Collectively the (cross-beverage) segments of the industry coordinate through organizations like the World Association of the Alcohol Beverage Industries (WAABI) that, despite its name, is a U.S.-based national association. As WAABI (2005) notes on its website—which is targeted to members—coordination across the allegedly highly fragmented segments of the industry is not unusual:

> When issues of concern to the entire industry come to our attention, WAABI's Legislative Committee swings into action, notifying chapters and encouraging all members to express their views in writing to their elected representatives. WAABI also helps the industry by speaking out on current issues before other local community groups, distributing literature, and by writing letters to the editors of local and national publications. . . . Among recent issues we have taken action on are: excise taxes, advertising restrictions, teenage drinking, warning labels, drunk driving legislation, and others. Through WAABI, you can stay abreast of the issues and take actions to protect your future.

Fraternizing with the Enemy

Beyond the issue of trade organizations, the global alcohol industry exhibits several trends that further confirm the appropriateness of terms like Big Alcohol. As the World Health Organization notes in its Global Status Report on Alcohol:

> There are three main global alcohol industries: beer, spirits and wine. They share a common trend away from labour-intensive products with little brand identity and decentralized production, and towards capital-intensive production of global brands heavily supported by marketing budgets. Increasing concentration of ownership is another general trend, most visible in the beer and distilled spirits industries. The leading alcohol marketing companies are nearly all headquartered in developed nations, rank among the world's largest transnational corporations, and rely on large marketing budgets to dominate the market and extract oligopoly profits. (2001:8)

Additionally, major alcohol corporations, while seemingly engaged in intensive competition with rivals for market share, often are close collaborators when in comes to sales. For example, SABMiller, the second largest beer brewery in the world, sells Guinness and Kilkenny (made by "rival" Diageo) in Hungary, Budweiser (produced by "rival" Anheuser-Busch) in Italy, and Amstel (made by "rival" Heineken) in South Africa. The multinational alcohol companies have found that it is more profitable to divide up the world markets, sell the products of other companies in their "home" regions, and reduce the costs of head-on competition. As Diageo CEO Paul Walsh noted during an interview in 2005:

> Regarding beer, the way that we will develop our beer market position is to partner with other beer players where we think we will benefit from a broader portfolio of offerings. You've seen that recently with the deal we

announced with Heineken in Russia, and that will be the strategy going forward. (The Cantos Transcripts 2005)

The point is not that there is no competition in the industry. For the most part, however, the sharpest edges of competition are controlled to protect everyone's bottom line. Corporate consolidation (e.g., increasingly multinational corporations like Foster's Group, an Australian-based beer and wine giant, produce more than one category of alcoholic beverage) coupled with pressure from wealthy nations for trade liberalization have turned the Western-based alcohol industry into a global business dominated by multinational megacorporations. These entities are capable of wielding powerful political influence because of their deep pockets, big advertising budgets, aggressive promotional efforts, and willingness to use their resources to achieve, in the words of an Anheuser-Busch (1997:3) annual report, "one overriding objective—enhancing shareholder value." As Anheuser-Busch boasted in a subsequent annual report to shareholders: "The scale and resources of Anheuser-Busch create a unique set of competitive advantages over any other brewers, enabling us to successfully meet the challenges before us" (2005:6). Moreover, as the American Medical Association observes, "The industry's political muscle is effective. Advertising and tax reform have been largely thwarted by industry lobbying efforts in state and federal legislatures" (2002:8).

Muscle

Thirty out of the 34 senators elected in 1998—half were Republicans and half Democrats—accepted contributions from the alcohol industry totalling more than $400,000. In the years between 1999 and 2004, the alcohol industry contributed over $37 million to congressional campaigns for offices in both the Senate and the House of Representatives, over $285,000 to two presidential campaigns, and $53 million to state and local campaigns (Mann 2006). The majority of the industry's considerable lobbying budget (approximately 63 percent) goes to the Republican Party. The primary target of political spending by Big Alcohol is the prevention of tax increases on alcohol sales. To achieve this goal, the industry has set up a number of political action committees. For example, the National Beer Wholesalers Association (NBWA), which has been named by *Fortune* magazine as one of the most influential lobbying groups in the country, donated $2.5 million in 2004 alone to several friendly congressional candidates. One of the directors of the NBWA was a major fundraiser in President George W. Bush's 2004 re-election campaign.

Beyond direct contributions, the industry makes various kinds of indirect donations as well. It is not uncommon for alcohol producers and trade associations to provide free or discounted alcoholic beverages for fundraisers or other events sponsored by or for members of Congress. Both beer- and wine-tasting festivities, for example, are popular social events on Capitol Hill. Additionally, the industry hosts events to express its appreciation to members of Congress for taking the leadership on issues of industry concern. The alcohol industry also contributes millions of dollars directly to the major political parties.

At the state level, there is considerable variation in the tax rates on alcohol, which broadly reflects the distribution of the industry across the nation. In Missouri, where the headquarters of Anheuser-Busch is located, the state tax on a gallon of beer is six cents. By contrast, Vermont, which lacks a major brewing industry, collects 26 cents on a gallon of beer. The same patterns are repeated for other sectors of the alcohol industry (Mann 2006). Similarly, industry contributions tend to reflect the relative strength of the two dominant national parties in state legislatures. In California, for example, during the 2003–2004 legislative session, the top money-getter from the alcohol industry was Michael Marchado, a democratic state senator and owner of a family farming operation in San Joaquin Valley. Marchado, who received over $27,000 from various alcohol industry sources (compared to $16,000 for the next highest recipient), sits on a number of key committees, including the Select Committee on the California Wine Industry. Wine is a major industry in California. Although wine is produced in 48 states, California's $16 billion wine industry produces almost 90 percent of the wine grapes grown in the country. In all, alcohol interests contributed over $600,000 to California state lawmakers during the 2003–2004 legislative session (Marin Institute 2006a).

Notably, a 2001 national public opinion survey found that 54 percent of participants believed that alcohol taxes should be increased, while another poll found that 71 percent supported raising funds by increasing the federal beer tax by several cents on each bottle to achieve the same level of taxation that exists on liquor (Richter, Vaughan, and Foster 2004). The beer lobby, however, has been able to blunt the influence of the public on law makers' voting patterns on this issue and keep taxes on beer especially low.

Sleight of Hand

As was seen in the case of Big Tobacco in the last chapter, things often are far from what they at first appear to be in the world that alcohol built; spirits of deception linger around every corner. Often concealed, for example, is the coordination that occurs between the tobacco and alcohol industries (e.g., in opposing smoking bans on indoor or outdoor sites, which the alcohol industry sees as a threat to taverns and other alcohol outlets). Crossovers involving tobacco corporations owning alcohol companies (or both being owned by a larger entity) also occur. Philip Morris, for example, fully owned the Miller Brewing Company and aggressively marketed Miller beers for several years until the operation was merged with South African Breweries in 2002, which subsequently became known as SABMiller. Altria Group, Inc., the new, more obscure (less tobacco-associated) name of Philip Morris, received 430 million shares of SABMiller from the Miller operation (which had developed about $2 billion in debt), stock that was valued at approximately $3.4 billion. The shares in SABMiller owned by Altria Group gave the latter a 36 percent economic interest in SABMiller and a 24.9 percent (up to 28.7 percent by 2006) voting interest in the London-based company, including three seats on the board of directors (Altria Group, Inc. 2003). The rationale for the move was provided by Graham Mackay, the CEO of South African Breweries, who explained: "The transaction represents a new chapter in our development, taking SABMiller to the number-two position globally, and positioning it to be a major participant in the ongoing consolidation of the global beer industry" (quoted in Guzzinati 2002:2). With total sales in 2004 of $11.3 billion and a gross profit of $645 million (Marin Institute 2006a), SABMiller is well on its way to achieving this goal. Similarly, UST, Inc., is a holding company with annual revenue of $1.8 billion that unites two primary subsidiaries: the U.S. Smokeless Tobacco Company and International Wine and Spirits Ltd.

Don't Drink the Water

Alcohol corporations hide other things as well, including illegal behavior. In 1981, for example, the executives at Coors learned that the water used to brew their beer was dangerously polluted. The culprit was Coors itself, a company that prides itself on being "committed to environmental responsibility" and to "environmental stewardship" (Coors 2006). Cancer-causing solvents like TCA, PCE, TCE, 1,1–dichloroethylene, and 1,2–dichloroethen, used to clean new beer cans before filling, had for several years been dumped into a cracked sewer line that leaked the solvents into four springs used to brew Coors beer. The substances involved were exceptional in their toxicity. For example, 1,1-dichloroethylene is ranked as one of the most hazardous known compounds (i.e., among the worst 10 percent of dangerous chemicals) for both ecosystems and human health. In addition to being carcinogenic, among its multifarious and grave threats to human health, 1,1–dichloroethylene is suspected of being a developmental toxicant (damaging to the in utero fetus), a kidney and liver toxicant, a respiratory toxicant, and a skin toxicant. Federal environmental protection law required Coors to immediately report the perilous leak to government authorities. Coors, fearing that such a report would spark a public relations and marketing disaster, did not report the problem. Notes Baum, "As Coors executives admitted almost a decade later, the company decided to keep the contaminations secret. . . . [Instead, company] engineers quietly began pumping the tainted waters" (2000:248). One of the polluted springs was pumped into Clear Creek, the first water source for Coors when the company founder built his brewery next to it in 1876. Other springs were pumped out to other sources of running water. The toxins washed away to unknown destinations with untold consequences for unidentified species, including possibly humans. From the company perspective, the problem was solved; Coors was saved.

Several Big Players

The alcohol industry includes innumerable independent bars and taverns, microbreweries, neighborhood retail outlets, and local distribution companies. There are, as well, alcohol titans, who are the true setters of the course and definers of strategy in the world of Big Alcohol. These mega-companies, acting in consort, drive the industry. The names of some of the big players in the alcohol industry, like Coors and Miller, are fairly well known, others less so. Brands and divisions change hands as corporations reshape, redefine, and reposition themselves to meet the challenges of global success and the pressures—including those from health critics—that come with selling commodities that are linked to a considerable amount of human misery, disease, and death.

Diageo: Empire Builder

As noted above, one of the contemporary giants of the alcohol industry is known as Diageo, an invented name formed by uniting the Latin word for day (*dia*) and the Greek word for world (*geo*). In the company's view, "We take this to mean every day, everywhere, people celebrate with our brands" (Diageo 2006). This is without doubt true, although the picture is not quite as rosy as Diageo suggests. In a study of 21st birthday celebrations, for example, Neighbors and coworkers (2006) found that of 164 study participants who reached legal age, 90 percent reported drinking as part of the festivities, 75 percent went to a bar to celebrate, 61 percent drank until their blood alcohol content (BAC) rose above the legal driving limit, and 23 percent got drunk. There were no differences between men and women in the study.

An alternative interpretation of the Diageo name, seeking to establish a terminological tie to ancient empires, is not mentioned in company promotional materials. Nonetheless, with operations that bridge the supposedly separate worlds of beer, wine, and spirits, Diageo is a global corporate empire builder with sales in over 180 nations, staffed by an army of over 20,000 employees, with offices in 80 countries, and a world headquarters in London. Its well-known brands include Smirnoff, Johnnie Walker, Seagram's 7 Crown American whiskey, Guinness, Baileys, J&B,

Captain Morgan, Cuervo, Tanqueray, Crown Royal, Beaulieu Vineyard wines, Chalone Vineyards wines, and Sterling Vineyards wines.

Diageo was formed in 1997 through the merger of Guinness and GrandMet. By 2005, its net global profit was approximately $25 billion. Like most corporations, Diageo is focused on future growth, especially in the international market. In particular, the company has its eyes and hopes pinned on Brazil, Russia, India, and China as sites for expanded profits. But Diageo also looks to the past, to the 18th- and 19th-century origins of the inventors of the brands that came under its umbrella, including Giacomo Justerini who arrived in London in 1749 and founded a company that developed J&B whiskey; Arthur Guinness who in 1759 signed a 9,000-year lease on an unused brewery in Dublin and began making a dark porter stout beer; Jose Cuervo who in 1795 received a license to produce tequila in Mexico; John Walker who in 1820 established a small grocery shop where he applied an approach for blending tea to the making of malt whiskey; the clergyman's son Charles Tanqueray who in 1830 abandoned his family profession to set up a small gin distillery in London; and to Piotr Smirnov who in 1886 was made the official producer of vodka for the imperial Russian court. The effort to blend past and future, old and new, and tradition and innovation emerges as a strong theme at Diageo, but more broadly throughout the alcohol industry.

Alcohol companies, in their respective carefully constructed self-images, do not make cheap wines that are passed around in bottle gangs of Skid Row men and drunk from crumpled paper bags; instead they produce the lubricants of conviviality and fuel celebrations of life. Further, the alcohol industry is not in the business of flooding college students with messages that Thursday-through-Saturday-night binge social drinking, rapid high-volume drinking games, throwing up on dorm room floors, and suffering a head-splitting hangover are normal, the things college students are suppose to do; rather, the alcohol industry is in the business of assisting consumers, as Diageo (2006) indicates on its website, to "mark big events in their lives and brighten small ones." Certainly, from their point of view, Big Alcohol companies like Diageo are not involved in helping to maintain a structure of economic and social inequality by specifically marketing some of their products to poor and working people, rather they produce "premium drinks" that provide communities and individuals with "tax revenues and possible health benefits as well as the enjoyment that the responsible consumption of alcohol brings" (Diageo 2006).

Anheuser-Busch: Legacy Builder

Another giant of the alcohol industry, which will be examined in some detail to illustrate features of many alcohol companies, is Anheuser-Busch. The largest brewery in the U.S. (with control of 50 percent of U.S. beer sales), Anheuser-Busch has as a company motto, the phrase "A Legacy of Quality." This slogan effectively expresses an attribute and an origin that are critical to the corporation's desired public image. Indeed, like many older companies Anheuser-Busch has celebrated organizational origin myth. Origin myths, as anthropology teaches us, provide explanations of how things came to be as they are. But they are more than mere explanations, in addition they "function to assure, encourage, and inspire. They are . . . literary creations: narrative epics, full of drama and romance, of novelty and imagination, of quest and conflict" (Carneiro 2000). Mythologizing Anheuser-Busch, in fact, is something of a company predilection. Early in the 20th century, in fact, its directors turned to Greek mythology as a source of images to promote its products. One promotional piece for Budweiser in 1904, for example, used a story about Zeus assuming the form of an eagle and flying the boy named Ganymede up to Mount Olympus to serve as the cup-bearer to the gods. In the Anheuser-Busch adaptation, called "The Modern Version of Ganymede," Budweiser is depicted as the new nectar of the gods. The promotion was commissioned by Adolphus Busch to celebrate the selection of Budweiser over various Bohemian beers in competition in Prague.

As told on its website, the company's origin myth begins with Adolphus Busch:

> In 1864, Adolphus Busch joined the fledgling brewery that would later become Anheuser-Busch. While the company's early years were demanding, he proved up to the challenge. His keen vision, bold initiative, marketing savvy and passionate commitment to quality were his legacy, and the high standards he established have been adhered to by those who follow. The distinctive contributions made by each succeeding generation of the Anheuser-Busch family clearly show that the history of Anheuser-Busch isn't a story about a company. It is a story about people. People with dreams and perseverance and a passion for the brewing business, who have led the company through challenging and turbulent times. (Anheuser-Busch 2006a)

Through the identification of the founder and his elevation to the status of a cultural hero and "a visionary . . . a man whose ideas were ahead of his time" (Anheuser-Busch 2006a), the company begins to establish an honored pedigree, inspirational values, deep cultural roots, and a thorough integration with the most celebrated traditions and ideals of American society (while not dwelling much on the foreign origins of the founder). Key to the company's telling of its origin tale is the focused effort to: (1) demonstrate that Anheuser-Busch and its "first family" have been tested and have proven their worth; the company and the people who created and fostered it succeeded in the face of significant adversity (affirming a core American value concerning the rewards of hard work and personal responsibility); (2) company leadership is balanced, blending cognitive skill with passion (and hence is both innovative and trustworthy); and (3) Anheuser-Busch is not a faceless entity run from the top floors of a mirrored sky scraper; nor is it an oppressive or exploitive profit-hungry machine; rather, it is, at its core, a very human enterprise made up of real people who are in the business "of making friends" (Anheuser-Busch 2006a).

After his arrival in America at age 18, Adolphus Busch moved to St. Louis, the biggest river town north of New Orleans, and home to a growing flood of immigrants in the mid-19th century. He found work as a clerk on the St. Louis waterfront and, using inheritance from his prosperous family in Germany, formed a company that sold brewery supplies. One of his customers was Eberhard Anheuser, co-owner of the Bavarian Brewery (later changed to Anheuser-Busch Brewing Association, and eventually to Anheuser-Busch, Inc.). The two German immigrants got to know each other and in a fateful move, on March 7, 1861, in a celebrated double wedding within the St. Louis merchant class, Adolphus married Lilly Anheuser, and his brother, Urlich, married her sister Anna, Eberhard Anheuser's daughters.

Expressing his commitment to business, in later years Adolphus liked to tell the story of how he was late for his own wedding because he was closing a deal in North St. Louis. A few years after the wedding, Adolphus went to work for his father-in-law and was sent to Germany to learn the brewing business. Eventually, Adolphus sold his supply business and used the money to buy out Eberhard Anheuser's business partner. Thus were united, in the company's origin myth, the two men "who would be *destined* to change forever the way beer would be brewed—and marketed—throughout the world" (Anheuser-Busch 2006a; italics added).

Author and journalist Dan Baum (2000) offers a contrasting picture of Adolphus Busch:

> Busch didn't care if he made the best beer possible; he just wanted to make the most beer possible. He wanted to become the first national brewer in an age when nationwide marketing was unknown. . . . Busch didn't even like beer. . . . Once when he offered a visiting journalist a drink, the fellow ingratiatingly asked for a Busch beer. "Ach," Busch said in his heavy German accent, "that slop?"

Even though the company has its roots in the German brewing tradition and its premier product, Budweiser, has a distinctly German name, part of the mythologizing of Anheuser-Busch has been its thoroughgoing Americanization. This process began with wrapping bottles of Budweiser in what the company refers to as the "familiar red, white and blue . . . label, known to generations of loyal beer drinkers" (Anheuser-Busch 2006a). In fact, the original Budweiser labels were printed in German with a Hohenzollern double-headed eagle in the upper-right corner, as well as an American eagle with a union shield in the upper-left corner. Within days of the U.S. declaration of war on Germany on April 6, 1917, however, all German words and the Hohenzollern double-headed eagle were eliminated from the Budweiser label, and German disappeared from the everyday language of workers in the Anheuser-Busch brewery. Further, affirming his Americanization, on the night that war was declared against Germany, August Anheuser, at a dinner meeting at the St. Louis Club, formally pledged loyalty to the United States and had his pledge sent to President Wilson. He also donated $100,000 to the Red Cross "hoping to show both his loyalty and generosity" (Hernon and Ganey 1991:92).

Painless Punishment.   In the midst of the First World War, it was already evident that the nation was sliding toward Prohibition. One target of the prohibitionist movement was the working-class saloon, seen by many as a hatching ground of corruption, immorality, and social unrest. At the time, saloons were not independently owned; many were controlled by the breweries. A controversy broke out at the end of the war when it was revealed that the saloons in East St. Louis, many of them owned by Anheuser-Busch, were breaking the law and staying open on Sunday. The violation was investigated by U.S. District Judge Kenesaw Mountain Landis, the man later credited with resolving the infamous Black Sox betting scandal in baseball, an achievement that led him to be selected as the sport's first commissioner.

> The results of [this] inquiry were highly embarrassing for [Anheuser-Busch]. An agent of Anheuser-Busch, called to testify, calmly announced that the brewery controlled thirty-two saloons in the community and that all of them stayed open on Sunday and had done so for the past ten years. . . . Only a day earlier, [Augustus A.] Busch told reporters that lawless saloons were responsible for the spread of prohibition sentiment. (Hernon and Ganey 1991:107)

This was not the first or last time that the company was charged with ignoring the law for personal gain or to expand profit. Other examples are known. In 1915, the attorney general of Texas filed antitrust charges against seven Texas breweries, including the Galveston Brewing Company, for attempting to interfere with the Texas political system by donating money to the Texas Brewers' Association to fight state prohibition. August Anheuser, as the paid president of the American Brewing Association of Houston, as well as an officer of the Lone Star Brewing Company of San Antonio and an investor in the Texas Brewing Company of Fort Worth, was called as a witness. August responded by having his name removed from corporate documents that linked him to the companies being charged with antitrust violations and refused to travel to Texas to take the witness stand. Nonetheless, letters he had written to the Galveston Brewing Company were entered into evidence. These letters instructed the brewery to increase the price of beer and use the extra profit to fund antiprohibition forces in Texas. Ultimately, the Texas brewers plead guilty and paid a fine of almost $300,000. August Anheuser got off without so much as a slap on the wrist.

Other times, the company was not so lucky. In 1978, Anheuser-Bush paid a then record $750,000 settlement with the Bureau of Alcohol, Tobacco and Firearms (it was not labeled as a fine, a common courtesy accorded legal corporations) for making payoffs to improve beer sales. Six years later, in another settlement, the company paid $2 million to end a price-fixing charge. The incident, involving potential violation of the Federal Alcohol Administration Act, stemmed from an attempt to monopolize beer sales at ballparks, race tracks, and similar venues across the country. Although Anheuser-Busch denied wrongdoing and attempted to minimize the significance of the episode, the company, "regulators charged . . . engaged in what can be characterized as predatory trade practices" over a number of years (Hernon and Ganey 1991:384).

In the late 1980s, two vice presidents of the company were arrested for cheating the IRS through a kickback scheme with an advertising agency. The subsequent federal trial aired a considerable amount of company dirty laundry. It was revealed that top executives routinely accepted expensive gifts in large quantity, including Rolex watches, computers, and televisions. One of those convicted, Joseph Martino, vice president for sales, explained his actions by saying getting regular kickbacks from businesses that engaged in commerce with Anheuser-Busch was simply part of corporate culture. During the eight years he was employed by the company, Martino said he "witnessed incredible greed and corruption at the highest levels of the company," including "flagrant personal misuse of corporate and thus shareholder funds" and "a lot of hiding behind the polished corporate image" (quoted in Hernon and Ganey 1991:381). Reaping the benefits of legality, huge profits, and top-flight lawyers, however, Anheuser-Busch avoided significant legal consequences for any criminal activities.

See You in Court.   In addition to its visits to criminal court, like most corporations, Anheuser-Busch has faced civil challenges by those claiming they have suffered significant damages because of company actions. In one of the larger suits against the company, the family of the former baseball homerun-crown holder, Roger Maris, sued Anheuser-Busch for terminating their lucrative Gainesville and Ocala, Florida, beer distributor contract. In the words of the Maris family lawyer, "There is no doubt in my mind that we are arguing this case today because of greed. . . . They are big, they're rich, they are powerful and they think they can do whatever they want whenever they want and how they want. We are defending what is right" (quoted in *Columbia Daily Tribune* 2005). The company responded that the termination was legal and was prompted by customer dissatisfaction with the service the Maris family was providing. In court, this assertion was disputed by a former beer distributor employee who testified that reports of customer dissatisfaction were falsified. In August 2001, the jury appeared to agree and rendered a verdict in favor of the Maris family. Family members were awarded an initial $50 million plus any additional accumulated prejudgment interest on the jury award. Ultimately, the company settled and paid the Maris family approximately $120 million. In another widely reported court action against the company, a rock band, the Standells, filed a million-dollar suit asserting that Anheuser-Busch used its song "Dirty Water" on commercials without permission from the band. According to the Standells' lawyer, "An advertiser decided to turn an artist into a pitchman without their consent. . . . That's morally wrong" (quoted in Fontenot 2006).

Up From Prohibition

Historically, one of the biggest challenges faced by Anheuser-Busch was Prohibition (which banned the manufacture and sale but not the possession, consumption, or transportation of alcoholic beverages). During these dark days, from 1920 to 1933, Anheuser-Busch stayed in business and kept its 70 city blocks of buildings busy by switching to the production of beer-like soft drinks such as root beer and ginger ale, near beers (with an alcohol content of less than one-half of one percent), syrups, ice cream, and a diverse array of other commodities, enterprises it abandoned in 1942.

There were 1,400 breweries in the U.S. prior to the start of Prohibition. Less than a quarter of them re-opened after its repeal; Anheuser-Busch was one of them. To mark the end of the 13 years of Prohibition, Anheuser-Busch introduced its now emblematic Budweiser Clydesdale horse team, which was used to deliver the first case of post-Prohibition Budweiser beer to former governor of New York, Al Smith, in front of the Empire State Building. The company returned to profitability based on beer and other sales within three years of the close of Prohibition. When the Bavarian Brewery was purchased by Eberhard Anheuser in 1860, the company was the 29th largest of the 40 breweries in St. Louis at the time. In subsequent years, Anheuser-Busch has grown to be the biggest brewery in the world and controls about 10 percent of global beer volume. One indicator of the corporation's global perspective was displayed during the 2006 World Cup in Germany; Anheuser-Busch plastered its logo on Berlin's soccer stadium walls. Notably, company ads were in Chinese. The target viewers for this advertising were not the 70,000 soccer fans gathered in the stadium, but the one billion people watching on television from Asia.

Stepping on the Micros. Like tobacco companies, Anheuser-Busch was quick to sponsor television programs, beginning with *The Ken Murray Show* in 1950. Beyond beer (including brands sold in Canada, England, Argentina, Mexico, Chile, and China, among other countries), the company has operations in theme parks (e.g., Busch Gardens), packaging, aluminum recycling, malt production, real estate, turf farming, and transport services. Despite its vast size, the company remains ever-conscious of potential competitors and is not averse to reaching into its deep pockets or exercising its considerable muscle to stymie rivals, even small ones. One target has been the many local microbreweries that have popped up around the country and around the world. Like all small start-up companies, microbreweries face many challenges, as Nigel Jaquiis (1998) observes:

> The toughest, perhaps most frightening, opponent the local brewers face is Anheuser-Busch, the spiteful giant upon whose turf the micros have dared to venture. Imagine Goliath, pumped up on steroids, putting the squeeze on David's underfed, disorganized little brother, and you have some idea of what happens when the worlds of industrial and microbrewing collide. "Bud," says [Portland, Oregon] local beer expert Fred Eckhardt, "doesn't want any competition."

Anheuser-Busch's primary strategy to thwart the microbreweries, according to Philip Van Munching (1998), a former beer importer and author of *Beer Blast*, is to denigrate, regulate, and replicate its microcompetitors. In addition, Anheuser-Busch began leaning heavily on distributors not to carry the products of microbreweries on its beer delivery trucks. By using appealing inducements, such as two cents per-case cash payments and providing distributors a $1,500 per-truck painting allowance, Anheuser-Busch attempted to gain what it called "100–percent mind share," that is, getting distributors to give their undivided attention to Anheuser-Busch products at the expense of all others. Although Anheuser-Busch's strategies are aimed at all competitors, big and small, it is primarily the microbreweries, which lack other distribution systems, that are hardest hit by such maneuvering. To further accomplish its aim, Anheuser-Busch, as well as other big players in the beer industry, have brought out their own "small label" beers, or, as they have become known among independent microbreweries, "pseudo-micros."

Getting a Conscience.   These activities notwithstanding, the modern, world-reaching Anheuser-Busch (2006a) corporation presents itself as a socially conscious, public spirited, people-oriented organization, with a strong commitment to "giving back" to the community. As the company asserts, "Anheuser-Busch continues to lead the alcohol beverage industry in promoting responsibility . . . and our commitment will continue in the future as we share the message that *Responsibility Matters*."

During the historic storm season of 2005, in the days after the devastating Katrina and Rita hurricanes slammed into New Orleans and surrounding coastal sections of Louisiana, Texas, Mississippi, and Alabama, many residents of the hardest hit areas lacked clean water. Anheuser-Busch responded and rushed 2.5 million cans of fresh drinking water to the victims of the storms. Company trucks were made available to the Red Cross to deliver food, water, power generators, and other supplies. More broadly, Anheuser-Busch (2006a) emphasizes:

> Our packaging group and four of our breweries supplied 9.4 million cans of drinking water to relief agencies following hurricanes and other natural disasters in 2005. This is the equivalent of a bumper-to-bumper convoy of semi-trailer trucks 2 miles long. Since 1988, Anheuser-Busch has supplied more than 59 million cans of drinking water to those in need.

While at first blush the company seemed to be living up to its claim to being a socially responsible corporation, the Marin Institute (2006b), a California nonprofit organization concerned with alcohol advertising and alcohol abuse prevention, has questioned whether the company's true motives were not gaining name recognition and increasing profits. According to the institute:

> Such generosity might appear to be goodwill and genuine concern for hurricane survivors. In reality, such actions are always designed to serve the long-term interests of the alcohol industry. Creating goodwill by packaging water in Budweiser beer cans—delivered in Budweiser trucks—is just another example of how the alcohol industry exploits vulnerable people to pad its bottom line. This strategy is most apparent in times of disaster, when victims often turn to substances like alcohol to cope with stress.

In the weeks after storms, as the flood waters began to recede and local governments shifted their focus from the immediate crisis to the longer-term process of caring for survivors and reconstructing damaged communities and infrastructures, a concerted push emerged from the alcohol industry to convince lawmakers to roll back restrictions and regulations on the industry and to give special tax breaks to local liquor stores, alcohol retail outlets, and other businesses in areas damaged by the storms. For community organizations that had been involved in alcohol abuse prevention in the hurricane-affected areas prior to the storms, this effort to promote alcohol sales was particularly disturbing. Sharon Ayers, former executive director of the Louisiana Coalition to Prevent Underage Drinking, for example, observed, "Alcohol sales are soaring across the state. Beer was one of the first things that ran out at stores after the storm. But no one is paying attention to it; there's not enough money to adequately deal with alcohol issues in times of crisis" (quoted in Marin Institute 2006b).

The previous chapter began with an exploration of how the world is seen (and talked about) by Big Tobacco corporations. Does the world look different to a legal alcohol company? In fact, as discussed below, there are some notable differences in the world as perceived by these two different kinds of legal drug companies.

Seeing the World as an Alcohol Corporation

The world as conceived by Big Alcohol appears to be structured especially around four key functions: production, both of current products and the development of new ones; distribution; marketing, including promotion and advertising; and point of sale outlets. These functions exist in a spatial dimension worldwide and a temporal dimension, which involves looking back in time as well as planning for and facing the future. Management skill, referred to within the industry variously as leadership and ingenuity and involving a combination of "good policies" and "good people," is the attribute that alcohol companies see as allowing them to succeed. Success is ultimately measured in terms of payoffs to shareholders but is tracked and assessed in terms of several indicators of growth, including expanded production and sales volume, increases in control over a portion of the market, entering new markets, acquiring/introducing new brands, and expanding the workforce. The ability to operate effectively across both place and time and in terms of one or more of the core industry functions is also an element of success. Management capacity and motivation, having "the right stuff," is imbued with magical qualities and mythologized as a product of good breeding.

Shades of Difference

No doubt these features in varying ways can also be found as influences in the world seen by tobacco companies. However, several historic factors, some impacting only the tobacco industry and some only the alcohol industry, contribute to differences in tobacco and alcohol company conceptions of their worlds, including: (1) the ways tobacco and alcohol traditionally were integrated into everyday social life, with the former filling a more solitary, briefer, time-out niche in day-to-day social practice (the cigar being something of an exception here) and the latter occupying a more social, celebratory role; (2) the end of Prohibition and the legal segmentation of the alcohol industry into distinct producers, distributors, and retailers through the "tied-house" laws (which prohibited the kind of pre-Prohibition saloons that were "tied" to particular breweries) with the intention of blocking the vertical integration of the alcoholic beverage industry; (3) the enduring effects of the "failure" of Prohibition on subsequent considerations of alcohol controls; (4) the long-term effects of the rising tide of establishing the lethality of tobacco use, the credibility lost by tobacco companies through their disingenuous denial of addiction and harm, the impact of the tobacco settlement on public attitudes about smoking, and tobacco company efforts to regain public credibility through routine acknowledgement of harm within a context of continued and even expanded production and sales; and (5) the centrality of the farm in the worldview of the tobacco industry versus the brewery/distillery/winery—i.e., the factory—in the alcohol industry (although the vineyard remains an important icon among wine makers).

As a result of these various factors, tension between the industry and the wider society are, for the most part, lower in alcohol than in tobacco (but see chapter 8), and the "romance of alcohol" (e.g., shopping for special brands for particular events and occasions, learning about the best brands, trying new brands, matching brand type to meal content, toasting, and drinking as a social, celebratory event) remain strong. The factory motif in alcohol, in turn, is tied to a forward-looking "conquer the future" posture, while the future of the tobacco industry remains uncertain.

Myth Makers

The origin myth remains a strong element in the alcohol industry, as does romantic myth-making generally. According to Jean Kilbourne, an expert on alcohol advertising, advertising is a continual process of constructing and selling myths:

> Alcohol advertising [creates] a climate in which dangerous attitudes toward alcohol are presented as normal, appropriate, and innocuous. Most important, alcohol advertising spuriously links alcohol with precisely those attributes and qualities, happiness, wealth, prestige, sophistication, success, maturity, athletic ability, virility, creativity, [and] sexual satisfaction, that the misuse of alcohol usually diminishes and destroys. (Kilbourne 1988:10)

Additionally, Kilbourne notes, alcohol advertising "drastically inhibits honest public discussion of the [health and social problems associated with drinking] in the media and creates a climate in which alcohol is seen as entirely benign" (1988:12).

One of the fundamental myths of the alcohol industry—which the tobacco industry is very concerned about promoting as well—is, as indicated, the absolute failure of Prohibition. According to the myth, people did not stop drinking during Prohibition, but continued to do so clandestinely, while organized crime developed to supply the national thirst for beverage alcohol. Historians, however, are in less than complete agreement with Big Alcohol about the failure of Prohibition. As Jack Blocker (2006: 241) points out, "Prohibition did work in lowering per capita [alcohol] consumption" as well the frequency of an array of diseases linked to drinking. As for the impact of Prohibition on organized crime, the latter both predates Prohibition and has significantly outlived the repeal of the 18th amendment. Even repeal of the ban on alcohol was not a response to the failure of Prohibition. Rather it reflected changing concerns and attitudes produced by the beginning of the Depression, an event that convinced voters that contrary to the promises of the temperance movement prohibition did not produce prosperity.

Frankenstein's Laboratory

Like the tobacco industry, the laboratory is also a key place in the world of Big Alcohol. Careful focus on each step in the production process has a long tradition among beverage alcohol makers. One of the issues of concern among beer manufacturers, for example, is enhancing what is called the "drinkability" of their products. This term refers to the fact that when beer drinkers' palates become fatigued (i.e., the beer begins experientially to loose its flavor) they stop drinking. The challenge for beer manufactures is how to adjust beer chemistry to motivate consumers to drink more than one or two beers per drinking occasion, a goal that would seem to fly in the face of industry claims about supporting responsible drinking. In fact, in an effort to increase beer consumption, "Almost every brewer is constantly changing their beer," reports Henry von Eichel, president and CEO of the hops producer John I. Haas, Inc., "but no one likes to talk about it" (quoted in Join Together 2006a). The parallel here to the manipulation of nicotine levels by tobacco companies is evident.

The laboratory is also the site of creation of new products, critical to a world of niche marketing of targeted brands. In recent years, alcohol companies have been focusing on the development of new, less traditional products that appear to be targeted to younger drinkers.

> An increasing number of alcohol producers are making it easier for young people to get drunk and wired at the same time. In October [2005], Anheuser-Busch rolled out Be ("B-to-the-E")-caffeinated beer infused with ginseng and guarana extract. This year [2006], Jim Beam and youth-friendly Starbucks partnered to produce Starbucks Coffee Liqueur. Now, Patron Spirits Company has caffeinated Coffee Liqueur Tequila, and Wingard recently released Everglo—a lime-green blend of vodka and tequila infused with caffeine. (Marin Institute 2006c)

One product that especially has caught the attention of people who work in alcohol abuse prevention is a new group of alcohol products that have been called "alcopops," or flavored malt beverages (although their alcohol content actually comes from distilled spirits), as they appear to many to be designed—both because of the flavoring and the soft drink–like packaging—to appeal to older teenagers. The industry denies this assertion. Alcopops fit into the wider category of alcoholic beverages known as FABs (flavored alcoholic beverages), which were first introduced during the 1980s beginning with wine coolers. FABs are marketed to youth internationally (Mosher and Johnsson 2006).

In March 2006, in response to the concerns of parents, law enforcement, and legislators, the California Senate Select Committee on Children, Youth and Families held a hearing on alcopops in San Diego. Assemblywoman Lori Saldaña (D-San Diego), sponsor of a state bill to change the classification of the alcopop products from beer to distilled spirits (and thereby raise the tax rate on alcopops), testified that the fruity drinks have become so popular with young people, particularly girls, that they have acquired the nickname "cheerleader beer" (Branscomb 2006). Saldaña further reported that the similarities between a bottle of the Seagram's alcopop called Pineapple Coconut Calypso Colada, which is filled with sweetened blue alcoholic liquid, is so similar to alcohol-free Jones Soda that it is difficult for parents to know what their teens are drinking. Also at the hearing, San Diego Police Chief William Lansdowne, who testified in support of the increased taxing of alcopops, affirmed that the city's biggest "drug" problem is alcohol. In her testimony, Sierra Papp, cochair of the San Diego County Youth Council, lamented, "It's really unfortunate that the alcohol companies feel the need to target youth just to gain profits" (quoted in Branscomb 2006).

Seeing the world like an alcohol corporation, in sum, means a lot of "not seeing," as part of a well-crafted effort to shape what everyone else sees, hears, knows, and desires. This approach to the world, in the end, befits the producer of a commodity known for its considerable capacity to impact perception as well as consciousness.

Behind the Myth Making: The Social Costs of Alcohol

A survey carried out in England by the Health Education Authority (BBC News 1998) found that more that half of study participants believe that alcohol is good for your health. The primary health benefit according to participants is reducing stress. The alcohol industry also has a history of emphasizing potential health benefits of drinking. In recent times, this emphasis has focused on alleged heart benefits of low levels of drinking. As extolled by alcohol industry defender, David Hanson (2005c), the litany of benefits of drinking sounds like a 19th-century ad for a patent medicine:

> Moderate drinkers tend to have better health and live longer than those who are either abstainers or heavy drinkers. In addition to having fewer heart attacks and strokes, moderate consumers of alcoholic beverages . . . are generally less likely to suffer hypertension or high blood pressure, peripheral artery disease, Alzheimer's disease and the common cold. Sensible drinking also appears to be beneficial in reducing or preventing diabetes, rheumatoid arthritis, bone fractures and osteoporosis, kidney stones, digestive ailments, stress and depression, poor cognition and memory, Parkinson's disease, hepatitis A, pancreatic cancer, macular degeneration (a major cause of blindness), angina pectoris, duodenal ulcer, erectile dysfunction, hearing loss, gallstones, liver disease and poor physical condition in elderly.

More vulnerable to public opinion, the alcohol industry itself tends to be more circumscribed in its health claims for it products, while still calling attention to studies that suggest moderate drinking can lower risk of heart disease.

As the Global Burden of Disease study (Murray and Lopez 1996) found, however, the problem with promoting drinking on the basis of its benefits for a healthy heart is that alcohol tends to kill and cause illness at relatively young ages while the protection it confers for cardiovascular diseases takes effect at older ages. Moreover, industry statements about the benefits of drinking for the heart are never accompanied by discussion of other research showing that drinking increases the risk of developing an irregular heartbeat known as atrial fibrillation (Frost and Vestergaard 2004). Nor does the industry tend to admit the full cost to U.S. society, let alone other societies, related to alcohol abuse, a figure that was estimated to be almost $230 million in 2005, more than cancer (which was estimated to have cost $196 billion in 2005) and also more than obesity ($133 billion) (Mann 2006).

Additionally, recent research has begun to suggest that the notion that moderate drinking helps prevent heart disease may be erroneous. An international research team from the Canada, the United States, and Australia (Fillmore et al. 2006) analyzed over 50 studies linking drinking patterns and premature death from all causes including coronary disease. The study team found that prior research suggesting heart benefits associated with moderate drinking made the error of lumping into the "abstainers" category people who had cut down or quit drinking because of declining health, increasing frailty, use of conflicting medication, or growing disability. As a result, statistically the amount of disease among abstainers rose while that among drinkers fell. An examination of studies that did not make this error of assignment found that there was no evidence of health benefits associated with moderate drinking.

Another social cost of alcohol abuse is crime. As John Dilulio summarizes:

> Sixty percent of convicted homicide offenders drank just before committing the offense. Sixty-three percent of adults jailed for homicide had been drinking before the offense. Sixty percent of prison inmates drank heavily just before committing the violent crime for which they were incarcerated. The relationship between poverty and homicide is stronger in neighborhoods with higher rates of alcohol consumption than in those with average or below-average rates. Numerous studies report a strong association between sexual violence and alcohol, finding that "anywhere between 30 and 90 percent of convicted rapists are drunk at the time of offense." Juveniles, especially young men, who drink to the point of drunkenness are more likely than those who do not drink to get into fights, get arrested, commit violent crimes, and recidivate later in life. (1996:15)

Like certain criminal acts, motor vehicle accidents can be considered violent and are more likely to occur when drivers have been drinking. It is estimated that approximately 40 percent of motor vehicle accidents in the U.S. involve the use of alcohol. A review of data from the National Epidemiologic Survey on Alcohol and Related Conditions by Chou et al.

(2006) found that in 2001–2002 more than 23 million (or just over 11 percent) of American adults reported engaging in drinking while driving or as a passenger in a motor vehicle (with passenger drinking being more frequent than driver drinking). Our awareness of the important role of alcohol in vehicular and other types of accidents as well as in cases of homicide or physical assault is diminished by the fact that it tends to get unreported in media accounts of those events (Slater et al. 2006).

The National Highway Traffic Safety Administration has determined that judgment and information processing are affected when BAC levels rise above .05, and concentration and speed control abilities are impacted as well above .07. In the year 2000, alcohol played a role in over one-fourth of motor vehicle crashes in Colorado. That year, BAC levels between .08 and .09 were involved in an estimated 600 motor vehicle "accidents" in the state, resulting in 17 deaths and 500 injuries (Pacific Institute for Research and Evaluation 2001). While denying any responsibility for the large number of people killed, permanently injured, or otherwise harmed by the mixing of alcohol and driving, alcohol companies in recent years have urged their customers to drink responsibly.

Globally the alcohol toll was estimated to be three-quarters of a million lives in 1990 and has spiraled up since then. While it was estimated that the disability-adjusted life years lost (a combination of cases or premature death, disability, and days of sickness) due to alcohol comprised 3.5 percent of all loss in 1990, by 2000 it had grown to 4 percent worldwide (World Health Organization 2001). In Australia, for example, research shows that more people "are drinking at dangerous levels, resulting in high numbers of deaths and injuries, and high health costs" (Khadem 2006:5). Alcohol is the "second largest drug-related cause of death in Australia [after tobacco] and the main cause of deaths on Australian roads" (Khadem 2006:5). In 2004, 25 percent of 14–19-year-old Australians were found by the Australian Bureau of Statistics to engage in either daily or weekly drinking.

Especially at risk, however, are resource-poor countries, or poorer sites within comparatively wealthier locations (e.g., especially poor neighborhoods, like squatter settlements), in which the consumption of alcoholic beverages has been going up but an adequate infrastructure does not exist to handle the health and social consequences. In some parts of the world, such as Central and Eastern Europe, alcohol abuse has contributed to what the World Health Organization (2001:1) reports as "an unprecedented decline in male life expectancy." Notably, from the perspective of Big Alcohol, these are prime growth markets for the industry's future. Overall, the World Health Organization concludes that "alcohol is a significant threat to world health" (2001:1).

The Drink Tab

A precise health and fiscal assessment of the costs of drinking is found in a study carried out by the Institute for Health and Aging and the Institute for the Study of Social Change (Marin Institute 2004) for the state of California. The conclusion of this analysis is that alcohol problems in the state come with "a heavy price tag—more than $500 per year for every California taxpayer." For the year 2001, the total cost was $17.8 billion, which included health care for people with a drinking problem, alcohol abuse treatment and prevention, the value of lives lost prematurely to alcohol abuse, and costs incurred by the criminal justice system handling inebriants. Of these, lives lost prematurely to alcohol abuse and its related diseases had the biggest cost. In 2001, 13,000 people in the state died as a result of drinking abuse (27 percent whose death was caused directly by alcohol, 39 percent who died of an alcohol-related medical diagnosis, and 34 percent who died of an injury resulting from drinking). The study found that the total value of alcohol-related lost productivity was $8 billion. As a result of taxes, fines, and fees paid by the alcohol industry in California in 2001—an issue the industry is quick to bring up when itemizing the contributions of alcohol to society—the analysis found that a total of $330 million came into state coffers. Consequently, while the industry reaped an enormous profit on alcohol sales in the state in 2001, "California was still left with a $17.46 billion tab" (Marin Institute 2004).

Underage and Under the Influence

One of the most vulnerable populations with reference to alcohol abuse is youth. Each day in the United States it is estimated that over 5,000 people under 16 years of age drink alcohol for the first time. The average age that children start drinking is 13, and nearly 7.2 million young people describe themselves as "binge drinkers" (Center on Alcohol Marketing and Youth 2006a). Additionally, each day, three teens die in drinking-involved vehicle accidents (National Highway Traffic Safety Administration 2005), and at least six additional youth die from a range of other alcohol-related causes, including suicide, homicide, drowning, and falls. According to the U.S. Centers for Disease Control and Prevention (CDC), alcohol is involved in one-fourth of the deaths among 15- to 20-year-old males and one-sixth of deaths among females in this age range (Center on Alcohol Marketing and Youth 2006a). Short of contributing to mortality, teen and young adult use of alcohol has multiple other adverse consequences, some of which take their toll later in life. In Britain, for example, the Office for National Statistics (Life Style Extra 2006) announced that there were over 8,000 deaths in the country that could be directly linked to the use of alcohol during the year of 2004, about double the number recorded in 1991. Much of the increase occurred among men and women between the ages of 35 and 54 years (although increases were notably greater among men). Given the time it takes to develop alcohol-related life-threatening health problems, such as chronic liver disease, the rising mortality data suggest that binge-drinking among people in their 20s is an important cause of the rising number of alcohol-related deaths.

In recent years, an expanded level of research involving brain scans and skills testing of drinkers shows that heavy drinking during adolescence affects how the brains of young people develop as well as levels of brain activity, findings that suggest short- or even longer-term brain damage (Brown and Tapert 2004). Moreover, research affirms that the earlier in life an individual begins consuming alcohol, the greater the number of consequences he/she suffers later in life, with those who begin drinking before age 15 being four times more likely to become dependent on alcohol (Grant and Dawson 1997), seven times more likely to be in an alcohol-related car or other vehicle accident, and at least 10 times more likely to be involved in alcohol-related violence (Hingson and Kenkel 2004) than those who wait until they are 21 to begin drinking. In a study of over 40,000 adults in the United States, Hingson and coworkers (2006) found that almost half of those who began drinking before they were 14 years old developed a dependence on alcohol, usually within 10 years of taking their first drink. Among those who did not begin drinking until they were 21 years old, only 9 percent became alcohol dependent. This research suggests the possibility that as was reported in chapter 3 for nicotine, very early exposure to alcohol affects the developing adolescent brain in ways that makes a person significantly more vulnerable to developing a long-term dependence on alcohol. According to Scott Swartzwelder, a neuropsychologist at Duke University who has studied the effects of alcohol on the brain cells of adolescent and adult rats:

> Clearly, something is changed in the brain by early alcohol exposure. It's a double-edged sword and both of the edges are bad. . . . Teenagers can drink far more than adults before they get sleepy enough to stop, but along the way they're impairing their cognitive functions much more powerfully. (quoted in Butler 2006:1)

While alcohol companies deny marketing their products to youth, the advantages of doing so in terms of attracting a new generation of long-term customers is evident.

In this light, patterns of alcohol advertisement become clearer. According to a study by the CDC (Associated Press 2006c), in 2004 just under one-half of all advertisement for beer, wine, and liquor on radio were aired on youth-oriented programs. Especially targeted were alternative rock and hip-hop stations. Ads on alternative rock stations, for example, comprised one-fourth of youth exposure to alcohol industry advertisements. Although the Beer Institute, the Wine Institute, and the Distilled Spirits Council joined together in 2003 to announce that they would limit advertisement on youth-oriented programs, the CDC concluded that the alcohol industry has failed to live up to this promise. The study found that ads for Colt 45 Malt Liquor were most likely to air on youth-oriented programs, while Bud Light had the greatest number of ads on youth-oriented programs.

An important difference between the products sold by the tobacco industry and those sold by the alcohol industry is that if used as recommended by the manufacturer, tobacco injures and kills its consumers, while alcohol, if used as recommended by the industry in its public pronouncements about drinking, namely encouraging people to drink in moderation, usually will not. The problem, as this examination of the health costs of drinking suggests, is that an enormous number of people are, in fact, injured and killed each year because of alcohol consumption. In terms of the cold statistics, while one-third of smokers die because of tobacco, only one-tenth of drinkers die because of alcohol. Still, in the United States alone, this means that 100,000 drinkers a year die because of alcohol-related causes (Saffer 2006). Moreover, from a profit perspective, in terms of the amount of their respective levels of alcohol consumption, two vulnerable groups, underage and pathological drinkers, are "the alcohol industry's most valuable customers" (Duran and Gavilanes 2006).

Selling Alcohol to the Poor

Needless to say, alcohol is sold to everyone, not just the poor, and the alcohol industry would be more than happy to welcome more middle-class and upper-class consumers to the ranks of its customers. Because the rates of alcohol consumption in wealthier classes have fallen over time, the alcohol industry must find alternative markets if shareholders are to be rewarded for buying company stock. They discovered, as did crack dealers in the mid-1980s, even the poor can be a profitable market.

The eagerness of the alcohol industry to sell alcohol to the poor is illustrated in a community struggle that took place in the year 2000 in Portland, Maine. Carl Flipper of the Humboldt Neighborhood Target Association in North Portland and his neighbors noticed one day that a large billboard near the local high school was displaying an ad for 40-ounce bottles of Olde English 800, a Miller Brewing Co. malt liquor that community members asserted is marketed primarily in poor, minority neighborhoods. The ad showed characters in gang attire partying with the large bottles of Olde English, a product known on the street as OE. Said Flipper:

> When I first saw the ads, I was offended . . . I stayed mad a long time because all I could see was gang members in the 'hood having a good time drinking large containers of beer. This is not the image we want portrayed to our young people. (quoted in Join Together 2000)

Flipper's concern was well founded in that existing research indicates that there are two periods of heightened vulnerability to substance abuse: early adolescence and during the transition to early adulthood. These are, at the same time, life stages during which many inner-city urban youth spend large amounts of time on the street and are likely to be exposed to street billboard advertising.

Liquid Crack in 40-Ounce Bottles

Flipper well knew OE's target audience; as stated in an older marketing brochure for OE, it is "brewed for relatively high-alcohol content (important to the ethnic market!)" (Allen-Taylor 1997). Notes *Modern Drunkard Magazine* (2004): malt liquor is

> the beer [that is] so strong they don't even call it beer—they call it liquor. The brew from the bad of town, the staple of gangstas and punk rockers, barrios and trailer parks. Strong, cheap and raw. Served up in a big bottle that hangs in your hand like a blackjack.

Indeed, on the street, with its high alcohol content (double that of regular beer and equivalent to five shots of whiskey in the common individual container, one 40-ounce bottle) and its concentration of corn syrup and other sweeteners that are thought to accelerate intoxication, malt liquor has the nickname "liquid crack." In the graphic description of journalist Douglas Allen-Taylor (1997):

> Throwing back a 40 [is] the equivalent of someone standing behind you with a baseball bat, teeing off on the back of your head every time you take a swallow. You leave your brains on the pavement when you walk away. If you can walk away.

Recognizing the implications of the billboard campaign, the local community in Portland organized in protest, and Miller, feeling the heat of bad publicity, backed down, at least to a degree. Although large OE billboards were removed from the neighborhood, the company announced that commercials promoting Olde English would continue on local radio and TV and in print media. Ronald McClaron, Miller's director of corporate relations, told community representatives:

> No one in corporate headquarters viewed the billboards as offensive, nor would we ever encourage underage drinking. . . . We aren't responsible for all of the drinking problems in your community, but we are canceling the campaign immediately. (quoted in Join Together 2000)

A Steady Diet of Alcohol Commercials

How responsible is the alcohol industry for drinking problems in low-income minority communities? As the *Report of the Secretary's Task Force on Black and Minority Health* noted, African Americans "suffer disproportionately from the health consequences of alcohol . . . [and] appear to be at a disproportionately high risk for certain alcohol-related problems" (U.S. Department of Health and Human Services 1985:130). Additionally, the age-adjusted death rate from alcohol-induced causes for African Americans is 10 percent higher than is the case for the general population (National Center for Injury Prevention and Control 2005).

Research indicates that while abstinence rates in the African American population overall are higher than in the general population, the prevalence of heavier drinking is greater (Galvan and Caetano 2003). Moreover, while African American youth and young adults traditionally drank less than their white counterparts, a higher prevalence of frequent heavy drinking was found among African Americans between 18 to 29 years of age: Frequent heavy drinking among white males in this age group declined between 1984 and 1995 from 32 percent to 16 percent but increased among African Americans of the same age from 17 percent to 18 percent (Caetano and Clark 1998).

Furthermore, researchers have identified poverty as an important factor in increased levels of drinking and its consequences. The Center for Science in the Public Interest and the Minnesota Institute of Black Chemical Abuse (1986) conducted a survey of health professionals who work with African Americans with a drinking problem, which confirmed that poverty is the most important factor influencing drinking. Similarly, Shaila Khan and associates (2002) studied the immediate and long-term effects of poverty and unemployment on alcohol abuse and found that an increase in poverty produces a corresponding increase in both the level of alcohol use and the frequency of alcohol-related problems. The relationship of poverty to alcohol consumption and its consequences are not completely straightforward, however: recent unemployment leads to a decrease in alcohol consumption; if unemployment endures, and becomes chronic, as is disproportionately common in inner-city ethnic minority neighborhoods, alcohol use goes up.

Despite the seriousness of this health dilemma, the Center for Science in the Public Interest (1986) has long maintained that rather than a rigorous national public health response "the lion's share of what is being said and done about alcohol in the black community consists of a steady diet of alluring commercial marketing campaigns designed to promote alcohol consumption among blacks." Like the OE billboards in Portland, much of this marketing is targeted to African American youth and young adults. An analysis by the Center on Alcohol Marketing and Youth (2006b) of exposure of African American youth to alcohol advertising printed in magazines, played on radio, and shown on television for 2003 and 2004 found that:

- Even as youth exposure to alcohol advertising in magazines has been declining, African American youth ages 12 to 20 are regularly exposed to significantly more magazine advertising for beer and distilled spirits than are youth in general, including 17 percent more beer and ale ads and 43 percent more distilled spirits ads in 2003, and 21 percent more beer and ale ads and 42 percent more distilled spirits ads in 2004. While 97 percent of all youth saw an average of 113 alcohol ads in magazines, 99 percent of African American youth saw an average of 150 alcohol ads in national magazines in 2004.

- In nine of the 10 largest radio markets in the country in 2003 and in six of the 10 top markets in 2004, African American youth hear more radio alcohol advertising per capita than youth in general.

- During the summer of 2004, advertisements for a single brand, Colt 45 Malt Liquor, accounted for almost a third (32 percent) of all radio alcohol advertising heard by African American youth.

- Alcohol advertising appeared on all 15 of the most-watched television programs among African American youth in 2004. During that year, the alcohol industry spent just under $5 million to buy commercial time on these programs. Black Entertainment Television, a cable television network that targets African American audiences, was the number-one outlet for overall alcohol spending in 2003–2004, as well as for spending on programs that generate the greatest youth exposure to alcohol advertising among African American youth. In 2004, for example, 72 percent of alcohol advertising dollars received by Black Entertainment Television was for commercials shown on just 10 programs on the channel. These programs were twice as likely to be seen by youth ages 12 to 20 than by adults.

Commodifying Culture

The pattern of targeted advertising is no different in inner-city Hispanic neighborhoods. Describing the experience of 18-year-old Sandra Villarda of the San Diego Youth Council, the *Wall Street Journal* reports that she began to feel

> besieged by beer billboards on her drive down El Cajon Boulevard to San Diego City College. Every day, the ads greeted her, for Bud Light on one block, Miller Lite on the next. "Mas Calor! Mas Sabor! Mas Fiestas!" one Miller Lite billboard read, "More Heat! More Flavor! More Parties." According to Villarda, "There is a lot of pressure to drink in this community." (Jordan 2006:1)

A study conducted by Maria Luisa Alaniz, professor and chair of the Social Science Department at San Jose State University, and Robert Parker of the Prevention Research Center affirms Villarda's experience. The study found that the typical Hispanic student in the San Francisco Bay area passes between 10 and 61 alcohol billboards each day on the way home from school. Alaniz also found five times as many alcohol ads in Latino neighborhoods as in predominantly non-Latino white neighborhoods (Alaniz 1998).

Additionally, researchers affiliated with the study examined alcohol advertising inside liquor stores, on billboards, and in restaurants that feature women and alcohol and found that many showcase scantily clad women holding a beer bottle or a glass, some standing, some lying down. One of the advertisements documented in the study, a point of purchase ad for Olde English found inside a liquor store, pictured a Latina dressed in black against a tiger-striped background. The tiger is one of the advertising symbols for Olde English. The ad reads: "El Tigre te desea" (the Tiger wants you). Alaniz sees alcohol advertising campaigns of this sort both as an attack upon Latina womanhood and as an attempt to "commodify" Latino culture (Alaniz and Wilkes 1995). According to Alaniz:

> Malt-liquor ads are raunchier than the rest. . . . If a beer ad puts a woman in spandex, the malt-liquor ad puts her in leather, often astride a can or a bottle. They are the worst. . . . The advertising campaigns of the alcohol industry aimed at the Latino population are insulting our culture and history. . . . [Advertising is potent because Latinos] are virtually invisible in other sectors, such as school curriculum and the media. Essentially the only positive image they see reflected of themselves is associated with alcohol. (quoted in Allen-Taylor 1997)

In one of her studies, Alaniz overlaid maps of alcohol outlets, such as bars and liquor stores, with maps of the distribution of crime in two California cities. The study documented a strong correlation between the presence of alcohol outlets and criminal activity. Additionally, the study found that alcohol-outlet density in Latino communities was much higher than in other areas. In a 1.2-square-mile radius in Redwood City, with a high concentration of Mexican Americans, 59 alcohol outlets were found. The state average for the same size area was 30. In their book, *Alcohol and Homicide*, Parker and Rebhun point out that the high density of alcohol outlets in poor, inner-city neighborhoods reflects

> the relative power of alcohol producers and wholesalers who supply liquor outlets, banks who loan money to store owners, and state regulators whose activities are more oriented toward the interests of alcohol industry lobbying groups than the regulation of that industry and the relative powerlessness of the poor and unemployed individuals and groups who live in greater concentration in these areas of high outlet density. (1995:24)

Anheuser-Busch is one of the sources of the ad binge in Latino communities. In 2006, the company created a new division and hired a new vice president who is specifically charged with marketing beer to Latinos. Anheuser-Busch budgeted $60 million for ads in the Latino media, two-thirds more than the 2005 budget. Similarly, at SABMiller, $100 million was earmarked for three years of TV advertising to Latinos on Univision, while Molson Coors Brewing Company followed Anheuser and named a vice president responsible for expanding the Hispanic market. As a result of such efforts, like their African American peers, Latino youth see more magazine ads, hear more radio commercials, and are exposed to more advertisements on television for alcohol than non-Latino white youth (Center on Alcohol Marketing and Youth 2006c). In the assessment of Felix Alvarez, a professor at the National Hispanic University:

> The alcohol companies are trying to take over Latino culture by sponsoring festivals and institutions. . . . They give scholarships to Latino educational institutions, they give grants to civic groups like the Hispanic Chamber of Commerce, they give "Hispanic Achievement Awards" and then do full ads on the awards in the Hispanic press to make sure we all know about it. . . . The alcohol companies don't do this because they love us. . . . They do this for two reasons: one, so that Latino culture will be closely associated with drinking; and two, so that Latino organizations will be less likely to speak out against drinking. (quoted in Allen-Taylor 1997)

Although the alcohol industry admits stepping up advertising targeted to Latinos, Marlene Coulis of Anheuser-Busch discounts that the goal of this cash outlay is to expand the market among Latinos. According to Coulis, "We would disagree with anyone who suggests beer billboards increase abuse among Latino or other minority communities" (quoted in Jordan 2006:1). Counters Katherine Culliton of the National Latino Council on Alcohol and Tobacco Prevention: "Latino youth are drinking more than black or white youth, with all the concurrent negative health and social consequences. We believe this is a result of beer companies aggressively targeting Latino youth" (quoted in Jordan 2006:1). Support for Culliton's assertion is found in recent studies with youth that show that exposure to alcohol advertising plays a measurable role in underage drinking. Snyder et al. (2006), for example, followed youth over a 23-month period in 24 media markets and found that for every extra alcohol ad they saw, drinking went up 1 percent. Additionally, for every additional dollar per capita spent by the alcohol industry on advertising in a specific media market (over the average of $6.80), the youth in the sample drawn from that market drank 3 percent more. Similarly, but from the opposite direction, Saffer and Dave (2006) found that a 28 percent decrease in youth exposure to alcohol advertising produced a 4 to 16 percent reduction in overall drinking and an 8 to 33 percent drop in binge drinking. Moreover, one way to get youth to drink more, research has shown, is to give them promotional material, such as alcohol-branded T-shirts and related items. A study of 2,000 middle school students, for example, found that those who owned items that exhibited alcohol brands were more likely to initiate drinking than those who did not own branded items (McClure et al. 2006).

In review of the recent literature, Gerald Hastings and colleagues (2005) conclude that although making categorical statements about cause and effect is difficult in the social sciences, studies with sophisticated designs provide increasingly compelling evidence that alcohol advertising has a direct effect on increasing adolescent drinking. At the same time drinking rates rise so do the negative, often severe consequences of drinking. Because of social inequality, however, the capacity of communities to respond to such consequences is not evenly distributed. As Guillermo Brito, executive director of the National Latino Council on Alcohol and Tobacco Prevention, observes, the "industry must also be aware that there is disparate impact of alcohol ads [because] Latino youth have less access to prevention and treatment" (quoted in Landa 2005).

Takin' the Night Train

As the discussion above suggests, throughout the alcohol industry specific brands are targeted to particular segments of the potential consumer market, which is segmented by the industry by ethnicity, region, age, and gender, but also by the customer's ability to pay. Chateau La Mondotte Saint-Emilion 1996 wine, for example, at $600 a bottle, is not marketed to factory workers. Customers of this luxury brand do not work on commodity production lines at General Motors or Delmonte. When asked how he felt about the fact that an enormously successful hip-hop performer like Jay-Z, who has recorded rap songs about being a drug dealer, favors $300-a-bottle Cristal champagne, and regularly features it being drunk from the bottle in his videos, Frederic Rouzaud, head of Louis Roederer, maker of the luxury brand, snobbishly replied, "We can't forbid people from buying it. I'm sure Dom Perignon or Krug [whose top-of-the-line champagnes sell for $475 and $225 respectively] would be delighted to have their business" (quoted in Givhan 2006:C1). "In matters of style and status," notes Robin Givhan, "companies like to pick and choose, always seeking the right image and the upper hand" (2006:C2). Conversely, two-dollar-a-bottle Night Train Express wine is not marketed to businesspeople earning six-figure salaries. Rather, Night Train and other cheap wines, which have double the alcohol content of table wines, are known variously on the street as bum wines, street wines, fortified wines, wino wines, or twist-cap wines, and they are marketed to the poor, the desperately poor.

A number of years ago, Alix Freedman (1988:3) wrote an exposé on the wine industry focus on bottom drawer products. It began:

> In the dim light of a cold February morning, a grizzled wino shuffles into the Bowery Discount liquor store muttering, "Thunderchicken, it's good

lickin'." Fumbling for some change, he says: "Gimme one bird." Raymond Caba, the store clerk, understands the argot and hands over a $1.40 pint of Thunderbird, the top seller in what he calls "the bum section." . . . The ritual is repeated a thousand times a day in dead-end neighborhoods across the country. Cheap wines with down-and-dirty names—and an extra measure of alcohol—are the beverage of choice among down-and-out drunks, but winos are an embarrassment to the big companies that manufacture these wines. With rare exceptions, they aren't eager to acknowledge their own products.

Both Thunderbird and Night Train are produced by the nation's largest wine company, E. & J. Gallo Winery. This information does not show up on the labels of the products however. Rather, on the label of Thunderbird the producer is listed as Thunderbird Ltd., while the Night Train Express bottle lists Night Train Limited as the manufacturer. Similarly, neither product can be found on the E. & J. Gallo Winery "portfolio of wines" on the company's website. Rather, the company stresses:

> For almost 70 years, the hallmark of the E. & J. Gallo Winery has been the quality of its products. The company understands that it can only be sound when it focuses on long-term success achieved by consistently offering consumers the highest quality product for the best value. (E. & J. Gallo Winery 2006)

Paul Gillette, the publisher of the *Wine Investor* in Los Angeles, is quoted by Freedman (1988:4) as saying, "Makers of skid-row wines are the dope pushers of the wine industry." The parallel to crack cocaine is clear. In his study of a largely African American community in the Northeast that he gave the pseudonym Fayerville, Kojo Dei reports a 44-year-old female informant told him "the problem in this neighborhood is not crack, it's booze. The cheap wine 'n' liquor is the real killer. Alcohol is what's destroying the Black family, not crack" (2002:20).

Street wines of the sort that Dei's informant complained about are inexpensive to produce. The product comes in a no-frills container, and is only advertised by word of mouth. Often not found in suburban liquor outlets, street wines, as Freedman (1988:4) observes, "are staples of the bulletproof liquor stores of low-income neighborhoods." Adds Neil Goldman, who was chief of the alcoholism treatment unit at New York City's St. Vincent's Hospital when interviewed by Freedman (1988:5), "The industry is manufacturing this for a select population: the poor, the homeless, the skid-row individual." Nonetheless, street wines are quite profitable. Freedman (1988) noted that representatives of the makers of Wild Irish Rose reported that the net profit margin is 10 percent higher on street wines than on table wines. Sales tend to be steady and strong, as the products have something of a captive market—alcoholics. As a former executive at Manischewitz Wine Company told Freedman (1988:5), "It's lots and lots of money, but it doesn't add prestige."

People like Joe and Jane

While the alcohol industry does not tend to like the fact that many of its customers are poor or near-poor and struggling to make it, sometimes it is useful to stress the working-class status of many alcohol consumers. In an effort to counter efforts in the 109th Congress to increase federal excise taxes on beer, for example, the Anheuser-Busch (2006b) company developed a profile of their average customer, a couple they dubbed "Joe and Jane Six Pack," with an annual household income of no more than $45,000 and one or two children (which was said to be true of 52 percent of Anheuser-Busch customers). Most families like that of Joe and Jane Six Pack, the company pointed out, do not own their own home but are apartment dwellers. Additionally, "Compared to other young, married males, the regular male beer drinker," like Joe, "is less likely to have graduated from college." Among women beer drinkers, 33 percent are heads of the household, and 70 percent do not work in white-collar jobs. In arguing against taxes on beer, the company claimed that such taxes "hit lower-income families five times as hard as upper income families." For people like Joe and Jane, "beer is one of the simple pleasures" of life. For alcohol companies like Anheuser-Busch, selling beer or other alcoholic beverages to people like Joe and Jane is big business. One result is that the negative consequences of abusive drinking hit lower-income families many times harder than they do upper-income families, contributing significantly to the drugging of the poor.

CHAPTER 5

Global Pharmaceuticals
Belowground Features
of an Aboveground Industry

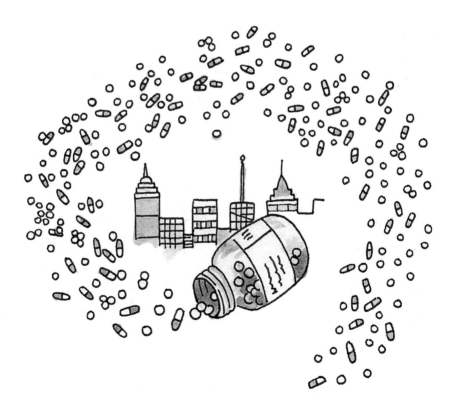

A Rich Man's World: The Coming of Big Pharma

A Chronology of Key Moments

"The story of the pharmaceutical industry" as K. S. Rajan (2006:22) observes, "has arguably been one of the most dramatic stories of industrial growth in the twentieth century." Part of the tale of the rise of the modern pharmaceutical industry involves an intertwined history of what might be called "snake oil" and power drugs." While the former consist of compounds that have been marketed as wonder cures but do not, upon objective evaluation, appear to have any real beneficial effect at the biological level, the latter are compounds that have the chemical capacity to significantly affect human biology and/or mood. Another part of the story involves the role played (or not played) by government regulation in both thwarting the marketing of snake oil and controlling the marketing of power drugs that, despite their efficacy, also can have toxic side effects. While the pathway taken was not linear, it is possible to identify a number of key moments in the rise of the contemporary global pharmaceutical industry, or what has been called Big Pharma:

- The emergence of the indigenous patent or propriety medicine industry in the U.S. following the War of Independence, a development that provided a foundation upon which the pharmaceutical industry would blossom

- The world flu pandemic of 1889–1892, which pulled a number of dye manufacturers, most importantly Friedr. Bayer & Co., into using their production facilities and broad knowledge of chemistry to conceive, develop, test, and market new medicines to treat flu (an event some see as the definitive origin point of the pharmaceutical industry)

- Development, primarily during the 19th century, of the first wave of "power drugs," a group of alkaloids—substances with nitrogen-containing molecules, like morphine, that have a noticeable effect on humans (and other species)—resulting in a marked increase in the number of brands and kinds of patent medicines on the market and a corresponding growth in chemical dependence and addiction

- A transition of patent medicines from local cures into more regional or, in some cases, national products, and of the organization of patent medicine production from cottage industry to industrial company, resulting in significantly increased profit, spiraling advertising budgets, and enhanced lobbying to contest government regulation

- National exposure of the dangers of unregulated health products, leading to the first regulatory laws, a culling of the patent medicine pharmacopoeia, and a clearing of the health product field for the emergent modern pharmaceutical industry

- Development of the second wave of "power drugs," the sulfa antibacteria, antifungal medicines, beginning with prontosil, discovered by German physician and chemist, Gerhard Domagk, in 1935, and sparking a marked expansion in the number of pharmaceutical companies

- Development, during and after World War II, of the third wave of "power drugs," including antibiotics like penicillin but including a range of other drugs that set the stage for the full florescence of the modern pharmaceutical industry

- Globalization of the pharmaceutical industry, characterized by worldwide distribution of products, multinational mergers, enormous productive capacity, and a growing concentration of control over access, coupled with a countervailing diversion of some drugs from the legal to the illegal trade

- Emergence of gene-splicing biotechnology promising the fourth wave of "power drugs," namely bioengineered medicines, generating both hopes of new levels of efficacy and fears of "science gone wild"

Within this chronology, four elements of the story of the pharmaceutical industry are especially important to the role of Big Pharma in the drugging of the poor.

First, as Petryna and Kleinman (2006:1) indicate, "marketing and advertising had their beginnings in the pharmaceutical industry" and spread from there to other commodities, including alcohol and tobacco. Hyped-up pharmaceutical product promotion, including direct-to-consumer advertising, has both a long history and a measurable impact. Specifically, 150 years of often intense pharmaceutical advertising has contributed to a cultural expectation of coping with negative experiences and personal distress through chemistry:

> Drug manufacturers seeking new markets and bigger profits urge everyone to feel better fast ("relief is only a swallow away"), and attempt to persuade

physicians and the public that unpleasant human feelings are abnormal—an "illness" that should be corrected with drugs." (Hills 1980:118)

A report by the Consumers Union (2006), publisher of *Consumer Reports*, for example, found that the use of prescription sleeping pills has gone up by almost 32 percent during 2001–2006. An important factor in this rise, according to the Consumers Union, is the heavy television and other direct-to-consumer advertising of a new class of anti-insomnia medications like Ambien, Sonata, and Lunesta. Big Pharma spent over $4 billion in consumer advertising during 2005, which represents a fivefold jump since 1995 (reflecting the 1997 decision by the FDA to allow television advertising of prescription drugs). Desiring the kind of fully restful sleep depicted in television commercials, consumers have pressed doctors for prescriptions while overlooking the risks associated with the new class of sleeping pills, including dizziness, day-after sleepiness, cognitive impairment, dependency, and rebound insomnia. The Consumers Union inspected the FDA's Adverse Events Reporting System data for Ambien and Lunesta in 2005 and found over 150 incidents of reported confusion, aggression, hallucination, and injury, including 70 hospitalizations and nine deaths. In the spring of 2006, for instance, Congressman Patrick Kennedy of Rhode Island reported that he took Ambien and an anti-nausea drug just prior to crashing his car in the middle of the night near the Capitol, thinking he was expected there for a vote. Moreover, as Yi (2006:A6) notes, "By heavily promoting drugs that treat symptoms rather than illnesses . . . patients may be driven to look for quick fixes instead of finding a solution." For the pharmaceutical industry, sales of prescription insomnia medications provided another type of quick fix, namely for its cash flow problems. Sales of these medicines produced almost $3 billion dollars in profits for the industry in 2005.

Second, historically, one of the first pharmaceuticals to be aggressively advertised through newspapers, magazines, and other venue was Dover's Powder, of which opium was a central ingredient. Indeed, addictive substances like heroin, cocaine, morphine, nicotine, and alcohol were all critical to the take-off phase of the pharmaceutical industry. Dover's Powder was produced in Britain, the source of most medicines used in the colonies prior to the Revolution. Very likely, the same ships that transported Dover's powder and other proprietary medicinal across the Atlantic to the colonies returned to Britain filled with American tobacco (as well as dried cod fish, some of which was then shipped to the Caribbean and traded for rum). After the War of Independence, American entrepreneurs launched their own medical commodities manufacturing, and from it ultimately emerged the U.S. pharmaceutical industry. In this domain, drugs that alter moods, relieve pain, and have the potential for dependence and addiction continue to play a major role. In particular, certain classes of commonly abused drugs, including painkillers, tranquilizers, stimulants, and sedatives, because they have such a huge market, are of keen interest to pharmaceutical companies.

Third, from the beginning, deception, half-truth, and grandiose claims have been key elements in the pharmaceutical promotional toolkit. Other forms of manipulation—including the use of strong-arm tactics if necessary—also have been standard tools of the trade in the selling of pharmaceutical products to consumers, especially with regard to countering government regulation but also in containing "bad press." Full truth in advertising is as alien to the pharmaceutical world as rehabilitation is to penal institutions: it may happen but it is really not what the system is set up to do or what it does best.

Finally, the entire pharmaceutical industry rests on an unquestioned acceptance of medical commodification; rather than a basic survival resource in which people have an inherent right, manufactured medicines (although often made of naturally occurring substances or having their origin in indigenous healing practices) are the private property of the pharmaceutical companies—or in the case of patents, their intellectual private property—access to which is governed by ability to pay. Since profit is the bottom line, continuously expanding production is highly valued. All markets are good markets, and when possible, establishing new markets is the name of the game.

Each of these points, both as characteristics of the pharmaceutical industry generally and factors in the drugging of the poor, is developed in this chapter.

The Birth of Advertising

During the 18th century, patent medicines—mixtures of various sorts that, despite their common referent, actually lacked legal patents—were among the first products promoted by the advertising industry. Indeed, several of the sales strategies that continue to be widespread in advertising—such as the use of consumer testimonials, expert and celebrity endorsements, niche marketing to specific consumer groups (e.g., women), and the use of give-away items as a promotional mechanism, as well as some techniques that have only recently been adopted by the modern pharmaceutical industry—such as direct-to-consumer promotion of medicinal products—were pioneered by the promoters of patent medicines. Branding, which has become important in global product marketing, also had its origin in the sale of patent medicines, which commonly were given unique personalized names, such as Ayer's Cherry Pectoral, Mrs. Winslow's Soothing Syrup, Scott's Emulsion, and, as noted, Dover's Powder. These product names (of which well over 200 are known)—some of which are still being sold—in part reflect a period before mass industrial capitalism depersonalized the relationship between products and their producers. At the same time, branding—along with claims of secret formulation—was critical to the makers of patent medicines because local pharmacists were more than happy to make income-producing generic versions of popular nostrums.

Advertising became critical to the patent medicine industry once it was realized that it allowed contact with consumers on a national level. By the latter part of the 1800s, some of the bigger patent medicine manufacturers were spending hundreds of thousands of dollars or more a year on advertising. The makers of Scott's Emulsion, for example, were budgeting over $1 million a year for marketing by the 1890s (Inciardi 1986).

In addition to their role in launching broad-based commodity advertising, the patent medicines played a crucial part in the growth of the newspaper industry—both as a source of revenue and as promoters of newspaper circulation. The national newspaper, *USA Today*, for example, is owned by the Gannett Corporation, which began in Maine in the mid-1800s circulating the periodical *Comfort*, a vehicle for the promotion of a patent medicine called Oxien. Almanacs also began with the patent medicine industry, many of which were distributed free of charge to help promote specific cure-alls advertised within. Another set of items given away by some patent medicines were picture cards, a practice taken up as well by the tobacco industry and other product lines, leading to modern sports and other collectors cards. Gombaults's Caustic Balsam, for example, which claimed to be effective in treating rheumatism, sprains, and sore throats in humans and lameness, strained tendons, and wind puffs in horses, issued a series of cards depicting champion race horses on one side and product uses on the other. Additionally, some modern hygienic and quasi-medicinal product lines, such as shampoo, deodorant, breath purifiers, and toothpaste, began as patent medicines. Assorted other products, including soft drinks and bitters (used as a flavoring in cocktails), began as popular remedies as well.

The Exotic Contents of Patent Medicines

Patent medicine advertising often celebrated the fact that the remedies contained exotic, rare, or secret ingredients. One type of nostrum, the liniments, for example, claimed to include an extract derived from snakes—snake oil—that had powerful healing properties. Typical was Clark Stanley's Snake Oil Liniment which gained widespread popularity after its inventor drew large, spellbound crowds to his booth at the 1893 World's Columbian Exposition held in Chicago. Outfitted in stylized cowboy attire, Stanley claimed that he slaughtered hundreds of rattlesnakes and extracted their essential oils for his magic potion. Advertisements for the oil claimed that it was "a wonderful pain destroying compound" and "the strongest and best liniment known for the cure of all pain and lameness" (quoted in Fowler 1997:10–12). Specific diseases and health problems cured by the use of Stanley's remedy included "rheumatism, neuralgia, sciatica, lame back, lumbago, contracted muscles, toothache, sprains, swellings . . ." as well as "frost bites, chill blains, bruises, sore throat, [and] bites of animals, insects and reptiles" (quoted in Fowler 1997:10–12). Like other patent medicines, Stanley maintained that his product was of Indian origin and that he had learned about it from a Moki Pueblo medicine man.

In 1917, following the passage of Pure Food and Drug Act (which was vehemently but unsuccessfully opposed by the patent medicine lobby), the federal government seized a shipment of Stanley's cure-all, tested its contents, and found that it was composed primarily of mineral oil, as well as beef fat, red pepper, and possibly contained traces of turpentine and camphor (perhaps to provide a medicinal aroma) (Fowler 1997). In the aftermath of this exposure, the terms "snake oil" and "snake oil salesman" came to mean quack medicine and charlatan, respectively, and Stanley's Oil lost its market.

One of the products still available in pharmacies today—although the family-owned business was sold to Cooper Laboratories in 1968—that can trace its origin to the era of patent medicines is Lydia E. Pinkham's Vegetable Compound, a medicinal that was specifically marketed to women. Developed in the late 19th century by Lydia Estes Pinkham after her husband went bankrupt, it was advertised on the backs of newspapers and in women's magazines as a proven cure for "all those painful Complaints and Weaknesses so common to our best female population" (Finley 2005), a euphemistic and class-conscious reference to menstruation. Because her picture appeared on the compound's label, Pinkham became one of the most widely recognized American women of her era.

Using an approach still prominent in pharmaceutical advertising today—the selling of disease to consumers—ads for this commodity "played on the theme of the [inherent] pain and suffering of being a woman and featured glowing testimonials from women who claimed to have been healed from all manner of dysfunction and disease by the compound" (Eskind Biomedical Library 2006). Moreover, advertisements for the compound emphasized women's responsibility for their own suffering, another marketing idea that has not been lost in contemporary direct-to-consumer pharmaceutical promotion. As one compound ad read: "Any woman . . . is responsible for her own suffering who will not take the trouble to write to Mrs. Pinkham for advice" (quoted in Eskind Biomedical Library 2006). This particular approach backfired when a social reform women's magazine, *Ladies Home Journal*, reported that Lydia Pinkham had been dead for over two decades when the ad was run (a point the magazine made by publishing a picture of Pinkham's grave). The fact that Lydia Pinkham had died in 1883 did not deter the company from continuing to play on her name and image. In response to the controversy these ads provoked, the company quickly announced that it was actually Pinkham's daughter, Jennie who answered all consumer letters.

This deceit also was exposed when another magazine, *Collier's Weekly*, published an article about the bank of typists (taught to promote the use of the compound in their responses) who actually answered the many letters sent by women to the company.

Although Pinkham was active in the temperance movement, and used several temperance leaders to promote her product, the Vegetable Compound was composed of almost 20 percent alcohol. The highest sales volume for the product, in fact, was during the era of Prohibition, suggesting that consumers were well aware of its most active ingredient. Other ingredients of the compound, some of which are still used in herbal medicines, included unicorn root (*Aletris farinos*), life root (*Senecio aureus*), black cohosh (*Cimicifuga racemosa*), pleurisy root (*Asclepias tuberosa*) and fenugreek seed (*Trigonella foenum-graecum*), although the contents have changed periodically over time.

Many other patent medicines had high alcohol content as well. Dr. Hostetter's Stomach Bitters and Hostetter's Bitters, for example, both had potent amounts of alcohol, the latter being over 40 percent alcohol, which is greater than the alcohol content of high-powered 80 proof whiskey. One remedy, Old Dr. Kaufmann's Great Sulphur Bitters, which contained a significant amount of alcohol, not only hid this fact but in its ads even advised consumers to "Never Use Cheap Rum Drinks Which Are Called Medicine" (quoted in Holbrook 1959:159).

Another common ingredient of patent medicines was opium or one of its derivatives (e.g., heroin), which at the time was seen even among physicians of the day as nature's cure for an array of health problems, including body pain, cough, nervousness, TB, diarrhea, dysentery, cholera, athlete's foot, baldness, and cancer. Some remedies containing opioid drugs were marketed as "women's friends," substances said to be effective in pacifying overly agitated and nervous women who were thought by many physicians to be emotionally unstable because of the unsettling effects of having a hormone-producing uterus. Other nostrums that were rich in opioids were advertised as soothing syrups for cranky babies suffering from colic. One patent medicine, Kopp's Baby Friend, a mixture of sweetened water and morphine, was promoted as the perfect way to calm restless babies. Given its contents it undoubtedly had this effect. A morphine-based remedy, Mrs. Winslow's Soothing Syrup, which also claimed to be effective in calming irritable, teething babies, included in its advertisements a customer testimonial that praised the syrup's powerful effects on cranky children: "makes 'em lay like the dead til mornin'" (quoted in Eskind Biomedical Library 2006). For some children, overdosing with opiate-laced patent medicines, however, insured that morning never came.

A study done in Boston in 1888 of the contents of prescriptions purchased from several pharmacies (most of which sold patent medicines) found that of the 10,200 prescriptions filled that year, 15 percent contained opiates and that opiate-based patent medicines had the highest sales (Eaton 1888). As a result, people of all walks of life became addicted to these drugs. Benjamin Franklin, for example, was a user and "was almost certainly addicted to opium in his declining years," as were other colonial leaders (Booth 1996:30).

Another common substance found in patent medicines was cocaine. Initially, cocaine was added to wine to give it extra potency. This practice began toward the end of the 19th century when Corsican wine maker, Angelo Mariani, imported coca leaves from Peru to add to a new wine he developed called Vin Coca Mariani. An instant success, the wine was publicized as being capable of lifting the spirits and eliminating fatigue. The beverage soon came to the attention of John Styth Pemberton of Atlanta, Georgia, a pharmacist who worked in the patent medicine industry. In 1885, Pemberton launched a medicinal drink that he registered under the title French Wine Coca. He claimed that his new product was an effective nerve stimulant that could combat fatigue and headache (precisely the reasons coca leaves have been chewed in South America for centuries). A year later, Pemberton added several additional ingredients and began to market his product as a nonmedicinal refreshment or soft drink under the name Coca-Cola. Before long, over 40 soft drinks were spiked with cocaine. By the 1890s, the patent medicine industry began marketing cocaine as a reliable cure for everything from alcoholism to venereal disease, even as a therapy for addiction to the opiate-based patent medicines. Only as it became clear that cocaine was going to be made illegal during the early years of the 20th century was it removed as a component of Coca-Cola and replaced with another stimulant, caffeine. A decocainized extract of the coca leaf is still used to flavor Coca-Cola. The success of the soft drink, however, insured that "Coca" would remain in the product's widely recognized name.

The Great American Fraud

Although patent medicines were widely used, the public did not have certainty about what they were consuming, although the notion of consumer rights has its roots in the eventual exposure of the patent medicine industry. The "Great American Fraud" is the aptly chosen title of a widely read series of magazine articles on patent medicines penned by muckraking writer Samuel Hopkins Adams (1905) for *Collier's Weekly*. He began the series by declaring:

> Gullible America will spend this year some seventy-five millions of dollars in the purchase of patent medicines. In consideration of this sum it will swallow huge quantities of alcohol, an appalling amount of opiates and narcotics, a wide assortment of varied drugs ranging from powerful and dangerous heart depressants to insidious liver stimulants; and, in excess of all other ingredients, undiluted fraud. For fraud, exploited by the skillfulness of advertising bunko men, is the basis of the trade.

Adams' writings, filled with witty sarcasm and pointed accusation, were intended to stir what he felt was a naive citizenry. He succeeded in this and helped to spark popular demand for protection from the patent medicine industry and to push Congress into passing the Pure Food and Drug Act in 1906 (Pines 2006), a law that specified that a drug's label could not be false or misleading, and further required that the presence and amount of 11 substances, including alcohol, heroin, and cocaine, had to be included on the product's label. In 1911, however, the Supreme Court, in a notably antipublic/pro-industry ruling, determined that the Pure Food and Drug Act's prohibition of falsifications applied to only the ingredients in proprietary medicines not to claims about efficacy in curing disease. In other words, the Supreme Court decided that the blatant falsehoods about curative powers that appeared regularly in patent drug promotions were perfectly legal. Adams (1905), having already concluded that "None of these 'cures' really does cure any serious affection" and that if users recover it is only because they were suffering from self-limiting disease and would have recovered anyway, was astonished by the decision of the high court. He launched a second series for *Collier's Weekly* on the deceptive claims of the patent medicine companies. Despite the intervention of the Supreme Court, the Pure Food and Drug Act severely hampered the often reckless patent medicine industry, forcing many companies that had been dishonest about the contents of their products out of business.

In 1912, the Pure Food and Drug Act was amended to cover the efficacy issue, but it was not fully enforced because now the government had to prove in court that when manufacturers made fanciful claims about the alleged curative powers of their products they intended to defraud consumers. As a result, the government lost several court cases even though there was little doubt that manufacturer statements about their products were not credible. The patent medicine industry had learned an important lesson that was not lost on corporations in many other domains of production: having legal status allows a company to use profits gained in defrauding the public to shield itself from government attempts to protect the public from harm.

To make its case about the dangers of many patent medicines, the Food and Drug Administration put together a display of killer medicinal commodities that it did not believe should be allowed to be on the market. The exhibit included

> Banbar, a worthless "cure" for diabetes that the old law protected; Lash-Lure, an eyelash dye that blinded many women; . . . Radithor, a radium-containing tonic that sentenced users to a slow and painful death; and the Wilhide Exhaler, which falsely promised to cure tuberculosis and other pulmonary diseases. A reporter dubbed this exhibit "The American Chamber of Horrors," a title not far from the truth since all the products exhibited were legal under the existing law. (Kurian 1998)

Despite this initiative, for the most part there was limited federal effort to do much about the public sale of dangerous medical products, until, as is so often the case historically, disaster struck and the public was mobilized to prod the government into action against the dangerous practices of legal corporations.

The Antifreeze Drink

In 1937, a Tennessee pharmaceutical company began marketing a sulfa drug for children under the name Elixir Sulfanilamide. As it turned out, a solvent used in the product, diethylene glycol, was a highly toxic chemical analogue of antifreeze. Over 100 customers were killed, many of them children. A graduate pharmacology student at the University of Chicago who worked on the team that discovered the noxious ingredient in the Elixir was a Canadian woman named Frances Oldham Kelsey. She would later gain national fame in the case of another toxic pharmaceutical (see below). The public was outraged by the findings on the contents of Elixir Sulfanilamide and demanded government action, leading to passage of the Food, Drug, and Cosmetic Act of 1938.

The new law, first of all, required that drugs be labeled with clear directions for safe use. Second, it obliged companies to obtain pre-approval of all new drugs before they could be marketed, a significant shift in the government's sense of its rightful powers to protect the public. Third, false therapeutic claims for drugs were banned. Finally, the new law formally authorized factory inspections and conferred other new powers on the Food and Drug Administration. As this list suggests, ways to protect the public from killer commodities were at hand but were not codified into law until there was pressure from an agitated populace outraged to discover, belatedly, that its welfare was not being well guarded by the government, a lesson that has had to be learned again and again by consumers over time.

Soon after the new law was passed, the Food and Drug Administration (FDA) began identifying a list of drugs, such as the sulfas, that it determined would require a prescription from a physician before they could be sold, a move that was unsuccessfully opposed by the emergent pharmaceutical industry. Elixir Sulfanilamide notwithstanding, the sulfa drugs, referred to earlier as the second wave of "power drugs," had been found to be quite efficacious in the treatment of infection.

The sulfa drugs entered into pharmaceutical production by way of the dye industry, when, in 1932, a German chemist and pathologist, Gerhard Domagk, discovered that a red dye called Prontosil was effective in countering a range of bacteria. Through careful chemical analysis he was able to show that it was the sulfanilamide section of the Prontosil molecule that was responsible for the dye's antibacterial properties. Eventually, it was learned that the reason sulfanilamide controlled infection was because it interfered with the metabolic functioning of bacteria (namely, the synthesis of needed folic acid), an important lesson for future pharmaceutical development.

During this period and for another decade, two particular classes of second-wave pharmaceutical drugs, those that were readily diverted for illicit street use, the amphetamines and barbiturates, "required more regulatory effort by FDA than all other drug problems combined" (Kurian 1998). Ultimately, with the passage of the Drug Abuse Control Amendments in 1965, and subsequent legislation in 1968, a new illicit drug control agency, which ultimately was given the name Drug Enforcement Administration (DEA), was created. The DEA would come to be well-known internationally through its lead role in the War on Drugs.

A New Crisis

The next event to significantly shake up the emergent pharmaceutical industry was the disaster caused by the drug Thalidomide, a sedative and antiemetic medicine that lessened the effects of morning sickness among pregnant women. Produced by the pharmaceutical company Grünenthal between 1957 and 1961, it was sold primarily in Germany and Britain, as well as in almost 50 other countries under an array of names. Before the drug could be approved for use in the United States, however, it was found to cause severe birth defects. Ultimately, 12,000 babies in 46 countries were born with birth defects caused by Thalidomide, of which only 8,000 survived until their first birthday.

Notably, Thalidomide had successfully passed safety tests on animals before being administered to humans. Grünenthal (and later several other manufacturers) promoted Thalidomide as a nontoxic medicine that had no side effects and was "completely safe for pregnant women" (Burkholz 1997). As the number of affected children began to mount, however, it came to light that given the intended users—pregnant woman—the proper tests, namely those involving pregnant animals, were never done. During a lawsuit that followed in the wake of mounting birth defects, it was discovered that some of the tests that were performed by the manufacturer were either poorly designed or that the findings that were reported were fraudulent. Later animal tests by Blake and coworkers (1982), which showed that Thalidomide in fact produced birth defects in some animal species, affirmed that had appropriate and ethical tests been performed on the drug it would never have won approval for use by pregnant women in Germany or Britain. According to Widukind Lenz (1992), the German physician who, along with Australian gynecologist, William McBride, first reported a suspected link between Thalidomide and birth defects:

> Grünenthal continued to deny the *teratogenic* effects of thalidomide for years, but there was a growing suspicion that this was not due to honest ignorance but to the purpose of weakening the accusations against the firm. In some

countries, e.g. Belgium, Brazil, Canada, Italy and Japan, thalidomide continued to be sold for several months (after withdrawal of the drug from West German and British markets).

In Germany, a criminal lawsuit was filed against seven Grünenthal executives in 1968. They were charged with marketing a drug that caused bodily harm without proper testing, failing to respond in a timely fashion to reports of significant side effects caused by the drug, and attempting to suppress damaging information about their product. The suit was dropped when Grünenthal agreed to pay compensation to the victims of Thalidomide, and no one was sent to jail for their involvement in what some consider a case of mass murder and mayhem. Similar settlements were reached in other countries.

In the United States, the manufacturer of Thalidomide had contracted with the Richardson-Merrell pharmaceutical company of Cincinnati to apply for Food and Drug Administration approval of the drug. It was assumed by the company that the process would be straightforward and encounter as few problems as had been the case in Germany or Britain. A brand new FDA pharmacologist, Frances Oldham Kelsey, was assigned to review the drug for approval. After studying the documentation submitted by Richarson-Merrell, however, Kelsey was not satisfied with the application. She found that the clinical reports submitted by the company "were more on the nature of testimonials rather than the results of well-designed, well-executed studies" (quoted in Bren 2001) and refused to clear the drug without fuller documentation on testing for potential side effects among unborn babies. Despite her requests, Kelsey was unable to get Richardson-Merrell to turn over the requested documents and the reason ultimately became clear. As noted, the appropriate tests had never been performed.

Instead, Richardson-Merrell began to pressure the FDA to approve the drug for sale, as it was in use already in countries around the world. Kelsey, having learned firsthand while at the University of Chicago about the potential dangers of pharmaceutical drugs being rushed to public use, firmly held her ground. Dr. Joseph Murray, Richardson-Merrell's representative, repeatedly called Kelsey and visited her in her office at the FDA. Frustrated by her unwavering stance, he went to her superiors and complained that she was difficult and nit-picking. The company was particularly anxious to have the drug on the market by Christmas because this is the high season for sedative use. But Kelsey knew from research she had performed during the Second World War that it was possible for drugs to pass the placental barrier between mother and unborn child. She wanted to make perfectly sure that this did not happen with Thalidomide. Kelsey recalled that she already "had accepted the fact [that she] was going to get bullied and pressured by industry" (quoted in Bren 2001) while working for the FDA, and was not intimidated by Richardson-Merrell.

As a result of Kelsey's resolve, untold numbers of additional children were spared damaging exposure to Thalidomide. The story of Kelsey's role in averting a Thalidomide disaster in the United States gained headlines in the *Washington Post* on July 15, 1962 (Mintz 1962), and in many newspapers thereafter. President John Kennedy, who awarded Kelsey the President's Award for Distinguished Federal Civilian Service, stated at the award ceremony, "Through high ability and steadfast confidence in her professional decision she has made an outstanding contribution to the protection of the health of the American people" (National Library of Medicine 2004). In 2000, Kelsey was inducted into the National Women's Hall of Fame in Seneca Falls, New York, and, all the while, up into her 80s, she continued to work at FDA's Center for Drug Evaluation and Research.

Although, because of Kelsey, Thalidomide was never approved for use in the United States, Richardson-Merrell distributed over two million Thalidomide tablets to over 1,000 doctors around the country on what the company called an investigational basis. As a result, the drug was given to almost 20,000 patients in the United States, including several hundred pregnant women, resulting in 17 U.S. children being born with Thalidomide-related deformities. In 1998, the FDA approved Thalidomide for the first time under the brand name Thalomid as a treatment for erythema nodosum leprosum, a debilitating complication of Hansen's disease (leprosy). More recently, interest in the drug has developed among cancer and AIDS researchers.

By the time of the Thalidomide crisis, as reflected in the number of countries in which the drug inflicted untold suffering, the pharmaceutical industry had fully achieved a central place in the world of global drug capitalism. Rather than marking a new era of cautious government regulation of the Big Pharma, Thalidomide signaled the emergence of a powerful industry capable of sustaining seemingly devastating exposure without suffering much real damage.

Strategies of the Modern Pharmaceutical Industry

The modern pharmaceutical industry emerged from the ashes of the patent medicine and defined its place in society through an interrelated set of strategies, including: (1) making successful claims of efficacy; (2) influencing strategic elites; (3) courting biomedicine; (4) suppressing contrary findings; (5) silencing critics; (6) buying science; and (7) intimidating the FDA; each of which will be assessed in turn below.

Claims of Efficacy

By the mid-1800s, as noted, pharmaceutical companies began discovering a number of potent alkaloids, including morphine, strychnine, quinine, nicotine, and cocaine that could be put to use in the production of medicinal commodities. These formed the first wave of efficacious "power drugs" that could be shown to have real impact on users. Morphine, for example, was extensively employed during the American Civil War to control pain resulting from wounds and injuries as well as during amputations. For 19th-century surgeons working the battlefields of the bloody internecine conflict, morphine came to be seen as a wonder drug, the one real medicine at their disposal that had some benefit for their patients. Other approaches available to physicians of the era included prescribing alcohol for pneumonia, cutting a patient's wrists for bloodletting, and pouring burning alcohol on a wound. For internal injuries various substances, including turpentine, mercury, and chalk, were administered. To the degree that any of these substances had healing properties, their benefits were often outweighed by the damage they inflicted. Morphine, by contrast, proved to be an admirable painkiller and remains in the arsenal of modern biomedicine.

The sulfa drugs, as indicated, constituted the second wave of efficacious pharmaceuticals. Even with their addition to the modern armament of medications, the incipient pharmaceutical industry still had a limited number of effective commodities to market. During the middle of the 20th century, however, the whole world of the pharmaceutical companies was transformed through the discovery of a diverse group of new medicines. It was at this time—the third wave—that drugs like penicillin, streptomycin, and chloramphenicol (the first broad spectrum antibiotic) came into use (with war—in this instance, World War II—again being a significant influence on the development of the pharmaceutical industry). During the late 1940s and early 1950s, corticosteroids, tetracycline, oral contraceptives, antihistamines, tranquilizers, amphetamines, diuretics, and various other pharmaceutical products were added to the list of third-wave efficacious pharmaceuticals.

Through this stepwise process of discovery and demonstrated efficacy, but also through the conscious use of advertising and the media to aggressively promote its successes, the pharmaceutical industry was able "to transform [itself] from a commodity chemicals business (with individual pharmacists compounding the dose) to one heavily concentrated in several large firms and dependent on large investments in research and marketing" (Petryna and Kleinman 2006:2). The result was the creation of a new branch of legal drug capitalism, a domain that was to grow to leviathan dimensions. Total retail spending on prescription drugs was $155 billion in 2001, almost double what it was in 1997. Spending reached $500 billion in 2003, a year in which pharmaceutical companies achieved an industry profit rate of over 14 percent compared to about 4.5 percent in other arenas of manufacturer (Angell 2004).

Pharmaceutical companies have tended to concentrate their resources on the development of drugs with the greatest potential for profit (i.e., most potential users) while shying away from exploring medicines that will not be used by enough people to insure significant financial gain (e.g., drugs to treat chemical addiction). Most pharmaceutical company attention currently is on the development of drugs to reduce blood cholesterol and triglyceride levels, anti-ulcer drugs, and antidepressants.

In recent years, the drug industry has witnessed several megamergers that have recast and significantly narrowed the pharmaceutical world, including the unification of Glaxo Wellcome and SmithKline Beecham, Pfizer and Pharmacia, and Sanofi-Synthelabo and Aventis. Additionally, serving as venture capitalists, wealthy pharmaceutical companies increasingly are helping to promote biotechnology and a novel approach—gene splicing—to the making of new drugs. Often such efforts begin with smaller biotech companies that either sell their findings to the pharmaceutical companies or are purchased by them outright once they have a promising new drug in the development pipeline. As Rajan states, in this activity, "pharmaceutical companies almost act like the investment banks of the drug development enterprise" (2006:24).

Where this will lead in terms of the future drugging of the poor remains to be seen, but it is clear that various so-called designer drugs, like fentanyl, that are products of molecular manipulation of existing substances, are already having a painful impact on the street, including causing numerous overdose deaths among street drug users. First synthesized in Belgium during the late 1950s, fentanyl is 50–80 times more potent than morphine. Thinking that fentanyl is just a hyped-up version of heroin, street users often inject the drug at tragically high doses. According to the U.S. Department of Justice, fentanyl has been linked to hundreds of both fatal and nonfatal overdoses across the Midwest, Northeast, and mid-Atlantic since late 2005. Between November 2005 and May of 2006, for example, 64 people died of fentanyl overdoses in Chicago alone, while it accounted for almost 100 deaths during this period in the greater Detroit area (Smalley 2006).

Courting Strategic Elites

Biomedicine, today, is the dominant medical system in the world, but this was not always the case (Baer 2004). At the time of the Civil War, for example, given the limited capacity of what would become modern biomedicine, an array of alternative healing traditions competed for prominence. The success of biomedicine in overcoming its adversaries, such as homeopathy, was, in part, a result of its ability to offer strategic elites an ideological rationale for discounting the roles that political, economic, and social conditions play in the production and spread of disease. The alliance that formed between the leading figures in biomedicine and key decision-making members of the industrial upper class "ultimately permitted biomedicine to establish political, economic, and ideological dominance over rival medical systems in the United States" (Baer et al. 2003:329). The emergent pharmaceutical industry, which came to serve as a frequently crossed bridge linking biomedicine and industry, was a crucial element in forging this consequential alliance. As pharmaceutical companies gained control of an expanding medicinal arsenal and won physicians to their use in treating patients, they provided strong support for narrowly responding to disease as an individual phenomenon rooted in nature (and caused by pathogens). That diseases were not randomly distributed, that the poor suffered a far greater disease load than the wealthy, and far greater mortality (including shorter lifespans) as a result could be downplayed if disease was thought to be caused by randomly dispersed pathogens striking individual victims who, in turn, could be treated with powerful and profitable pharmaceutical medicines. On this foundation, a whole array of pharmaceutical treatments emerged that are not specifically linked to contesting pathogenesis but treat conditions like depression, ulcers, diabetes, cholesterol, and high blood pressure that even more overtly reflect social conditions and relationships.

To help underwrite its relationship with strategic elites, the pharmaceutical industry regularly has made large contributions to the major political parties; in fact, the industry consistently is one of the highest contributors to political campaigns. As M. Asif Ismail (2005) summarizes:

> The pharmaceutical and health products industry has spent more than $800 million in federal lobbying and campaign donations at the federal and state levels in the past seven years, a Center for Public Integrity investigation has found. Its lobbying operation, on which it reports spending more than $675 million, is the biggest in the nation. No other industry spent more money to sway public policy in that period. Its combined political outlays on lobbying and campaign contributions are topped only by the insurance industry. The drug [companies'] huge investments in Washington—though meager compared to the profits they make—have paid off handsomely, resulting in a series of favorable laws on Capitol Hill and tens of billions of dollars in additional profits.

In 1990, for example, according to data released by the Federal Election Commission (Center for Responsive Politics 2006), drug manufacturers donated over $2 million to members of the U.S. House and Senate. In the years leading up to Congress' passage of the Medicare Modernization Act, which set prescription drug benefit standards for Medicare in 2003—a bill that held great promise of benefiting Big Pharma—the generosity of contributions escalated. During this period, hand-outs from pharmaceutical manufacturers to House and Senate members (and presidential candidates) jumped to over $6 million dollars. The top recipient was George W. Bush, who benefited from over $500,000 (compared to just under $280,000 for his opponent). Pfizer, Inc., was the biggest contributor, dropping over $1.5 million in the campaign coffers of both Republicans and Democrats, although almost 70 percent went to Republicans. The top recipient among senators and congressmen was Senator Richard Burr (Republican, North Carolina), who sits on the U.S. Senate Committee on Health, Education, Labor and Pensions, which is charged with oversight of the Food and Drug Administration. Other members of the committee who were running for office in 2004, both Republicans and Democrats, also were beneficiaries of pharmaceutical campaign donations. In that the Medicare Modernization Act partially reversed previous cuts in reimbursements to pharmaceutical companies, the expenditures were far more than made up for in new revenue.

Lobbying is another strategy fruitfully used by the pharmaceutical industry in shaping its relationships with strategic elites. The industry employs thousands of lobbyists, many of whom are former federal officials (including, in 2004, more than 15 former senators and more than 60 former members of the U.S. House of Representatives). When the industry was focusing its efforts on passage of favorable language in the Medicare Modernization Act, Pharmaceutical Research and Manufacturers of America, the industry trade group, hired the newly formed lobbying firm of Larson Dodd, LLC, to join its efforts. This company was founded by the former health policy advisor to Senate Majority Leader Bill Frist, who was the chief sponsor of the Medicare bill, and the former legislative director to Kay Bailey Hutchison, the fourth-ranking Republican in the Senate.

In 2003, the year that the Medicare Modernization Act was being voted on, the industry spent over $115 million on lobbying the government (Ismail 2005). One of the benefits for the industry that stems from this kind of lobbying campaign is that the U.S. government contributes a significant amount of money to the development of new drugs, primarily in the form of either tax breaks or direct subsidies to the industry. Nonetheless, pharmaceutical drugs tend to cost more for consumers in the United States than in any other part of the world. This is so, in part, because while many countries regulate drug prices, the pharmaceutical industry "has been able to block a host of measures aimed at controlling prices in the United States" (Ismail 2005).

Campaign donations also are freely distributed by the pharmaceutical industry to candidates for U.S. state offices. In 2004, for example, the Big Pharma donated over $5 million to individuals running at the state level. That year, the industry spent another $22 million on lobbying efforts in a number of key states (Center for Public Integrity 2006). The top spender ($4.5 million) was the Pharmaceutical Research and Manufacturers of America.

Influencing strategic elites does not stop at the border of legality. In fact, as Australian researcher John Braithwaite argues:

> Every scholar who has surveyed the comparative evidence on bribery in international trade has concluded that pharmaceuticals is one of the most corrupt, if not the most corrupt, of industries. My own research . . . found evidence of substantial bribery by 19 of the 20 largest American pharmaceutical companies. There is evidence of bribes being paid to every type of government official who could conceivably affect the interests of pharmaceutical companies: bribes to cabinet ministers to get drugs approved for marketing, bribes to social security bureaucrats who fix prices for subsidised drugs; to health inspectors who check pharmaceutical manufacturing plants; to customs officials, hospital administrators, tax assessors, political parties, and others. (Braithwaite 1986)

While corporate crime is not a rare event across industries, drug companies commit three times as many serious to moderately serious violations of the law than companies in other industries (Braithwaite 1984). A noted example of bribery involving pharmaceutical companies came to light in 1989. The exposure of lucrative payoffs by some pharmaceutical companies to officials at the FDA to accelerate the approval of their drugs for the market began when a rival company hired private detectives who, after a year of investigation, "caught FDA agents red-handed taking bribes in exchange for expediting drug approval" (Ausubel 2000:278). Some of the evidence in the case came from regular covert examinations of FDA garbage dumpsters. Private detectives found evidence during their dumpster-diving ventures that some companies were submitting fraudulent trial data and paying off officials to use the false information to speed approval of their products.

Courting Biomedicine

In Hollywood they call it "shwag," high priced promotional items given free to celebrities so that they, as their images appear in the mass media, will be seen sporting a company's products; in effect, a one-by-one approach to product placement. The purpose is somewhat different in the world of medicine but the ultimate goal is the same. U.S. doctors write four billion prescriptions each year, choosing from an array of 15,000 available prescription drugs. They also recommend use of over-the-counter medicines, of which there are 300,000 on the market (Combined Wire Services 2006). Freebies from the pharmaceutical industry are intended to court physician awareness and increase selection of company medicines, a practice that has long been a component of medical culture. It is difficult to spend much time in a doctor's office without seeing pens, note pads, mugs, magnets, and other giveaway items stamped with the logos of various pharmaceutical companies and their products. Pharmaceutical largesse, from a medical student's first stethoscope to free vacations for more established practitioners, is a common feature of industry–doctor relationships. Industry "gifts" to doctors include paid phone cards, expensive tickets to sporting events or other entertainment,

passes to golf courses, and consulting fees for attending sales presentations in vacation settings. As Earl Mindell reports:

> The ultimate drug company "bribery" is sending an M.D. on an exotic vaca-
> tion and including CME courses along with it. The physician spends a few
> hours a day listening to lectures on how to prescribe the company's drugs
> and the rest of his time on the beach or golf course. (1999:13)

Most continuing medical education classes taken by physicians are paid
for by pharmaceutical companies, activities that many physicians see as
"verging on infomercials" for company products (Hensley 2002)
although necessary to keep their medical licenses up to date. Additionally, notes Jay Cohen (2006), a physician who has attended numerous
medical conferences, "The drug industry's presence at some medical
conferences is so pervasive, sometimes it is hard to tell whether they are
medical conferences or pharmaceutical advertising conventions." The
preliminary program of the American Psychiatric Association's June
2006 meeting in Toronto, for example, included at least 45 symposia
sponsored by the major pharmaceutical companies.

Another strategy of the pharmaceutical companies is the use of free
samples. Each day, 90,000 drug company representatives visit doctors'
offices and drop off samples as well as accompanying literature and study
findings for the drugs the companies want to promote, such as newly
launched drugs or those that have failed to catch on with physicians previously. Notes Jerome Kassirer (2006), author of *On The Take: How Medicine's Complicity with Big Business Can Endanger Your Health*:

> While lobbying groups spend about $2 billion to convince politicians to do
> their bidding, pharmaceutical companies spend nearly 10 times that much
> to influence the nation's 600,000 to 700,000 physicians to prescribe the
> newest and most expensive drugs.

Concern within the American Medical Association and other medical
societies has led to the development of voluntary guidelines to encourage
limits on the acceptance of pharmaceutical company gifts of more than
token value. There is little evidence that these guidelines have had much
effect. Many doctors continue to accept drug company promotional items
while asserting that their judgment is not influenced by exposure to promotions and sales pitches. Studies suggest otherwise. Doctors' prescribing
patterns, it has been found, are significantly affected by pharmaceutical
company incentives (Brett et al. 2003).

Suppressing Contrary Findings

One of the dilemmas faced by the pharmaceutical industry is that
sometimes even their own carefully designed and controlled studies produce undesirable findings. Unwelcome study results may indicate that a
heavily invested company product is far less efficacious than was

expected or that it produces significant adverse side affects, as happened in the case of Thalidomide. While companies respond in different ways to such a turn of events, one not uncommon strategy is the "outright suppression of data" (Healy 2006).

An increasingly well-known example of blocking the public release of adverse clinical trial findings occurred in the case of Vioxx and other related COX-2 (cyclooxygenase) nonsteroidal anti-inflammatory drugs (e.g., Celebrex and Bextra). At the beginning of 2004, Vioxx reigned as an exceedingly profitable painkiller (e.g., while similar chemically to aspirin, the drug was sold for 100 times the price of aspirin) that was especially coveted by arthritis sufferers because it deadens pain but, unlike other nonaddictive painkillers, does not cause gastrointestinal problems including bleeding. In a dramatic reversal, Vioxx ended the year as disgraced killer commodity permanently removed from the drug market (Singer and Baer in press). During the period that it was being sold as a prescription drug, it is estimated that Vioxx may have contributed to 25,000 heart attacks and strokes (Bazerman and Chugh 2006). Even more disturbing was the testimony of David Graham, associate director for science in the Office of Drug Safety at the FDA, before a Senate Finance Committee hearing. Graham revealed that according to his calculations between 88,000 to 138,000 people may have died because of Vioxx, putting the drug at the top of the list of known deadly pharmaceuticals to be released to the public.

Significantly, the first evidence of the drug's dangerous features began to appear years before it was withdrawn from the market and possibly even before it was brought to the market by its manufacturer, Merck & Co. As a result of the various laws passed during the 20th century, a new pharmaceutical drug must go through a multistep process of testing, ending with human trials, first for safety and then for efficacy in addressing its target health problem(s). Vioxx successfully passed through this clinical trial process. Outcomes of this research showed that Vioxx was free of the adverse stomach effects of conventional nonsteroidal anti-inflammatory drugs (such as aspirin) and achieved the same painkilling and anti-inflammatory effects of the conventional compounds. As is the standard, findings from this research were published in respected medical journals and, as a result, Vioxx received FDA approval for use in the treatment of pain. To insure that sales lived up to expectations, the makers of Vioxx invested millions of dollars in advertising targeted to doctors as well as to potential consumers. Recognizing the benefits of Vioxx for patients suffering from chronic pain, doctors began churning out prescriptions for the drug, 100 million of them in the Untied States alone while the drug was on the market.

Less clear to doctors, and certainly unknown to most patients, was the fact that at the time that Merck was preparing Vioxx for clinical trial testing, the company was facing the loss of highly profitable patent protections on several of its major earners and, to keep stockholders smiling, was in critical need of a new star on its list of marketable drug products. As a result, Merck was committed to insuring that Vioxx was a success. Troubling the atmosphere of hope and excitement about Vioxx within the company were several early warning signs that there might be major problems with the drug. The public—and those who had been taking and prescribing the drug, as well as FDA officials—learned of these early problems when, on November 1, 2004, two months after Vioxx had to be taken off of the market, the front page of the eastern edition of *The Wall Street Journal* featured an article by Anna Wilde Mathews and Barbara Martinez:

> When Merck & Co. pulled its big-selling painkiller Vioxx off the market in September, Chief Executive Raymond Gilmartin said the company was "really putting patient safety first." He said the study findings prompting the withdrawal, which tied Vioxx to heart-attack and stroke risk, were "unexpected." But internal Merck e-mails and marketing materials as well as interviews with outside scientists show that the company fought forcefully for years to keep safety concerns from destroying the drug's commercial prospects. (Mathews and Martinez 2004:A1)

As it ultimately became clear, Merck first recognized there were significant problems with Vioxx as early as the mid- to late-1990s. When clinical trials were being organized, Merck officials and scientists began discussing how to shape the trials so that they would minimize the higher level of heart problems that they feared would develop among subjects given Vioxx compared to people on conventional pain medications. According to Mathews and Martinez:

> A Nov. 21, 1996, memo by a Merck official shows the company wrestling with this issue. It wanted to conduct a trial to prove Vioxx was gentler on the stomach than older painkillers. But to show the difference most clearly, the Vioxx patients couldn't take any aspirin. In such a trial, "there is a substantial chance that significantly higher rates" of cardiovascular problems would be seen in the Vioxx group, the memo said. . . . A similar view was expressed in a Feb. 25, 1997, e-mail by a Merck official, Briggs Morrison. He argued that unless patients in the Vioxx group also got aspirin, "you will get more thrombotic events"—that is, blood clots—"and kill [the] drug." (2004:A1)

By 2000, Merck fully recognized that use of Vioxx was linked to an increased rate of heart and other cardiovascular problems:

> On March 9, 2000, the company's powerful research chief, Edward Scolnick, e-mailed colleagues that the cardiovascular events "are clearly there" and called it a "shame." He compared Vioxx to other drugs with known side effects and wrote, "there is always a hazard." But the company's public statements after Dr. Scolnick's e-mail continued to reject the link between Vioxx and increased intrinsic risk. (Mathews and Martinez 2004:A1)

As these revelations came to light, the editors of the *New England Journal of Medicine*, which had published the positive clinical trial findings on Vioxx, realized they had been duped. They published a hard-hitting editorial in the journal indicating that the authors of the Vioxx paper had intentionally concealed information about the heart attacks among patients on the drug.

For four and a half years, as the drug was being prescribed to millions of people, Merck struggled to find evidence to prove the safety of Vioxx and to insure its continued availability and, from the standpoint of profit making, productivity. All the while, company employees who promoted Vioxx were trained to skillfully dodge direct questions, including those from physicians, about risks associated with the drug. A training brochure developed by Merck, for example, informed its promotional staff:

> If a doctor said he was worried that Vioxx might raise the risk of a heart attack, he was to be told that the drug "would not be expected to demonstrate reductions" in heart attacks or other cardiovascular problems and that it was "not a substitute for aspirin." This wasn't a direct answer. (Mathews and Martinez 2004:A1)

Rather, it was a way to get doctors to prescribe both Vioxx and aspirin, which would mask the harmful side effects of Merck's product.

In the pointed assessment of Georges Halpern (2005), as expressed in his paper in the medical journal *Inflammopharmacology*, the Vioxx story is one of greed, deception, and death. Merck knew it could bring a dangerous drug to market because it "faced a possibly complicit, toothless and bloodless FDA, and used every maneuvering to fleece the patients. We must now reflect on attitudes that we thought only belong to the tobacco industry" (Halpern 2005:419). Notably, in September of 2006, Merck released a 1,700-page report on a 20–month investigation of the Vioxx case. The $21 million report, funded by the company, found that "senior management acted responsibly in its development and marketing of . . . Vioxx" (Agovino 2006). Specifically, the report concluded that Merck "management acted with integrity and had legitimate reasons for making the decisions that it made, in light of the knowledge available at the time" (quoted in Agovino 2006). Mark Lanier, an attorney representing some Vioxx customers who are suing Merck, called the report "an absurd, expensive . . . public relations stunt" and questioned whether anyone would consider "a jury independent if I paid them $21 million" (quoted in Agovino 2006). Merck admitted that none of who served on the investigative panel were asked about conflicts of interest with the company.

Importantly, the Vioxx case is not a unique event. As Harris Coulter (1991:18) stresses, "Frightful examples of dishonesty, fraud, negligence, and other kinds of wrongdoing in clinical trials have been staple fare for readers of the daily press since the 1970s, when Congressional committees and subcommittees renewed their interest in the topic." In the shadow of the Vioxx scandal, for example, it came to light that contrary to what had been reported in scientific journals about the success of treating children with antidepressant drugs: "In clinical trials with children antidepressants had not been shown to work, that there was a doubling of the risk of suicidal activity" among children given antidepressants compared to those who were given a placebo (Healy 2006:76; Law 2006). Moreover, company documents showed that GlaxoSmithKline, which sponsored the clinical trials, had plans to publish only positive results. When these documents were discovered, the manufacturer was sued for fraud by the New York State attorney general. Rather than face an embarrassing trial, the company settled with New York out of court.

Silencing Critics

As Healy (2006:67) aptly observes, "In addition to accentuating the positive, pharmaceutical companies have always been prepared to minimize the negative." One approach to achieve this end has been to tighten the purse strings on newspapers (which make a lot of money on advertising by pharmaceutical companies), medical and scientific conferences (which often are funded by Big Pharma), taking critics to court (knowing that the company has far deeper pockets to support lawyers over a protracted court case than do most researchers), and making veiled or even outright threats. In the case of Merck and its failed wonder drug Vioxx, when researchers began to sense something was amiss with the drug and to ask increasingly pointed questions about its safety, the company went on the attack. A number of scientists complained to the *Wall Street Journal* about actions taken by company officials that appeared to be intended to get them to stop questioning Vioxx. One researcher, Gurkirpal Singh of Stanford University, reported that he was threatened by Merck and told that if he continued to give lectures that criticized the company he would "flame out" (implying that his career would be ruined). Dr. James Fries, who wrote to Merck to complain about its efforts to silence Singh, told the *Wall Street Journal* that there had been "a consistent pattern of intimidation of investigators by Merck" (Mathews and Martinez 2004:A1).

Another researcher who complained about company pressure was Joan-Ramon Laporte of the Catalan Institute of Pharmacology in Barcelona, Spain. During the summer of 2002, Laporte, a well respected scientist, edited a document published by his institution that included several criticisms of Merck's handling of Vioxx that previously had been published in the British medical journal *Lancet*. Not long after, Laporte received a correction statement from Merck that they wanted him to publish. He told the company that he did not see a problem with the original publication and did not intend to publish the correction. As a result, Merck filed suit in a Spanish court against Laporte and his employer demanding a public correction of inaccuracies in the institute's publication. In January 2004, the court ruled in favor of Laporte, saying that the institute's publication accurately reflected debate within the medical community about Vioxx and ordered Merck to pay court costs.

Company efforts did not stop there, however. In March of 2004, Laporte was slated to be a keynote speaker at an annual pharmaceutical conference for Spanish family practitioners and other physicians. In previous years, as is common in the medical world, Merck had helped pay for the gathering. Prior to the 2004 conference, however, a Merck representative informed the conference organizer that the company wanted Laporte dropped from the program. When this idea was rejected as undue interference, Merck withdrew the approximately $140,000 it had committed to the conference. Later, a corporate lawyer for Merck would assert that the company supports "open and vigorous scientific debate" and "never has had a policy of retaliating against scientists" but Merck also "has a right to defend its medicines against false claims" (Mathews and Martinez 2004:A1). In pulling Vioxx from the market, of course, the company, in effect, admitted Laporte and other critics were right: Vioxx was an extremely dangerous compound.

Buying Science

"Just how tainted has medicine become?" This question was asked in an editorial published in *Lancet* in 2002. The editorial gave as one example a study of the relations between authors of clinical practice guidelines (used by doctors in setting treatment plans for patients) and the pharmaceutical industry. The study found that almost 90 percent of authors working on the guidelines received research funding from or served as consultants to a pharmaceutical company. Further, over half had connections with the very companies whose drugs were discussed in the guideline they were developing.

Similarly, an investigation of connections to the pharmaceutical industry among the 170 panel members who contributed to the selection of diagnostic criteria included in the *Diagnostic and Statistical Manual of Mental Disorders* (DSM), the standard text of psychiatric diagnoses, found that 56 percent had one or more financial ties to pharmaceutical companies (Cosgrove et al. 2006). Moreover, Cosgrove and colleagues found that all of the members who served on the panels that developed the sections of the DSM entitled "Mood Disorders" and "Schizophrenia and Other Psychotic Disorders" had financial links to the pharmaceutical industry. The types of financial connections to pharmaceutical companies found among panel members included research funding (42 percent of panelists), consultancies (22 percent), and serving on an industry speakers' bureau (16 percent). These researchers concluded that while connections to the industry were significant across panels, they were especially strong in those diagnostic areas where pharmaceuticals are the first line of treatment.

These examples suggest one of the many ways in which the pharmaceutical companies buy science. Another strategy reflecting an even more sinister Faustian bargain involves the ghostwriting of scientific articles on the findings of drug research. As Ana Mathews points out:

Many of the articles that appear in scientific journals under the bylines of prominent academics are actually written by ghostwriters in the pay of drug companies. These seemingly objective articles, which doctors around the world use to guide their care of patients, are often part of a marketing campaign by companies to promote a product or play up the condition it treats. . . . The practice of letting ghostwriters hired by communications firms draft journal articles—sometimes with acknowledgment, often without—has served many parties well. Academic scientists can more easily pile up high-profile publications, the main currency of advancement. Journal editors get clearly written articles that look authoritative because of their well-credentialed authors. (2005:1)

David Healy (2006), based on a review of articles prepared by Current Medical Directions, a ghostwriting firm, found that the company was involved in preparing journal research articles, review articles, abstracts, journal supplements, product monographs, expert commentaries, and textbook chapters. Remarkably, he concluded that up to 75 percent of the articles that appear in major medical journals on randomized clinical trials conducted on pharmaceutical products may be ghostwritten. While some might consider this figure to be on the high side, Mathews (2005) reports on a poll of 71 freelance medical writers that was conducted by the American Medical Writers Association. The poll found that 80 percent said they had written at least one article that omitted mention of their contributions. Additionally, Healy found that the most cited articles on pharmaceuticals are ghostwritten, perhaps because, being prepared by professional writers rather than pharmaceutical researchers, they are easier to understand. Finally, he concludes, a pattern found in ghostwritten articles is the omission of negative findings on side effects. Ghostwriting, in short, is another way that pharmaceuticals suppress undesirable findings, win FDA approval, and make the world safe for profits.

Intimidating the FDA

To assess the state of science at the FDA, the Union of Concerned Scientists (2006) and Public Employees for Environmental Responsibility distributed a survey to almost 6,000 FDA scientists, of which almost 1,000 responded. The results of this study suggest that the FDA is a nervous and troubled agency. Hundreds of scientists reported that scientific work at the FDA was subject to significant levels of interference, jeopardizing the agency's ability to protect public health and safety. Science, some respondents said, no longer plays a very important role in the FDA's regulatory decisions. Key findings of the survey included:

- Almost 20 percent agreed with the statement: "I have been asked, for non-scientific reasons, to inappropriately exclude or alter technical information or my conclusions in an FDA scientific document."

- Over 60 percent of respondents reported that they know of cases in which "Department of Health and Human Services or FDA political appointees have inappropriately injected themselves into FDA determinations or actions."
- Less than half agreed with the statement "The FDA routinely provides complete and accurate information to the public."
- Forty percent indicated that they could not publicly express "concerns about public health without fear of retaliation."

When he was called before a U.S. Senate committee to testify about Vioxx, FDA whistle-blower David Graham (2004) stated:

> The public expects national drug regulators to complete research . . . in their ongoing efforts to protect patients from undue harm. But, too often, the FDA saw and continues to see the pharmaceutical industry as its customer—a vital source of funding for its activities—and not as a sector of society in need of strong regulation.

As part of his job at the FDA, Graham completed an epidemiological study with Kaiser Permanente in California to assess the heart attack risk of high-dosage Vioxx. This study, like others, found that Vioxx significantly increased the risk of heart attack, but when Graham (2004) presented his findings to the FDA's Office of New Drugs, it triggered "an explosive response." Graham testified that he was pressured to change his conclusions about Vioxx and his recommendations about banning the drug. Unless findings were changed, Graham was told, he could not present his findings, as planned, at the International Conference on Pharmacoepidemiology. Graham (2004) further testified:

> My experience with Vioxx is typical of how [the FDA] responds to serious drug safety issues in general. . . . Vioxx is a terrible tragedy and a profound regulatory failure. I would argue that the FDA, as currently configured, is incapable of protecting America against another Vioxx. We are virtually defenseless. It is important that this Committee and the American people understand that what has happened with Vioxx is really a symptom of something far more dangerous to the safety of the American people. Simply put, the FDA and its Center for Drug Evaluation and Research are broken.

Subsequent investigation found that almost one-third of the individuals who serve on advisory boards set up by the FDA to provide objective recommendations concerning FDA approval for drugs and other medical products have direct financial connections to companies whose products need FDA approval but that these individuals rarely excuse themselves for conflict of interest (Alonso-Zaldivar 2006:A12).

Overproduction of Pharmaceuticals

According to the Drug Enforcement Administration (Rannazzisi 2006), the percentage of youth and young adults abusing prescription drugs is second only to marijuana and ahead of cocaine, heroin, methamphetamine, and other illicit drugs. Diversion of some drugs, as Lovell points out, "is certainly a nonnegligible source of revenue for the pharmaceutical maker" (2006:160). As early as the 1970s, in an article in the journal *Transaction*, James Graham (1972) pointed out the striking production levels for amphetamines by American pharmaceutical companies and the politics underlying this arrangement:

> The American pharmaceutical industry annually manufactures enough amphetamines to provide a month's supply to every man, woman and child in the country. Eight, perhaps ten, billion pills are lawfully produced, packaged, retailed, and consumed each year. . . . Th[e] industry has skillfully managed to convert a chemical, with meager medical justification and considerable potential for harm, into multi-hundred-million-dollar profits in less than 40 years. High profits, reaped from such vulnerable products, require extensive, sustained political efforts for their continued existence. The lawmakers who have declared that possession of marijuana is a serious crime have simultaneously defended and protected the profits of the amphetamine pill-makers.

Amphetamine was first synthesized in Germany in 1887, but its potential as a profitable medicinal stimulant was not realized until the late 1920s. By the early 1930s, the pharmaceutical company Smith, Kline and French began marketing the over-the-counter Benzedrine inhaler, which provided a spray of Amphetamine Sulphate to relieve the symptoms of nasal congestion, asthma, hay fever, and the common cold. Before long, a number of up-and-coming jazz musicians discovered that inside the inhaler was a strip of paper soaked in the drug that could be sucked on to produce a "rush" which they felt enhanced their musical performance. By the 1950s, diversion of amphetamines for nonmedical use began to spread beyond small circles in the music world to college campuses and within a decade amphetamine had become "one of the half-dozen most popular street drugs" (Goode 1984:176), especially on the West Coast.

The growing street use of amphetamines, the vast majority of which came from legal pharmaceutical manufacture (although a small underground industry had begun to emerge as well), led to congressional efforts to control production by the mid-1960s. Senator Dodd of Connecticut later stated during congressional hearings that pharmaceutical corporations used their considerable financial capacity and political connections to "vigorously oppose . . . passage of (the 1965) act. I know very well because I lived with it, and they gave me fits and they gave all of us fits in trying to get it through" (quoted in Graham 1972). Asserting that the appearance of an underground nonmedical market for legally produced pharmaceutical drugs was not an "accidental development," Dodd went on to implicate the pharmaceutical industry:

> Multi-hundred-million-dollar advertising budgets, frequently the most costly ingredient in the price of a pill, have, pill by pill, led, coaxed, and seduced post-World War II generations into the "freaked-out" drug culture. Detail men employed by drug companies propagandized, harried and harassed doctors into pushing their special brand of palliative. Free samples in the doctor's office are as common nowadays as inflated fees. (quoted in Graham 1972)

Overprescription of drugs by physicians—which provides a key source for illicit diversion—has been traced to advertising efforts of the pharmaceuticals. Increasingly, the advertising campaigns of the pharmaceutical industry are targeted via the mass media directly to consumers, creating a demand for pharmaceutical psychotropics and other drugs.

There is another aspect of overproduction and diversion of pharmaceutical drugs, namely, that potential misuse is not calculated into the assessment of the negative effects of drugs during the early stages of pharmaceutical clinical trials. While negative effects on clinical trial subjects are closely scrutinized, the potential of a drug to be diverted into illicit use, and as a result cause considerable harm, is not examined in determining a drug's safety for human use.

These concerns about overproduction notwithstanding, in 1970 Congress passed the Comprehensive Drug Abuse Prevention and Control Act, which focused most attention on illicit production of pharmaceuticals rather than on legal overproduction and diversion. This law, which was fundamental to launching the War on Drugs by the Nixon administration, was a clear victory for the pharmaceutical industry. As Graham (1972) wryly observes:

> The victory could not have been secured without the firm support of the Nixon administration. The end result is a national policy which declares an all-out war on drugs which are *not* a source of corporate income. Meanwhile, under the protection of the law, billions of amphetamines are overproduced without medical justification.

Senator Thomas Eagleton of Missouri, reflecting on the passage of the law, remarked, "When the chips were down, the power of the drug companies was simply more compelling" than the protection of public health (quoted in Graham 1972).

Although the wave of nonmedical use of amphetamines subsided—only to be replaced some years later by a much more extensive epidemic involving the related drug methamphetamine—the pattern of nonmedical diversion of powerful pharmaceuticals was well established. With reference to anabolic steroids and related pharmaceuticals that are sidetracked for nonmedical use by athletes and body builders, for example, Swedish Police Inspector Gunnar Hermansson notes:

> Some big pharmaceutical companies are responsible for a great part of the anabolic steroids and testosterone products that are found in the black market. Bearing the nowadays restricted medical use of anabolic steroids in mind, compared to the huge amounts of these products seen outside of medical control, there has to be a considerable legal overproduction in the world. The manufacturers are probably not unaware of this fact. (2002:1)

While the pharmaceutical industry produces medicines that contribute significantly to the ability of people to cope with living in a world of diseases, there is as well an enduring and unambiguous pattern within the industry of inflicting harm if it serves the cause of making a profit. As Braithwaite notes, the list of corporate crimes in the pharmaceutical industry is long: "bribery and fraud, misrepresentation in advertising, breaches of laws which ensure the sterility and purity of products and antitrust offences, . . . [are] all widespread" in Big Pharma (1986:47). It is within this context that the pharmaceutical companies aggressively produce adequate quantities of drugs to meet both legal and illegal demand. The corporate mind-set driving overproduction of pharmaceuticals, corporate fraud, or other habitual crimes of the pharmaceutical industry are revealed by the interviews that Braithwaite was able carry out with pharmaceutical industry executives. As one of them stated:

> I don't follow the corporate rules when it doesn't suit me. No one does. That is, if you're credible you can get away with it. We're credible because we perform well. If we were running at a loss, I'd be fired for breaking the rules. But because we're doing well, it's a good management decision. (1986:391)

As a result of the way pharmaceutical companies see the world, namely as an array of markets that must be penetrated and shaped to perform by any means necessary, many pharmaceutical products regularly find their way into illicit use and contribute to the drugging of the poor. As Braithwaite observes, there is a cruel irony in the fact that "people who foster dependence on illicit drugs such as heroin are regarded as among the most unscrupulous pariahs of modern civilisation. In contrast, pushers of licit drugs tend to be viewed as altruistically motivated purveyors of a social good" (1984:23).

Pharmaceutical Street Drugs

Pharmaceutical drugs have found a home on the street and are playing an increasingly important role in the drugging of the poor. The 2005 Partnership for a Drug-Free America's Partnership Attitude Tracking Study (PATS), which surveyed over 7,000 teenagers in grades 7–12, for example, found that Latino youth may be at special risk for diverted pharmaceutical drugs and abuse of over-the-counter pharmaceuticals as well. The practice of "pharming"—using a host of medicines and chemical products to get high—is becoming increasingly entrenched among Latino youth. While use of other illegal drugs among Latino youth commonly is lower than other ethnic groups, the study found that one in five Latino teenagers (21 percent) has used prescription drugs to get high while one in eight (13 percent) of the Latino youth in the study reported using cough medicine to get high. Reference to the use of prescription cough suppressant medicine that contains codeine mixed with soft drinks has been found in the lyrics of several hip-hop performers for example (Leinwand 2006). Additionally, the study found that many teenagers are not aware of the risks of misusing prescription and over-the counter-drugs. Notably, almost half of Latino teenagers reported that prescription medicines are safer than illegal drugs. Just over half reported that the reason pharmaceutical drugs are appealing is that they are not illegal, while 35 percent reported they are appealing because they have fewer side effects than other street drugs (Garay 2006).

Another indication of the diffusion of pharmaceutical drugs in low-income populations was found in the second wave of the Hispanic Health Council Drug Monitoring Study (Vivian et al. 2005). This survey was conducted with 242 outreach-recruited, out-of-treatment street drug users and included a battery of questions about the use of narcotic analgesics (NAs) including Vicodin (hydrocodone), OxyContin (oxycodone), Percocet (which also contains oxycodone), Demerol (meperidine), and Darvon (propoxyphene), synthetic opiates that are capable of providing symptom-relief from pain as well as euphoric effects. Results of the study indicate that NA use is widespread in the inner city among both men (20 percent) and women (25 percent) of varying ages. With respect to ethnic identity, it appears that whites in the inner city are somewhat more likely to abuse NAs (40 percent) than other ethnic groups (15 percent of African Americans, 17 percent of Latinos in the sample).

Results also identified some other characteristics of NA users. Of particular note is the fact that they were more likely than nonusers to also use tranquilizers (48 percent vs. 11 percent) and to associate with other people who also illicitly use prescription drugs (44 percent vs. 16 percent). These findings are notable for several reasons. First, mixing opiates and tranquilizers is particularly dangerous and puts users at high risk for overdose. Indeed, the NA users in the sample were found to be significantly more likely to report drug-related overdose (35 percent) than nonusers (21 percent). Additionally, the fact that NA users associate with others involved in the nonmedical use of prescription drugs suggests that there may be social networks of people in the inner city involved in prescription drug diversion. Moreover, an important trend in the data was an association between NA use and reported infection with hepatitis C even after controlling for injection drug use, age, ethnicity, and gender, suggesting that illicit use of NAs may play an important role in the local spread of disease.

Though motivations for use were not explored directly in the Hispanic Health Council study, some inferences might be drawn from findings on self-reported psychiatric symptomatology among NA users. NA users in the sample were significantly more likely to report problems with anxiety than individuals who did not report NA use (35 percent vs. 21 percent). The appeal of NAs for some people may be that they provide an effective means of self-medicating emotional upset.

A subsample of participants who reported using NAs in the past 30 days (n = 52) were asked additional questions about their use of these pharmaceutical drugs. While some of the participants reported using NAs for several years, the majority of participants (61 percent) were recent initiates, having used these drugs for one year or less. A sizeable percentage of this subgroup of newer users reported fairly intense or regular use of NAs following initiation (70 percent reported frequencies of use ranging from daily to several times per week). The most frequently mentioned source of NAs (58 percent) were street drug dealers, while 43 percent indicated that they have sold prescription drugs themselves.

As these findings indicate, pharmaceutical drugs are now available and are being used on the inner-city street. Increasingly, in fact, they are becoming dominant drugs on the street. According to the Drug Enforcement Administration (2006), the percentage of state and local law enforcement agencies reporting high or moderate availability of diverted pharmaceuticals increased each year from 2002 to 2005, and at a higher rate than any other category of drugs.

In sum, a range of pharmaceutical drugs are, like heroin and cocaine, but also like alcohol and tobacco, readily available for purchase on the street to address the needs of the poor. In this, pharmaceutical drugs are playing an ever-greater role in the drugging of the poor.

CHAPTER 6

The Belowground
Illicit Drug Industry

Cartels or Corporations?

In *Understanding Globalization*, sociologist Robert Schaeffer states:

> The expansion and spread of drugs and narcotics, which are sponsored by international drug cartels and mafias based in different countries, are seen by some as a component of globalization, even though they involve the production and trade of illegal goods by criminal organizations. (2003:4)

As argued in chapters 1 and 2, there is no clear reason why the illegal nature of a group of commodities and the organizations that produce and distribute them should raise doubts about whether their rapid, consequential, and worldwide spread and impact should be considered an expression of globalization. Global illicit drug sales have been estimated to now be $300–$500 billion each year (even higher in some estimates), rivaling the annual intake for the pharmaceutical industry, which totals about $300 billion. Illicit drug use occurs in numerous countries, including low-resource nations, especially those involved in transshipment (including storage and repackaging) along the route leading from countries of production to countries of final destination and consumption. It is estimated by the United Nations Office on Drugs and Crime (2006) that at least 200 million people, or about 5 percent of the global population between the ages of 15 and 64, have used illicit drugs at least once during the last 12 months (compared to 28 percent who smoked tobacco). Because of a global flow due to technological advances in communication and transportation and the re-ordering of social relationships and daily life experiences, the illicit drug cabinet of American society (and a growing portion of other countries as well) is now well stocked with a wide assortment of mind altering, mood adjusting drugs from around the world.

The key developments that have enabled the trade in illicit drugs to become a fully global commerce parallel those found in the international production and marketing of legal drugs. To take but one example, without doubt injection drug users in Mumbai, India; Lagos, Nigeria; and Seattle, USA have their differences. Nonetheless, as a result of globalization, many of those who turn to injection drug use anywhere tend to have much in common, including leading marginalized lives at the edges of mainstream society, using commercially produced hypodermic needles, injecting heroin directly into their veins for its rapid psychotropic effects, falling prey before long to drug addiction, and being at high risk for syringe-mediated HIV and other infection. In all three of these seemingly disparate places, people's lives are being reconfigured in important ways by "common economic, political, and environmental developments: increased competition, fluctuating interest rates, the introduction of new technologies, a change in climate . . . and the scourge of violence and drug use" (Schaeffer 2003:15).

While transnational "corporations" are the critical organizations at play in the production and distribution of legal drugs, Schaeffer uses the interchangeable terms "cartels" and "mafias" to label the organizations that produce and distribute illicit drugs. He notes:

> The mafias that came to control the global drug trade in the 1970s, 1980s, and 1990s grew out of regional crime gangs that emerged in Europe [e.g., the mafioso in Sicily and mafiyas in the former Soviet Union], the Americas [e.g., the Italian American Cosa Nostra, the Colombian drug cartels], and Asia [e.g., Chinese Triads, Japanese Yakuza] during the previous century. (Schaeffer 2003:339)

As he explains, the term mafia had its origin on the Mediterranean island of Sicily in the 1860s following a successful uprising that pushed the Spanish out and led ultimately to unification with other city-states on the Italian peninsula to form the Kingdom of Italy, the first consolidation of this region since the fall of the Roman Empire. But the new government was weak, especially in Sicily, and a political vacuum emerged. Freeing the peasants from legally binding obligations to landlords left productive relationships and processes in a shambles. While it was on the horizon, a full market economy with its distinct wage labor system had not yet taken hold. As a result, there was no socially legitimate and mutually accepted system for land owners and landless peasants, opposed social classes with competing interests, to enter into contractual relationships for the purposes of making a living.

This void came to be filled by the one entity that, because of the successful uprising, had social credibility and the organizational structure to mediate patron/peasant/merchant relations, provide protection to all parties from the self-interested actions of the others, and to enforce contracts. This entity consisted of bands of armed former soldiers who had helped drive out the Spanish. Following the local patriarchal extended family model, these groups tended to be lead by *mafioso* or "men of honor," respected elders with experience, authority, and stature, as well as a willingness to use force to maintain their positions and impose their decisions. Rather than a unified system, mafioso formed small, independent, local gangs composed of relatives and friends called *cosca*.

As they emerged and developed, the various cosca collaborated and competed, forming alliances and sometimes violent rivalries. They were united in their embrace of the cultural concept of *omerta* (honor), which included never cooperating with government authorities. Says Schaeffer, "It is these informal groups that are described by journalists as 'the mafia,' but they are more like a trade association composed of affiliated competitors than a corporation made up of members organized into a single hierarchy" (2003:340).

With the turn of the 20th century, thousands of Sicilian peasants and other rural Europeans migrated to the United States. Most poured into burgeoning urban centers like New York City, where the newcomers were crowded into ethnic enclaves in slum areas with little assistance in finding their way in this new world. Under these conditions, reconstituted mafias (usually linked to mafioso families in Sicily and their methods and organizational patterns) stepped in to broker relations among governmental bodies, political party bosses, employers, and Italian (and other) communities and their workers. The new entities grew to be far larger, wealthier, and more complex (e.g., they included affiliated members and associates with Jewish, Irish, or other ethnic backgrounds) than their Sicilian progenitors.

Each of the (at one time) 25 or so U.S. mafia "families" were independent and carried their own names, which usually were taken from a particular patriline, such as the Gambinos in New York, the Patriarcas in New England, and the Genoveses in Pittsburgh (cousins to the Genovese family in New York). These families often were rivals, jockeying for turf and profit, and sometimes fighting bloody battles. To limit bloodshed and resulting public and police attention, control competition, increase regional or national collaboration, and routinize business operations, in the early 1930s the mafia families formed a "National Commission," composed of family bosses, especially those in New York or with New York connections, as an overarching authority.

Initially, the commission was headed by Salvatore Maranzano, originally of Castellammarese de Golfo in Sicily, who used an army of 600 "soldiers" to eliminate or intimidate rivals and proclaim himself "Boss of Bosses" during a secret mafia meeting inside a social hall in the Bronx, New York. Maranzano established lines of authority and drafted the organizational structure that guided the American mafia for the remainder of the 20th century. Critical to Maranzano's victory was Salvatore "Lucky" Luciano, who, in addition to being most responsible for introducing the illicit drug trade into the mafia's business operations (with the aid of his childhood friend, Jewish gangster Meyer Lansky), also was one of the first younger leaders of the mafia to press for an end to disruptive, internecine warfare. Realizing that once enthroned Maranzano was not inclined toward power sharing, Luciano and Meyer arranged for him to be killed by four assassins dressed as police officers in his real estate office on Park Avenue on September 10, 1931. Over the next 24 hours, three other old-guard mafia bosses also were murdered by the young turks:

> With the slate wiped clean, Luciano and Meyer Lansky reorganized the National Commission. . . . Patterned after the hierarchical structure of modern corporations, the Commission was a tightly controlled bureaucracy of crime based on patriarchy, and empowered to settle jurisdictional disputes as they arose, particularly in cities like Las Vegas, which has always been considered "open territory" for organized crime penetration. (Lindberg 2001)

Although the FBI long denied the existence of the commission, it changed its tune after discovering 65 high-ranking mafia bosses from as far away as Italy, Cuba, Los Angeles, Dallas, Chicago, Tucson, and Kansas City at a meeting at the sprawling mansion of Canada Dry Bottling Company president Joseph Barbara in Endicott, New York, on November 14, 1957. While various issues were on the agenda of the meeting, including Vito Genovese's bid for recognition in New York City, the group was to decide whether or not to put out a contract for several federal narcotics officers who were threatening the mafia's profitable illicit drug trade. In a single stroke, the new corporate nature, deep involvement in drug trafficking, and mafia connections to legal corporations were made public.

While the "mafias" and "cartels" that developed in Asia, South America, Mexico, Africa, and Eastern Europe each have their own histories, ritual and formal structures, and methods of operation, they share features with the Sicilian crime families. According to Schaeffer (2003:344), all of these illicit organizations have engaged in protection and vice industries, adhered to strong behavioral codes, "act[ed] with both courtesy and cunning, demonstrate[ed] both compassion and revenge, and display[ed] great energy," and, to add another feature they have in common, made immense profit from illicit drugs. Moreover, they have tended to evolve from smaller gang-like entities into corporate structures.

In each case examined below, legal barriers influenced the organizational structures and methods of operation of the entities involved in the production and distribution of illicit drugs. Calling these entities cartels or mafias, however, and treating them as completely distinct from legal corporations obscures more than it reveals, including the features all producers/distributors, legal and illegal, share as a result of their involvement in global drug capitalism. Also hidden by such terms is the level of collaboration between illegal and legal corporations, ties that suggest both are very much alike in making decisions based on what financial managers call "the bottom line."

The Heroin Business

Existing archeological evidence indicates that the source of heroin, the flowering opium poppy plant (*Papaver somniferum*), evolved in the Fertile Crescent region between the western Mediterranean Ocean and Asia Minor, from which it spread, very likely with human assistance, to the Far East. It is not known how or initially why the plant came to be cultivated by humans, although the practice is thousands of years old as is knowledge of the effects of its consumption on human experience. Only cultivated or at most semiwild populations of the plant remain today and only in "pioneer habitat created and maintained by humans either consciously, in the form of cultivated fields, or unconsciously, in the form of 'waste areas' or disturbed environments adjacent to or in the near vicinity of these fields" (Merlin 1984:54). Although wherever it is grown the opium poppy has local medicinal and other uses, as the source of medicinal morphine it can wind up as a legal drug commodity. Nevertheless, most of the opium poppy under cultivation in the world is converted into heroin within the informal economy of illicit drug capitalism.

Heroin first entered the market as a legal commodity, produced and aggressively advertised by the Bayer pharmaceutical company as a cure-all for a range of health problems and discomforts. In the United States, it remained legal to buy heroin for about 15 years. By the time its addictive potential was firmly established and Bayer stopped making the drug, thousands of people in the United States were addicted. When sale and use of heroin was banned, many of these individuals became the initial underground market for this powerful central nervous system depressant. Additionally, there was a growing cadre of poor and working-class users "who had begun experimenting with drugs in such decidedly nonmedical establishments as brothels and saloons" (Courtwright et al. 1989:3–4); ethnic and class prejudice against the latter helped to fuel the passage of laws and the establishment of court precedents penalizing heroin use.

The Global Hourglass of Heroin (and Cocaine)

In the production of illicit drugs like heroin (and cocaine as well), there is a global hourglass model in operation: production begins with large numbers of poor farmers who reap little profit from growing the opium poppy (or, in the case of cocaine, coca bushes) in Asia or South America, and the final product ends up in the hands of large numbers of poor (as well as nonpoor) consumers in the United States, Europe, or elsewhere, many of whom can afford only small purchases, enough to sustain themselves through a single day. Between these two populations of poor people are the illicit drug capitalists who reap the real profits of the multibillion-dollar illegal drug industry and those they employ, directly and indirectly, to process and move the product along various pathways into consumers' hands. This system, which developed in the aftermath of the criminalization of heroin possession early in the 20th century, has its historic roots in the illicit alcohol trade of the Prohibition era.

The individuals who first saw an exploitable opening for quick profits from the criminalization of heroin came from the Jewish enclave on the lower east side of New York City. These individuals not only recognized there was a significant demand for heroin following the federal prohibition of its use, they also had the connections in Europe to buy drugs legally from pharmaceutical companies and the means and experience from their involvement in alcohol smuggling to bring heroin clandestinely into the United States (Singer 2006b). The early heroin traffickers set up acquisition, processing, and distribution systems that remain the models for contemporary heroin commerce. Moreover, the original Jewish heroin importers demonstrated to others in the criminal underworld, especially members of the Italian American mafia organizations, that illicit drug importation and distribution was feasible, enormously profitable, and, unlike bootlegging or rum running, not likely to vanish as a result of legalization. While some members of the mafia were somewhat ambivalent about involvement in the heroin trade, as noted earlier, one up-and-coming mafia leader, Lucky Luciano, a man with strong links to the Jewish underworld, fully realized the profit-making potential of heroin.

Lucky Strikes

By the 1930s, Luciano and his Jewish partners were running a growing heroin business in New York City. But District Attorney Thomas E. Dewey, tracking Luciano's rise in the criminal underworld, targeted him for arrest and prosecution. In 1936, Luciano was convicted on over 60 prostitution-related charges and was sentenced to up to 50 years behind bars. He was released, however, ten years later and deported to Italy in exchange for using his influence on the docks of New York City to aid the U.S. Navy during World War II. He also may have convinced his associates in Sicily to aid in the Allied landing there. Back in his native Sicily, Luciano was able to rebuild the illicit heroin business. As a result, by the 1950s, heroin was again flowing into the United States and the number of users began to expand significantly, beginning in poor African American and Puerto Rican neighborhoods and expanding outward.

Globalization and the Heroin Industry

Globalization has had significant impact on the heroin business. Indeed, Brzezinski has called heroin "the ultimate global commodity." Moreover, he notes:

> Beneath its veneer of violence, narcotics trafficking is a surprisingly sophisticated industry, marketing-driven just like any consumer-products business. . . . From source to street, pushing drugs shares many common elements with hawking soda pop or cigarettes. It requires lots of working capital, steady supplies of raw materials, sophisticated manufacturing facilities, reliable shipping contractors and wholesale distributors, the all-important marketing arms and access to retail franchises for maximum market penetration. (2002:24)

In short, there has been a steady movement in what Brzezinski (2002) calls "the heroin business model" toward the reigning corporate models of global capitalism. While violence remains part of the game, globalization has led to the establishment among heroin and other drug corporations of "strategic alliances to cooperate . . . rather than fight . . . through subcontracting arrangements, and joint ventures, whose business practice closely follows the organizational logic of . . . 'the network enterprise' characteristic of [global business in] the Information Age" (Castells 1998:172). One expression of this shift occurred in the mid-1990s in New York and surrounding areas. Up until that point, the East Coast had been the market territory primarily of Chinese organizations (that had largely supplanted the Italian mafia in the local drug trade). In an effort to enhance profits, however, Colombian cocaine producers had retooled to include heroin in their product lines (which entailed learning about the planting and care of opium poppy, methods for harvesting opium and converting it into high-grade heroin, and marketing the drug). Like modern businessmen, the Colombian drug capitalists brought in experienced consultants to assist them in their restructuring, namely individuals from Asia with heroin production experience. Among other things, they taught their employers how to grow poppy, information that was passed on through various networks to small farmers involved in coca plant cultivation.

To Market, to Market

Unlike coca, opium poppy can be grown high in the mountains on small plots of land. Typical producers are poor, family farmers who grow poppy because they know it brings in somewhat higher prices than other crops they might plant. They often know little about what happens to the sap produced by the poppy after they sell the substance to eager buyers. From the fields, poppy sap is transported to hidden laboratories for conversion to heroin and from there to distant markets in the United States or elsewhere. When the Colombians began bringing their heroin to market, they used their connections in the Latino communities of New York and contiguous areas. The potential emerged for a bloody turf war between the Colombians and Chinese in the East Coast heroin trade. "Astonishingly," notes Brzezinski (2002:54), "what broke out was almost entirely a price war," of the sort commonly "fought" by legal corporations, which the Colombians ultimately won. On the street, the effect has been the availability of much purer heroin at lower prices.

At present, there are three primary heroin/opium trade routes in the world (World Health Organization 2006):

- from Latin America (Mexico, Colombia, and Peru) to North America (especially the U.S.);

- from Myanmar/Lao PDR to neighboring countries in Southeast Asia, and to Asia (notably China), and to Oceania (mostly Australia); and

- from Afghanistan to neighboring countries (especially Iran), to the wider Middle East region, to Africa, and to Europe.

The Heroin Business Model

Other features of the new heroin business model that reflect the impact of globalization include:

Gateway Marketing. One of the explanatory models for the pathways taken during individual drug use careers is known as the "gateway hypothesis." According to this proposition, individuals who take up the use of psychotropic drugs tend to begin with certain "starter drugs" that serve as the "gateway" into the use of a range of other mind-altering substances, often following an identifiable sequence. The most common starting points for drug use among youth in the United States, for example, are tobacco and alcohol, as these drugs are readily available and legal among adults, even though they are banned among children. After gaining familiarity with these starter drugs, the most likely gateway into illicit drug use is through smoking marijuana.

Interestingly, examination of organizations involved in illicit drug trafficking suggests the existence, as well, of a *gateway marketing pattern*. The individuals, for example, who would rise to prominence and public visibility as the so-called "cocaine drug lords" of Colombia, began their careers in the illicit drug trade smuggling cigarettes during the 1950s and moved on to marketing marijuana during the 1960s. In Mexico, illegal drug capitalists began their careers by smuggling duty-free cigarettes and alcohol across the U.S. border during the 1970s, and moved on later, first to marijuana, and then cocaine, heroin, and methamphetamine trafficking. Those who built the heroin trade in the east and the Midwest began during Prohibition, smuggling contraband alcohol into the United States, and with the end of Prohibition switched to heroin and other illicit drugs.

This pattern of *commodity transition*, beginning first with tobacco and/or alcohol and switching over time to other drugs, is seen as well among legal corporations and reflects an organizational pattern involving: (1) learning routines of operation; (2) monitoring risks; and (3) seizing opportunities to exploit specialty niche markets. As Peter Drucker

(1993:26) noted in his classic account of General Motors, the first law of the corporation is: "produce goods with the maximum economic return." In contemporary "corporate-speak," successful illicit drug entrepreneurs are quick to identify "new platforms" for growth (i.e., new products) while "capitalizing on existing assets" (e.g., using transport and marketing experience gained with the original drug product for use with the new drug product). In such transitions, drugs like heroin and cocaine come to be targeted because they are well suited to long-distance trade (in that they have far less bulk than tobacco or marijuana and can be more easily hidden than alcohol), and have a high value-to-weight ratio that more than covers transport costs (about on par with diamonds) (Gootenberg 2005).

Decentralization and Flexibility. The readiness to shift to new, higher-yield products reflects two idealized features of contemporary global corporations: *decentralized operations* and *maximum adaptive flexibility*. While this trend was already underway in the later part of the 20th century, it accelerated rapidly in what often is referred to in corporate-speak as "the post-9/11 business environment." Corporations now see the world differently than they used to. At the start of the 20th century, the push among emergent corporations was toward rapid growth, increased complexity, and centralized decision making. Major companies like General Motors or DuPont sought to integrate the multiple steps that comprise production and distribution into a centrally managed enterprise. Today, by contrast, in the face of increased global competition in the "9/11 environment":

> Corporations are reorganizing into what Bennett Harrison calls "networked production." They pursue "lean production" by downsizing in-house operations to "core competencies" and farming out work to "rings" of outside suppliers. Corporations construct "strategic alliances among one another, both within and, especially, across national borders." Harrison describes this "emerging paradigm" as concentration of control combined with decentralization of production. (Brecher and Costello 1998:1)

This decentralized corporate model is believed to produce maximum flexibility to allow appropriate and timely response to changing conditions in the market and in a volatile global community in which treacherous wars break out suddenly, governments rise and fall, epidemics erupt and spread, and terrorism strikes. This is no less true for illicit corporations than their legal counterparts.

Notably, as Brzezinski (2002:26) emphasizes, "September 11 and its new world of heightened border controls has made decentralization doubly important for international [drug] smuggling networks, be they Chinese, Colombian, Turkish or Nigerian." The "slimming down" process now seen in illicit drug corporations also is an adaptive response to the War on Drugs, which, since 9/11, has been publicly linked by government spokespersons and their prevention messages to international terrorism. In the aftermath of 9/11, the U.S. Border Patrol added over 2,000 agents and National Guard units began patrolling the nation's borders. As a result, drug exporters in Mexico developed new methods to get around enhanced border protection, such as partnering with groups involved in smuggling people into the U.S., sewing heroin into the stomachs of puppies exported to the country, or digging new tunnels under the borderline. Additionally, the decision makers in the heroin business as well as other illicit drug sectors "have adopted the mantra of their more enlightened [legal] corporate cousins . . . that size does not necessarily create efficiency, and that to survive you have to stay nimble" (Brzezinski 2002:26). As a result, despite enhanced border controls and interdiction efforts, the heroin business remains strong.

Outsourcing. A key element of decentralization in the contemporary corporate world is outsourcing, which involves the contracting with other companies for the performance of specific tasks in the production and distribution processes. Corporations cite a number of benefits of outsourcing, including accessing highly specialized skills found in other companies (perhaps located in other countries), protecting the corporate image (e.g., contracting out telemarketing and using this contractual relationship to deny direct wrongdoing when offshore contractors are cited, as they regularly are, for violating "no call" laws), reducing operating costs, addressing lack of in-house capacity during periods of expansion, and giving up responsibility for hard-to-manage functions.

Today, transport, as well as other functions in the heroin business, is outsourced to specialized companies. Some of these entities, like Nigeria Express and the Arellano Felix Organization, specialize in smuggling heroin across borders to its final destination. Street sale of heroin commonly is farmed out to independent youth gangs. While the term street gang conjures up particular images of wayward and violent teenagers, research has shown that there are different kinds of youth gangs. One type, that Siegel (1998) labels the "criminal gang," operates like a business and like its legal counterparts attempts to limit behaviors by its members that may be bad for business (besides the selling of illegal drugs or other illegal but profitable enterprises). In his study of a Chicago public housing project, for example, Sudhir Venkatesh (1997) ethnographically documents how street gangs took over the distribution of crack during the 1980s with business-like efficiency. One such youth gang in Los Angeles, in fact, has taken as its name "The Businessmen."

Outsourcing of retail street sales offers illicit drug corporations the same kind of protection gained by legal corporations when they outsource problematic functions (e.g., removal of medical waste) to the lowest bidder. Additional features of the role of gangs in the street marketing of drugs are examined in the next chapter.

Contract Manufacturing.   Contract manufacturing is a form of out-sourcing in which production itself is farmed out to another entity that has low labor costs (e.g., because it operates in a country in which wages are extremely limited) and is capable of delivering great quantities of the desired product (e.g., low-priced cell phones, toys, electronic compo-nents, etc.). In contract manufacturing, the real profits are made by designers and distributors not the actual manufacturers. Moreover, con-tract manufacturing frees the distributors from the challenges of labor recruitment, maintenance, and control, those all become someone else's worry. As a result of the advantages it offers, contract manufacturing has become a widespread feature of global capitalism and many contract manufacturing companies have emerged around the world.

Heroin is well suited to specialized production because its manufac-ture is capital intensive and complicated. In the Golden Triangle area of Asia, temporary facilities are used to avoid detection. They are set up to fill a particular order and can be quickly dismantled if threatened. Various chemicals must be acquired and shipped to the production site, including calcium hydroxide, which is used to cook the raw opium extracted from poppy plants into morphine; liquid ether from India and ammonium chloride from China, which are used to convert the morphine into low-grade heroin (called "brown sugar"); and acetic anhydride, which is used to transform brown sugar into high-grade 90 percent pure No. 4 heroin. Like legal contract manufacturers, the producers of the drug reap only a tiny portion of its final street value; producers sell a kilogram of heroin to distributors for under $3,000. In New York City, this amount has a wholesale value of over $200,000 and a far greater retail value.

Target Marketing and Microbranding.   In his book *Strategic Position-ing,* Paul Temporal (1999) identifies three types of branding. In the first, called "corporate branding," a company tries to get its name associated in customers' minds with high-quality products or services. The goal is to convince people that if they buy something from your company, they will get the best product available. In the second, called "house brand-ing," the company and its product are played up together. This approach may be used when a company is known but it is hard to introduce new products in a tightly competitive market. The final strategy is called "product branding," in which the corporation seeks to build up the name of each of its individual products, devoting corporate resources to insure that each product's targeted consumer populations are aware of its name, its value, and its uses, while the name of the corporation it comes from may be more obscure. The goal is to have the consumer identify with a product and seek it out by its brand name. In product branding each new product can be positioned precisely for a specific market.

While these various forms of branding are not new and have been used to sell products for generations, with globalization there has been a heavy emphasis on a focused variant of product branding known as "microbranding." This involves producing and marketing products that are intended to appeal to a very specific "demographic" (i.e., age/gender/ ethnic or other segment of the market) and entails concentrated advertisement to this market segment. Recent efforts to market pharmaceutical drugs specifically to African Americans (on the basis of having been developed to meet their unique "biology characteristics") is an example of microbranding. Like other forms of pharmaceutical marketing, constructing the market—i.e., getting people to identify with the market label and use it in purchasing decisions—is more then half of the battle.

Increasingly, the illicit drug industry has begun marketing specific "brands" to niche market segments, such as promoting heroin that is pure enough to be snorted to suburban youth who fear needles and being infected with AIDS. Brzezinski, for instance, describes the sale in Baltimore of small vials of heroin with color-coded plastic caps that denote variation in purity and price designed to appeal to the widest possible customer base. He observes that if this approach to marketing "sounds incongruously like something out of an MBA textbook, that's because it is: the strategy is called microbranding, and it is the reason so many different varieties of Coca-Cola sit on grocery shelves these days" (2002:24). In places where heroin is sold in bags, brand names, often taken from movies, song lyrics, or other sectors of popular culture, are stamped onto the package, and when buyers learn about a particularly strong brand from their friends they ask for this brand by name. While brand names in the heroin business have a shorter shelf life than do those of many legal consumer products, their appearance on the street is driven by the same marketing principles applied by legal corporations.

Cocaine: From Cottage Industry to Global Complexity

Illicit cocaine production began as a cottage industry, with amateur equipment in makeshift laboratories, sometimes located in private homes, designed to convert small amounts of coca leaves into the much more potent cocaine powder. Initially, transport systems were simple, with individual couriers (called "mules") carrying small quantities of cocaine hidden in luggage or in other personal effects on commercial airline flights from Colombia for delivery to a pre-arranged buyer in the United States. During the 1970s, several of the initial founders of the Colombian cocaine industry carried comparatively small amounts of cocaine into the United States for direct sale. During these early smuggling ventures, they came to recognize the potential of the North American market and used their time during drop-offs in the U.S. to explore opportunities for larger-scale illicit export and distribution operations.

During this early phase in the development of the global cocaine industry, the various steps in the production and sale of the drug came to be segmented into independent operations handled by different sets of small-time players. As the U.S. demand for cocaine took off in the early 1980s, the opportunity emerged for the drug's illicit producers to significantly expand their operations, consolidate their organizations, and greatly increase the amount of cocaine brought to market. Explained Juan Ochoa, one of the founders of the Colombian cocaine industry:

> The business worked in the following way. The supply people would bring it [coca paste] initially from Peru and Bolivia, and they would process it in labs here in Colombia. From [them], you would buy the cocaine and you would contract it with someone to send it to the United States. Maybe it was through air or perhaps some maritime way, and there someone would receive it. . . . That agent would be in charge of sending it to other clients, from California, from New York, from different states. The person in the United States would be in charge of receiving the money and sending it back to Colombia. That's the way it would work. (FRONTLINE 2000)

Directors of the new cocaine companies realized that the primary focus of the U.S.-led War on Drugs was marijuana smuggling; that and the fact that powder cocaine is far easier to move clandestinely across borders and into the U.S. than bulky marijuana facilitated the cocaine smugglers' efforts.

According to Juan Ochoa, before long several alternative business models began to appear among the informal sector companies that comprised the illicit cocaine industry:

> One [approach] was to buy the [already prepared] cocaine [from local producers] and to send it [to a partner in the U.S.], and [the] partner would sell it there. The other way would be to have your own lab where you would process it. You'd have your own way of transporting it, a plane or a boat or something like that. You send it at your own cost. Another way, you'd end up having to subcontract with other people to do the different stages, like processing, transport, and the transfer of sales to the person that you had contracted in the United States. (FRONTLINE 2000)

To realize the vast profits they sensed could be made from expanded cocaine production, however, a number of groups of producers who operated out of several key cities, most notably Medellín and Cali, Colombia, began to coalesce their operations to form large, more comprehensive illicit drug corporations, entities that soon would come to be known to the outside world as the Colombian "cocaine cartels."

Cocaine Confederations

Before long the industry was controlled by several regional confederations (e.g., the so-called "Medellín cartel," the "Cali cartel") of independent companies that were composed of directors and managers, chemists, pilots, and other operatives. The confederations worked together for mutual benefit (e.g., to set wholesale prices, to share intelligence about common threats, to arrange transport) and to profit from economies of scale. Especially, they "collaborate[d] to improve smuggling logistics or to thwart government counternarcotic efforts" (Clawson and Lee 1998:19). High-volume export efforts led to the development of "complex coordination of many activities: air, sea, and overhead transport; aircraft refueling and maintenance; drug loading and unloading and storage; delivery of bribes to appropriate officials in transit countries" and many other tasks (Clawson and Lee 1998:38).

Initially, there were about ten cocaine confederations. Carlos Toro, a close associate of Carlos Lehder, who, along with George Jung established a very lucrative and well-run cocaine enterprise, recalls how the confederations began to form:

> Carlos Lehder approached Pablo Escobar [an original founder of the cocaine industry] and he told him [about working together], he is the one who said to Escobar, we have to change the way we're doing business. . . . Carlos earned that elevation in his power when they saw that he had tremendous capabilities of getting organized and doing things. They saw that he was a man that could transport anything. He had alternative routes and he [knew how] to scramble frequencies. He had radio people. Carlos became the most important ingredient of the whole pie. . . . And that's how the cartel got started. Carlos was a very good pilot. Carlos can fly anything. He can fly a helicopter, he can fly a Citation, a Turbo Commander, you name it. And he knew the islands extremely well. (FRONTLINE 2000)

Lehder, who had a fascination with Hitler and would dress in Nazi uniforms, carefully planned his operation, including how to translate his cocaine profits into a run for the Colombian presidency (L. Smith 2006).

As Toro's statement suggests, the "body-packing" individual "mule" was superseded by the use of small aircraft and speed boats capable of hauling as much as 1,000 kilograms of cocaine at a time. Bigger laboratories, some on the scale of industrial factories, were built to process greater quantities of coca leaves. One of these, at a site in Colombia named Tranquilandia, was raided by the Colombian national police and the DEA in March 1984. The laboratory was part of a hidden city carved into the jungle, 250 miles from the nearest road and accessible only by aircraft. Fourteen laboratory complexes had been constructed at the site, which was serviced by a runway that could handle DC-3 airplanes. During the raid, 22,000 pounds of refined cocaine, with a street value of over a billion dollars, was confiscated. Seven planes that were used to fly the finished cocaine to market also were seized at the site as well as various chemicals and equipment needed to transform coca leaves into refined cocaine powder.

Despite the size of this seizure, it had little impact on cocaine availability or price in the United States. Startled by this turn of events, the DEA admitted that the scale of the cocaine industry was far greater than they had imagined. The discovery of Tranquilandia also confirmed the level of consolidation that had been achieved by the Medellín cocaine corporation.

To supply Tranquilandia with leaves for processing into pure cocaine, small farmers had been recruited to plant coca bushes. Thousands of families flocked to coca-growing areas, trying to escape extreme poverty by acquiring a small plot of land on which to grow coca plants for the drug industry. Like the small farmers who grow opium poppy in Asia, they received only a miniscule amount of money for what would become a product worth billions of dollars.

Flying Money

Initially, profits from cocaine sales were returned to the Colombian-based drug corporations as cash. Jung reports:

> The money would go back [to Colombia] packed into Chevy Blazers exported out of the United States. . . . Carlos owned a place down there, a dealership, and was purchasing Chevy Blazers in the United States and then money would be packed into the door panels and what-have-you and they'd be shipped out of the country into Colombia. And later, as time wore on, I said, "We don't have to go through all that. We can fly legally out of the country. Why the hell not just fly the money back down?" (FRONTLINE 2000)

Ultimately, the volume of cash became too great for small aircraft to serve as a practical or dependable means of moving tens of thousands of pounds in small bills throughout the year. Consequently, more sophisticated money laundering schemes were hatched. Dick Gregorie, an assistant United States attorney in the Southern District of Florida, identified some of the money laundering approaches developed by the cocaine corporations:

> What's happened is that the money launderers have been able to develop businesses which are cash business, [for example] restaurants. . . . Jewelry has become a great way to launder money. You can buy it here in the U.S., take it down to South America, resell it, and the money is laundered. You can purchase real estate in the United States for an ungodly sum, then . . . sell it back to someone in South America, and the money is laundered. If you go and look at some of these businesses [in Miami], nobody goes in them, nobody goes out of them. . . . We had a baby store that literally had no parking in front of it. Yet when we looked at the receipts, they were recording several million dollars a month going into their accounts. Well, we knew it wasn't from the sale of baby clothes. (FRONTLINE 2000)

Laundered drug money was also invested in the formal economy, including in "trucking and freight companies, race tracks, banks, natural gas companies, the dairy industry, [and] the tourism industry" (Clawson and Lee 1998:255). Furthermore, illicit drug money was invested in legal pharmacies and pharmaceutical manufacturing companies. Cocaine profits allowed the heads of the cocaine corporations to live like kings.

The cocaine corporations recruited outside investors, usually Colombian businessmen from the formal economy who would purchase part of a cocaine shipment. In other words, a kind of informal stock market was formed in illicit drug shares. In this arrangement the cocaine corporations "provided the cocaine and served as the shipping agent. If the shipment was successful everyone made money. If not they were insured" (Duzan and Eisner 1994:198). The insurance was provided by Pablo Escobar, who received about 10 percent of the U.S. price for each cocaine shipment. If the shipment was confiscated by the police or otherwise lost, Escobar replaced it. Through such schemes, Escobar was able to gain a central role in the Medellín-based operations. To protect himself from arrest for his illicit activities, Escobar ran for office and in 1982 was elected as an alternative to the Colombian House of Representatives, gaining him immunity from prosecution. Escobar became so wealthy in the cocaine trade that *Forbes* listed him as the seventh richest man in the world in 1989.

With expansion came a degree of specialization. While the cocaine corporations provided overall management, many tasks (smuggling, sales, money laundering, police monitoring, and enforcement) were subcontracted to smaller groups and freelancers. Illicit drug capitalists based in Cali, Colombia, for example, paid $200,000 a month to set up and maintain a joint counterintelligence and enforcement operation (Sheridan 1995). Some of this money was used to bribe officials (including heads of state in some countries) and the police, and to support a private army to carry out the business decisions made by corporate heads.

Cocaine and Broccoli

The only major hindrance to industry growth was the threat of arrest. As Carlos Toro (FRONTLINE 2000) explained, contingency planning became a core business practice:

> The DEA was the greatest fear. The DEA was indeed the only force capable of . . . [putting] us out of business, and put us in jail and extradite us and do whatever was necessary. . . . [The] DEA knew about the operations. That was the paranoia that kept the group so well armed and so well protected. There were contingency plans of blowing airplanes and blowing the airstrip and dynamiting the whole thing. . . . We [had] plans of escape and we [had] boats and speedboats and cigar boats and all kinds of equipment, as plan B or plan C to evacuate.

These plans were focused on a small island in the Bahamas known as Norman's Cay, one of 700 islands that comprise the country, which was the hub of Lehder's cocaine corporation. Before Lehder's arrival, the island had been developed as a residential community with a yacht club and a marina. In 1978, however, a Bahamian company called International Dutch Resources (IDR) began aggressively buying up island property. IDR, it turned out, was a front set up for Lehder by a legal Bahamian trust company that managed his working capital (L. Smith 2006). During the early 1980s, Lehder's airstrip on the island received daily cocaine flights from Colombia. From there, cocaine was loaded onto smaller air and sea craft and transported 96 miles to Florida or to elsewhere in the United States.

Despite back-up planning, Lehder was arrested in 1987, at which point his net worth was estimated to be $2 billion. Although an object of great disdain among federal officials, given his vast and detailed knowledge of the global cocaine trade, Lehder had something of tremendous value to the antidrug warriors in the U.S. government. In 1992, he cut a deal to provide information that was used to indict and convict Panama president Manuel Noriega on drug trafficking and money laundering charges. Afterward, Lehder disappeared, to a hidden prison cell according to the DEA, to a comfortable life in the prisoner protection program according to other sources.

While the War on Drugs has never stopped the cocaine trade, it did impact how business was done by the cocaine capitalists. Numerous innovative strategies were developed to secretly transport cocaine to the United States. Gilberto and Miguel Rodriguez Orejuela, for example, purchased a fence-post plant and lumber mill, and Miguel developed a method for hiding cocaine in hollowed out lumber and in concrete fence posts, which were then exported to compatriots in Miami. Other strategies included hiding cocaine in chlorine cylinders and in frozen broccoli and okra. When he was the head of the DEA in Miami during the 1990s, Tom Cash called Miguel's concealment schemes "brilliant."

Although there were many independent operators in the cocaine trade, Colombian cocaine corporations maintained their own marketing units in key American cities. These cells were closely tied to their Colombian bosses. In New York City, for example, a major illicit market given the large number of local drug users, the Cali cocaine corporation established

> ten to twelve marketing subsidiaries, or "cells," each comprising ten to twelve salaried employees. . . . Cell directors reported directly to the home office in Cali, where the directors made all key decisions on the cell's activities—they set prices, determined the amounts of cocaine to be sold, and approved prospective buyers. (Clawson and Lee 1998:40)

Relations also were established with drug trafficking groups in other countries to facilitate smuggling (including drugs for weapons exchanges). A number of Mexican organizations became key partners with the Colombians and later set up their own production and distributions systems as the Colombian companies came under increasing military pressure from the joint U.S.–Colombian antidrug war. This offensive ultimately forced changes in the South American cocaine production and distribution system, including decentralization. Although many of the earlier Colombian illicit drug capitalists were arrested, the industry itself, in changed form, continues as a force shaping contemporary drug use dynamics. In Lupsha's (1992) apt phrase, "The players change but the game continues." This dynamic was well expressed by the lawyer for Gilberto and Miguel Rodriguez Orejuela when the Cali-based brothers, aged 67 and 63 respectively, pled guilty and were sentenced to 30-year prison sentences in Miami in exchange for dropped charges against 28 other family members: "The best chess players understand that every now and then you must sacrifice some important pieces for the safety and security of the entire board" (Join Together 2006b).

The New Game

The cocaine "game" continues, and it is not just the players but how the game is played that has changed as well. The new "atomized game" involves the development of:

> Newer, less-structured and "flatter" organizations . . . most of which operate [as] small autonomous cells that are linked via Internet chat rooms and cellular phones protected by the very latest in encryption technology. Unlike the previous cartels, these "boutique" groups typically contract out the majority of their jobs to specialists who work on a job-to-job basis rather than as part of an integrated structure. (Rabasa and Chalk 2001:14)

The U.S. border with Mexico has become the chief point of entry for cocaine smuggling into the United States in recent years. The DEA estimates that as much as 65 percent of the cocaine that comes into the country crosses this border. From there it is dispersed through wholesale purchase by local, independent distribution units located in major cities across the United States. Illicit drug capitalists in Colombia continued for a long time to oversee the wholesale side of the cocaine trade in the northeastern part of the United States, but a number of Dominican illicit drug companies have expanded their control in this region in recent years.

Similarly, in the United Kingdom, *The Economist* (2004) reports that the cocaine market is opening up:

> London-based Colombian importers who traditionally controlled the import and wholesale trades now contract freely with British entrepreneurs. A recent trend is for Britons living in Spain to deal directly with Central American suppliers before selling on to Colombians in London or directly to an army of middlemen. New importation routes open frequently, sometimes as a result of police activity. . . . One of the biggest domestic seizures this year came from a warehouse in west London. Among a shipment of pineapples and vegetables from Ghana were ten kilos each of cocaine and marijuana.

In South America, new wholesale companies have emerged in Bolivia and Peru, creating further decentralization. Venezuela has become an important transit country for cocaine produced in Colombia. At the same time, Venezuela plays a key role in production as a primary conduit for needed precursor chemicals as well as a fiscal hub for drug money laundering. Ecuador is another growing transit country, while countries of the Southern Cone—Argentina, Chile, Paraguay, and Uruguay—are secondary transshipment sites for cocaine bound for the United States and Europe. As a result of these transitions, the old patterns of vertical consolidation, top-down organization, and micromanagement by the Colombian corporate leaders have faded into history. The modern cocaine corporations are well adapted to the post-9/11 business environment.

Crack: A Market Innovation

One of the significant shifts in the cocaine trade began in the mid-1980s with introduction of a ready-to-smoke form of cocaine known variously as crack, rock, or ready rock. As Jacobs points out, in business, legal or illegal, "[t]hose who fail to evolve, adapt, and diversify are doomed" (1999:122). Crack represents an adaptation to changing conditions in the illicit drug trade:

> Crack was a marketing innovation. It was a way of packing a relatively expensive and upscale commodity (powder cocaine) in small, inexpensive units. So packaged, this form of smokeable cocaine (crack) was then sold . . . to a whole new class of customers: residents of impoverished inner-city neighborhoods. Reinarman and Levine (1997:2)

The precise origin of this innovation is not known but there are some suggestions in the available evidence that it was first produced in the Caribbean among middle-men partners of the Colombian drug corporations. Agar (2003), for example, points out that shifts in patterns of cocaine production, such as outsourcing, and the movements of populations, including the migration of people from the Caribbean to Miami, Los Angeles, and New York, were important social changes that helped to foster the development and spread of a new product like crack.

The invention of crack marked the beginning of a shift in the cocaine trade from an emphasis on the high-end marketing of expensive snortable powder to a reliance on poor and working people as the primary cocaine market. A tenth of a gram of crack cocaine commonly is packaged in vials or glassine bags and sold for as low as $3 or less on the street, a price affordable to even unemployed, homeless individuals. While the crack "high" is intense, it is short-lived, pushing those who are dependent on the drug into a cycle of continual fund-raising through both licit and illicit ventures.

Cocaine is a primary substance in the drugging of America's poor. In her book, *Behind the Eight Ball: Sex for Crack Cocaine Exchange and Poor Black Women*, for example, Tanya Telfair Sharpe (2005) documents the involvement with crack of poor, marginalized African American women, including an examination of the role of crack-addiction in their turning to prostitution. Sharpe points to the effects of long-term social exclusion and systemic racism in undermining the self-image of poor African American women as the critical element in crack use, crack-related commercial sex, and related health problems.

Researchers who have studied the relationship between drug use and sex work point out that the diffusion of crack use on the street was associated with the appearance of a more desperate tone in day-to-day street life, marked by a decreasing price for commercial sex, less control over sex activities by sex workers, a resulting increase in riskier behaviors, and greater level of degradation and humiliation of the sex worker by drug dealers who controlled access to crack. A multicity ethnographic study of HIV transmission associated with sex-for-crack exchanges involving interviews with 340 active crack users (Ratner 1993), for example, found that crack-addicted prostitutes were reporting a significant jump in the number of customers per day. As one participant in a Miami study, a woman who began prostituting in a crack house in exchange for regular access to crack reported to Inciardi and co-workers:

> [The houseman] calls in this guy Stoney. He was working "lookout" across the street. And right there he says, . . . "let Stoney come in your mouth." He wanted me to do it right there, in front of five, six people. . . . And after Stoney, I did three others in the room, and by midnight I had done 30 more. (1993:59)

The Miami site in the multicity study found that only 23 percent of women involved in sex for crack/money exchanges always used condoms during vaginal intercourse, and only 14 percent reported always using condoms during oral sex. To assess the role of crack use in AIDS risk, Logan and colleagues (1998) compared a sample of women crack users who exchanged sex for drugs or money with women crack users who reported that they were not involved in such exchanges. They found these two groups of women had similar drug use patterns and had initiated drug use at similar ages. Those who exchanged sex for crack, however, had more sexual partners, a greater frequency of unprotected oral sex, were more likely to use drugs before and during sex, and had a higher rate of sexually transmitted diseases.

Risk of exposure to violence is also common among commercial sex workers who use crack. In her book *Tricking and Tripping: Prostitution in the Era of AIDS*, based on an ethnographic study of women crack users and commercial sex in Atlanta, Clare Sterk reports the case of a research participant who told her:

> The guys think about us as their fucking property. Like they own us because they give us some smoke. . . . You see this black eye? . . . I got beat up because he couldn't get it up. I had been rubbing and sucking him for a long time. He was bleeding, and he wanted to go on. . . . Finally he gave up and made me have sex with this other girl. (2000:70)

The turn to commercial sex work among crack-addicted women is not random and may be predicated on prior life experiences. As a participant in the Hispanic Health Council's study of drug use and intimate partner violence in Hartford reported:

> I was suffering from depression, you know [since being raped by her stepfather], and I never got help for it so. Then I had my oldest son, after my oldest son, I moved out. . . . I left my apartment, went into a shelter and got me another apartment . . . had another baby from another man. Then I started doing drugs. That's when I got into doing drugs . . . doing dope, I started doing dope. I was already twenty-one. First I was sniffing then I got into doing shooting up . . . I started hanging around with people that was shooting and stuff. So let me try it . . . that's when I really got into the heavy, doing dope. I started learning how to [do] crack cocaine, I started smoking it. I lost my apartment, I went through a lot, you know. I started even selling myself, just to get the drugs, drug money for the cocaine, for my habit and stuff. (Singer 2006a:20)

As these accounts suggest, crack has played a significant role in the drugging of the poor, and in their exposure to HIV and other blood-borne diseases. At the same time, it has been linked with an enormous increase in the imprisonment of poor users and with significant emotional suffering. In this sense, crack is intricately linked to the complex system of addiction, imprisonment, and disease that supports the reigning structure of social inequality.

Methamphetamine

The amphetamines/methamphetamines comprise a chemical family of semisynthetic stimulant drugs (sometimes called amphetamine type stimulants or ATS) with continued but limited medical utility and considerable potential for addiction (Lucas 1985). Amphetamine was first synthesized from benzylmethyl acetic acid in 1887 by Lazar Edeleanu, a Romanian chemist living in Germany, but its stimulant properties were not fully recognized and the substance, which its discoverer named phenylisopropylamine, was largely forgotten until the late 1920s, about the time a Japanese scientist was discovering methamphetamine. Chemically, the two substances are the same, with the addition in methamphetamine of a single molecule of methyl (i.e., one atom of carbon with a set of usually three hydrogen atoms). Drug researchers—both professional and underground—know that adding methyl to a psychoactive drug alters its effects, including both the duration and potency of the high it produces. This occurs because methyl adds improved fat solubility to amphetamine increasing its ability to penetrate the brain. Additionally, the crystalline nature of methamphetamine powder makes it water soluble, and thus a perfect candidate for injection.

Methamphetamine was widely prescribed in the United States during the 1950s and 1960s, primarily for the treatment of depression and obesity, reaching a peak of 31 million prescriptions in 1967, mostly to women. Desoxyn, the pharmaceutical brand name of methamphetamine, is still used to treat several conditions, including attention deficit disorder and attention deficit hyperactivity disorder, narcolepsy, and obesity. This class of drugs has been dubbed "the most American of drugs" because they stimulate effort and a sense of busyness, facilitate long hours of work (e.g., driving through the night among long-haul truckers), enhance the user's experience of work intensity, and create a frenetic sense of industriousness; their effects embody key American values about hard work leading to success. The connection of these drugs to hard work and success, however, is illusory, and their regular use tends to push the consumer to a narrow focus on drug use and away from other life pursuits, including productivity. Because their longer-term regular use can cause tremendous damage to the life and health of the user, and considerable suffering for the user's immediate social network, these drugs do, in fact, give expression to another, less-hallowed, American value, namely: making a profit at the expense of good health and well-being (Baer et al. 2003).

Amphetamine was first diverted for illicit psychotropic use in the 1940s and 1950s, emerging during the 1960s, a period of significant increase in the number of people using drugs illicitly and in the total number of drugs available for use, as "one of the half-dozen most popular street drugs" (Goode 1984:176), especially in the western region of the United States. Daily injection (every 4–8 hours) became common in a population of younger users who called themselves, and were called by others, "speed freaks" or "meth-heads."

After smoking or injecting methamphetamine, users rapidly experience a powerful, pleasurable, and psychologically addictive "rush" lasting for several minutes, which is then followed by a prolonged high. In pill form or snorted, the drug does not produce a rush but instead the user experiences a significant increase in energy as well as a depressed appetite. While this mode of ingestion may at first appear benign to casual users who often function "normally" in society, addiction, involving intense craving and the need to use larger doses to achieve desired effects, is a common sequelae. After binging on methamphetamine for several days, a routine called "a run," users learned to ease the discomfort of the crash by using barbiturates or heroin, which in turn, led to many "speed freaks" becoming addicted to the opiates. This practice prompted an eventual switch to primary heroin for many users as its effects were easier to manage and less stressful on the body. In light of its effects individually, socially, and environmentally, the current spread of methamphetamine has been called "a perfect storm of complications" (Lineberry and Bostwick 2006).

The Meth Makeover

The experiential short-term effects of methamphetamine reported by users include euphoria, wakefulness, enhanced self-confidence, feelings of heightened strength, aggressiveness, talkativeness, loss of appetite, prolonged initiative, and, as noted, ritualistic busyness. Reproducing desired effects, however, tends to require increasing the doses over time. As the drug is metabolized by the body, withdrawal symptoms begin to set in, including intense craving, deep melancholy, a sense of meaninglessness, extreme fatigue, lack of initiative, and unprovoked fear. Suspicion of others and hostility also are common, as is violence. Additionally, Gail Tominaga and coworkers (2004) found that injury patients who tested positive for methamphetamine were more likely to have self-inflicted wounds.

Some of the dramatic behaviors seen in longer-term methamphetamine users may be the consequence of the drug's apparent neurotoxic effects. With prolonged use and resulting damage to the terminal section of brain neurons, methamphetamine is believed to produce a reduction in overall brain dopamine levels, resulting in some cases in symptoms that resemble Parkinson's disease. Additionally, the drug causes increased heart rate and raised blood pressure, which over time can lead to irreversible blood vessel damage in the brain, leading to strokes. Even with limited methamphetamine consumption, users report suffering from irritability, insomnia, confusion, tremors, convulsions, anxiety, paranoia, and aggressiveness (National Institute on Drug Abuse 2004a). Other negative effects include respiratory problems, irregular heartbeat, and anorexia. Through damage caused to the brain, cardiopulmonary system, and other body systems, as well as through hypothermia, methamphetamine use can be lethal.

Methamphetamine is also linked with the spread of HIV/AIDS and other blood-borne infectious diseases like hepatitis. The drug can facilitate HIV/AIDS both as a result of the direct and indirect sharing of drug injection equipment and through the promotion of sex with multiple partners. Some have linked the jump in HIV infection among men who have sex with men (MSM) after the initial reductions that were achieved early in the epidemic to the spread of methamphetamine. Notes Owen, "there is no firm scientific data showing conclusively that crystal meth is behind the rise, but anecdotal evidence from doctors in New York [suggests] that the drug plays a role in anywhere from 50–75 percent of new cases of HIV in the city" (2004:4). Similarly, health officials in several states have expressed strong concern about the link between methamphetamine and increasing rates of HCV (hepatitis) infection. Additionally, methamphetamine is known to have a dramatic impact on a user's appearance. Meth heads often suffer marked physical deterioration, with those who use regularly looking 10 and 20 years older than they really are after just a few months of use, a transition that has been called "the Meth makeover."

On the Road with meth and the Yaks

Methamphetamine came into widespread use during World War II when it was distributed by both sides in the conflict to enhance the fighting capacity of troops. The Japanese air force distributed the drug to Kamikaze pilots because it made them more alert and they could fly for longer periods of time. Large quantities of the drug that had been stockpiled by the Japanese military fell into the hands of the Yakuza, or Yaks as they are popularly known, Japan's large and tightly organized crime and illicit drug corporations. Dating from the end of the feudal era, the Yakuza groups, which traditionally were characterized by rigid internal hierarchies and kin-like rituals of respect and obligation to organizational superiors, have a history of diverse criminal activity, including protection, extortion, and gambling. The Yakuza say that they are descendents of the communal guards who protected their respective villages from marauding bandit groups during the feudal era. Thus, they see themselves as underdog folk heroes who stood up for the poor and the defenseless.

Unlike the American Mafia, the Yakuza are not underground companies but operate more or less in the open. Their access to military stockpiles of methamphetamine stemmed from their close ties with ultra-conservative sectors of the Japanese government and military (Hill 2003). The Black Dragon Society, the most prominent Yakuza group before World War II, for example, included many right-wing and nationalist government officials as members. They also acted as spies for the government during the war, a task that was enhanced by their involvement in prostitution, and were engaged, as well, in the opium trade and other illegal profit-making schemes. Additionally, the Yakuza provided thugs to the government to break up workers' strikes and organizing efforts.

Like the cocaine companies of Columbia, the Yakuza engage in community works, and for the same reasons. After the devastating January 17, 1995, Kobe earthquake (in which over 5,000 people died), for example, the Yamaguchi-gumi, the powerful Kobe-based Yakuza group (which rakes in about $2 billion in annual drug profits) directed by Yoshinori Watanabe, provided disaster relief, an action that was widely reported in the media because their efforts came much faster than those provided by the government.

Outside of Japan, the Yakuza have a foothold in Japanese communities in Hawaii and California, and used these to introduce methamphetamine to the United States. It is through Hawaii and California that the drug first began to spread across the United States; later, Mexican illicit drug corporations largely took over the Hawaiian and California methamphetamine markets and have developed new markets across the country.

In the late 1980s, under the influence of the Yakuza, a new wave of stimulant use developed, coming this time especially via two forms of methamphetamine: 'crank' and 'ice,' the former is a powder that can be smoked, snorted or injected, while the latter is a crystalline substance that is usually smoked. Different forms of the drug have noticeably different effects on the user and, from the perspective of drug dealers, create the possibility of attracting more customers (with differing drug preferences). The shipment of methamphetamine to Hawaii was initiated by a subgroup of the Yamaguchi-gumi corporation. These Yakuza recruited couriers to smuggle the drug as passengers on commercial airline flights. According to the DEA (Casteel 2003), many of the couriers were unwitting accomplices who received paid vacations in exchange for transporting golf clubs, bottles of shampoo, or other items filled with methamphetamine. In 1998, there were 24 ounces of heroin and 26 ounces of crystal methamphetamine seized by law enforcement officials in Hawaii. Six years later, there was less than an ounce of heroin seized compared to 785 ounces of crystal methamphetamine. Far and away, methamphetamine had become the "drug of choice" in paradise (Farnsworth 2004).

How Not to Fight a War on Drugs

Home production of methamphetamine began during the 1980s. Until the late 1980s, law enforcement officers found only small labs producing the drugs, operated primarily by biker gangs. At the time, methamphetamine production and use were small-scale compared to what they would become in a few years. To shut down the so-called Mom and Pop labs, the DEA, at the request of Gene Haislip, the third ranking officer in the DEA at the time, tried to block lab access to chemicals like ephedrine, an alkaloid derived from several related plants in the Ephedra family, that were needed for methamphetamine production. Although Haislip's efforts received a supportive response from the president and Congress, he quickly ran into a stone wall thrown up by the chemical and pharmaceutical industries. According to Haislip, antidrug warriors like himself and the chemical and pharmaceutical companies live in two different worlds.

> They live in the business community, where the name of the game is to make money and sell product, supposedly for legitimate purposes, whereas we in law enforcement, we see the other side of it. We see the harm that these same drugs and chemicals can do when they slip from the legitimate to the illicit. . . . They don't see that side. They don't think of that side, because that's not the business they're in. So they are always a little bit concerned about what DEA does in a situation like this, and sometimes more than a little bit. They know who to talk to and who to go to in Washington. They're highly skilled, very well organized and very well funded, and they can be quite formidable. (FRONTLINE 2005a)

In 1988, Congress amended the Controlled Substances Act of 1970 to include provisions both requiring full reporting on the import and export of bulk ephedrine and authorizing the DEA to stop shipments of controlled chemicals like ephedrine from U.S. suppliers to companies outside the country that were suspected of diverting them to drug traffickers. Officials at the DEA working to stop the flow of methamphetamine thought they had scored a slam dunk. They were certain of this when they began to see the effects of the new legislation. Recalls Haislip:

> It wasn't long before we saw the effect, because at that moment, the problem was a diversion of bulk ephedrine almost exclusively from domestic sources. Pretty soon what we saw is the [illicit] traffickers on the West Coast were reporting they couldn't get their ephedrine. They were trying to burglarize suppliers and did in some cases. Ephedrine was selling on the street per kilo for almost what cocaine was selling. They were desperate. (FRONTLINE 2005a)

At the same time, hospital and other health sources began to report drops in methamphetamine-related deaths and injuries, further confirming to the DEA that they has scored a big victory in the War on Drugs. This feeling of success was short-lived, however, as before long the quantity of methamphetamine on the street returned to the same level as before passage of the new legislation. The DEA was stunned. Something had gone terribly amiss.

The source of the problem soon became clear when searches of newly discovered methamphetamine labs produced enormous quantities of empty packets of cold medicine tablets that contain ephedrine and pseudoephedrine. As many of the packets had French instructions, the DEA concluded that the tablets had been brought in from Canada. As it turned out, the revised law specifically excused over-the-counter medicines containing the precursor drugs from the record-keeping and reporting requirements. Why had this exemption been codified into law? The DEA soon discovered it was because of effective lobbying by the pharmaceutical companies intent on protecting a lucrative market from regulation. As Steven Suo, an investigative reporter for the *Oregonian* who wrote an insightful series on the methamphetamine epidemic in Oregon in 2004, concluded:

> Meth was still a very small problem confined to the West Coast. . . . If all of Haislip's initial ideas had actually been implemented back in the 1980s when meth was a small problem, it may never have gotten out of hand. This is in many ways an unnecessary epidemic in the sense that the government has [had] numerous opportunities to stem the supply of the drug and has pretty much missed each of those opportunities along the way, both due to industry lobbying and due to its own wavering interest in the problem. (FRONTLINE 2005b)

In 1997, the law was changed again. This time, however, according to Suo:

> The DEA finally got the ability to regulate wholesale distributors of pseudoephedrine like they'd been trying to do for the preceding decade, [but]

they really were not prepared to actually carry out that mission. People who were licensed to sell pseudoephedrine by the DEA were not typically shut down, even if their product ended up turning up in meth labs. The DEA would send out 20, 30, even 40 warning letters without ever shutting these people down. As a result of that, in a number of high-profile cases, people who have been licensed by the DEA ended up turning around and supplying millions of pills to the super labs in California. (FRONTLINE 2005b)

Meth Labs in Mexico

Instead of being halted in its tracks, methamphetamine use spread from California and the northwest coast, eastward across the country during the 1990s and into the 21st century. Treatment data showed the incidence of methamphetamine-related health problems moving clearly upwards, more sharply than for any other drug.

The spread of methamphetamine was associated with numerous reports of increased violence, damaged lives, and disrupted communities. In February 2003, for example, several members of the Soldiers of the Aryan Culture, a Utah motorcycle gang, were arrested on various charges including operating a methamphetamine ring throughout the state. The gang, run as a military unit both in the prison system and on the street, adhered to a strict code of conduct that required its "soldiers" to study white supremacy literature and participate in the gang's drug production and distribution system. Some of defendants in the case, all of whom were addicted to methamphetamine, were accused of maiming one rival, of attempting to kill seven additional individuals, and of making violent threats to others in an effort to maintain control of drug trafficking in Utah. Increasingly, however, as the 1990s progressed, biker gangs like the Soldiers had to compete with Mexican drug companies for control of the methamphetamine trade, a clash that the Mexican corporations consistently have won.

Established Mexico-based illicit drug companies entered the illicit methamphetamine trade in the mid-1990s and moved quickly to control the production and distribution of the drug. Mexico-based groups are now believed to control between 70 and 90 percent of methamphetamine production and distribution in the United States (Brouwer et al. 2006). The advantage these groups have is access on the international market to large quantities of the assorted chemicals needed to produce methamphetamine as well as control of heroin, cocaine, and marijuana smuggling and distribution networks, especially in the western United States but increasingly across the Midwest and South as well. To increase production, the Mexican illicit drug companies acquired several large laboratories in Mexico that can turn out significant quantities of very pure methamphetamine. "Superlabs," those capable of producing more than ten pounds of methamphetamine in a 24-hour period, also are found in California. Notably, in 2001, 298 superlabs were seized in the United States by police, up from 168 the prior year. In Mexico, primarily in the Baja California border towns of Mexicali and Tijuana, 24 superlabs were raided compared to two the previous year. In 1992 U.S. authorities seized 6.5 kilograms of methamphetamine that was being smuggled across the border, primarily in concealed compartments in passenger cars, by 2001 1,370 kilograms of methamphetamine were confiscated at the border, suggesting a significant jump in the availability of this drug in the United States (Drug Enforcement Administration 2005; Glittenberg and Anderson 1999).

In addition to cars driven across the border, other methods are used for bringing the drug into the United States, including walking through tunnels that are dug under the U.S.–Mexico border. Like methamphetamine produced in California, once in the United States, Mexican methamphetamine is transported using various means, including tractor trailers, private cars, and on motorcycles steered by outlaw motorcycle gangs. At times, couriers board commercial airlines to move the drug across the country, and parcel delivery services are also used. When the drugs reach their destination, they are sold wholesale to local dealers, including local street gangs who control illicit street drug sale locations. These groups, in turn, dilute the relatively pure Mexican methamphetamine with additives such as caffeine, methylsulfonylmethane (a nutritional supplement), or other adulterants in order to increase profits. The diluted "meth" is then packaged in various smaller quantities for sale by street dealer teams. Street prices for methamphetamine varied during the period from 1992 to 2003, when the cost per gram was between $50–$200 and a single dose sold for about $10–$20.

A Pound of Methamphetamine

Even today, not all methamphetamine production occurs in Mexico. Smaller, covert methamphetamine labs continue to be found in many parts of the United States. In 2003, 8,000 such labs were raided by police across the country (Butterfield 2004). These laboratories use various recipes to produce methamphetamine. One formula combines the phosphorous from the ignition strips on matchboxes with pseudoephedrine from over-the-counter cold medication and iodine. Production of just one pound of methamphetamine creates six pounds of waste that contains corrosive liquids, acid vapors, heavy metals, flammable solvents, and other harmful substances that can cause disfigurement or death if they come in contact with the skin or if their fumes are inhaled.

Tragically, police found more than 3,000 children, the offspring of lab operators and workers, living in the methamphetamine labs they seized in 2003 (Butterfield 2004). All of these children were at risk, both because of the poisonous chemicals that are released during the cooking process, which tend to be heavier than air and thus cluster at children's levels closer to the ground, and because lab explosions and fires are fairly common occurrences as a result of the volatile chemicals in use and the makeshift operating conditions of most underground labs. Moreover, to save money and avoid detection, operators of methamphetamine labs have been known to dump their toxic waste into common sewage systems, in open fields, into the large trash dumpsters of businesses, along the sides of roads, in national parks, on beaches, or at other public sites. The clean up of a single site can cost up to $50,000.

Shop[liFt]ing For Precursors

Often, methamphetamine labs are detected because of the producers' need for large quantities of coffee filters, acetone, camp fuel, lye, cold pills, and matches. One clear tip-off for the police that a methamphetamine lab is operating in an area is that large quantities of these items are suddenly being shoplifted from local stores.

To limit access to certain precursor chemicals needed to produce methamphetamine, a number of states have passed laws requiring certain cold medicines to be moved from open racks in pharmacies to behind the pharmacy counter. This strategy has resulted in a significant reduction in the number of small labs, but not necessarily in the availability of methamphetamine, which can still be smuggled from Mexico in large quantities. Consequently, while the number of labs being discovered by the police has fallen sharply in many parts of the country, the quantity of methamphetamine has not significantly diminished. Expecting eventual police detection, methamphetamine laboratory operators are often well-armed, and their laboratories are sometimes booby-trapped and equipped with cameras for scanning the surrounding area.

From the Sticks to the Streets

The National Survey on Drug Use and Health (Substance Abuse and Mental Health Services Administration [SAMHSA] 2003), found in 2002 that 12.4 million Americans who were age 12 and older had tried methamphetamine at least once during their lifetimes (5.3 percent of the total population); the study also found that the majority of individuals who had used the drug during the previous 12 months were between 18 and 34 years of age. The Drug Abuse Warning Network (DAWN) has also compiled data on methamphetamine use. DAWN is a hospital-based system for monitoring emergency room (ER) visits for drug-related health problems (e.g., overdoses, "bad trips," car accidents involving drugs). As part of the DAWN system, ER patient charts in sentinel hospitals are reviewed to identify any patient mentions that have been written in the patient's chart by ER staff. A review of DAWN's data set found that "there has been a large increase in the abuse of methamphetamine" in recent years (Greenblatt and Froerer 1997:1). This conclusion was based on data showing:

> Large increases in methamphetamine admissions to publicly funded treatment facilities occurred between 1992 and 1995. Most activity occurred in the western region of the United States, but methamphetamine abuse also appears to be increasing in the Midwest and in some southern States.

Notably, DAWN data for subsequent years showed a continued eastward spread of methamphetamine. The greatest national increases in hospital admissions for methamphetamine use in 1995–2002 occurred in Newark (which had a 574 percent increase), New Orleans (507 percent increase), and Baltimore (500 percent increase) (SAMHSA 2003). Additionally, SAMHSA's Treatment Episode Data Set (TEDS) from this same period showed that the ATS hospital treatment admission rates at sentinel sites increased from 10 admissions per 100,000 to 52 admissions per 100,000 patients for those aged 12 and older (SAMHSA 2003).

As contrasted with prior waves of new drug use in the United States, rural areas have been especially heavily hit by the spread of methamphetamine. For example, Sioux City, Iowa, with a total population of only 84,000, has emerged as a regional center for methamphetamine trafficking because it sits at the intersection of Iowa, Nebraska, and South Dakota. Although Mexican drug gangs control the methamphetamine trade in Sioux City, small-time independent producers, called "cooks," operate labs in more rural parts of the state. Small labs produce less than an ounce at a time. Iowa police found two methamphetamine labs in 1994; in 1999 they raided 803 labs. "For every one that learns to cook, they teach 10," says Marti Reilly, a police drug task force spokesman, "It's kind of the Amway pyramid thing" (quoted in Bonné 2001:1).

While methamphetamine use has often been associated in the media with white urban and rural working-class users, the drug has diffused to various ethnic and sexual minority populations, and to the poor. Research in New York indicates the spread of methamphetamine use among African American and other gay men of color. According to Barbara Warren (National Coalition 2004:1), "A decade ago, we watched as cocaine use grew into a crack epidemic in communities of color . . . we are trying to prevent crystal meth use from exploding into an epidemic among men of color." Other ethnic minority populations, like Latinos, have also started to use methamphetamine, creating a potential for even greater diffusion. Diaz (1998), for example, has described methamphetamine use among gay Latino men. As noted earlier, methamphetamine has spread to many sectors of the gay-identified and wider MSM community. Gorman and Carroll (2000), for example, report on the use of methamphetamines among MSM in Puget Sound, Washington. These researchers identified a number of MSM user subgroups, including those who use methamphetamine as part of their involvement in party circuits, those who use it in gay baths and sex clubs, transgendered/transsexual methamphetamine users, and a group of HIV+ men who use methamphetamine to self-medicate their HIV symptoms.

Wake-Up Call

One indication of the movement of methamphetamine from white to ethnic minority users comes from a study conducted by the Hispanic Health Council (HHC) in Hartford, Connecticut. After years of monitoring patterns of drug use in the city, HHC researchers began to spot an upsurge in reported recent use of methamphetamine among low-income inner-city Puerto Rican, African American, and white users for the first time in 2005, as indicated in an interview with a 36-year-old African American male who has been a street drug user in Hartford for 14 years:

E: Where do you get [methamphetamine] from?

R: All over.

E: All over in Hartford, like in all neighborhoods?

P: In all neighborhoods, yup. . . . You could go on the street right now and ask people, "where crystal meth at" and they'll tell you where it's at.

E: And how much do you pay for it?

R: You pay like for crack, 10 dollars, 20 dollars, or up, it's like a glass and you smoke it. . . . Methamphetamine that makes you to stay up for like three or four days. . . . It's worst than crack. It's like. . . . Like I said, crack, if you smoke it, it gives you like 15 minutes high, with crystal meth, you get three, four days, it's wilder. . . . When you are high on meth you cannot come down, you want no more, you are wired already, cuz it's like I said, it takes like three or four days. . . . The next day you still feel it in you, cuz it's meth. It's clear like a diamond, so you smoke that, it's like . . . you're wired.

E: How new is crystal meth [in Hartford], when did you start seeing it?

R: I started seeing that . . . let's see, like five or four months ago . . . (Singer et al. 2006b:211)

Similar accounts were provided by other participants in the study. These users reported several different sources, from a drug dealer with biker connections who sells methamphetamine and other drugs close to a Hartford music club and operates a "get off" house nearby where customers can stay high for two or three days, to a seller with New York connections who deals methamphetamine in a nearby suburb. Additionally, in 2005, police in a town near Hartford raided two clandestine methamphetamine labs. A police officer involved in the raids reported, "I am concerned that Connecticut is going to see more of this. . . . We need to use this as a wake-up call . . ." (Seay 2005:5). Indeed, many countries have had a methamphetamine wake-up call in recent years as the drug has diffused across the planet, often displacing heroin or other drugs as the most commonly used "hard drug" on the street.

Ecstasy and Club Drugs: Ups and Downs of the Market

Ecstasy is a designer drug—that is, its production involves the molecular manipulation of an existing substance. Formally known as MDMA (3,4–methylenedioxymethamphetamine), Ecstasy has both psychedelic and stimulant effects on users, lasting for several hours. The drug originally was discovered by German chemists working for Merck Pharmaceutical Company and was patented in 1914. Afterward, it faded into near oblivion until during the 1960s some individuals on the West Coast of the United States discovered that it might have therapeutic uses because it left users feeling highly sociable and euphoric. Within a few years, the drug diffused from therapeutic to the nonmedical underground use. Early in this process, it was test marketed by would-be distributors under the name Empathy, which does reflect one of its interpersonal effects. Ultimately, the drug acquired the name Ecstasy, and it is under this label that it has spread around the world.

Kitchen Labs

Production of Ecstasy during the takeoff phase of its popularity often took place in small, sometimes mobile, minilaboratories, often called "kitchen labs" by their owners. Initially, many of these labs were set up in Belgium and the Netherlands, and later, to lower product costs, they were established in Eastern Europe. Poland, in particular, became active in Ecstasy manufacture and its product gained a significant share of the Ecstasy market in northern and Eastern Europe. Ecstasy labs also have been found in the United States and the Middle East.

The equipment of a kitchen lab generally includes several heaters, various distillation flasks and funnels, and access to sources of running water, electricity and a waste pipe. The makeshift production process was designed to be transferable, with all of the needed equipment able to be packed up into the back of a van and moved to a new location every few weeks to diminish the likelihood of detection by the police (Doward and Thompson 2003). Additionally, as Agar and Reisinger (1999) point out, Ecstasy producers lowered their risk of being caught by locating needed production processes, including the mixing of ingredient chemicals, producing Ecstasy tablets, and preparing tablets for international shipment, in different sites. Maintaining a "fluid and modular structure," within and across allied drug dealing organizations, as well as globally across countries with players of diverse nationalities (as contrasted with the ethnic-centered Mafia model), is the postmodern style of the Ecstasy industry (Agar and Reisinger 1999:367).

Loosely organized underground companies, initially composed of Israelis or Russians, and later of people from other countries as well, commonly run Ecstasy factories. These groups recruited Americans, Israelis, and western Europeans to serve as couriers. Express mail services, commercial airline flights, and airfreight shipments also have been used to bring bulk quantities of Ecstasy to its primary markets in the United States and Europe.

Beginning in the mid- to late-1990s, several Triads—illicit drug and other crime corporations in China—began to corner the market on the raw ingredients needed to produce Ecstasy. One of the chemicals controlled by the Triads is piperonyl methyl ketone (PMK), a synthesized derivative of the sassafras tree whose bark is used to make aromatherapy oils. Today, with diminishing production in Brazil and Vietnam, only a small number of Chinese chemical companies produce PMK, ostensibly for use in the perfume industry. Taking advantage of China's burgeoning trade relationships with other countries, the Triads began to distribute the chemicals to local producers around the world. For this purpose, the Triads created a series of front companies to buy and ship the chemical. Surprisingly, in 2006, in his International Narcotics Control Strategy Report to Congress, President George W. Bush noted that he had "removed China . . . from the list of major drug transit or major illicit drug producing countries because there is insufficient evidence to suggest that China is a major source zone or transit country for illicit narcotics that significantly affect the United States" (Bush 2006). Whether this assertion reflected the actual situation or what was politically expedient remains unclear.

From Up to Down in the Ecstasy Trend

Common in the illegal drug industry is the rapid rise in popularity of a particular drug, a growing number of users, geographic diffusion in the use of the drug, and the incorporation of new and more diverse groups of consumers. After a sudden rise in use rates, at some point a peak is hit and users begin abandoning the drug, although some segments of the drug-using population may continue as regular and enduring customers. This rise-and-fall pattern broadly reflects overall trends in Ecstasy use, and this pattern can also be found among a variety of legal commodities as well, such as toys that are very popular for one or two years and then become marginal parts of the vast toy market. In another commodity pattern, the product begins to get used by a few people but it never really catches on with a large customer base. In the illicit drug market this pattern is seen with drugs like Datura or Bufotenine. On the opposite side are products like Wham-O's popular "Frisbee," which remain widespread across multiple generations of users. In terms of drugs, marijuana reflects this pattern of use.

One important window on changing drug use trends in the United States that serves as a monitor of shifting prevalence in Ecstasy use over time is the DAWN study conducted between 1999 and 2000, showing that the number of drug-related ER episodes rose by an alarming 20 percent for 12- to 17-year-old patients and 13 percent for 18- to 25-year-old patients, while remaining level for older age groups. Further, DAWN data show that ER mentions of Ecstasy in participating hospitals jumped from 250 in 1994 to 2,850 in 1999, and increased another 58 percent to 4,511 in 2000. As these data suggest, during the 1990s there was a significant leap in the number of youth using Ecstasy. By 2001, the number of Ecstasy initiates in the United States had risen to almost two million. The National Survey on Drug Use and Health (Substance Abuse and Mental Health Services Administration 2003) found that 15 percent of 18- to 25-year-olds surveyed had tried the drug at least once. Similarly, the DEA (Drug Enforcement Administration 2001) reported seizing fewer than 200 Ecstasy tablets in 1993, almost 175,000 in 1998, over 1 million in 1999, more than 3 million in 2000, and more than 5.5 million in 2001. Ecstasy has been illegal in the United States since 1985 after several researchers testified that it caused brain damage in rats. The DEA included Ecstasy as a Schedule I controlled substance, the most restrictive designation, and the one applied to drugs like heroin.

The growing appeal of Ecstasy among adolescents and young adults sufficiently alarmed the National Institute on Drug Abuse (2004b) and a number of other health organizations to issue an alert about the dangers of Ecstasy use. According to the alert:

> A number of our Nation's best monitoring mechanisms are detecting alarming increases in the popularity of some very dangerous substances known collectively as "club drugs." This term refers to drugs being used by young adults at all-night dance parties such as "raves" or "trances," dance clubs, and bars. MDMA (Ecstasy), Rohypnol, ketamine, methamphetamine, and LSD are some of the club or party drugs gaining popularity. NIDA-supported research has shown that use of club drugs can cause serious health problems and, in some cases, even death. Used in combination with alcohol, these drugs can be even more dangerous. Thus, we are issuing this alert to aid communities in identifying and responding to this threat to the health and safety of their young people.

As indicated above, Ecstasy did not achieve popularity on its own, but initially was completely intertwined with a group of drugs, some newer, some older, and many having hallucinogenic properties, that were connected by the context of their use and the sociodemographic characteristics of their users: youth-oriented raves and late-night music/dance club scenes frequented by middle-class, suburban, white adolescents and young adults. As Boeri and coworkers point out, the term rave is applied to various kinds of social events, including:

(1) the underground or "real" raves; (2) the "weekend" raves; and (3) the "commercial" or publicly advertised raves. The underground raves are described as all night and/or two-day-long events that rely on alternative modes of advertisement. The "weekend" raves, usually called "parties," are weekly events held in empty anchor stores at deserted strip malls whose location may be found at online dance happening sites. These events are called "weekend" raves because they are held only on weekend nights. The advertised raves are held at well-known clubs that are rented for various dance or concert events and are commercial in economic and promotional terms. (2004:833)

Club drugs as a group, in short, are party drugs, intended by users to enhance social interaction and immediate gratification. As this alternative social milieu emerged and spread from Europe to the United States and from larger gateway to smaller hinterland U.S. cities, with it came a colorful cultural array of objects and behaviors. As one ethnographic account of the club scene described:

Lots of people were dancing, and many had glow sticks. A few were swinging them around to make interesting patterns in the air. Other people sat on the ground or stood around the periphery of the dance floor. I saw a number of people sucking on lollipops and tossing mini glow sticks around in their mouths. I saw two different people with glow-in-the-dark, white, finger-less gloves on their hands. . . . Many were rubbing their friends' arms or giving them back massages. One [guy] had a toy in the shape of a sphere that glowed in the dark. When the guy moved it, it changed shape. At one point, he focused on a woman in her thirties. They sat down together on the floor facing each other. He moved the sphere in front of her face, made designs in the air with his gloved hands, and rubbed her body with the gloves. Two other men were also in this position right next to them. . . . Many people had jars of Vicks VapoRub and also nasal sticks. They put *Vicks* on their own faces and on each other's [faces]. They also blew *Vicks* into each other's faces. I saw a few people holding onto another's shoulders and carefully shaking the person back and forth as part of the *Vicks* "ritual." (Eiserman et al. 2003:22)

In a reversal in use patterns, the Monitoring the Future Study (National Institute on Drug Abuse 2003) found that Ecstasy consumption among high school students began declining during the years 2002 to 2003. Among 10th and 12th graders surveyed in 1996, the annual prevalence of Ecstasy (that is, those who reported using the drug during the previous year) was 4.6 percent in both grades. Seven years later, the annual prevalence had decreased to 3 percent among 10th graders and 4.5 percent among 12th graders. At the same time, in Europe, the dance club scene began to unravel, with some of the most famous clubs attempting to rebrand themselves as more sedate, reflecting part of the movement away from Ecstasy. The same trend may be moving across the Atlantic, hastened as well by new federal drug legislation called the Illicit Drug Anti-Proliferation Act, also known as the "Rave Act," which strengthens existing laws under which property owners are deemed responsible for any drug use on their premises. The slowing of the Ecstasy wave is also suggested by the findings from the 2002 Partnership Attitude Tracking Study which showed a decline in the percentage of adolescents who reported using the drug (compared to 2001).

Ecstasy on the Street

In "The Agony of Ecstasy," Benjamin Wallace-Wells (2003), editor of the *Washington Monthly*, traces the movement of Ecstasy from a suburban-ite party drug to an inner-city street drug, arguing, "In recent years, the Ecstasy market has expanded beyond the rave scene, and more sophisti-cated and dangerous drug organizations have begun to elbow in on what had been mostly a friend-to-friend, white suburban trade." By "more sophisticated and dangerous drug organization," Wallace-Wells means urban street gangs like the Latin Kings. Put differently, while the produc-tion of Ecstasy has long been an underground corporate business, indeed, a very big business that has produced billions of dollars in profits for manufacturers, at the user level Ecstasy was embedded in a dense social scene that celebrated the credo: "Peace, Love, Unity, Respect," and Ecstasy was known among users as "the hug drug." In such a context, giving Ecstasy pills away free to friends was not uncommon, a gift that expressed and consolidated personal rather pecuniary ties. Schensul et al. (2005:63), for example, based on ethnographic research in dance clubs and on the street in Hartford, Connecticut, reports that many of the young people interviewed in the Pathways Project received their first Ecstasy pill "from friends free of charge." At the same time, however, from early in the rave scene, profit-seeking behavior lived side-by-side with gift giving. Explained one participant in the Hartford study:

> In the drug world . . . nothing is free. It is true, nothing in life is free, nothing. Unless you're the one who supplies it. Then it is free to you. Other than that, it's not free, just how it goes I guess. (quoted in Schensul et al. 2005:58)

This individual went on to explain that after her first purchase of Ecstasy, she found friends in her neighborhood who were selling the drug. Personal relationships remain important in acquiring drugs, primarily as a way of being sure they are real and are safe (a regular problem with Ecstasy, which is often adulterated and may contain no psychotropic substances).

In Atlanta, Boeri and coworkers found increasing numbers of young adults from disadvantaged neighborhoods reporting use of Ecstasy.

> In terms of their daily lives, many described being unemployed, having dropped out of school, having witnessed and or been involved with crimi-nal activities, including selling drugs and seeing little opportunity for upward social mobility in life. Typically, they used in or near neighborhood bars. (2004:847)

These researchers found that people who used Ecstasy at neighborhood bars in the inner city were primarily African American, usually older than rave scene participants, and they commonly drank alcohol with their Ecstasy pills, for which they paid as little as $5 a pill and regularly bought 10 or 20 pills at a time. Moreover, inner-city African American Ecstasy users interviewed by Boeri and coworkers indicated that they use the drug frequently, with weekend nights being the most common time of use. In addition to mixing Ecstasy with drinking alcoholic beverages, a number of individuals reported mixing it with methamphetamine, its distant chemical cousin. One method of Ecstasy use in this population is called "hotrailing," which involves heating a glass tube at one end until it is red hot, holding this end close to a line made from crushing Ecstasy pills, and snorting on the other end inserted in the user's nose.

As use of Ecstasy has moved to the street, a process Wallace-Wells (2003) calls "streetification," not only the way the drug is used but even its contents appear to be changing. Groups involved in the distribution of heroin and cocaine have gotten into the Ecstasy business and they have begun cutting Ecstasy with drugs like methamphetamine, perhaps as a way of making Ecstasy addictive and insuring return customers. At the same time, selling Ecstasy appears to be a good business move among illicit drug selling operations. As Rob MacCoun, a professor of public policy and law at the University of California-Berkeley, has observed, like any businesspeople, street drug sellers "want to meet the diverse needs of their market" (quoted in Wallace-Wells 2003). As street customers began asking for the drug, drug sellers realized they should find a way to sell it that would limit the risk of losing customers to their competitors.

As part of this change, Ecstasy is now being sold outside, in public locations, where it is used on the street or even at home alone. Illicit drug sales on the street tend to increase the violence associated with a drug because street sellers are vulnerable to being robbed. Because they cannot call the police when this happens, there is a tendency to take matters into their own hands and begin carrying weapons (Singer 2006b).

One indication of the movement of Ecstasy to new contexts and populations of users has been the appearance of references to the drug in hip-hop music. As Boeri and coworkers note, in hip-hop and rap songs the drug has

> a sexual connotation. For example, Missy Elliot places ecstasy in the club/ dance bar scene in her song, *4 My People*: "This is for my people, my ecstasy people/C'mon, c'mon, get down, get down/I'm at the bar now, and I'm buying drinks/And I got this feeling, and it's all over me/I wanna dance with you, and lick your face/Take me on the dance floor to feel some ecstasy." (2004:844–845)

Seeing the World as an Illicit Drug Corporation

Chapters 3, 4, and 5 presented discussions of how legal drug corporations "see" the world. In light of the foregoing examination of the underground domain of drug capitalism, the dual question is raised; how do illicit drug corporations see the world and how does this compare with the vision of their legal counterparts? From the emic or insider perspective of the large illicit drug corporations it would appear that unlike the developmental nation-state, which Scott (1998) argued sees the world in terms of a grid-like pattern of manageable sectors, drug capitalists see the world is a simplified *global loop*. The first half of this loop constitutes a pathway for the outward flow of illicit drugs from areas of production to areas of consumption (e.g., the U.S., Europe) and, on its return route of illegal profits from the global periphery to where the illicit drug corporation is based. This way of seeing emphasizes fluidity rather than set points, motion instead of a cartography of fixed territories, and routes rather than the land- and seascapes they traverse. It is a way of seeing that transcends the "embedded statism" (van Schendel 2005:39) (i.e., the taken for granted conception of the world in terms of countries, cities, and topographical features encased within nation-state borders) traditional to Western society since the French Revolution. Instead, this perspective "depends heavily on the persuasive value of the arrow" as a visual code of movement across national borders, as if the latter were (as in a sense they are) imaginary lines only of importance in so far as they mark changes in language, currency, and the friendliness or corruptibility of local officials to the movement of illicit commodities. Along the loop, only laws made and enforced by the illicit drug corporation matter as there is an unfailing indifference to local laws.

The global loop is highlighted along its pathway by several nodes of critical activity, all of which are connected: sites of plant growth (for heroin, cocaine, and marijuana) and procurement, locations of drug processing, points of storage and transshipment, delivery depots for passage to retail sales partners, and money laundering operations. None of these are fixed locations; they all shift over time. New small farmers are recruited in a different country or region if law enforcement targets existing cultivation (e.g., a shift from Peru to Colombia for coca bush planting). Drug laboratories shift their location frequently; some are even built as mobile units. Transshipment sites are adjusted to respond to police pressure and to the emergence of new opportunities (e.g., corruptible officials). Trading partners change and local distribution groups come and go (often to jail). Laundering operations are under constant police investigation, and hence new sites and schemes are always being developed and put "online." As this account suggests, flexibility and secrecy (indeed, invisibility) are highly valued while any particular locations of drug-related activity, even those that had at one point in time proved to be useful and highly profitable, are abandoned without hesitation or much regret.

Because of the pressure of law enforcement, the global loop functions as a battle plan (in which making profits and not getting caught constitutes winning). Illicit drug corporations are in a constant state of war, sometimes with each other but always with law enforcement locally and globally. As a result, pathways that comprise the active loop at any point in time are shrouded in enforced secrecy. Secrecy protects profits and profits are king. Killing to defend this system and protect the corporation is valorized. As Hoffer (2006:108) notes, at the street level the drug business "is a social behavior with economic outcomes," but at the global level it is raw economic behavior with social consequences (e.g., the impact of bribery on trust in government).

Two social entities matter most in the optics of illicit drug corporations: collaborators and enemies. The former are the various partners (e.g., traders, smugglers, dealers) that help move drugs around the loop and profits back to the corporate center (e.g., money laundering institutions). The latter is law enforcement, especially the DEA but many other criminal justice organizations as well, including national militaries in countries like Colombia. Given their importance to the flow of illicit drugs and drug-related profits, illicit drug corporations expend sizeable resources on intelligence gathering to allow careful assessment of the trustworthiness of the potential collaborators and the imminent threat presented by antidrug forces.

With full globalization, illicit drug organizations fragment into linked but separate constituent parts, and, as a result, the way illicit drug organizations see the world has changed. Today, drug capitalism is dominated by "less-structured and 'flatter' organizations" (Livingstone 2002:106) and, accordingly, they have a narrower and more disjointed vision of the world. Such entities may not embrace a vision of the world as a simplified loop, but rather more like a relay runner, they see what is just ahead and right behind and devote all of their energy to passing the product on and reaping the benefits of performing a limited but critical part in a much more complex process. The optics of drug capitalism have shifted, moving from a lower-power lens that shows the big picture but few details to a more focused and constricted vision with abundant details. Interestingly, both approaches seem to work (as they are adapted to differing conditions of threat and opportunity); both have contributed to the delivery of illicit drugs to every state in the union and to every city in every state, and a good number of towns, villages, and hamlets besides. Moreover, both have brought drugs in abundance to poor.

CHAPTER 7

Drugging the Poor

> If the rich could hire other people to die for them, the poor could make a wonderful living.
>
> —Yiddish Proverb

Cannabis and Class

People use drugs for many different reasons, and whatever it is that initially prompts them to try a particular drug may be quite different from what motivates them to continue to use the drug over time. Curiosity, for example, is for many people an important trigger of initial drug use and first use of particular drugs, but it is not likely to be a cause of continued or longer-term use. Of particular concern to the approach presented in this book is the effect of poverty and interrelated forms of social oppression on the impetus to start and continue using drugs. While people of all social and class backgrounds use drugs, how does being poor and being subjected over time to the emotional, psychological, and social costs of poverty—and the various forms of structural violence and social deprivation, including discrimination, residential and dietary insecurity, internalized oppression, prolonged social stress, and health disparities—impact motivations for drug use, patterns of consumption, and consequences of drug exposure?

As a case in point, it is generally known that marijuana is the most widely used illicit drug in the United States and beyond. For the year 2004, the national Monitoring the Future Study conducted by the National Institute on Drug Abuse (2005) found that almost 15 million Americans over 12 years of age used marijuana at least once in the month prior to being surveyed. Furthermore, about 50 percent of high school students have used an illicit drug, primarily marijuana, by the time they graduate. Some of these users were from quite wealthy families, which raises a question that is rarely addressed: why do rich people use drugs?

Several studies of teenagers from affluent backgrounds, in fact, show heightened levels of substance abuse compared to the middle class. Two factors, perceived social pressure to achieve and isolation from parents, have been identified as motivations to use drugs among the children of the well-to-do (Luthar 2003). Very likely boredom, desire for adventure, and challenging parental authority are additional influences on drug use in the children of the upper class. Family drug use patterns are another factor, as the use of marijuana by other family members is an important influence on whether an individual begins using the drug. Conversely, family tensions can play a key role the initiation of marijuana use. Coping with anxiety, loneliness, depression, the challenges of growing up, and the stress generated by everyday life problems are further reasons people become involved in marijuana use.

In a study of motivations for using marijuana among people who had been diagnosed with psychosis compared to motivations for use among those without such a diagnosis, Green and colleagues (2004) found that the most commonly reported reasons for smoking marijuana in their psychiatric sample was positive mood alteration (36 percent), coping with negative emotions (27 percent), and as a way to enhance participation and enjoyment of social activities (38 percent). In the matched control group of undiagnosed individuals, the most commonly reported motivations for using marijuana were more narrow and included seeking relaxation (34 percent) and a way to enhance social activities (49 percent). Finally, research has shown that people who were physically or sexually abused as children are more likely to use marijuana and other drugs than those who were not abused (Harrison et al. 1997).

While some of the identified motivations for marijuana use cut across social class boundaries, are there distinctive patterns of and incentives for drug use among the poor? Further, does drug use impact low-income populations in ways that are different from more affluent groups? One answer to these questions is found in a study by Wilson and colleagues (2005) of the relationship between a person's sense of social disorder in the neighborhood where he/she lives and his/her sense of hope, on the one hand, and marijuana and other drug use on the other. Using a sample of middle school students, these researchers found that increased marijuana use was associated with greater perception of neighborhood disorder as well as with a lower level of hope.

Another answer to the questions raised above comes from a study of marijuana use in the U.S. adult population for the years 1991–1992 and 2001–2002 that analyzed data collected in both the National Longitudinal Alcohol Epidemiologic Survey and the National Epidemiological Survey on Alcohol and Related Conditions. In this study, Compton and coworkers (2004) at the National Institute on Drug Abuse and the National Institute on Alcohol Abuse and Alcoholism found that the number of people reporting the use of marijuana was essentially the same in both of the time periods under study, but the prevalence of drug abuse or dependence (based on the definitions provided by the American Psychiatric Association's *Diagnostic and Statistical Manual of Mental Disorders, Fourth Edition, DSM IV*) increased markedly from the beginning of the 1990s to the beginning of the 21st century. The DSM IV defines marijuana abuse as repeated instances of use under hazardous conditions; repeated, clinically meaningful impairment in social/occupational/educational functioning; or legal problems related to the use of marijuana. Marijuana dependence is defined as increased tolerance, compulsive use, impaired control, and continued use despite physical and psychological problems caused or exacerbated by marijuana use. Moreover, the study found that increases in the prevalence of abuse or dependence were most evident among young African American men and women and young Hispanic men. Specifically, the study identified an increase of 224 percent in marijuana abuse and dependence among African American men and women aged 18–29, and an increase of 148 percent among Latino men aged 18–29.

To the degree that the African American and Latino participants in the study reflect patterns among lower-income individuals generally—which, given the disproportionate number of these two ethnic minorities among the poor, this is likely—these findings suggest that there are *important class differences in marijuana use and consequences*. While both rich and poor people use marijuana, the poor suffer greater negative outcomes, including a greater likelihood of becoming dependent on the drug. Like so much else in society, it appears, drug use is not equal; it is more punishing for the poor in several ways. Additionally, these studies, as well as other research on various other drugs, indicate that while the poor do not necessarily consume more drugs than other social classes, they may have somewhat unique drug use motivations. These patterns draw attention to the likelihood that social factors other than patterns of drug use per se are of prime importance in understanding the drugging of the poor.

The Social Life of Drugs in the Everyday Life of the Poor

In 1986, Arjun Appadurai (1986b) edited an anthropological volume entitled *The Social Life of Things: Commodities in Cultural Perspective* in which he and other contributors traced the life course and social meanings invested in and derived from material objects in economic circulation, ranging from oriental carpets to medieval religious relics. In this book and the follow-up volume, *Commodification: Things, Agency and Identities* (van Binsbergen and Geschiere 2005), the argument was made that looking at commodities as if they lead social lives provides a heuristic for understanding the role objects play in interpersonal relationships, in the everyday construction of value and desire, and in the development of personal identities.

Material culture theorists involved in the study of the social life of things argue that objects have biographies (Kopytoff 1986), including phases of existence before and after they are commodities. They are, from a cultural standpoint, different things at different times in their unfolding life histories. These differences also may reflect spatial transitions; things may be different in different places, just as pieces of the moon became something different, culturally, when they were brought to the earth and displayed under glass in a museum in Washington, D.C., or when a rock mined by black hands from the ground in South Africa becomes a diamond ring on a white hand in a wedding ceremony in Iowa.

A number of researchers have applied this framework to drugs, primarily pharmaceutical products and coffee (e.g., Whyte et al. 2002; Weiss 2005). In light of the goals of this book, the question emerges: what is the social life of drugs, licit and illicit, in the everyday lives of the poor?

Social Life Begins

Commodities do not come into existence automatically. They are brought into being through social processes and as an expression of social relationships. Heroin, for example, does not initially have a distinct social life at all; during the initial phase of its existence it is an invisible constituent part of cultivated poppy plants, which often are planted and tended by people who may have little knowledge of what ultimately will become of their harvest. Drugs are not an issue to these poor farmers. They cultivate poppies because poppies fetch a higher price than other crops that might be grown. Poppies, in other words, are of interest to peasant farmers as a means of survival, of feeding their children, of maintaining a way of life in a world of threat, scarcity, and change. This is the poppy as it is seen and understood by people like Mariana Almendro, who grows a small plot of flowering poppies in Colombia:

> Clinging to a steep hillside 9,000 feet high in the Andes, Mariana Almendro's tiny garden is a gorgeous blanket of red, violet and pink opium poppies. Profitable, too, producing a milky gum that brings about $115 a pound from buyers who turn it into heroin. A Guambiano Indian living on a reservation a half-hour drive from the nearest paved road, Almendro, 48, sees nothing wrong with her illegal crop. "It just brings in a little money for food," she said. . . . One acre of poppies yields about 11 pounds a year of milky gum that hardens into opium, worth about $1,250 [11 pounds of heroin was worth about $400,000 on the streets in the U.S. at the time]. In comparison an acre of onions brings about $30. "No one is rich here. This is just to be less poor," said Almendro, a widow living with her three children in a one-room adobe hut up a steep and winding gorge. (Tamayo 2001:A1)

People like Mariana Almendro grow some crops to feed their families and grow others (like the poppy) with the intention of selling them for cash, with which they can purchase food or other items they cannot grow or make. For these people, the poppy and the gummy latex it produces mean a chance to stay a little ahead of financial ruin and even starvation.

Addiction, "mixing up" (adding water to drug powder in preparation for injection), "works" (drug paraphernalia), "mainlining" (shooting drugs into a vein), "skin popping" (shooting drugs into a muscle), "morning shot" (first injection of the day), "get off house" (a place to use drugs), "chasing the dragon" (inhaling heroin smoke), overdosing, going "cold turkey," "clocking" (selling drugs on the street), and all of the other images, behaviors, and meanings that are part of the understanding of substances like heroin for a drug addict in Miami or Seattle are not part of the daily life or storehouse of meanings drawn on by Mariana.

The poverty that drives small farmers to take up poppy cultivation is rooted in national and international economic inequalities and the playing out of political economy at regional and global levels. Based on an assessment of the global distribution of wealth,

> the overall picture . . . is one of growing inequality and [a growing] global gap between rich and poor. The richest 50 individuals in the world have a combined income greater than that of the poorest 416 million. The 2.5 million people living on less than $2 a day—40% of the world's population—receive only 5% of global income, while 54% of global income goes to the richest 10% of the world's population. But the problem is not just one of inequality between countries. . . . [I]n the last 20 years the unequal distribution of income . . . within many countries has grown worse. Of the 73 countries for which figures are available, 53 (comprising over 80% of the world's population) have recorded an increase in inequality of distribution. (Martens 2005:3)

At the same time, once they are engaged in poppy cultivation, small farmers soon learn that very powerful forces are at odds over the plants they grow. Their fields might be fumigated by government airplanes; soldiers may come to uproot their crops or even shoot community members; armed combatants, at war with the government, may have a keen interest in what they are growing; and certainly buyers are very ready to take possession of their harvest. Consequently, small farmers know that there are risks inherent in cultivating poppies, even if the reasons are not always completely clear; but then, what are the options? And when has life not been risky for people like Mariana? For them, the poppy is a small hedge against a far greater risk.

Life in the Lab

Once the sap of the poppy is sold to buyers, it is moved clandestinely to sites where it is converted into heroin, commonly in secret laboratories that often are hidden in the forest, in rugged hilly areas, underground, or in other surreptitious off-the-map locations. In places like rural Afghanistan, where raw opium is used as a form of currency and can be "spent" by farmers to buy food in stores, "clandestine labs churn out so much product that the average heroin price in Western Europe tumbled to $75 a gram from $251 in 1990, adjusted for inflation, according to the United Nations Office on Drugs and Crime" (Shishkin and Crawford 2006). The opium industry accounts for at least 35 percent of the total gross domestic production in the country, is the largest employer, and the biggest exporter (Barker 2006). In 2005, Afghanistan earned almost $3 billion from opium exports, or about 52 percent of the country's gross domestic product of $5.2 billion.

In the labs, people known as "cooks" place raw opium into a barrel and heat it over a fire. The product is filtered through a simple flour sack and laid out to dry in the sun. Electric mixers are used to blend the product with two different acids. According to a man who worked in one of the labs in Afghanistan, "what you get in the end is a beautiful thing—pure heroin" (quoted in Shishkin and Crawford 2006). Many of the people who toil in the labs—daily mixing and pouring the chemicals and managing the processes that turn hard dark lumps of opium sap into white powder heroin—are not much different from the people who grow the poppies to begin with. They are people like 18-year-old Nilofar from a small Afghan village (*PakTribune* 2006). Both of Nilofar's parents are dead and, after her wedding, her husband died too. With few alternatives, she and her 16-year-old sister went to work in a heroin lab; it was the only work around, the only means of survival they could find. Then she got sick because of the toxic substances she was exposed to during the process of making the heroin. Her sister got sick as well. In fact, many of the lab workers she knew were suffering from health problems, including rashes, asthma, blood deficiencies, diarrhea, and stomach upset. In Nilofar's case, as well as that of her sister, the problem was nerves. She wanted to go to the doctor but could not afford to pay for it.

As generally is the case, the health of workers is a reflection of their social relations with their employers. Workers who have struggled and won rights and concessions from their bosses tend to live and work under healthier conditions than those who have been unable to persuade employers to protect workers from occupational or environmental dangers (Levy and Sidel 2006). Working in an illicit trade, it is hard for drug lab workers to organize; certainly it is all but impossible to pressure the government to come to their aid, as is sometimes possible in legal industries. As a result, they are at the mercy of their bosses and their subordinate social position may literally be etched in their bodies in the illnesses they suffer from the kind of work they do.

In the lab, the "thing" of concern is no longer a bright pretty flower, a blanket of sun-lit color covering a steep hillside, a safety rope for the marginalized and impoverished. Just as its form and appearance have been radically transformed in the processes and relationships of production, so too has the complex social life it leads been changed. While it still retains its role as a meager means of livelihood for the poorest of the poor, it has at the same time begun to take on its new broader and far more contradictory "job" as a shadowy source of physical suffering: the medicine that relieves but does not heal; the remedy that takes far more than it yields; the lie that embodies all the lies between the rich and poor.

Out in Circulation

From the labs, the processed heroin must be bagged in small quantities and transported, usually through a circuitous route, often through various middlemen, to the market. Nilofar was one of those who briefly played a role in this process. Seeking to raise the money needed to see a doctor, she agreed to transport processed heroin to India. But, like many others at her level at the bottom of the illicit transport system, she was caught in the Kabul airport and taken to prison. On a ledger somewhere she would be recorded as evidence of progress in the War on Drugs, a sign that victory is near. But making heroin did not mean drugs or altered states of consciousness to Nilofar, nor did it mean bountiful profit and a luxurious lifestyle. To her, heroin was only a means to survival under the harshest of economic, social, and health conditions, a slender and shaky tightrope suspended above catastrophe.

The same could be said of Shudi Nurasov, a skinny 37-year-old man from Tajikistan. Nurasov was caught by Tajik border guards navigating the calm waters of the Panj River, the first phase on the long voyage taken by Afghani heroin northward on its zigzag route to Europe. Dressed in a green skullcap and a dirty knee-length Afghan shirt, a tired and bedraggled Nurasov was caught steering an inner tube taken from a heavy truck tire, across which were laid several wooden boards. With him were 20 one-kilo bags stamped with an oval in which it was written at the behest of an underground promotional specialist: "AZAD PRIVATE FACTORY. The Best of all Export. Super White." Inside the bags was $24,000 worth of high-grade heroin. Nurasov told the border guards that he had been recruited by a man he met in prison who entrusted him with transporting the drugs to Tajikistan and returning with the money from selling them, two-thirds for the owner of the drugs and one-third for Nurasov (Shishkin and Crawford 2006).

Heroin was new to most people in Tajikistan. They had no idea how dangerous or addictive the drug could be. As one Tajik youth who became addicted to heroin stated, "It was very prestigious, we saw drugs in movies" (quoted in Shishkin and Crawford 2006). To this youth, like so many others who have become addicted to heroin, the drug represents modernity, a point of contact with the valued West. Although produced in nearby Afghanistan, heroin possessed the aura of the West, a glittery place, as seen in the movies, of fancy cars, enormous homes, an endless supply of electronic gadgets, food aplenty, and, perhaps most important of all, glamour and prestige. In injecting heroin, this individual was not taking an illegal drug, he was participating in a world he had come to venerate, but into which he had little other means of entering. Drugs looked to him not like a dead end but a doorway to the promised land.

Out on the Streets

Some of the heroin from Afghanistan, and much more from South America and Mexico, reaches the United States. It finds its way into the country, as discussed in the last chapter, through various clandestine portals; it travels by way of every kind of moving vehicle, going by highway, waterway, and airway, as well as by the mail and courier service, and even on foot to every corner of the land, where, commonly, it is sold by local dealers to a steady stream of customers, many of them poor. One of the differences between the wealthier and poorer social classes is that drugs are not very visible in the streets and gathering places of suburban neighborhoods, even if they are being used by many residents, especially youth; by contrast, "In the impoverished inner-city neighborhood, the drug trade is everywhere, and it becomes ever more difficult to separate the drug culture from the experience of poverty" (Anderson 1999:29). For example, in Larimer, the hard-up section of Denver that Hoffer (2006:23) studied, it appeared to him there was "a heroin dealer on every corner" although some dealers "sold heroin out of their homes and did not directly market their wares on the street to strangers" (Hoffer 2006:5).

In Hartford, Connecticut, an impoverished city and hub for the sale of illicit drugs to the wider region, the sociogeographic profile of heroin and other illicit drug sales reflects patterns of neighborhood/ethnic segregation, the distribution of late-night dance clubs and bars, and the location of after-hours, open air "hot spots" at which commercial sex and drug purchases are concentrated and interconnected, as well as the location of academic institutions (Singer and Mirhej 2004). Heroin finds most of its customers on the south end of the city, in the heart of the Puerto Rican community. It also is sold at several south-end bars that cater to whites or to a mixed clientele. Additionally, at times, small "mom and pop" stores or bodegas have been involved in the city's drug trade.

A primary path taken by heroin on its way to Hartford is the highway system that connects New York and Connecticut, such as Highway 95 along the Connecticut shore and, from the coast, Highway 91 that links New Haven with Hartford. Some drug distributors interviewed in Hartford report that they periodically drive to New York to buy drugs. Higher-level distributors also bring heroin into the city via the highways, usually by employing paid couriers and sophisticated methods of drug concealment. For example, when heroin is transported into Connecticut from New York City by car it may be hidden in specially developed hydraulic compartments or "traps" in the vehicle's engine or body.

The drug often arrives in Hartford in bulk form and is "cut" locally with adulterants like powdered milk or even PCP to enhance dealer profit.

Once the drug is cut, it is packaged into small plastic bags for street sale for $5–$10 a bag (varying by time and place). As a result of cutting, the heroin people consume is a quite different "thing" than the heroin produced at the point of origin. At times, the actual heroin content in a bag may be quite low, at other times, it can be so high as to cause overdoses.

All of the equipment needed to complete these tasks (e.g., a scale, a sealer machine, etc.) are lightweight and highly portable. In November of 2003, for example, when Hartford police raided a heroin factory in a residential apartment on the south end of the city, they found 387 grams of heroin (with a street value of $150,000), seven grams of crack ($174,000), a heat sealer to secure the plastic bags, two stamps to press the drug-dealing group's logo into the bags, packaging materials, cutting agents, and a hand-operated grinder. Frequently, leading members of street gangs, individuals with sufficient stature and resources and contacts in the drug selling world, purchase drugs from the middlemen in New York and hire members of their gang or less formally organized crew of friends to pick up the drugs and transport them back to Hartford. From the heroin users' perspective, it is a seller's market; addicted buyers have few options.

Consumption and the High-Country Blues

In his 1974 novel, *The Milagro Beanfield War*, which was made into a movie directed by Robert Redford, activist/author John Nichols tells the tale of the dirt-poor New Mexico town of Milagro, population 426, and the fight of town residents, a colorful collection of memorable characters, against powerful big business interests that divert water from their community. The citizens of Milagro are Hispano or Norteño, people who trace their ancestry to the early Spanish settlers of the Southwest. Their language is enlivened by archaisms that date back to the original settlers from Spain. While the book is fiction, it effectively captures the lives and social struggles of the salt of the earth inhabitants of the picturesque Española Valley, a place known to many through the remarkable landscape paintings of Georgia O'Keefe.

Since the appearance of Nichols' much admired book, the people in some of the tight-knit communities of Española Valley have been engaged in another struggle against a different powerful foe. As Angela Garcia (2006), a New Mexican resident and graduate student in anthropology at Harvard reports, since the mid-1990s, the Valley has had the highest per capita rate of heroin addiction in the country, even higher than New York, Baltimore, and Chicago, and a rate of heroin-related mortality that is over four times the national average. From 1995 to 1998, there were 85 reported heroin-related deaths in the Valley. In 2003, there were 41, a striking number in a location with a population of only 20,000 people.

Heroin came to the Valley by way of various sources, including residents who left the town to work in the big city, where they became addicted prior to their return home. Another source was Vietnam War veterans who brought their addictions home from the battlefields of Southeast Asia. Until the 1990s, however, drug use was not very visible in the Valley; it was hidden behind community doors and shielded by family secrets. Then things suddenly changed:

> "Before, everything was in private," says Silviano Maestas, a 52-year-old Valley resident and recovering addict. "It was a small group of guys, not bothering anyone. Pero things changed, no?" Suddenly, Silviano says, heroin use was "al aire libre," out in the open. "People didn't care no more who saw them, or what they did to get it." Strung-out addicts wandered the streets, often hitching rides to meet their dealers. Hypodermic needles turned up everywhere, even in the holiest places: in churchyards and cemeteries, and in the acequias, or irrigation ditches. The emergency room at the Española Hospital became a dumping ground for overdose victims—many of them abandoned by companions who feared arrest. Month by month, the death toll mounted. (Garcia 2006)

The skyrocketing rates of heroin use in the Valley finally became a national news story in the fall of 1999, when 150 police and other law enforcement agents raided the seemingly quaint village of Chimayó, home of the famous El Santuario de Chimayó Church (where pilgrims come to get "healing soil" from a hole in the church floor), and arrested 31 suspected drug dealers as part of a broader interstate effort known as "Operation Tar Pit." The crackdown was named for the unusually pure brand of black tar heroin arriving from Mexico that was contributing to the high number of overdoses among Valley residents.

A common theme of mass media reporting on drug abuse in places like Chimayó is bafflement about how heroin could have such damaging impact in a place of awe-inspiring natural beauty, implying thereby that in the popular imagination

> heroin belongs more to urban ghettos than historic villages of cottonwoods and adobe chapels, as if poverty and addiction cannot exist in a bucolic setting. Perhaps it is precisely because this landscape has been so powerfully represented by generations of American artists—who typically render the land as scenery without people—that visitors are blind to the possibility of such a contradiction. (Garcia 2006)

This is the issue that has guided Angela Garcia's doctoral research in the Valley. Since 2004, she has interviewed drug counselors, health care providers, religious leaders, land activists, and heroin addicts. Why heroin? Why here, she asks. The first answer that she hears from many people of different walks of life is the enormous disparities of wealth and access that characterize the region. Chimayó is a relatively short drive from Santa Fe, a place of expensive boutiques and pricey art galleries, a city made wealthier by high-income seasonal residents and cash-rich pleasure- and curio-hunting tourists. Garcia draws attention to this close-up encounter of rich and poor, noting the work of fellow anthropologist Philippe Bourgois (2003) and his studies of impoverished drug users living (in impoverished tenements and under bridges) amid the great wealth of cities like New York and San Francisco. Public policies in such places have favored urban gentrification and the needs of the wealthy while producing growing despair among the poor.

> In the Española Valley, the inequality is palpable. Many locals blame the Los Alamos National Laboratories for the region's deepening chasm between rich and poor. Since the 1940s, the Labs have demanded a local "nonprofessional" work force—maintenance and security crews, for example. Today, the Labs are the largest employer of Valley residents. During rush hour, the Old Los Alamos Highway, which connects Española with the "Atomic City," is bumper-to-bumper with frustrated commuters. Meanwhile, back at home, many of the old family farms lie untended. (Garcia 2006)

Los Alamos, whose population is 90 percent white, is the wealthiest county in the United States, with a median household income of over $90,000 and a poverty rate of under 3 percent. A study conducted by *American City Business Journals* (Thomas 2004) found that in terms of quality of life Los Alamos County, which is a half-hour drive from Sante Fe, topped the list as the best place to live in America. By contrast, Rio Arriba County, which encompasses much of the Española Valley, is one of New Mexico's poorest counties. One in five Valley residents lives below the federal poverty line.

Beyond the damaging effects of poverty, Garcia's research points to the importance of close, kin-base social networks. Addiction spreads along family lines, passing from one generation to the next. Reports one of Garcia's (2006) study participants, Marta, a 28-year-old addict awaiting sentencing for drug dealing, "Family is everything." It is an expression Garcia has heard many times since beginning her research in the Valley. Marta tells that her mother was also an addict and that she remembers well the

> terrible nights in her childhood, when her mother agonized in "las maleas"—the sharp, shooting pains in the limbs and the profuse sweating brought on by withdrawal. She would be all upset, crying, Marta says. "You're a kid, and you're scared they're gonna die. And, basically, you'll do anything to make them feel better," she says. "Sometimes, the only thing you feel like you can do is get them high." Marta knows what las maleas feel like. She began using heroin with a boyfriend when she was 16. . . . Within a year, Marta had developed a serious habit, and her mother started supplying her with drugs for the same reasons that Marta had supplied her mother with them. "Lo que pasa es . . ." Marta starts to explain, then

switches to English, as if to set the record straight: "The thing is, nobody wants to see their kid in pain." (Garcia 2006)

Beyond poverty and enmeshed family ties, Garcia found that an enormously important force pushing addiction in the Valley—the very issue addressed in Nichols' novel—is the steady separation of people from the land that has been their traditional source of livelihood, identity, and communality. She relays the case of Joseph, who was raised in a village named Hernandez made famous by an Ansel Adam's 1941 photograph entitled "Moonrise." Joseph never heard of the photograph, but he knows heroin well, and he knows the cemetery pictured in the photograph; it is a place he used to go to inject drugs.

> As in many Hispano families, he and his siblings were groomed for traditional agriculture. But they didn't see a financial future in it. "Little by little, we had to sell the land," he says. And as the family acres were slowly parceled off and sold, Joseph's heroin addiction worsened. (Garcia 2006)

Joseph was in the New Mexico State Prison in Santa Fe for burglary in 1998 when his family sold their Hernandez home for "next to nothing." When he was finally released from prison, the family home belonged to strangers. Now Joseph lives in a trailer park, lost, detached, and frustrated, feeling that as things are is not as they were intended to be.

In one clear sense he is right. The original Spanish settlements in the Valley were based on land grants from the Spanish throne. According to those grants, much of the land was held in common, owned by the community, and could not be sold by individual community residents. Shortly after the Mexican-American War, however, the U.S. government, working hand-in-glove with land speculators, invoked a process of "adjudication" that questioned and undermined the validity of many land grants in the state. The U.S. Supreme Court, in a colossal example of misplaced memory, found that there was no precedent for common land ownership in U.S. policies or British common law, a frequent source for judicial decision making. In fact, this form of land tenure was well-known to English common law, and throughout Medieval Europe, including Spain. Thus, the mistaken interpretation by the courts of common lands in New Mexico was not due to a historical absence of this form of land tenure in England or the United States.

As a result of such events, much of the land held by Hispanos was legally stolen and fell into the avaricious hands of developers, the U.S. Forest Service, or the Bureau of Land Management. Of course, the land that was "lost" is still there, including the land on which the now wealthy town of Los Alamos sits; "Every Hispano can see it" (Garcia 2006). In a somewhat cruel irony, local drug treatment advocates have suggested that it would be therapeutic to use participation in farming activities in the treatment of the Valley's numerous Hispano addicts. No one has considered the option of giving them back their land, however.

The theme of loss is not unique to the Hispano heroin addicts of New Mexico. It is a common one among long-term heroin users generally. Many feel they have traded away their self-esteem and anything else of value they ever had for drugs. Pondering this painful dilemma, however, only sets off a craving for drugs to self-medicate their distress.

Illicit and Licit Drug Mixing

Polydrug use and drug mixing have become dominant patterns in contemporary street drug consumption. According to the Substance Abuse and Mental Health Services Administration (2005), over half of all patients admitted for substance abuse treatment in publicly funded facilities in the year 2002 reported polydrug use, with younger users being more likely than older ones to report polydrug use patterns. Among polydrug users, alcohol was the most common substance reported (76 percent), marijuana was second (55 percent), followed by cocaine (48 percent), and opiates (27 percent).

At least five different patterns of drug mixing have been identified by ethnographers: (1) direct mixing of two or more drugs for simultaneous consumption, such as the use of what is commonly known on the street as a speedball, a mixture of heroin and cocaine; (2) simultaneous use in which two or more drugs are used at the same time and mixed in the body, such as drinking while snorting cocaine; (3) sequential use, such as the common pattern of smoking a cigarette after injecting heroin; (4) substitution, in which one available drug replaces a more desirable drug that is not available; and (5) binge mixing, in which various drugs are taken during the course of an extend "run" (staying "high" for two or three days at a time). As Earleywine and Newcomb (1997) point out, there have been few studies that compare these various drug mixing strategies and whether they, in fact, constitute distinct drug use patterns with differing health or other effects. Using a community sample, they found that the two most commonly simultaneously used drugs were marijuana and alcohol, followed by alcohol and cigarettes. Neither simultaneous nor concurrent use (i.e., sequential mixing) predicted drug-related symptoms, but simultaneous use did have more impact on users than concurrent use. Ethnographic research, involving direct observation of drug use in natural settings, reveals the complex nature of drug mixing as captured in the following accounts of street drug use.

Drug Mixing among Puerto Rican Crack Dealers in New York: In the mid-1980s, anthropologist Philippe Bourgois and his family were living in East Harlem preparing to carry out a study of inner-city poverty when the crack epidemic hit full force. Working in the immediate neighborhood where he was already living, Bourgois (2003) was able to develop relations with a number of young crack dealers and users, leading to his book, *In Search of Respect: Selling Crack in El Barrio*. As he hung out with dealers, Bourgois recorded multiple instances of routine drug mixing. This often involved mixing crack, heroin, and alcohol: "On cold nights after the Game Room [a crackhouse within an arcade] was closed, we would often take refuge in a housing project stairwell where Primo and Benzie would sniff speedballs [a mixture of heroin and cocaine] and we would drink malt liquor until well past daybreak" (Bourgois 2003:95). Drug mixing, including combining illegal and legal drugs during late-night makeshift social gatherings, in short, was routine among the people Bourgois studied. On many nights, they would open a small bag of heroin and another of cocaine, using a key or other tool to scoop up a small amount of white powder to hold to their noses, snorting and chatting about daily events, remembrances of days gone by, and jumbled plans to quit drug use and lead a different life, while passing around a 40-ounce bottle of malt liquor or rum.

Drug Mixing among Inter-City African American Heroin Addicts: The Heroin Lifestyle Study was carried out by a team of qualitative researchers in four major U.S. cities: Chicago, New York, Washington, D.C., and Philadelphia. In each city, former heroin addicts conducted open-ended interviews with African American men who injected heroin at least once a day and had never been in drug treatment. The men said they began using heroin for various reasons: curiosity, heightened status among peers, strong peer pressure, and media sensationalism. Most of the men in the study "remember[ed] their second shot of heroin as the beginning of a long descent from the peak experience of their first injection" and "a futile attempt to recapture the first experience—in short, the beginning of a never ending search for the perfect high" (Beschner and Bovelle 1985:87). Before long, the men were not using just heroin, but an assortment of other drugs in the course of a typical day including "alcohol, both hard liquor and wine, . . . [and] marijuana" (Walters 1985:32). One of the participants, Ron from Chicago, described his morning to an interviewer saying:

> Woke up and smoked a joint. Went into the bathroom where I have my works [injection paraphernalia] laid out. Had my little ol' shot of heroin. . . . Got me a glass of wine and hit the streets. I was feeling pretty good.

Another participant, Jim from Chicago, reported

> I went back and bought myself a bag of reefer [marijuana]—this was about eight o'clock now. Smoked some and came back in the street and messed around with the fellows. Drank some wine and went in and partied for an hour [injected heroin]. That was about eleven o'clock. (Walters 1985:32)

This kind of legal/illegal simultaneous and sequential drug mixing appeared to be the norm among study participants.

Drug Mixing among Street Drug Users in Hartford: The Drug Monitoring Study was carried out by the Hispanic Health Council in three waves of data collection between 2003 and 2006, using a mixed method of survey interviews and open-ended qualitative interviews with not-in-treatment drug users recruited through street outreach (Singer et al. 2006b). Participants ranged in age between 18 and 60 years, and included both men and women who were African American or Latino. Approximately 40 percent were homeless and 60 percent reported no employment. Of the 241 participants in the third wave of data collection, about 58 percent reported current use of crack cocaine, 57 percent reported powder cocaine use, 58 percent reported marijuana use, and 33 percent reported heroin injection, among a range of other illicit or illicitly acquired pharmaceutical drugs, including sedatives, painkillers, and methamphetamine.

Additionally, three-quarters of the participants reported that they currently drink alcoholic beverages. The majority of participants who drink reported that they use alcohol to "take the edge off" or to "come down" from the effects of other drugs. As one participant, a 52–year-old African American woman, commented: "Cuz the high, yeah it cuts the edge off of it too, but it makes you feel better, yeah it makes it better, it does" (quoted in Singer et al. 2006c:505). A motivation for drinking in this sample of drug users, in other words, was to modulate the experience of being under the influence of other drugs.

Cocaine, participants reported, is the drug most likely to be mixed with drinking, followed by marijuana and heroin. One participant, a 37–year-old African American man, explained, "When you smoking crack it [alcohol] calms you down. You know what I'm sayin', it will calm you down so it's like two combined together just like mellow it out" (quoted in Singer et al. 2006c:204). Participants also mentioned using alcohol to get to sleep after a several-days "cocaine binge" or to help them stay calm when using cocaine. At the same time, participants explained that cocaine use allowed them to continue drinking and stay awake for a longer period. Another purpose of drinking, according to people interviewed in the study, is as a "backup high" when other drugs are not available (72 percent) or are unaffordable (70 percent). As one participant, the 52-year-old African American woman quoted above, explained, if drugs are not readily available she drinks instead, more so than she would have if she had not really wanted drugs: "I would drink more . . . I would drink more. . . . Cuz, it's worth more, but I don't need it as much. I was with the liquor when I don't have no crack. I got to get me where I want to go" (quoted in Singer et al. 2006c:205).

Mixing Pharmaceuticals and Street Drugs: The nonmedical use of prescription drugs has become widespread, with painkillers being the most commonly diverted class of pharmaceutical drugs. Painkillers come in many brands, with Vicodin, OxyContin, Percocet, Demerol, and Darvon among the most common to find their way into nonmedical use. Their appeal, in addition to deadening pain, is that in sufficient dosage they can also produce euphoric effects. While most focus has been on diversion to the suburbs and to white users, it has become clear that there is considerable movement of pharmaceutical drugs to inner-city street drug sellers and users.

The Hartford Drug Monitoring Study also looked at the diversion of pharmaceutical drugs to the inner city and the mixing of them with other drugs. The study found that diversion occurs when people fake medical conditions that are treated with pain medication, steal and forge prescriptions, steal medicines from hospitals or pharmacies, visit multiple doctors and present the same health problem, collaborate with "pill pushers" (doctors who are willing to dispense large quantities of pharmaceutical drugs for a profit), or purchase unused pills from someone with a legal prescription. During the study, researchers identified a local street site in and around a fast-food restaurant as a place where illicit pill sellers and buyers meet to do business, and business, it was observed, was often brisk. Several nearby bars also were reported as sites where pharmaceutical drugs are sold. One individual who purchased pills at this site reported:

> I was startin' to get heavy into Xanax. I was shootin' up. Plus I was takin' aspirin bottles, emptyin' them out, puttin' water and Xanax, and dope, and sniffin' it while I'm drivin'. I was really bad. I mean I'm bad now but I'm talkin' . . . you know where I was, I didn't even have my right mind with the Xanax.

One of the contexts in which drug mixing occurs among the poor involves blending methadone and other drugs. Although methadone substitution is one of the most available forms of treatment available to low-income drug users, it is also a way of controlling the poor, keeping them on drugs rather than providing them with drug-free residential therapy of the sort wealthier drug users can access. Many opiate users feel, however, that methadone has helped them stabilize and reclaim their lives. Nonetheless, methadone clinics must contend with a common pattern of mixing tranquilizers with methadone. The Drug Monitoring Study found that of the individuals interviewed in the third wave of data collection, 43 had at some point been on methadone. Of these, 54 percent reported mixing methadone and tranquilizers. Additionally 49 percent reported having mixed methadone with other opiates such as heroin or OxyContin.

Street observation through the Drug Monitoring Study also identified various ways in which the material culture of drug use is mixed across types of drugs. Nip bottles, plastic versions of the small, one-per-drink, liquor bottles served on airplanes, are converted by drug users into crack pipes by inserting a straw through a hole drilled through the plastic; a perforated piece of aluminum foil is placed across the top of the bottle to hold the crack, which is heated from above with a lighter. The concave bottoms of beer cans are used as cookers to mix drug powder with water. Also, cigars are hollowed out and filled with cocaine, PCP, marijuana, or other drugs. Tobacco pipes serve as marijuana pipes, just as cigarette wrapping paper is used to prepare marijuana joints. Cigarettes are dipped in PCP fluid and smoked. While these examples reflect the tendency of drug users to "make do" and use items that are handy to facilitate drug use, they also reflect the fact that the items mentioned above are "on hand" because they are also being consumed by street drug users.

As these several accounts suggest, in the context of consumption among the poor, issues of legality and illegality vanish; licit and illicit drugs are routinely mixed in various ways and with several different motivations. What is important among low-income consumers is not the legal status of a drug, but rather its availability and contribution, in conjunction with other drugs, to medicating the overt and hidden emotional injuries of life, including those rooted in class, ethnic, or other oppression.

Modulating Moods

The Self-Medication Hypothesis and the Drugs of Solace

In 1985, Edward John Khantzian, MD, of Harvard University published an article on self-medication and drug use in the *American Journal of Psychiatry*. For this contribution, Khantzian has been called the Father of the Self-Medication Hypothesis. Khantzian's perspective on drug use developed out of three decades of clinical work with patients as well as a series of studies he conducted. In working with addicted patients, Khantzian noticed that they often had histories of difficulties with aggression, including problems of rage and depression that had long preceded their involvement with drugs. He also found that many of them reported that use of heroin gave them relief from dysphoric feelings of restlessness, anger, and rage.

In addition to various articles on self-medication, Khantzian wrote the book *Treating Addiction as a Human Process* (1999) to address the clinical implications of his hypothesis. At the root of habitual use of drugs Khantzian (1989, 1990, 1991) argues are two key factors: human suffering and problems with self-regulation. The primary urge driving the continued use of drugs, he asserts, is not a search for euphoria or even simple pleasure but rather seeking relief from the burden of personal suffering. It is for this reason that Spanish-speaking drug users refer to drugs as *la cura* (the cure). Whatever the longer-term problems drugs cause, in the short-term they allow users to regulate their lives by helping them cope with an otherwise overwhelming emotional burden.

What is the nature of suffering among the poor that makes drugs seem appealing? A large piece of the answer has been provided by William Dressler, a medical anthropologist involved in the study of the impact of perceived disparities on the experience of stress. One type of stress that he has found to be common among the poor is caused by the experience of relative deprivation associated with frustrated consumer aspiration; in other words, people are stressed by valuing and wanting things they cannot have. Dressler has found that in many communities there tends to be a widely shared understanding of what is the acceptable standard of living, which commonly, as it turns out, is what would be described in the United States as middle class (Dressler 1999). As one of the African American drug users interviewed in the Heroin Lifestyle Study expressed it:

> There was a time in my life when I wasn't using any drugs, when I tried to have the middle-class American dream. . . . I had those dreams too. . . . But that's all it has been is dreams and visions because you can never reach the type of success that they [white people] can. (quoted in Beschner and Brower 1985:20)

In one study, Dressler looked at what African Americans living in a small southern city considered important in defining a successful life. He found that owning a home and a car, having central heating or air conditioning, a telephone and a television, a VCR and cable TV, a microwave oven, and a washer and dryer were considered to be critical markers of success. Dressler coined the phrase *cultural consonance in lifestyle* to label the degree to which an individual had succeeded in achieving the cultural model of success for his/her community. He then compared this measure against health and found that individuals who fail to achieve their cultural ideal of success report higher levels of perceived stress and suffer greater levels of adverse health outcomes, such as elevated blood pressure. Individuals who felt they had achieved their cultural ideal of success had a 20 percent lower risk of hypertension than those who failed to achieve their ideal.

In a classic work in sociology, Robert Merton (1968) referred to this kind of situation as "double defeat" because not only do individuals feel they have not succeeded, but in addition, because of the American cultural expectation that individual effort will lead to upward social mobility, they tend to blame themselves for their failure. In fact, there are greater structural barriers to upward social mobility out of poverty in the U.S. compared to other developed nations like France, Germany, Sweden, and the Netherlands. As Alesina et al. (2001:39) note, in the U.S. "the political system is geared towards preventing redistribution." In other words, structurally imposed social inequality produces not only poverty but also the experience of personal failure, which, in turn, leads to self-reported higher levels of perceived stress as well as greater frequency of hypertension.

It is in this context that Cameron and Jones (1985) coined the term "drugs of solace." The poor use drugs like alcohol, tobacco, heroin, and cocaine because they provide solace, even if for a short time, from the daily social stress of perceived personal failure and associated feelings of damaged self-worth. Ironically, because drug use is stigmatized, and heavy users commonly are perceived not only as social deviants but also as the very embodiment of deviancy in our society, the solace drugs bring comes with a significant price. As a result, life for a drug user often is a vicious cycle of perceived stress followed by self-medicating drug consumption and resulting social stigmatization and sense of damaged self-esteem (which triggers the desire, again, for solace from drugs). Moreover, because of the damaging effects of drug use (e.g., liver damage, HIV infection, cancer) this behavior, in turn, contributes to health disparities. Whatever harm wrought by legal and illegal drug use, including the significant amount of suffering they cause, at the moment of desire and use, drugs "work"; they provide what drug users are after—temporary escape from their prison of personal misery. The hard truth always comes back to haunt, but then there are always more drugs seeking those in need of being "fixed."

One research method that has been used to look closely at the feelings and experiences of drug users is diary keeping. In this approach, study participants are asked to keep a daily diary of their drug use and associated emotions, settings, and behaviors. As part of a study of contextual factors in risk, the Hispanic Health Council recruited a sample of not-in-treatment street drug users and asked them to record this information in a blank diary provided by the project (Stopka et al. 2004). Although some participants used the diary to discuss feelings unrelated to drug use, several documented how their emotional state may have influenced their drug use and vice-versa. One participant, whose diary frequently contained statements about feelings of guilt and depression, at times alluded to the need to inject in order to diminish such negative sentiments:

> 10:00 AM [in bus station]. Sat down next to a kid that just got out of jail and told him that I have been here for two days. I asked him for four dollars and he gave it to me. Feel bad at having to take money from good people so I can get high. What life I'm living. . . . I hope I don't get arrested for doing this [hustling]. Don't feel like I fit out here in this life. Feeling sad and mad about myself. Want to cry. Want my mother to hold me and take the pain away. This is wrong. Need to get high.

An example from another participant's diary expresses similar sentiments: "I stole $20.00 out of my mom's pocket book which I feel like shit about. I just wanted to be numb. I hate myself sometimes." As these examples suggest, numbing emotional pain with drugs is a frequent pattern among drug users.

From Stress to Trauma

Beyond stress, the poor are subject to various other emotional burdens, including trauma. Low-income individuals are routinely subjected to various kinds of traumatic experiences, but exposure to violence is one of the most frequent sources. Violence, in turn, comes in various forms, from witnessing street violence, to having a friend or loved one be the victim of violence, to being directly victimized. Intimate partner violence (IPV) has attracted growing attention from researchers because of its frequent association with posttraumatic stress and victim self-medication with drugs.

El-Bassel and coworkers (El-Bassel et al. 2005; Gilbert et al. 2000), for example, have found that women in drug treatment who have suffered domestic violence are more likely to have used crack cocaine in the past 30 days than their nonabused counterparts. These researchers found that IPV increases the likelihood of subsequent frequent drug use, a finding that "underscore how women may react to the negative sequelae of IPV by self-medicating with drugs" (El-Bassel et al. 2005:469). Similarly, Mardge Cohen and her colleagues (2000) report that exposure to domestic violence (lifetime or recent) is significantly associated with a history of drug use. The association between IPV and alcohol and other drug abuse by the domestic partner also has been well established (Amaro et al. 1990; Cunradi et al. 2002; Duke et al. 2006).

The self-medication model asserts that drug use relieves posttraumatic stress symptoms (at least for awhile) and brings on sleep. As a result, symptoms like anxiety, irritability, and even depression can be temporarily suppressed. Drugs, in effect, become a coping mechanism, although before long, users realize they must also cope with drug dependence and addiction (Brinson and Treanor 1988; Boudewyns et al. 1991).

Snapshots of Self-Medication among Drug Users

The process of self-medication with drugs can be seen in the words and deeds of frequent drug users, such a Marco. Marco lives in Tijuana on the Mexican side of the porous border between Mexico and the United States. When he needs to shoot up drugs, Marco often finds a place to crouch down in the shadow of the fence that marks the borderline. Without looking around to see who might be watching, Marco, who is homeless, pulls out a noticeably battered syringe and tries to find a place on his badly damaged arms tattooed with open abscesses oozing dark liquid. He pushes the needle in and jams down firmly on the charger sending the liquefied contents of a $5 bag of methamphetamine into his craving body. Why does he shoot up methamphetamine? Says Marco, because the powerful synthetic drug—which is manufactured in great quantities in clandestine labs throughout the area—"neutralizes" the painful realities of the jagged life he leads on the streets of the border town, adding "I don't see my family any more because I feel worthless." Tears welling up in his eyes, he whispers, "Drugs help me to forget what I lost" (Corpus 2006).

Another, quite different, example of self-medication with drugs is seen in the case of Sally DeJesus, who, free of illicit drugs, but also off of her antidepressant medication, began to fall into depression until presented with her old cure for feeling miserable:

> After years of heavy cocaine use, she had been clean and sober for 11 months, and pregnant for nine, when she ran into one of her old crack dealers in a convenience store near Flat Rock, N.C. She was feeling lousy. Anxious to keep her system clean while her baby was growing inside her, the 28-year-old mother of two had months ago quit taking her anti-depressant medications; partly as a result, she says, she had been terribly depressed. "I'd hide in the bedroom crying," she says. "I wouldn't eat. I didn't shower for weeks at a time." To make matters worse, she and her husband had gotten into a bitter fight that morning. So when the dealer offered to take her for a ride and get her high, DeJesus said yes. "As soon as I did the first hit, I knew I'd screwed up," she says. "But when you're an addict, sometimes your judgment just goes right out the window." (Beiser 2000)

Piri Thomas, in his autobiographic classic *Down These Mean Streets,* described how drugs took away all of his problems, until drug addiction became the main force driving continued use. In recalling his initiation into injecting heroin, he explained:

> There is something about . . . heroin—it's a super-duper tranquilizer. All your troubles become a number of bleary blurred memories when you're in a nod of your own special dimension. And it was only when my messed-up system became a screaming want for the next fix did I really know just how short an escape from reality it really brought. (1967:200)

Diane, a Puerto Rican woman interviewed in the Hispanic Health Council's SAVA II study, an examination of drug use among inner-city women, provided the following account of her self-medication of trauma and depression:

> I was eleven years old when I got raped and finally I waited like a year to tell. Finally I left my house, I ran away. . . . When I was nine years old they took us away from my mother, but then . . . she got custody of us again. I . . . ran away and went back to the foster home and . . . told . . . what had happened to me. I had gotten raped by my stepfather, and I could no longer live there. Because I was having bad dreams and stuff. So finally, they took us away from my mother . . .
>
> They were going to help me press charges against him and what not. But then a month later he passed away when we was going to go to court. And then from there I went back home. I left to Puerto Rico. I was going to stay with my grandmother, move to Puerto Rico, with my two oldest sisters. So, I left my mother and my baby sister, I left my baby sister with my mother. My mother couldn't take care of my baby sister, 'cause my baby sister wouldn't listen to my mother and my mother used to drink. And my

mother got so heavy, that already she wasn't functioning, everything wasn't the same, her memory come and go and stuff like this. So she wasn't really taking care of my sister. My sister would just go with her friends and sometimes don't even come home. Finally, my mother put my sister in a foster home, you know until I came back. But when I came back and found out that my mother had put my sister in a foster home, I had came back, and at that point I had got pregnant, I had got pregnant with my oldest son's father. I had gotten an apartment, I was still too young. I was only fifteen going on sixteen, so I was still too young I had to wait a year . . . for them to give me my sister, so I left my sister in the foster home . . . I had my son, and me and his father we had joint custody. I went through a lot 'cause I was suffering. I needed help really, I needed psychiatric help. . . . I was suffering from depression you know and I never got help for it. . . . First I was sniffing [heroin] then I got into doing shooting up. . . . I had moved into a shelter in Wethersfield, from Wethersfield I started hanging around with people that was shooting and stuff. . . . The lady next door she was selling dope. At that time there was twenty-dollar bags. . . . I got into [it] heavy, that's when I really got into the heavy . . . dope. I started learning how to crack cocaine, I started smoking it. I lost my apartment, I went through a lot, you know. I started even selling myself, just to get the drugs, drug money for the cocaine, for my habit and stuff.

As these accounts suggest, drugs are used by the poor to medicate the immediate emotional and psychological effects of the punishing world in which they reside. The pressing motivation to use drugs is often the desire to find relief from the ultimate forces (sexual abuse, a chaotic family life, fear of street violence, etc.) that put poor people at high risk for personal suffering—and hence for the use of drugs to self-medicate. These "forces" tend to grow out of what has been referred to as *structural violence*—poverty, discrimination, lack of decent housing, being forced to live in dangerous environments, and related factors. As Farmer (1997:280) notes, "the world's poor are the chief victims of structural violence."

The Role of Drugs and the Structuring of Inequality

Drugs and Poverty

As Philippe Bourgois has argued:

The painful symptoms of inner-city apartheid will continue to produce record numbers of substance abusers, violent criminals, and emotionally disabled and angry youth if nothing is done to reverse the trends in the United States since the later 1960s around rising relative poverty rates and escalating ethnic and class segregation. (2003:325)

These conditions, which can be still found in inner cities from coast to coast will, as Bourgois suggests, continue to produce individuals like

Manny Torres. Manny was born to a poor, inner-city Latino family in the Bronx, joined a criminal gang as a teenager, was involved in a life of criminality, and became a heroin addict when his uncle showed him how to mainline (i.e., inject into a vein). He found heroin to be the "ultimate tranquilizer" capable of anesthetizing "the whole damn ugly world" (Rettig 1999:13). Soon Manny had become the very embodiment of every caustic stereotype about drug addicts. By the time he was 20 years old, he was "a dope fiend, all screwed up" and on his way to prison (Rettig 1999:65).

Many years later, however—after completely turning his life around—Manny reflected on his tumultuous life and came to understand the political-economic origin of the involvement of poor people with drugs. He wonders how he personally is to blame for the route his life took, since his life, in fact, reflects a far broader social pattern.

> Why did I turn out to be a dope fiend? . . . Most of the people in my neighborhood turned out to be dope fiends. . . . Who are the real criminals? Most of the people in my generation in the Bronx turned out so-called bad. . . . One way or another they were wasted. (Rettig 1999:183–184)

Responding to an assertion in Durkheimian theory that the social role of criminals is to set the boundaries of acceptable behavior for the rest of society, Manny argued:

> That's fine if you're [born] on the right side of the tracks. But what if you are locked into the streets and locked out of the jobs because of your background or your dope habit? Hell, man, its simple for me to see, because I've been there. The social order created the drug problem and anything that comes of heroin addiction is their [the broader society's] fault. Personal breakdowns are an aspect of social breakdowns. (Rettig 1999:175)

In his own way, Manny expressed one of the major arguments of this book, namely that drugs, including both legal and illegal varieties, and often these mixed together at the point of consumption, contribute to maintaining an unjust structure of social and economic relations. Analyses of the role of drugs in upper-class dominance over the labor power of workers as well as the minds and bodies of the working class and the poor point out "a variety of ways in which drugs have been employed to palliate, control, and exploit labor" (Courtwright 2001:135). Drugs have proven to be useful because the concern of the corporate class is twofold: first, using labor to produce profit at the lowest level of investment (in reproducing and maintaining the working class), and two, minimizing restlessness and rebellious resentment arising from the experience of exploitation and relative deprivation. These dynamics play out not only on the consumption side but on the production side of illicit drugs as well:

> Jamaican teenagers who weed ganja fields are sometimes paid in kind, and are not infrequently high when they chop and pull [i.e., harvest marijuana].

> Cannabis is a popular adjunct to agricultural labor throughout the lands of the ganja complex. In the Punjab consumption increases by half during the harvest season. Colombian peasants boast that cannabis helps to them to *quita el cansancio*, or reduce fatigue; increase their *fuerza* and *ánimo*, force and spirit, and become *incansable*, tireless. (Courtwright 2001:136)

Similarly, in Europe, historically, workers received part of their pay check in the form of alcohol, a practice that was carried over to the colonies and maintained until industrialization pushed cottage manufacturing from the center stage of commodity production. A common pattern was for drinking to begin with the alcohol offered as payment for work and continue through to the bottom of workingmen's paychecks, keeping them, week after week, on the labor treadmill.

At the same time and as a result of these patterns and practices: "Drug use has . . . historically operated as an impediment to upward mobility" (Courtwright 2001:138). As well, it has functioned to pacify the poor and working classes (never completely, but often sufficiently) by diverting energies from collective action to individual palliative consumption and self-medication with solace drugs. This is not to say that drugs always are made available to the poor with the conscious intention of keeping them in check; indeed, making a profit is the primary reason both legal and illegal drugs are made so readily available to the poor.

Whatever the intentions of those who insure there is no shortage of licit and illicit drugs in poor neighborhoods, including the corporate captains of the alcohol, tobacco, pharmaceutical, and illicit drug industries, mollifying the poor, most of the time, is an observable effect. As Bourgois (2003:319) points out, "Self-destructive addiction is . . . the medium for desperate people to internalize their frustration, resistance, and powerlessness." Along with a dominant social ideology of individualism and self-blame for failure, a heavy police presence, forced incarceration of many community members, and the provision of limited access to benefits and services, legal and illegal drug use palliates the challenges brought about by social and economic inequality. Despite a noticeably widening gap between the rich and the poor, as has occurred in the United States and elsewhere in recent decades, social inequality is sustained day-in/day-out, in part, through the drugging of the poor.

The Roles of Drug Users in the Socioeconomic System

The role drugs play in containing the poor reverberates throughout the socioeconomic system. In her book, *Street Addicts in the Political Economy*, for example, Alisse Waterston (1993) analyzes the place of street drug users in the social structure of American society. Many who have addressed this question before her have described drug users as extreme deviants, and hence not quite a part of society, its institutions, economic dealings, and political processes. This kind of taken-for-granted demonization of drug users dates to the passage of the first federal antidrug laws early in the 20th century. The ultimate social effect of antidrug legislation has been to label drug users and dealers as heinous criminals, the bogeymen of contemporary society. Inner-city illicit drug use and sales have come to be synonymous with lack of control, senseless violence, and moral decay. Drug addicts as a group—which historically has included noted writers, playwrights, statesmen, and even physicians—have lost all credibility and social standing and have become "pretty much worthless humans in the popular imagination" (Kane and Mason 2001:471). As Goode (1984:218) emphasizes, "by the 1920s the public image of the addict had become that of a criminal, a willful degenerate, a hedonistic thrill-seeker in need of imprisonment and stiff punishment." In fact, as Courtwright et al. (1989:3) remind us, "Some extremists in the 1920s and 1930s even proposed firing squads as a permanent solution for the drug problem, on the theory that the only abstinent addict was a dead one."

More recently, drug users and drug dealers are depicted as naive handmaidens of modern-day terrorism, as the social embodiment of nightmarish evil and unlimited harm, and as threats to but not members of society. In other words, drug users serve an important social function as objects of blame: they, not structures of inequality in employment, housing, education, and ownership, are responsible for the social ills that plague everyday life. In Michael Agar's apt phasing:

> Drugs are great for what I call chemical scapegoating. The anthropologist Levi-Strauss once described totemism by saying 'animals are good to think with' [i.e., they provide readily available symbols to use in organizing conception]. Drugs, on the other hand, are good to *blame* with. (2006:20)

In opposition to commonplace perspectives, Waterston contends that drug users are not *in any sense* separate from society—except in the concerted effort to portray them so. Rather, she effectively argues, they play an important system-maintaining role at the bottom of the social ladder as an exploitable pariah subcaste of low-cost, drug-dependent workers. Although most street drug users do not sustain steady full-time employment, they do acquire temporary and part-time blue-collar jobs of diverse sorts, such as lawn care, construction and repair, street clean-up, and snow removal. Most of jobs they perform fall within the largely unregulated, underpaid, and usually somewhat hidden—and as a result highly exploitative—sectors of the informal economy. Sociologists of work long have recognized that the presence of a sector of semi-employed workers at the bottom of the labor pool is an effective means of lowering salaries in the general working class. This especially desperate set of workers who are resigned to accept socially marginal, low-status (yet often high-risk) jobs at minimum (or even subminimum) wages, and few if any employment benefits, serves to competitively pull down the pay scale for all other groups of workers up the ladder of blue and even white collar labor. Asserts Waterston:

> As a special category, addicts are politically weak and disconnected from organized labor, thereby becoming a source of cheap, easily expendable labor. Moreover, the costs of daily reproduction are absorbed by addict-workers themselves. The conditions of their reproduction are quite poor and occur at barely minimal levels. (1993:241)

Lower labor costs translate into higher profits. Moreover, when workers from the bottom of the labor pool are no longer needed, they can be easily cast off without fear of legal or labor action. Furthermore, because they are drug addicts, and as a result perhaps guilty of other crimes as well, they can be carted off to prisons where, even if they get out of hand, their behavior rarely threatens the wider society. In 1980, for example, 19 out of every 1,000 people arrested for a drug-related violation served time in prison; 12 years later this figure had increased by more than 500 percent to 104 incarcerations per 1,000 drug arrests. During this period, drug arrests accounted for approximately three quarters of the total increase in the number of federal prisoners. Importantly, drug possession is twice as likely as involvement in drug sales or manufacture to be the reason for a drug-related arrest (Chambliss 1994). The cost of incarceration is $20,000 per person, per year, producing an annual bill of $8 billion for the prolonged warehousing of drug offenders.

This system of warehousing portions of surplus labor in publicly funded prisons, Waterston (1993) stresses, has real benefits for capitalism: unneeded labor does not become an economic liability, as taxpayers pick up the tab for people in prison. Furthermore, imprisonment need not block corporate access to very low-cost labor, as many prison-based industries are linked directly or indirectly to private corporations (Chien et al. 2000; Singer 2004a).

Social Disparity, Health Inequality, and Drugs

Social disparity between wealthier and poorer sectors of the society has several dimensions that affect health. Educational attainment is an important health-related variable because people with higher educational achievement tend to be healthier than those with lower levels of education (Pappas et al. 1993). Education has both direct and indirect effects on health outcomes. For example, a direct effect is that education increases an individual's ability to access health information, while an indirect effect is seen in the fact that education is associated with an individual's standard of living and working conditions.

Income is another social indicator that has a close relationship to health status. Low income can contribute directly to poor health by lowering access to health care and indirectly as a determinant of living conditions and residential location. Poor health, in turn, can affect capacity to work and thus level of income. At the same time, poverty has, as noted, been found to be a strong predictor of and risk factor for poor health, disease, and drug use.

Although health disparities are strongly influenced by poverty, even among the poor there are notable differences in health. Poor health has been found to be especially high among poor people who live in areas with a high percentage of impoverished individuals and families in the local population. Thus, poor people in cities with smaller impoverished populations are at lower risk of dying than those in cities with large, highly concentrated impoverished populations (Budrys 2003), as is common in many American inner-city areas. Areas of concentrated poverty tend to have "poorer services, more crime, and more civil disruption" (Marmot and Bell 2006:37). Furthermore, studies of health status among the poor by location show that the *sociophysical environment* in which people live—that is, their lived experience of their surrounding community, including their awareness of threat, danger, stress, discomfort, and alienation from their local social environment—is a critical determinant of their health status. Feelings of hopelessness and powerlessness in a community have been found to be good predictors of health risk and health status, and, as well, the appeal of psychotropic drugs.

Aside from individual and structural factors, it is likely that cultural and linguistic factors also play a role in health care disparities. For example, while white families (enrolled in Title V special needs children's programs) report their primary unmet care needs are for day care, respite care, recreational programs, and home health aids, among their Latino counterparts the primary perceived needs have been found to be unresolved health care problems, rehabilitation therapy, health information, and support group access (Gannotti et al. 2004). Additionally, Latino families express different expectations of health care providers than do white families, increasing the opportunity for breakdowns in communication with physicians and other providers. Consequently, appropriate health care increasingly is being defined as care that includes attention to issues of *cultural safety*. This concept, developed in New Zealand, refers to the central acknowledgement by providers of the validity and fundamental importance of cultural values in the provision of effective health care (Ramsden 1990).

While various factors, such as exposure to environmental toxins, high levels of stress, lack of health insurance, exposure to street violence, and high rates of low birth weight and poor maternal diet (which produce life-long health deficits), contribute to greater levels of disease and premature death among the poor than among the wealthy, a significant contribution is added by drug use.

Cigarette smoking, for example, is strongly associated with risk of disease and death especially among lower-income men. Overall, the prevalence of various drug use-related diseases, including AIDS, heart disease, and stroke, reflect income disparities (Smith et al. 1996). Similarly, with reference to ethnicity, although, across all age levels whites have higher rates of alcohol use than African Americans, the negative consequences of alcohol abuse, including alcohol-related death, are more prevalent among African Americans. Among Latinos, the rate for alcohol-related cirrhosis of the liver is double the rate for non-Latino whites (National Center for Health Statistics 2003). Alcohol and tobacco threaten minorities disproportionately as a result of their role in cancer, cardiovascular diseases, stroke, and tuberculosis. Low-income ethnic minority populations suffer higher levels of adverse health effects from drug abuse, especially from illicit drugs, than the white population. Latinos, especially Puerto Ricans and Mexican Americans, for example, suffer the highest level of injection drug-related HIV/AIDS infection (Singer 1999).

In short, not only do the tobacco, alcohol, pharmaceutical, and illicit drug industries help to sustain social inequality and socioeconomic disadvantage, they also contribute significantly to health inequality. These factors are linked in two other ways as well: (1) poorer health is a barrier to upward social mobility, and (2) exposure to alcohol, tobacco, and other drugs in utero can have a life-long impact on individual health and capacity. When we add in the fact that the poor, especially low-income African Americans, Latinos, and Native Americans, are much more likely to be arrested for drug-related charges and to serve time behind bars for such offenses and that having a prison record is a barrier to improved socioeconomic status, *it becomes clear how a set of closely connected factors not only sustains social inequality but insures its reproduction across generations.*

By examining (1) the diverse parallels and direct connections between the tobacco, alcohol, pharmaceutical, and illicit drug industries as variously intertwined expressions of global capitalism and (2) the tendency of the poor and oppressed to use and mix the commodities produced, widely distributed, and heavily promoted by these industries to self-medicate the psychological and emotional injuries of inequality, (3) it becomes clear how multibillion dollar corporations and their exceedingly wealthy executive decision makers play a profound role in shaping the lives of the poor and the social and health conditions they endure.

CHAPTER 8

The People's War on Drugs

> Without war there can be no peace.
>
> —Congolese proverb

Reflections on Resilience

There is growing realization among social scientists, service providers, policy makers, and community members that low-income neighbors, including those living in many ethnic minority neighborhoods of major urban centers, are described much more often in terms of their problems rather than their strengths, their suffering and not their capabilities, their risks but rarely their resiliencies. While, as emphasized in chapter 7, there certainly are casualties in poor neighborhoods, including many individuals who fall victim to alcohol dependence, tobacco-induced diseases, and drug abuse and addiction, the so-called "slums" are home communities for millions of people who avoid such threats and lead productive, triumphant, and healthy lives. When we focus only on the multiple structural risk factors faced by these individuals (e.g., poverty, ethnic discrimination, hostile and threatening environments, lack of education, linguistic and cultural differences from the dominant population, conflict between school and home), we tend not to predict that many of them are as successful as they are.

Missing from a narrow risk-assessment approach, therefore, is a consideration of protective dynamics, including individual, family, and cultural factors (Aronson 2001), as well as the potential to be resilient. *Resilience*, which is defined as the capacity for and process of successful adaptation despite challenging circumstances (Todis et al. 2001), has come to be understood as including a range of components and characteristics, such as optimism, strong capacity for skill acquisition, having an internal locus of control and sense of personal agency, ability to plan for needs, facility at alternative thinking, and intergenerational support and the transmission of cultural heritage (McCubbin et al. 1998). In addition, individuals who demonstrate a high level of resilience commonly report life-course turning points and other significant life-changing experiences. Characteristics of resilient individuals include the ability to "bounce back" in response to setbacks; maintaining a "where there is a will there is a way" attitude; approaching problems as challenges, not barriers; and seeking windows of opportunity (see Glittenberg 2007).

Eddie Perez, the mayor of Hartford, Connecticut, exemplifies what has come to be recognized as a common resilience pattern. Born to an impoverished, female-headed, Puerto Rican family (seven brothers, one sister) that moved from the island to inner-city Hartford when he was 12, Perez became a member of the Ghetto Brothers street gang as a teenager. Because of his involvement with a community program, he went on to get an associate degree from a community college and, through V.I.S.T.A., to become a community organizer and activist, an experience that led him to eventually be elected the first Puerto Rican Mayor of Hartford. Trying to understand and learn from the resilience of such individuals has become a topic of considerable interest in the social and behavioral sciences.

The resilience and personal achievements of outstanding individuals, of course, does not change the fact that in a context of injustice—where a few have wealth beyond imagination, many others struggle to stay one pay check ahead of impoverization, and a large number of people lose that contest and fall into short-term or enduring poverty—health and well-being are not equitably distributed. Moreover, under such circumstances the health and health problems of one social class are intimately tied to those of other social classes (e.g., selling drugs to the poor provides wealth that can be used to protect the health of the rich).

The human costs of social disparity are significant and painful. However, at the community level, a focus on problems only tells part of the story. The full story must include accounts of how people acting in concert respond to discrimination, mistreatment, and structural violence. History has shown, time and again, that diverse social groups facing threatening conditions do not accept mistreatment, exploitation, and structural violence forever. They fight back! Calling on seemingly hidden and often unexpected reserves of energy and indignation, they form social movements and they resist the oppressive actions of those who certainly are wealthier and, initially at least, much more powerful. Included in this pattern of resistance is what might be called the emergent "People's War on Drugs."

An Alternative War on Drugs

The term "War on Drugs" can be traced to 1971 and the Nixon administration, which referred to the campaign as an "all-out offensive" against illicit, mind-altering substances. It is a "war" that has been waged by every presidential administration since then, and by many other countries besides the United States as well. This official War on Drugs is fought by the army and navy, the FBI, the coast guard, the border patrol, the DEA, the Bureau of Alcohol, Tobacco, and Firearms, and many other military, law enforcement, and criminal justice bodies against illegal drug companies, their allies, and their customers. For the most part, the war has been a failure: over 30 years of fighting and there is little to show. Billions upon billions of dollars have been spent waging this war, tens of thousands of mostly poor and working people have been arrested and put in prison, some have been killed, and enough drugs have been seized to keep the whole nation high for years and years. Nonetheless, illicit drugs on the street are evermore plentiful and cheaper. Moreover, pharmaceutical drug abuse is increasingly widespread, with huge quantities of psychoactive laboratory drugs being diverted from medical uses and added to the bountiful illicit supply of street drugs. Add to this bulging warehouse of mind altering substances vast quantities of alcohol and tobacco and the full scope of the drugging of the poor becomes disturbingly clear.

Because the official War on Drugs has failed—not only as reflected in its inability to stop the flow and use of illicit drugs, but also in its failure to ever consider alcohol and tobacco, the substances that by far take the biggest toll on human life, as items of concern or interest—people increasingly are fighting their own war against the drugs that plague their communities, including both licit and illicit substances.

Some of this resistance already has been described, such as the community demand for an end to "gangsta-oriented" malt liquor advertising in African American neighborhoods in Portland. This is not an isolated incident. The marketing of alcohol products in African American, Hispanic, and other low-income communities increasingly is generating national controversy and meeting a mounting degree of community opposition. Aggressive alcohol promotion has sparked protest demonstrations, the spray paint defacement of alcohol advertisement billboards, letter writing campaigns, visits to corporate offices, and demands for legislative action in communities across the country (Jernigan and Wright 1994). Malt liquor advertising, in particular, has generated outcry, leading to fines levied against the makers of St. Ides Malt Liquor for advertising practices that target youth and glamorize gang activity (Gallegos 1999).

Not Bowing Down to the PowerMaster

An exemplary community "fight-back" against a malt liquor manufacturer targeting an ethnic minority population began in June 1991 when the G. Heileman Brewery announced the release of a new brand called PowerMaster in Chicago. Offended by the crass attempt to prompt drinking in their community, two African American clergymen, Reverend George Clements and Father Michael Pfleger of St. Sabina Church, traveled to the manufacturer's headquarters in La Crosse, Wisconsin, intent on meeting company heads to express their concerns about the advertising campaign being launched for the high voltage beverage. In La Crosse, Heileman representatives told Clements and Pfleger that they were sorry but the company president, Thomas Rattigan, was away on business and no one else was available to meet with them. Rather than meekly accepting this corporate rebuke, the clergymen, in an act of civil disobedience, refused to leave and were subsequently arrested for trespassing. That the clergymen had traveled to Wisconsin to inform Heileman that the company was trespassing on the African American community of Chicago was of little interest to the arresting officers. As noted, a significant benefit of legality is the ability to call on the state and its capacity to exercise force to protect corporate interests. Clements and Pfleger ultimately were released on an $85 signature bond and firmly instructed by a Wisconsin judge to cease further protest or face longer-term imprisonment. They also were informed that they would have to return to La Crosse to face trespassing charges. Unbowed, the clergymen announced that their intention was return to the brewery to continue fighting against PowerMaster.

Once back in Chicago, the clergymen and their growing network of supporters wrote a series of letters to the Federal Trade Commission voicing objections to the wording used to promote PowerMaster. In July, the Bureau of Alcohol, Tobacco and Firearms responded and sent word to Heileman that approval of PowerMaster was being revoked because the product's name violated the Federal Alcohol Administration Act of 1935, which banned the labeling or advertising of beer as being "strong, full strength, extra strength or high test," all words that could be construed as indicators of a product's alcohol potency. Father Pfleger declared victory:

> When we are spiritually strong, there's no problem we cannot overcome. We have a serious alcohol problem in the African American community, and this means that something worse won't be added to it. . . . Big business better watch out if it's doing something wrong. (quoted in National Association of African Americans for Positive Imagery 2004a)

While it is unlikely that Big Business was particularly concerned about Father Pfleger's declaration, the incident affirms that an aroused populace can push the state to provide some level of protection of its health and social interests.

Not Down with Uptown

Even before the struggle over PowerMaster, and providing a model for the Chicago effort, activists in the African American community of Philadelphia had taken on the R. J. Reynolds Tobacco Company in response to the launch of a new cigarette brand clearly targeted to African Americans. Called "Uptown," the new menthol cigarette was to be test marketed in 1989 followed by a splashy introduction during Black History Month the following year. Taking advantage of planned festivities during the month, R. J. Reynolds decided to give away the cigarettes at various events and to play up the new brand using billboards, mass transit and bus shelter advertising placards, point-of-purchase displays in stores, and advertisements placed in various African American–oriented newspapers and magazines.

As word of R. J. Reynolds' plans reached the community, a number of organizations, mindful of high cancer rates in the African American population, expressed intense objection. A number of these groups, including the National Association for the Advancement of Colored People, the Black Clergy of Philadelphia, the Philadelphia Chapter of the National Black Leadership Initiative on Cancer, as well as several other organizations, joined together to form the Coalition Against Uptown Cigarettes. This consortium launched a vigorous campaign in the community and in the media expressing its ire at R. J. Reynolds. Several nationally known African American leaders also voiced opposition to the tobacco manufacturer. Seeing the handwriting on the wall, in January 1990 R. J. Reynolds cancelled the marketing test and suspended the production of Uptown. Out of this and similar struggles, the National Association of African Americans for Positive Imagery (NAAAPI), an organization dedicated to helping end the excessive marketing of alcohol, tobacco, and other harmful products to communities of color, was born in 1991.

The [Auto]Biography of Menthol X

Four years after the Uptown struggle, NAAAPI, aided by Churches Organized to Stop Tobacco (COST), successfully blocked the introduction of another cigarette, called Menthol X, targeted to African Americans, from gaining a customer base, leading its manufacturer to pull the cigarette from the market. Distinguished by the large "X" on the cover of the package as well as on the cigarette itself, the relatively inexpensive brand seemed especially aimed at the African American youth and young adult market. Leaders of the coalition organized to fight back against the Menthol X marketing effort. They recognized the insensitive attempt to link the disease-causing product to Malcolm X and

> were outraged that tobacco manufacturers were willing to exploit the name of such an important leader in the African American community. However, it had been done before. A few years earlier in South Africa, "Mandela" cigarettes were being marketed towards young South Africans in the name of "freedom." (National Association of African Americans for Positive Imagery 2004b)

In response to the negative publicity generated by NAAAPI, the manufacturer of Menthol X cigarettes received complaints from all over the country. Withdrawal of the cigarette from the market affirmed that it was possible for community social movements to push back Big Tobacco by organizing effectively and generating sustained and mounting negative publicity.

Another lesson learned by grassroots efforts to wage a People's War on Drugs is that winning individual battles does not mean that the war has been won. Two years after the defeat of Menthol X, R. J. Reynolds was back with Camel Menthols, and again the African American community was the target consumer audience. NAAAPI once again launched its own campaign called "Say No to Menthol Joe Community Crusade." The cigarette soon disappeared from the market. In subsequent years, NAAAPI initiated several more grassroots efforts to stop new cigarette, cigar, and alcohol beverage brands marketed to the African American community and was able to both initiate and help fund several local fight-back efforts by community coalitions and groups. It also sued the tobacco industry for predatory target-marketing menthol brand cigarettes to African Americans. Although the suit never reached a jury, it further added to the negative publicity that NAAAPI has been able to focus on tobacco companies.

Not So Nice in Nicetown

A typical local struggle against legal drugs erupted in the Nicetown-Tioga section of Philadelphia in 2004. Residents of the area were dismayed to discover that yet another liquor outlet, called A Wine & Spirits Shoppe, was opening in their neighborhood. Church leaders, dental students, and local residents of the neighborhood decided to stop the liquor store from opening. According to Reverend Jesse Brown Jr., pastor of Good Shepherd Lutheran Church and president of NAAAPI, a liquor store "lowers the quality of life and it breeds disruptive behavior. . . . The state [which owned the store] has become a pariah in this neighborhood. . . . They don't love North Philadelphia. They don't care what they dump on us" (quoted in Khabir 2004). The Reverend Franklin Bowers of nearby Greater Ebenezer Church added, "We have plenty of liquor stores in that area, and all the drugs you could possibly need" (quoted in Taussig 2004).

At a community demonstration at the site, at which participants chanted, "One, two, three, four, we don't want a liquor store," community anxiety was expressed about the store's close location to several churches, a day care center, and Temple University's dental, medical, and pharmacy schools. Over 500 people signed a petition demanding that the store be closed. Said Brown, "It's a non-negotiable issue. . . . We're going to use all means necessary to stop this" (quoted in Khabir 2004). Because the struggle, in part, involved legal issues—whether a proper variance was granted to allow a liquor store to be erected so close to two churches—the conflict ended up in court. Additionally, in an effort to expand the cadre of activists working to fight back against Big Tobacco and Big Alcohol, NAAAPI launched the Youth Prevention Project Training Institute, a skills building, community organizing project intended to actively involve youth in the struggle against the legal drug industry's placement, promotion, pricing, and targeting of their products to African American and other minority communities.

Nuestra Cultura no se Vende

The spirit of fighting back against the legal drug industries has blossomed as well in the Latino community. One example, from California, is *Cinco de Mayo Con Orgullo* (With Pride), a project begun in 2001 by Latinos and Latinas for Health Justice. The project developed out of the group's earlier *Nuestra Cultura no se Vende* (Our Culture is Not for Sale) campaign. The goal of the project is to reclaim the historic Mexican festival from exploitation by beer and spirits manufacturers who have turned the day into an annual "El Drinko del Cinco" celebration of excessive alcohol consumption.

Cinco de Mayo commemorates the battle of Puebla of May 5, 1862, a clash in which the smaller Mexican army under General Ignacio Zaragoza defeated the French colonial invaders sent by Napoleon III. The day is not widely celebrated in Mexico and is mainly a Puebla state event. Mexican Independence Day, September 16, which is celebrated nationally in Mexico, has not fallen prey to drinking promotion efforts in the United States. During the 1960–1970s, with the rise of the Chicano political and cultural movement, activists from the community adopted Cinco de Mayo as a day of cultural pride and victory against oppressors. As the early activist phase of the Chicano movement passed, the holiday became institutionalized in Mexican American neighborhoods as a cultural holiday celebrated through traditional cultural forms, such as the ballet folklórico, mariachi music, and Mexican food.

As these celebrations developed popular appeal within and beyond Latino communities of the Southwest, the alcohol industry, looking for ways to break into the rapidly growing Latino market, stepped in and began sponsoring local celebrations with cash donations. Before long, the holiday had been thoroughly transformed into an unrestrained drinking party above all else and, as such, was promoted successfully by the industry to Mexican Americans and non-Mexican American alike nationwide. Soon May 5th was setting alcohol sales records. As a result, many people on both sides of the border condemned Cinco de Mayo as a North American commercial contrivance rather than an authentic Mexican holiday. The cultural damage was even greater. As James Gogek (2004) remarks, in Cinco de Mayo alcohol advertising,

> the blatant stereotyping and perversion of Mexican culture . . . is flatly disgusting. A tequila ad shows a blender making margaritas on top of a Mayan pyramid at Chichen Itza, which is akin to using the Western Wall in Jerusalem to sell liquor. A beer ad shows half-naked models wrapped in bandoleras and other symbols of the revolutionary struggle, which would be like inserting half-naked women into an illustration of the Declaration of Independence signing and using it to sell whiskey.

To counter the alcohol industry, Cinco de Mayo Con Orgullo has taken a two-pronged approach. On the one hand, the project organizes alcohol-free cultural Cinco de Mayo celebrations in cities throughout California, as well as in several other states; issues community proclamations explaining the actual historical events and genuine cultural significance of the holiday; and puts on a play for youth audiences that decries the alcohol industry's exploitation of Cinco de Mayo celebrations. On the other hand, the project organizes visits to retail outlets to urge them to respect the cultural integrity of the holiday by refusing to display signs and in-store promotions that use Cinco de Mayo to sell alcoholic beverages. According to Bill Gallegos (quoted in Gogek 2004), a Latino alcohol prevention advocate:

> For kids searching for a sense of identity to have one of their few acknowledged holidays hijacked by the alcohol industry, so that the overwhelming theme of your culture is not the fight against social injustice but partying and getting drunk . . . they take our symbols and our traditions and use them purely for the sake of market share.

Cinco de Mayo Con Orgullo activities have garnered a lot of media attention. Various California newspapers, including the *San Diego Union Tribune, San Francisco Chronicle*, and the *Los Angeles Times*, have run in-depth articles about the alcohol-free holiday campaign. Nationally, activities of the group have appeared in *USA Today*, the *Wall Street Journal*, and the Internet service Join Together Online. A significant victory for the group was getting the city of San Diego, which hosts one of the largest Cinco de Mayo celebrations in the country, to prohibit alcohol and tobacco sponsorship of its annual celebrations. The sights of Cinco de Mayo Con Orgullo are now on similar initiatives at the state and national levels. Another accomplishment of the group was getting the Los Angeles Unified School District to adopt their training tools (which includes a PowerPoint presentation, educational video, community action kit, and samples of organizing tools including letters to the editor, municipal and county proclamations, and press releases) for classroom education and use by students and teachers.

Students as young as middle school age have been trained with the Cinco de Mayo Con Orgullo materials and have gone out into their neighborhoods and asked local merchants not to display Cinco de Mayo - themed promotions for beer and liquor. In other school-based projects, students have mapped the location of alcohol outlets including those that display culturally exploitive alcohol advertising. According to Bernardo Rosa, chairperson of the Southern California chapter of the organization, "Our ultimate goal is to train Latino communities across America to recognize and reject the exploitation of their celebrations by alcohol promotion" (quoted in Marin Institute 2006d). Additionally, the organization seeks to use cultural traditions like the Cinco de Mayo celebration as a protective factor in building community pride and reducing the appeal of tobacco and alcohol.

The alcohol industry has taken notice of the community movement toward alcohol-free celebration. In an effort to counter the trend, in 2004 marketing managers from the breweries began contacting Cinco de Mayo event organizers and offering them $10,000 donations to help support festival activities, provided the brewery could host a booth and advertise its products with banners and other promotional materials. Jovita Hurtado, an organizer for the San Diego celebration, received such a call and declined the offer. She reported that the company representative

> was surprised. . . . He said, "but this is Cinco de Mayo!" Then he wanted to take me to lunch and talk about it. He said this kind of event would be very hard to raise money for, except from the beer industry. He said his company could help take a load off our shoulders. (quoted in Gogek 2004)

Hurtado informed the brewery representative that the celebration was alcohol-free, a Cinco de Mayo Con Orgullo event.

No one knew better than Hurtado how in the past the alcohol industry has expropriated Cinco de Mayo. When she was younger, she enthusiastically celebrated the holiday by visiting the crowded bars in the Old Town section of San Diego, drinking malt liquor and tequila, participating in the drinking contests, and partying until the wee hours. Often the celebrating ended suddenly in drunken fights, drunk driving arrests, and girls getting beaten up by their boyfriends. In Los Angeles, the SWAT team had to be called in one year when a drunken riot broke out at a Cinco de Mayo festival. Then, in 1986, Hurtado's fiancé died in a drunk-driving car crash following a night of Cinco de Mayo partying. She became abstinent shortly there after.

At the national level, the National Latino Council on Alcohol and Tobacco Prevention has initiated the National Latino Conference on Tobacco Prevention and Control. In 2005, the theme of this annual conference was "Marketing Disease to Latinos: Advocating for Social Change." The goal of the conference, which was held in Puerto Rico, was to bring to the forefront how Latinos are portrayed in the media; it included training on how to use the media to gain support for community struggles and a presentation of analyses of how the legal drug industries use the mass media to achieve their marketing and sales objectives among Latinos.

"Beer, It's What's For Breakfast"

Part of the struggle in the People's War on Drugs is shaped by the fact that the well-funded effort of the drug industries to normalize consumption has impacted popular culture. Rather than emphasizing the risks of misuse, popular culture portrays legal drugs, especially alcohol, in humorous ways, often by playing up insubordinate or disobedient themes that have appeal to coming-of-age youth. One consequence of this industry-influenced imaging was discovered by parents in Portland, Oregon, when they opened their newspapers one August day and found a full-page ad announcing a back-to-school sale at Macy's that promised "all the best looks for back to the books" (Newman 2006). Featured in the ad was a T-shirt emblazoned with the slogan "Beer Pong," the name of a drinking game popular among underage drinkers. When Judy Cushing, the director of a substance-abuse prevention group, visited Macy's to investigate, she found several additional T-shirts in the teen section of the store with other drinking slogans, including "Beer, It's What's for Breakfast," and "I'm Working on My Six Pack," a play on an expression for toning stomach muscles.

When Cushing's group—which must contend with the fact that surveys show that almost 30 percent of high school juniors in Oregon report having binged on alcohol during the previous month—contacted the store's offices in protest, they were rebuffed by statements about letting the customers decide (as if customers had had some say in stocking the T-shirts and displaying them in the teen section or in newspaper advertisements to begin with). Instead of backing down, Cushing went to the TV media with a press release criticizing Macy's participation in the promotion of underage drinking. During the evening news, reporters from one TV station showed the T-shirts to customers as they were leaving Macy's and solicited their opinion. The reaction was unambiguously negative. As a result of the bad publicity, the offending T-shirts were pulled from store shelves in all Macy's and Bloomingdale's stores nationwide.

Fighting Illicit Drug Companies

Cleaning Up the Neighborhood

During 2006, Georgia NeSmith was facing eviction from the second-floor apartment in Rochester, New York, where she had resided since 1999. Her offense? NeSmith initiated a community battle to stop open drug dealing on the corner near her apartment. The site is well suited to illicit drug sales because it has a busy store that attracts a regular flow of pedestrians, which provides excellent camouflage for drug dealers as well as a steady stream of potential customers. Near the store are alleys that allow dealers and customers a quick escape when police patrol cars drive by. For suburban drug buyers who come into the city to "score drugs," the area offers easy access and egress. People can drive up, and dealers will approach the car and assess the client's needs. Once the deal is made, the customer can drive hastily away. Watching out her window, or while working in her front yard garden, NeSmith began taking careful notes on what she saw and posted her accounts on her personal Web log. She also took pictures of actual "hand offs" (quick exchanges of money for small plastic bags of white powder). Additionally, NeSmith became a frequent caller to 911 and developed ties with several high-ranking police officers who wanted to "clean up" the area. Says NeSmith (quoted in Flanigan 2006a), "People in poor neighborhoods have the same right to safety and security as people in rich neighborhoods."

In her efforts, NeSmith was not always secretive, however, and sometimes stood on her porch, telephone in hand, to try and scare illicit drug buyers away. As a result, the dealers knew who she was and what she was doing. While NeSmith's landlord, Jean Longchamps, said she understood NeSmith's desire to fight the drug dealers, she felt that her actions were too risky and took steps to evict NeSmith. In a letter to NeSmith, Longchamps explained, "I appreciate everything you are doing to clean up the neighborhood. . . . Unfortunately, I believe that some of your actions have put yourself, the house and other tenants in danger" (quoted in Flanigan 2006b). NeSmith vowed to fight the eviction in court, arguing that Longchamps "has caved in" to the criminals who bring down the quality of life in the neighborhood. The low simmering tension between landlord and tenant escalated after someone threw rocks through the windows of two apartments in the building. Later a rock crashed through NeSmith's car window. Afterward, Georgia NeSmith (2006) wrote in her on-line blog:

> The dealers of course are mad as hell at me and have been trying to re-take the corner. They thought smashing my car window would make me run and hide. Boy, they just don't get it, do they? Much more to write about all their stepped up efforts to try to intimidate me. Later on that. It's all theater. Ninety percent of their power lies in our ability to imagine what they MIGHT do. So I'm not buying it. Unfortunately, because my landlady bought into the mythology they love to create, they are now trying even harder.

NeSmith maintained that her eviction would send the wrong message and would only encourage the dealers. Hanif Abdul Wahid, a member of the local neighborhood association and a founding member of Rochesterians Against Illegal Narcotics, agreed but pointed out that the landlord–tenant dispute between Longchamps and NeSmith underscored the complicated challenge of fighting illicit drug sales. Activists working alone can frighten other residents; what is most needed is community organizing, according to Wahid. In fact, NeSmith (2006) agreed, noting:

> I would never have taken on this fight against the dealers . . . alone. I am working closely with neighborhood groups, including the Marketview Heights Community Action Group and Rochester Interfaith Action. I have sought the advice of members of my own faith community, the Rochester Society of Friends (Quaker), including others who have been involved in organizing against the drug trade.

As NeSmith discovered, fear is a potent enemy of the effort to build a People's War on Drugs and has contributed to the small scale of these types of efforts. For her part, NeSmith was undaunted by the opposition she encountered and vowed to continue to carry on the struggle despite the eviction.

Running a Block

One of the problems with grassroots antidrug efforts focused on one neighborhood is that illicit drug dealing is highly flexible; street drug markets are easily moved to new locations when the pressure from neighbors or the police begins to interfere with drug sales. In the case of NeSmith's neighborhood, her repeated 911 calls and police visits to her neighborhood led to a marked reduction in local drug activity. But the dealers did not go out of business, they simply shifted their operations to a new, less troublesome location. In the Frogtown section of Minneapolis, a high drug use area of the city, community members regularly used 911 to report dealer activity to the police. A police sweep of the area led to a drop in 911 calls. Using computer software to map drug calls received by the police, it was discovered that following the sweep, dealers moved a mere six blocks to the southwest and resumed business as usual (Laszewski and Roberts 2004).

Additionally, drug operations can be quite sophisticated. An example is seen in a drug selling area in New York City run by a gang member named Hector Santiago. Santiago deployed his "troops" with almost military precision. One member of the gang was posted as a lookout at each end of the block, with a youth on a bicycle riding up and down passing information on customers, police, and supplies. On the rooftop, a lookout with a walkie-talkie in hand spotted police cars entering the area and alerted gang leaders. On the street, gang members challenged anyone they did not recognize, asking what their business was in the neighborhood and intimidating them if they tried to park their cars. The actual drug sellers wore ski masks and maintained strict discipline. If one of the street sellers was arrested, Santiago continued to pay them as long as they didn't divulge information to the police. Similar configurations are found among many other street drug dealers. A Connecticut dealer explained:

> I was running my block, it was five or six of us. . . . We used to have one person that stayed at one end of the block and another at the other end, with walkie-talkies. And we'd talk to each other to see who was coming, cops, whatever, and we used signals off of the porch. We would use 5-0 to signal for the police coming. (Singer 2006b:69)

While organized to contend with rival gangs and with the police, the military-style formations maintained by gangs, with ranks and an expectation of discipline, can be mobilized to intimidate community resistance efforts. Brenda Scott, an antidrug activist and president of the Ebbets Field Houses Tenants Organization in Brooklyn, New York, found that

that some gangs are willing to use deadly force to maintain their hold on a neighborhood. During the summer of 2006, a bullet was fired through Scott's door but crashed into a jar full of pennies that she was saving, and no one was injured. She was left fearing for her life. "Sure, I'm scared," Scott told a reporter. "I don't want to die, but it's not going to stop me" (quoted in Associated Press 2006d).

Nonetheless, communities can grow so weary of feeling under siege by rival gangs—which may be engaged in ongoing armed feuds in which some of the victims are civilians caught in the cross fire—that they react and organize to push the dealers out. In Hartford, for example, on the north end of town, the community exploded when a seven-year-old girl named Takira Gaston was shot and killed by a stray bullet during a shoot-out among rival dealers. A wave of community protest followed, with repeated street demonstrations and marches, all of which were focused on condemning local drug dealers. Declaring Takira's death a civil rights issue, the Greater Hartford NAACP launched a "Peace in the City" campaign, while grassroots neighborhood groups such as Communities Against Drugs initiated a series of protest marches. Led by the Reverend Cornell Lewis, a substance abuse counselor, the group organized several weekend take-back-the-streets "campouts" on street corners heavily used by local drug dealers to ply their wares to the community. The goal of mobilizing the community, explained Lewis, was to shame and harass drug dealers until they leave the area. "People know where [the drug dealers] live, where they eat, where they park their cars, and where they sleep at night. Let's see how they like it when we show up at 8 o'clock on a Saturday morning," Lewis told the demonstrators.

During the campout, Lewis reported that the dealers sent a message to the demonstrators saying that while they understood community concerns, the protest was disrupting business. Lewis sent back a reply that the community did not appreciate the climate of violence produced by drug dealing by armed gang members. The gang members responded, according to Lewis, by sending over a man who rapped a song "about how he had a gat and an extra clip and was looking for someone to shoot. We asked him to leave" (quoted in *Drug War Chronicle* 2002). Cliff Thornton, leader of an anti–War on Drugs policy reform group called Efficacy, and subsequently the Green Party candidate for governor in Connecticut, publicly expressed doubt that Lewis' approach could accomplish much. Explained Thornton:

> They've been doing these marches and things for the last year-and-a-half. . . . They had a big sweep there last summer, but by November things were back to normal and in some places even worse. And even during the marches, I've seen people making drug deals right across the street. The dealers move when the heat comes, but then they come right back. This will not solve the problem. . . . This may be well-intentioned, but it's ineffective. (quoted in *Drug War Chronicle* 2002)

Lewis counters:

> These criminal elements are destroying our neighborhoods and they need to be dealt with now. . . . That's where our methods come into play. No drug dealer will stay in business if he can't make money, so we try to make it impossible for them to operate. . . . We've had some success in some neighborhoods. . . . I tell you what, come up with something better, then I'll listen, in the meantime we'll do what we think is necessary. (quoted in *Drug War Chronicle* 2002)

Lewis believes his strategy will work because he was able to use it successfully in his own neighborhood. There, he organized street blockades and set up video cameras and halogen spotlights to drive away illicit drug customers. He taught local residents to use binoculars so that they could see and then write down license plate numbers and call the police as often as they necessary. Despite several threats to Lewis' life, community support remained strong. Ultimately, knowing it would be easier elsewhere, the dealers left the immediate area. They did not, however, leave the north end of Hartford.

Favela Rising

The fight-back against the damaging effects of the illicit drug trade is fought on many fronts. One of those fronts is in the *favelas* or squatter settlements found in the major cities of Brazil. As noted in chapter 2, the illicit drug trade is rampant in many of the favelas, with well-armed drug organizations literally running some of the settlements. At the same time, the police have proven to be particularly brutal in countering illicit drug corporations in Brazil, including indiscriminate killings of favela members, whether they were involved in the drug trade or not. The residents of many favelas at times have felt as if they lived in a permanent war zone.

One such place is Vigá Geral favela, a densely populated settlement perched on the hillsides overlooking the wealthier seaside sections of Rio de Jainero. As portrayed in the movie *City of God*, drug-related violence in the favelas of Rio can be intense. After one particularly brutal retaliation by the police for the shooting of four policemen, an attack that left several dozen residents of Vigário dead on the streets of the community, some of the young adults, including individuals with backgrounds in the drug trade, decided it was time to make a change. They began a social movement in 1993 in direct opposition to the violent drug industry and to police oppression.

The first strategy of the founding members was to start a newspaper called *AfroReggae Notícias*, geared toward giving a positive perspective on black culture, especially various black musical forms like reggae and hip-hop—a response to the fact that social class in Brazil tends to be drawn on color lines. Once the newspaper was up and running, the group, now called Grupo Cultural AfroReggae (GCAR), was able to open a community cultural center. The center began offering classes for adolescent residents of the favela in dance, percussion, garbage recycling, soccer, and *capoeira* (an Afro-Brazilian martial art and dance form). Later, programs were offered for young children, as the movement began to grow. Intense, fast-paced musical performances by Banda AfroReggae, the movement's main band, became increasingly popular among community residents, especially young people, and gave the leaders a public stage on which to spread their message to youth about not becoming involved with the illicit drug trade. Before long, the group was running classes for community members on domestic violence, hygiene, and other topics, with programs for children, families, and the elderly. Other bands, including Banda Makala Música e Dança, Afro Lata, and Afro Samba, emerged within the movement, providing multiple vehicles to disseminate the pro-culture/ anti- drugs and drug violence message of GCAR.

In 2001, the movement spread to the neighboring—and often rival— favela of Parada de Lucas (whose drug traffickers had a history of armed battles with those of Vigário), and from there to additional favelas in Rio. As a result of the movement's hard work, drug-related violence has sig-nificantly diminished in Vigário, a success story in the People's War on Drugs that is depicted in the award-winning HBO documentary film *Favela Rising* (2006) by Jeff Zimbalist and Matt Mochary. Importantly, as this example shows, community fight-backs against illicit drug corpora-tions are winnable if they are integrated with longer-term community development and cultural development efforts.

La Lucha Contínua

The People's War on Drugs continues to struggle on. The struggle against drugs, their producers, and distributors has proven to be more effective in some places than in others, and, for the most part, has remained a local affair, rooted in grassroots community organizations, churches, and the unwavering will of local activists. A coordinated national effort has yet to appear, although several organizations have emerged that have sought to enhance coordination and support. In this sense, a full-scale social movement has yet to appear. Despite lack of national coordination, local groups share ideas and tactics, and the Inter-net has helped to spread information rapidly about local antidrug strate-gies and struggles. All of these efforts have benefited from the civil rights movement, which field tested the basic organizing tactics in play among community antidrug warriors.

It has been possible for the People's War on Drugs to win battles against even the richest legal drug companies, because profit can be affected by public relations. In an era in which the tobacco and alcohol industries have become highly sensitive to appearing socially sensitive and involved, bad publicity can be effective in getting megacorporations to change course, at least somewhat. The strategy of the legal drug industry when challenged by grassroots initiatives has been to deny all accusations but quietly (if community protest is sustained) remove the offending product from the market, only to replace it several years later with a new product intended to capture the same "demographic." The greater "win" for low-income communities has been in the negative publicity about the risks of smoking and drinking, as these have contributed to drop-offs in consumption by community members.

The struggle against illicit drug selling also has been conducted at the local level, often by ad hoc groups and coalitions. Even at the neighborhood level, support has been divided, as the effectiveness of direct nonviolent tactics targeted at street drug dealers has not been firmly established. As community members know, the people who stand on street corners and sell drugs are not the power wielders of illicit drug capitalism. Rather, they and their immediate customers are the two groups in the illicit drug trade that are "reachable" by community anti-drug activists. Further, it is widely recognized that drug corners are not highly invested, and dealers can pick up their bags of heroin, cocaine, marijuana, or other drugs and find another selling area within a few blocks of the original site. Also, it is hard for a community to sustain an antidrug campaign for long, and sooner or later it is often possible for the drug dealers, including a fresh crop of new ones that emerged since the last confrontation, to reclaim old territory.

In that it is poverty, inequality, racism, and related forms of structural violence that help drive drug use among the poor, it appears ever clearer that winning the People's War on Drugs rests in defeating these scourges.

References

Abraham, Itty, and William van Schendel
  2005 Introduction: The Making of Illicitness. *In* Illicit Flows and Criminal Things: States, Borders, and the Other Side of Globalization. W. van Schendel and I. Abraham, eds. Pp. 1–37. Bloomington: Indiana University Press.
Action on Smoking and Health
  1996 ASH Seeks Federal Investigation of Smoking in the Movies. Electronic document, http://ash.org/legal/eye.html.
Adams, Samuel Hopkins
  1905 The Great American Fraud. Colliers Weekly, October 7. Electronic document, http://www.mtn.org/quack/ephemera/oct7-01.htm.
Agar, Michael
  2003 The Story of Crack: Towards a Theory of Illicit Drug Trends. Addiction Research and Theory 11(1):3–29.
  2006 Dope Double Agent: The Naked Emperor on Drugs. Morrisville, NC: Lulu Books.
Agar, Michael and Heather Schacht Reisinger
  1999 Numbers and Patterns: Heroin Indicators, What They Represent. Human Organization 58:365–374.
Agbavon, Patrick
  2001 The Tobacco Industry and Tobacco Control Movement in Togo. Electronic document, http://www.essentialaction.org/tobacco/qofm/0201/togo.html.
Agovino, Theresa
  2006 Merck Report Absolves Managers on Vioxx. Yahoo Finance, September 6. Electronic document, http://www.biz.yahoo.com/ap/060906/vioxx_report.html?.v=6.
Alaniz, Maria
  1998 Alcohol Availability and Targeted Advertising in Racial/Ethnic Minority Communities. Alcohol Health & Research World 22(4):286–289.
Alaniz, Maria, and C. Wilkes
  1995 Reinterpreting Latino Culture in the Commodity Form: The Case of Alcohol Advertising in the Mexican American Community. Hispanic Journal of Behavioral Sciences 17(4):430–451.
Alesina, Alberto, Edward Glaeser, and Bruce Sacerdote
  2001 Why Doesn't the US Have a European-Style Welfare State? Harvard Institute of Economic Research. Cambridge, MA: Harvard University.

Allen-Taylor, J. Douglas
　　1997 Malt Assault. Sonoma County Independent, October 2–8. Electronic document, http://www.metroactive.com/papers/sonoma/10.02.97/latino-drinking-9740.html.
Alonso-Zaldivar, Ricardo
　　2006 FDA Pledges Conflict Reforms. Los Angeles Times, July 25: A12.
Alsop, Ronald
　　2002 Perils of Corporate Giving. Wall Street Journal, January 16: 1.
Altice, Frederick, Adrian Marinovich, Kaveh Khoshnood, Kim Blankenship, Sandra Springer, and Peter Selwyn
　　2005 Correlates of HIV Infection among Incarcerated Women: Implications for Improving Detection of HIV Infection. Journal of Urban Health 82(2):312–326.
Altria Group, Inc.
　　2003 2002 Annual Report. Electronic document, http://www.altria.com/AnnualReport2003/ar2003_07_2900.asp.
Amaro, Hortensia, Lise Fried, Howard Cabral, and Barry Zuckerman
　　1990 Violence During Pregnancy and Substance Use. American Journal of Public Health 80:575–579.
American Heart Association
　　2005 Tobacco Industry's Economic and Political Influence. Electronic document, http://www.americanheart.org/presenter.jhtml?identifier=11224.
American Medical Association
　　2002 Partner or Foe? The Alcohol Industry, Youth Alcohol Problems, and Alcohol Policy Strategies. Electronic document, http://www.ama-assn.org/ama1/pub/upload/mm/388/partner_foe_brief.pdf.
Anastasia, George
　　1998 The Goodfella Tapes: The True Story of How the FBI Recorded a Mob War and Brought Down a Mafia Don. New York: Avon Books.
Anderson, Elijah
　　1999 Code of the Street: Decency, Violence and the Moral Life of the Inner City. New York: W. W. Norton & Company.
Angell, Marcia
　　2004 The Truth about the Drug Companies: How They Deceive Us and What to Do About it. New York: Random House.
Anheuser-Busch Co., Inc.
　　1997 Annual Report. St. Louis, MO: Anheuser-Busch Companies, Inc.
　　2005 Annual Report. St. Louis, MO: Anheuser-Busch Companies, Inc.
　　2006a Company Web Site. Electronic document, http://anheuser-busch.com.
　　2006b Meet Joe and Jane. Electronic document, http://www.rollbackthebeertax.org/meet.
Appadurai, Arjun, ed.
　　1986a Introduction: Commodities and the Politics of Value. In The Social Life of Things: Commodities in Cultural Perspective. Cambridge: Cambridge University Press.
　　1986b The Social Life of Things: Commodities in Cultural Perspective. Cambridge: Cambridge University Press.
　　1996 Modernity at Large: Cultural Dimensions of Globalization. Minneapolis: University of Minnesota Press.

Arias, Donya
    2006 Tobacco Industry Misled Public for Decades, Federal Judge Rules. The Nation's Health, October: 1, 20.

Arias, Enrique Desmond
    2006 Drugs and Democracy in Rio de Janeiro. Chapel Hill: University of North Carolina Press.

Armenian, Haroutune, and Moyses Szklo
    1996 Morton Levin (1904–1995): History in the Making. American Journal of Epidemiology 143(6):648–649.

Arnett, Jeffrey
    2005 Talk is Cheap: The Tobacco Companies' Violations of Their Own Cigarette Advertising Code. Journal of Health Communications 10(5):419–431.

Aronson, Rosa
    2001 At-Risk Students Defy the Odds: Overcoming Barriers to Educational Success. Blue Ridge Summit, PA: Scarecrow Press.

Arthur, B.
    2006 Nothing's Going to Change. National Post, March 31: 12.

Associated Press
    2006a Tobacco Expected to Kill 1 Billion This Century. Electronic document, http://www.msnbc.msn.com/id/13803326.
    2006b Two Legal Cases Cost GE $22.5 million. Hartford Courant, July 22: E2.
    2006c Alcohol Ads Run on Youth-Oriented Radio. New York Times, August 31: 1.
    2006d Anti-Drug Activist Says Penny Jar Saved Her Life. Electronic document, http://www.wcbs880.com/pages/50253.php?contentType=4&contentId=163113.

Ausubel, Kenny
    2000 When Healing Becomes a Crime: The Amazing Story of the Hoxsey Cancer Clinics and the Return of Alternative Therapies. Rochester, VT: Healing Arts Press.

Baer, Hans
    2004 Toward an Integrative Medicine: Merging Alternative Therapies with Biomedicine. Thousand Oaks, CA: AltaMira Press.

Baer, Hans, Merrill Singer, and Ida Susser
    2003 Medical Anthropology and the World System. 2nd edition. Westport, CT: Praeger.

Balko, Radley
    2003 Back Door to Prohibition: The New War on Social Drinking. Electronic document, http://www.cato.org/pubs/pas/pa501.pdf.

Barker, Kim
    2006 Opium Boom Undermines Karzai. Hartford Courant, September 5: A2.

Baskin, Brian
    2005 Top 9 Employers in State Have 9,698 Getting Public Aid. Arkansas Democrat-Gazette, March 17: 1.

Bauer, Paul, and Rhoda Ullmann
    2001 Understanding the Wash Cycle. Economic Perspectives: An Electronic Journal of the U.S. Department of State 6(2). Electronic document, http://www.usinfo.state.gov/journals/ites/0501/ijee/clevelandfed.htm.

Baum, Dan
    2000 Citizen Coors. New York: William Morrow.

Bay City News
2005 Alameda County Suit Alleges Wal-Mart Cheated Workers. Bay City News, January 20.

Bazerman, M., and D. Chugh
2006 Decisions without Blinders. Harvard Business Review 84(1):88–97.

BBC News
1998 Gauging the Real Benefits of Drinking. Electronic document, http://www.news.bbc.co.uk/1/hi/health/231840.stm.

Beelman, Maud
2001 White House Sought to Soften Anti-Terrorism Legislation in Support of Tobacco Companies. Electronic document, http://www.publici.org/report.aspx?aid=284.

Beiser, Vince
2000 Fetal Abuse. Mother Jones Magazine. Electronic document, http://www.motherjones.com/news/feature/2000/06/fetal.html.

Berrigan, Daniel
1971 WikiQuote. Electronic document, http://en.wikiquote.org/wiki/Daniel_Berrigan.

Beschner, George, and Elliot Bovelle
1985 Life with Heroin: Voices of Experience. *In* Life with Heroin: Vices from the Inner City. Bill Hanson, George Beschner, James Walters, and Elliot Bovelle, eds. Pp. 75–108. Lexington, MA: Lexington Books.

Beschner, George, and William Brower
1985 The Scene. *In* Life with Heroin: Vices from the Inner City. Bill Hanson, George Beschner, James Walters, and Elliot Bovelle, eds. Pp. 19–30. Lexington, MA: Lexington Books.

Bezruchka, Stephen, and Mary Anne Mercer
2004 The Lethal Divide: How Economic Inequality Affects Health. *In* Sickness and Wealth. Meredith Fort, Mary Anne Mercer, and Oscar Gish, eds. Pp. 11–18. Cambridge, MA: South End Press.

Blake, D., G. Gordon, and S. Spielberg
1982 The Role of Metabolic Activation in Thalidomide Teratogenesis. Teratology 25(2):28A–29A.

Blocker, Jack
2006 Did Prohibition Really Work? American Journal of Public Health 96(2):233–243.

Bobak, M., P. Jha, S. Nguyen, and M. Jarvis
2000 Poverty and Smoking. *In* Tobacco Control in Developing Counties. Prabhat Jha and Frank Chaloupka, eds. Pp 41–61. Geneva: World Health Organization.

Bodenheimer, T.
1985 The Transnational Pharmaceutical Industry and the Health of the World's People. *In* Issues in the Political Economy of Health Care. J. McKinlay, ed. Pp 187–216. New York: Tavistock Publications.

Boeri, Miriam, Clare Sterk, and Kirk Elifson
2004 Rolling Beyond Raves: Ecstasy Use Outside of the Rave Setting. Journal of Drug Issues 34(4):831–859.

Bonné, Jon
2001 Scourge of the Heartland: Meth takes Root in Surprising Places. MSNBC. Electronic document, http://www.msnbc.msn.com/id/3071773.

Booth, Martin
    1996 Opium: A History. New York: St. Martins.
Borio, Gene
    2003 Tobacco Timeline. Electronic document, http://www.tobacco.org/
        resources/history/Tobacco_Historynotes.html#aamort.
Borowski, John
    2004 For Christmas, Will Coca-Cola Stop Acting Like Bit Tobacco? Common
        Dreams NewsCenter. Electronic document, http://www.commondreams.org/
        cgi-bin/print.cgi?file=/views04/1221-21.htm.
Boudewyns, P., M. Woods, L. Hyer, and J. Albrecht
    1991 Chronic Combat-Related PTSD and Concurrent Substance Abuse:
        Implications for Treatment of This Frequent "Dual Diagnosis." Journal of
        Traumatic Stress 4:549–560
Bourgois, Philippe
    2003 In Search of Respect: Selling Crack in El Barrio. 2nd edition. Cam-
        bridge: Cambridge University Press.
Boyer, Richard, and Herbert Morais
    1955 Labor's Untold Story. Pittsburgh, PA: United Electrical Radio &
        Machine Workers.
Braithwaite, John
    1984 Corporate Crime in the Pharmaceutical Industry. London: Routledge
        and Kegan Paul.
    1986 The Corrupt Industry. New Internationalist 165(November). Elec-
        tronic document, http://www.newint.org/issue165/corrupt.htm.
Branscomb, Leslie
    2006 Hearing Targets "Alcopops" Marketed to Underaged. San Diego Union-
        Tribune, March 11. Electronic document, http://www.signonsandiego.com/
        news/metro/20060311-9999-2m11alcopop.html.
Brecher, Edward, and the Editors of Consumers Union
    1972 Licit and Illicit Drugs. Boston: Little Brown & Co.
Bren, Linda
    2001 Frances Oldham Kelsey: FDA Medical Reviewer Leaves Her Mark on
        History. FDA Consumer Magazine, March–April. Washington, DC: U.S.
        Food and Drug Administration.
Brett, A., W. Burr, and J. Moloo
    2003 Are Gifts from Pharmaceutical Companies Ethically Problematic? A
        Survey of Physicians. Archives of Internal Medicine 163:2213–2218.
Brinson, T., and V. Treanor
    1988 Alcoholism and Post Traumatic Stress Disorder among Combat Viet-
        nam Veterans. Alcoholism Treatment Quarterly 5(3/4):65–82.
British American Tobacco
    1959 BAT Research & Development, Complexity of the P.A.5.A. Machine
        and Variables Pool, August 26. Minnesota Trial Exhibit #10,392.
    1962 A. McCormick, Smoking and Health: Policy on Research, Minutes of
        Southampton Meeting, Document #1102.01.
    1979 P. Lee, Note on Tar Reduction for Hunter, Tobacco Advisory Council,
        July 19 (L&D UK Ind 33).
    2006a Our Business. Electronic document, http://www.bat.com/OneWeb/
        sites/uk__3mnfen.nsf/vwPagesWebLive/
        C36DBD7910B585F680256BF40003316E?opendocument&SID=&DTC=.

2006b Public Smoking Restrictions. Electronic document, http://www.bat.com/oneweb/sites/uk__3mnfen.nsf/vwPagesWebLive/DO6HADSB?opendocument&SID=&DTC=&TMP=1.

Brook, Judith, Elinor Balka, Zohn Rosen, David Brook, and Richard Adams
2005 Tobacco Use in Adolescence: Longitudinal Links to Later Problem Behavior among African American and Puerto Rican Urban Young Adults. The Journal of Genetic Psychology 166(2):133–151.

Brook, Judith, Elise Schuster, and Chenshu Zhang
2004 Cigarette Smoking and Depressive Symptoms: A Longitudinal Study of Adolescents and Young Adults. Psychological Reports 95:159–166.

Broughton, Martin
2002 Speech at the British American Tobacco Annual General Meeting, April 16. Electronic document, http://www.bat.com/oneweb/sites/uk__3mnfen.nsf/vwPagesWebLive/DO52AELS/$FILE/medMD599JUB.pdf?openelement.
2003 Collective Action to Combat Counterfeiting. Key note speech to International Trademark Specialists and Brand Owners, May 6. Electronic document, http://www.bat.com/oneweb/sites/uk__3mnfen.nsf/vwPagesWebLive/DO52AELS/$FILE/medMD5MGHWG.pdf?openelement.
2004 Speech at the British American Tobacco Annual General Meeting, April 21. Electronic document, http://www.bat.com/oneweb/sites/uk__3mnfen.nsf/vwPagesWebLive/DO52AELS/$FILE/medMD5Y9GAV.pdf?openelement.

Brouwer, K., P. Case, R. Ramos, C. Magis-Rodriguez, J. Bucardo, T. Patterson, and S. Strathdee
2006 Trends in Production, Trafficking, and Consumption of Methamphetamine and Cocaine in Mexico. Substance Use and Abuse 41(5):707–727.

Brown, S., and S. Tapert
2004 Health Consequences of Adolescent Alcohol Involvement. In Reducing Underage Drinking: A Collective Responsibility, Background Papers [CD-ROM]. Pp. 383–401. Washington, DC: National Academies Press.

Brown and Williamson Tobacco Company
1982 What are the Obstacles/Enemies of a Swing to Low "Tar" and What Action Should We Take? July 2. Minnesota Trial Exhibit #26,185.

Brzezinski, Matthew
2002 Re-Engineering the Drug Business. The New York Times Magazine, June 23: 24–29, 46–55.

Budrys, Grace
2003 Unequal Health: How Inequality Contributes to Health or Illness. Lanham, MD: Rowman & Littlefield.

Burkholz, Herbert
1997 Giving Thalidomide a Second Chance. Electronic document, http://webmd.lycos.com/content/dmk/dmk_article_5462593.

Bush, George, W.
2006 International Narcotics Control Strategy Report. Washington, DC: Bureau for International Narcotics and Law Enforcement Affairs.

Business Information Analysis Corporation
1985 RJR Young Adult Motivational Research. R. J. Reynolds Tobacco Company. January 10. Bates No. 502780379-0424. Electronic document, http://www.rjrtdocs.com, http://www.library.ucsf.edu/tobacco/mangini.

Butler, Kathy
    2006 The Grim Neurology of Teenage Drinking. The New York Times, July 4: 1
Butterfield, Fox
    2004 Home Drug-Making Laboratories Expose Children to Toxic Fallout.
    New York Times, February 23:1.
Caetano, R., and C. Clark
    1998 Trends in Alcohol Consumption Patterns among Whites, Blacks and
    Hispanics: 1984 and 1995. Journal of Studies on Alcohol 59:659–668.
Cameron, D., and I. Jones
    1985 An Epidemiological and Sociological Analysis of the Use of Alcohol,
    Tobacco, and Other Drugs of Solace. Community Medicine 7:18–29.
Campaign for Tobacco-Free Kids
    2005 Special Report; Big Tobacco Still Targeting Kids. Electronic document,
    http://www.tobaccofreekids.org/reports/targeting.
Campbell, D.
    2002 Bush Tars Drug Takers with Aiding Terrorists. The Guardian, August 8.
Cantos Transcript, The
    2005 Diageo Preliminary Results. Interview with Paul Walsh. Electronic
    document, http://www.diageo.com/NR/rdonlyres/4DA6C679-AC5E-
    4F90-8E93-AB213FFCD958/0/PaulWalshInterviewTranscript.pdf.
Carneiro, Robert
    2000 Origin Myths. Thinkquest. Electronic document, http://www.library.
    thinkquest.org/C005854/text/types.htm.
Casteel, Steven
    2003 Narco-Terrorism: International Drug Trafficking and Terrorism—a Dan-
    gerous Mix. Statement before Senate Committee on Judiciary, May 20. Elec-
    tronic document, http://www.usdoj.gov/dea/pubs/cngrtest/ct052003.html.
Castells, M.
    1998 The Information Age: Economy, Society and Culture, vol. 3: End of
    Millennium. Oxford: Blackwell.
Castro, A., and M. Singer
    2004 Unhealthy Health Policy: A Critical Anthropological Examination.
    Walnut Creek, CA: AltaMira Press.
Center for Corporate Policy
    2005 Corporate Crime and Abuse. Electronic document,
    http://www.corporatepolicy.org/issues/FCPA.htm.
Center for Public Integrity
    2001 Tobacco Companies Linked to Criminal Organizations in Cigarette Smug-
    gling. Electronic document, http://www.publici.org/report.aspx?aid=353.
    2006 Pharmaceutical Industry Lobbying and Campaign Donations in All
    States. Electronic document, http://www.publicintegrity.org/rx/iys.aspx.
Center for Responsive Politics
    2005 Tobacco: Long-Term Contribution Trends. Electronic document, http://
    www.opensecrets.org/industries/indus.asp?Ind=A02.
    2006 Pharmaceutical Manufacturing: Long-Term Contribution Trends. Elec-
    tronic document, http://www.opensecrets.org/industries/indus.asp?Ind=
    H4300&cycle=2002.
Center for Science in the Public Interest
    1986 A Compilation of Alcoholic-Beverage Industry Political Contributions
    to Members of the Appropriations Committee of the U.S. House of Repre-

sentatives, 1997–1998. Alcohol Policies Project. Electronic document, http://www.cspinet.org/booze/underagedrinking.ondcp5.htm.

Center for Science in the Public Interest/Minnesota Institute on Black Chemical Abuse

    1986 CSPI/MBCA Questionnaire, November 1985–January 1986. Washington, DC: CSPI.

Center on Alcohol Marketing and Youth

    2006a Youth Exposure to Alcohol Advertising in Magazines, 2001 to 2004: Good News, Bad News. Electronic document, http://www.camy.org/.

    2006b Exposure of African-American Youth to Alcohol Advertising, 2003 to 2004. Washington, DC: Center on Alcohol Marketing and Youth.

    2006c Exposure of Hispanic Youth to Alcohol Advertising, 2003–2004. Electronic document, http://www.camy.org/research/hispanic1005/.

Centers for Disease Control and Prevention

    1999 Illegal Sales of Cigarettes to Minors—Ciudad Juarez, Mexico; El Paso, Texas; and Las Cruces, New Mexico. Morbidity and Mortality Weekly Review 48(19):394–398.

Chang, J.

    2005 Rio Slum Mourns Gangster. The Philadelphia Inquirer, December 11: 2.

Chambliss, W.

    1994 Why the Government is Not Contributing to the Resolution of the Nation's Drug Problem. International Journal of Health Services 24(4):675–690.

Chien, A., M. Conners, and K. Fox

    2000 The Drug War in Perspective. In Dying for Growth. J. Kim, J. Millen, A. Irwin, and J. Gershman, eds. Pp. 293–327. Monroe, ME: Common Courage Press.

Chou, S., D. Dawson, F. Stinson, B. Huang, R. Pickering, Y. Zhou, and B. Grant

    2006 The Prevalence of Drinking and Driving in the United States, 2001–2002: Results from the National Epidemiological Survey on Alcohol and Related Conditions. Drug and Alcohol Dependence 83(2):137–146.

Christian Aid

    2001 The Scorched Earth: Oil, War, and Corruption. London: Christian Aid.

Clawson, P., and R. Lee

    1998 The Andean Cocaine Industry. New York: St. Martin's Griffin.

Cohen, Jay

    2006 The Medical Profession's Culture of Corruption. MedicationSense.com. Electronic document, http://www.medicationsense.com/articles/may_aug_06/conflict_of_interest_060306.html.

Cohen, Mardge, Catherine Deamant, Susan Barkan, Jean Richardson, Mary Young, Susan Holman, Katheryn Anastos, Judith Cohen, and Sandra Melnick

    2000 Domestic Violence and Childhood Sexual Abuse in HIV-Infected Women and Women at Risk for HIV. American Journal of Public Health 90(4):560–565.

Columbia Daily Tribune

    2005 Maris Trial against Beer Giant Starts: Distributor Says Anheuser-Busch Intentionally Defamed It. Columbia Daily Tribune, August 2. Electronic document, http://www.showmenews.com/2005/Aug/20050803Busi006.asp.

Combined Wire Services

    2006 Study Finds Drug Errors Common. The Hartford Courant, July 1: A4.

Compton, Wilson, B. Grant, J. Colliver, M. Glantz, and F. Stinson
2004 Prevalence of Marijuana Use Disorders in the United States: 1991–1992 and 2001–2002. Journal of the American Medical Association 291(17):2114–2121.

Consumers Union
2006 Sleeping Pills: Are They Worth the Risks? Consumer Reports. Electronic document, http://www.consumerreports.org/cro/health-fitness/drugs-supplements/sleeping-pills-9-06/overview/0609_sleep-pills_ov.htm.

Coors
2006 Support of Environment Coors' Web Site. Electronic document, http://www.coors.com/factsheets/EnvironmentFactSheet.pdf.

Coreil, Jeannine, and Gladys Mayard
2006 Indigenization of Illness Support Groups in Haiti. Human Organization 65(2):128–139.

Corporate Crime Reporter
2005 Eli Lilly Pleads Guilty to Illegally Promoting Evista, to Pay $36 Million. Corporate Crime Reporter 1(1), December 21.

Corpus, Aline
2006 Mexico Drug Use Soars as U.S. Meth Labs Shift South. Reuters, May 9.

Cosgrove, Lisa, Sheldon Krimsky, Manish Vijayaraghavana, and Lisa Schneider
2006 Financial Ties between DSM-IV Panel Members and the Pharmaceutical Industry. Psychotherapy and Psychosomatics 75:154–160.

Coulter, Harris
1991 The Controlled Clinical Trial: An Analysis. Washington, DC: Center for Empirical Medicine.

Courtwright, David
2001 Forces of Habit: Drugs and the Making of the Modern World. Cambridge, MA: Harvard University Press.

Courtwright, David, H. Joseph, and Don Des Jarlais
1989 Addicts Who Survived: An Oral History of Narcotics Use in America, 1923–1965. Knoxville: The University of Tennessee Press.

Cressy, Peter
2000 Cultural Acceptance Seen as Key to Boosting Industry Sales. Night Club and Bar Magazine. Electronic document, www.nightclub.com.

Cummings, K., G. Giovino, and A. Mendicino
1997 Cigarette Advertising and Black-White Differences in Brand Preference. Public Health Reports 102:698–701.

Cunradi, C., R. Caetano, and J. Schafer
2002 Alcohol-Related Problems, Drug Use, and Male Intimate Partner Violence Severity among U.S. Couples. Alcoholism, Clinical and Experimental Research 26(4):493–500.

Custer Battles Ltd.
2006 Company Web Site. Electronic document, http://www.custerbattles.com/services/transformrisk.html.

Daniel, H., M. Johnston, and C. Levy
1981 Subject: Young Smokers—Prevalence, Trends, Implications, and Related Demographic Trends. March 31, 1981. Bates: 1000390803-1000390855 Exhibit 1. Electronic document, http://www.tobaccodocuments.org/youth/AmYoPMI19810331.Rm.html.

Davies, David
> 2003 External Forces, Facing the Future. Speech of the Phillip Morris International Senior Vice President for Corporate Affairs. Electronic document, http://www.philipmorrisinternational.com/PMINTL/pages/eng/press/speeches/DDavies_20031126.asp.

de Granados, Oriana Zill
> 2002 International Smuggling Overview. April 19. Electronic document, http://www.pbs.org/now/politics/smuggling.html.

Dei, Kojo
> 2002 Ties That Bind: Youth and Drugs in a Black Community. Long Grove, IL: Waveland Press.

DeJong, William
> 2004 What's in a Name, Let Me Count the Ways. Prevention File, Silver Gate Group. Spring:2–5.

Diageo
> 2006 Company Profile. Electronic document, http://www.diageo.com/en-row/Investors/CompanyProfile.

Diaz, Rafael
> 1998 Latino Gay Men and HIV. New York: Rougledge.

Diaz, T., S. Chu, J. Buehler, D. Boyd, P. Checko, L. Conti, A. Davidson, P. Hermann, M. Herr, and A. Levy
> 1994 Socioeconomic Differences among People with AIDS: Results from a Multistate Surveillance Project. American Journal of Preventive Medicine 10(4):217–222.

Dilulio, John
> 1996 Broken Bottles: Alcohol, Disorder, and Crime. The Brookings Review 14(2):14–17.

Doll, R.
> 1998 Uncovering the Effects of Smoking: Historical Perspective. Statistical Methods in Medical Research 7:87–117.

Doll, R., and Hill, B.
> 1950 Smoking and Carcinoma of the Lung. The British Medical Journal 221(ii):739–748.

Doward, James, and Thompson, Tony
> 2003 The Great Ecstasy Epidemic. The Observer, September 28. Electronic document, http://www.mdma.net/club-drugs/global-ecstasy.html.

Downie, L.
> 1971 Justice Denied. New York: Praeger.

Dressler, William
> 1999 Modernization, Stress, and Blood Pressure: New Directions in Research. Human Biology 71:583–605.

Drug Enforcement Administration
> 2001 Drug Trafficking in the United States, September 2001. Electronic document, www.dea.gov/pubs/intel/01020/index.html.
> 2005 New Jersey. Electronic document, http://www.dea.gov/pubs/states/newjersey2003.html.
> 2006 Pharmaceuticals. Electronic document, http://www.usdoj.gov/dea/concern/18862/pharm.htm.

Drug War Chronicle
2002 In Hartford, Neighborhood Drug Fighters and Drug Reformers Inhabit Parallel Universes. Electronic document, http://www.stopthedrugwar.org/chronicle/236/hartford.shtml.

du Plessis, Jan
2006 Speech given at the British American Tobacco Annual General Meeting. Electronic document, http://www.bat.com/OneWeb/sites/uk__3mnfen.nsf/vwPagesWebLive/DO52AELS?opendocument&SID=&DTC=&TMP=1.

Dube, A.
2005 Impact of Wal-Mart Growth on Earnings throughout the Retail Sector in Urban and Rural Counties. Berkeley: University of California, Berkeley Labor Center.

Duke, Michael, Wei Teng, Scott Clair, Hassan Salaheen, Pamela Choice, and Merrill Singer
2006 Patterns of Intimate Partner Violence among Drug Using Women. Free Inquiry in Creative Sociology 34(1):29–38.

Duran, Lauren, and Nancy Gavilanes
2006 More Than a Quarter of Underage Drinkers Meet Clinical Criteria for Alcohol Abuse or Dependence. National Center on Addiction and Substance Abuse. Electronic document, http://www.casacolumbia.org/absolutenm/templates/print-article.aspx?articleid=437&zoneid=56.

Duzan, Maria, and Peter Eisner
1994 Death Beat: A Colombian Journalist's Life Inside the Cocaine Wars. New York: HarperCollins.

E. & J. Gallo Winery
2006 World Class Quality. Online at: http://jobs.gallo.com/WorldClass/WorldClas.asp.

Earleywine, M., and M. Newcomb
1997 Concurrent versus Simultaneous Polydrug Use: Prevalence, Correlates, Discriminant Validity, and Prospective Effects on Health Outcomes. Experimental Clinical Psychopharmacology 5(4):353–364.

Eaton, V.
1888 How the Opium Habit is Acquired. Popular Science 33:665–666.

Edwards, L.
2005 Wal-Mart Chipping in for Advocates. Arkansas Democrat Gazette. Electronic document, http://www.nwanews.com/adg/Business/140371/print.

Eichenwald, Kurt
2003 Conspiracy of Fools: A True Story: New York: Broadway Books.

Eiserman, Julie, Merrill Singer, Jean Schensul, and Lorie Broomhall
2003 Methodological Challenges in Club Drug Research. Practicing Anthropology 25(3):19–22.

El-Bassel, Nabila, Louisa Gilbert, Elwin Wu, Hyan Go, and Jennifer Hill
2005 Relationship between Drug Abuse and Intimate Partner Violence: A Longitudinal Study among Women Receiving Methadone. American Journal of Public Health 95:465–470.

Eskind Biomedical Library
2006 The Name that Launched a Million Bottles. Electronic document, http://www.mc.vanderbilt.edu/biolib/hc/nostrums/pinkham.html.

Fahrenkopf, F.
2004 Testimony before the U.S. Senate Committee on Banking, Housing, and Urban Affairs. Electronic document, http://www.americangaming.org/Press/speeches/speeches_detail.cfv?ID=305.

Farmer, Paul
1997 On Suffering and Structural Violence: A View from Below. *In* Social Suffering. Arthur Kleinman, Veena Das, Margaret Lock, eds. Pp. 261–284. Berkeley: University of California Press.

Farnsworth, JoAnn
2004 The Hawaii Island Meth Initiative. Hili: County of Hawaii.

Farrow, Anne, Joel Lang, and Jennifer Frank
2005 Complicity: How the North Promoted, Prolonged, and Profited from Slavery. New York: Balantine Books.

Favela Rising
2006 Film Web Site. Electronic document, http://wwwfavelarising.com/default.php.

Ferguson, James
2005 Seeing Like an Oil Company. American Anthropologist 107(3):377–382.

Fillmore, Kaye, William Kerr, Tim Stockwell, Tanya Chikritzhs, and Alan Bostrum
2006 Moderate Alcohol Use and Reduced Mortality Risk: Systematic Error in Prospective Studies. Addiction Research and Theory 14(2):101–132.

Finley, Harry
2005 Lydia E. Pinkham's Medicine Business. Electronic document, http://www.womenshistory.about.com/gi/dynamic/offsite.htm?zi=1/XJ&sdn=womenshistory&zu=http%3A%2F%2Fwww.mum.org%2FMrsPink1.htm.

Fishman, C.
2003 The Wal-Mart You Don't Know. Fast Company 77:68.

Flanigan, Patrick
2006a Crime-Fighter's Car Window Smashed. Rochester Democrat and Chronicle, June 13: 3.
2006b Tenant's Crime-Fighting Leading to Her Eviction. Rochester Democrat and Chronicle, June 5: 1.

Fontenot, Robert
2006 Standells Sue Anheuser-Busch over their "Dirty Water." Oldies Music. Electronic document, http://www.oldies.about.com/b/a/256091.htm.

Forbes.com
2005 Web Site. Electronic document, http://www.forbes.com/personalfinance/philanthropy/2005/11/11/charities-corporations-giving-cx_lm_1114charity.html.

Foster, Susan, Roger Vaughan, William Foster, and William Califano
2006 Estimate of the Commercial Value of Underage Drinking and Adult Abusive and Dependent Drinking to the Alcohol Industry. Archives of Pediatric and Adolescent Medicine 160:473–478.

Fowler, Gene, ed.
1997 Mystic Healers and Medicine Shows. Santa Fe, NM: Ancient City Press.

Freedman, Alix
1988 Wines and Winos: The Misery Market: Winos are a Major Embarrassment to Big Companies Producing Cheap Wines. Saturday Evening Post, July–August: 4, 5.

Freifeld, Karen
    2006 Bank to Settle Money-Laundering Probe. Hartford Courant, September 28: E3.
Friedman, Jonathan, ed.
    2003 Globalization, the State, and Violence. Walnut Creek, CA: AltaMira Press.
Friedman, Thomas
    2006 The World is Flat: A Brief History of the Twenty-First Century. New York: Farrar, Straus and Giroux.
FRONTLINE
    2000 Drug Wars. Electronic document, http://www.pbs.org/wgbh/pages/frontline/shows/drugs.
    2005a The Meth Epidemic. Interview with Gene Haislip, September 20. Electronic document, http://www.pbs.org/wgbh/pages/frontline/meth/interviews/haislip.html.
    2005b The Meth Epidemic. Interview with Steven Suo. Electronic document, http://www.pbs.org/wgbh/pages/frontline/meth/interviews/suo.html.
    2006 Inside the Tobacco Deal. Electronic document, http://www.pbs.org/wgbh/pages/frontline/shows/settlement/case/dogs.html.
Frost, Lars, and Peter Vestergaard
    2004 Alcohol and Risk of Atrial Fibrillation or Flutter: A Cohort Study. Archives of Internal Medicine 164:1993–1998.
Gallegos, B.
    1999 Chasing the Frogs and Camels out of Los Angeles: The Movement to Limit Alcohol and Tobacco Billboards: A Case Study. San Rafael, CA: The Marin Institute for the Prevention of Alcohol and Other Drug Problems.
Galvan, F., and R. Caetano
    2003 Alcohol Use and Related Problems among Ethnic Minorities in the United States. Alcohol Research and Health 27(1):87–96.
Gannotti, M., L. Kaplan, P. Handwerker, and N. Groce
    2004 Cultural Influences on Health Care Use: Differences in Perceived Unmet Needs and Expectations of Providers by Latino and Euro-American Parents of Children with Special Health Care Needs. Journal of Developmental Behavior and Pediatrics 25(3):156–165.
Garay, Annabelle
    2006 Hispanic Teens Abusing Prescription Drugs. Associated Press, July 26.
Garcia, Angela
    2006 Land of Disenchantment. High Country News, April 6.
Gardner, Martha, and Allan Brandt
    2006 The Doctor's Choice is America's Choice: The Physician in U.S. Cigarette Advertisements, 1930–1953. American Journal of Public Health 96(2):222–232.
Geertz, Clifford
    1973 The Interpretation of Cultures. New York: Basic Books.
Gelberg, Lillian, and Lisa Arangua
    2006 Homeless People. In Social Injustice and Health. Barry Levy and Victor Sidel, eds. Pp. 176–189. Oxford: Oxford University Press.
Gilbert, Louisa, Nabila El-Bassel, Valli Rajah, Anthony Foleno, Jorge Fontdevila, Victoria Frye, and Beverly Richman
    2000 The Converging Epidemics of Mood Altering-Drug Use, HIV, HCV, and Partner Violence. The Mount Sinai Journal of Medicine 67(5&6):452–464.

Gittins, Ross
    2006 Capital Flows Are Altering Economist's World View. The Sydney Morning Herald, August 26: 40.
Givhan, Robin
    2006 Bubbly Boycott? Oh Please, Jay-Z, Just Chill. Washington Post, July 7: C1–2.
Glantz, S.
    1983 Tobacco Industry Response to the Scientific Evidence on Passive Smoking. Proceedings of the 12th World Conference on Tobacco and Health, Winnipeg, Manitoba, pp. 297–292.
Glittenberg, J.
    2008. Violence and Hope in a U.S.–Mexico Border Town. Long Grove, IL: Waveland Press.
Glittenberg, Jody, and C. Anderson
    1999 Methamphetamines: Use and Trafficking in the Tucson-Nogales Area. Substance Use and Misuse 34(14):1977–1989.
Global Partnerships for Tobacco Control
    2002 What is Big Tobacco Up to Around the World. Electronic document, http://www.essentialaction.org/tobacco/qofm/0201a.html.
Gogek, James
    2004 Cinco de Mayo Should Not be for Sale. Amitai Etzioni Notes. Electronic document, http://www.amitai-notes.com/blog/archives/000694.html.
Goode, E.
    1984 Drugs in American Society. New York: Doubleday Anchor.
Gootenberg, P.
    2005 Talking Like a State: Drugs, Borders, and the Language of Control. In Illicit Flows and Criminal Things: States, Borders, and the Other Side of Globalization. W. van Schendel and I. Abraham, eds. Pp. 101–127. Bloomington: Indiana University Press.
Gorman, Michael, and R. Carroll
    2000 Substance Abuse and HIV: Considerations with Regard to Methamphetamines and Other Recreational Drugs for Nursing Practice and Research. Journal of the Association of Nurses in AIDS Care 11(2):51–62.
Gottlieb, Henry
    2003 Press Is Refused Access to Files in Prudential Fraud Case. Electronic document, http://www.law.com/jsp/article.jsp?id=1061487996845.
Gottlieb, L.
    1989 The Range of Medical Abnormalities Resulting from Asbestos Exposure. In Sourcebook on Asbestos Diseases: Medical, Legal, and Engineering Aspects, vol. 4: Asbestos Medical Research. George A. Peters and Barbara J. Peters, eds. Pp. 1–35. New York: Garland Law.
Graham, David
    2004 Testimony to Congress. Electronic document,
        http://www.finance.senate.gov/hearings/testimony/2004test/111804dgtest.pdf.
Graham, H.
    1987 Women's Smoking and Family Health. Social Science and Medicine 25:47–56.
    1993 Hardship and Health in Women's Lives. London: Harvester and Wheatsheaf.

1994 Gender and Class as Dimensions of Smoking Behaviour in Britain: Insights from a Survey of Mothers. Social Science and Medicine 38:691–698.

Graham, J.
1972 Amphetamine Politics on Capitol Hill. Transaction 9(3). Electronic document, http://www.geocities.com/zoots90210.

Grant, B., and D. Dawson
1997 Age of Onset of Alcohol Use and Its Association with DSM-IV Alcohol Abuse and Dependence: Results from the National Longitudinal Alcohol Epidemiologic Survey. Journal of Substance Abuse 9:103–110.

Greaves, T.
2006 Water Struggles of Indigenous North America. *In* Globalization, Water & Health. L. Whiteford and S. Whiteford, eds. Pp. 153–184. Santa Fe, NM: School of American Research Press.

Green, B., D. Kavanagh, and R. Young
2004 Reasons for Cannabis Use in Men with and without Psychosis. Drug and Alcohol Review 23(4):445–453.

Greenblatt, Janet, and Joseph Froerer
1997 Methamphetamine Abuse in the United States. Washington, DC: Office of Applied Studies, Substance Abuse and Mental Health Services Administration.

Greenhouse, S.
2002 Suits Say Wal-Mart Workers Forced to Toil Off the Clock. New York Times, June 25: 3.

Guzzinati, Laurie
2002 Philip Morris Companies, Inc. Announces Agreement to Merge Miller Brewing Company into South African Breweries plc. Electronic document, http://www.altria.com/download/pdf/media_117_final_release.pdf.

Haar, Dan
2006 Elephant in the Room: Low Value of Work. Hartford Courant, January 15: D1–D2.

Halpern, Georges
2005 COX-2 Inhibitors: A Story of Greed, Deception and Death. Inflammopharmacology13(4):419–425.

Hammond, D., N. Collishaw, and C. Callard
2006 Secret Science: Tobacco Industry Research on Smoking Behaviour and Cigarette Toxicity. Lancet 367(9512):781–787.

Hanson, David
2005a What's Wrong with the Alcohol Industry. Electronic document, http://www2.potsdam.edu/hansondj/Controversies/1088618303.html.
2005b Anti-Alcohol Industry 101: Overview of the Anti-Alcohol Industry in the U.S. Online. Electronic document, http://www2.potsdam.edu/hansondj/Controversies/1122492295.html.
2005c Alcohol and Health. Electronic document, http://www2.potsdam.edu/hansondj/AlcoholAndHealth.html.

Hastings, Deborah
2006 Iraq Contract Fraud Alleged. Hartford Courant, July 22: E1–E2.

Hastings, Gerald, Susan Anderson, Emma Cooke, and Ross Gordon
2005 Alcohol Marketing and Young People's Drinking: A Review of the Research. Journal of Public Health Policy 26:296–311.

Healy, David

2006 The New Medical Oikumene. *In* Global Pharmaceuticals: Ethics, Markets and Practices. Adriana Petryna, Andrew Larkoff, and Arthur Kleinman, eds. Pp. 61–84. Durham: Duke University Press.

Hensley, S.

2002 When Doctors Go to Class, Industry Often Foots the Bill: Lectures Tend to Feature Pills Made by Course Sponsors. Wall Street Journal, December 4: A1.

Hermansson, G.

2002 Doping Trade. Play the Game. Electronic document, http://www.playthegame.org/Knowledge%20bank/Articles/ Doping%20Trade,-c-,%20Business%20for%20The%20Big%20Ones.aspx#.

Hernon, Peter, and Terry Ganey

1991 Under the Influence: The Unauthorized Story of the Anheuser-Busch Dynasty. New York: Avon Books.

Heyman, J., and A. Smart

1999 States and Illegal Practices: An Overview. *In* States and Illegal Practices. J. Heyman, ed. Pp. 1–24. Oxford: Berg.

Hill, Peter

2003 The Japanese Mafia: Yakuza, Law, and the State. Oxford: Oxford University Press.

Hills, S.

1980 Demystifying Social Deviance. New York: McGraw-Hill.

Hingson, R., T. Heeren, and M. Winter

2006 Age at Drinking Onset and Alcohol Dependence Age at Onset, Duration, and Severity. Archives of Pediatric and Adolescent Medicine 160(7):739–746.

Hingson, R., T. Heeren, R. Zakocs, A. Kopstein, and H. Wechsler

2002 Magnitude of Alcohol-Related Mortality and Morbidity among U.S. College Students Ages 18–24. Journal of Studies on Alcohol 63(2):136–144.

Hingson, R., and D. Kenkel

2004 Social, Health, and Economic Consequences of Underage Drinking. *In* Reducing Underage Drinking: A Collective Responsibility, Background Papers [CD-ROM]. Pp. 351–382. Washington, DC: National Academies Press.

Hirayama, T.

1981 Non-Smoking Wives of Heavy Smokers Have a High Risk of Lung Cancer: A Study from Japan. British Medical Journal 282(17):183–185.

Ho, D.

1996 The Influence of Coinfections on HIV Transmission and Disease Progression. The AIDS Reader 6(4):114–116.

Hoffer, Lee

2006 Junkie Business: The Evolution and Operation of a Heroin Dealing Network. Belmont, CA: Thomas.

Holbrook, Stewart

1959 The Golden Age of Quackery. New York: Macmillan.

Horton, James, and Horton, Lois

2004 Slavery and the Making of America. Oxford: Oxford University Press.

Hymowitz, N., C. Moulton, and H. Edkholdt

1995 Menthol Cigarette Smoking in African Americans and Whites [Letter]. Tobacco Control 4:194–195.

Inciardi, James
    1986 The War on Drugs: Heroin, Cocaine, Crime, and Public Policy. Mountain View, CA: Mayfield.
Inciardi, James, D. Lockwood, and A. Pottieger
    1993 Women and Crack-Cocaine. New York: Macmillan.
Ismail, M. Asif
    2005 Drug Lobby Second to None: How the Pharmaceutical Industry Gets Its Way in Washington. Electronic document, http://www.publicintegrity.org/rx/report.aspx?aid=723.
Jacobs, Bruce
    1999 Dealing Crack: The Social World of Streetcorner Selling. Boston: Northeastern University Press.
James, W., and S. Johnson
    1996 Doin' Drugs: Patterns of African American Addiction. Austin: University of Texas Press.
Jankowiak, William, and Dan Bradburd
    1996 Using Drug Foods to Capture and Enhance Labor Performance: A Cross-Cultural Perspective. Current Anthropology 37(4):717–720.
Jaquiis, Nigel
    1998 Microblues: How Bud is Mashing Local Breweries. Willamette Week, April 8. Electronic document, http://www.wweek.com/html/cover040898.html.
Jarvis, M., and J. Wardle
    1999 Social Patterning of Individual Health Behaviours: The Case of Cigarette Smoking. In Social Determinants of Health. M. Marmot and R. Wilkinson, eds. Pp. 240–255. Oxford: Oxford University Press.
Jernigan, D., and P. Wright, eds.
    1994 Making News, Changing Policy: Using Media Advocacy to Change Alcohol and Tobacco Policy. Rockville, MD: Center for Substance Abuse Prevention.
Johnston, David
    2002 Justice Dept's Inquiry into Enron is Beginning to Take Shape, Without Big Names. New York Times, January 16: C7.
Join Together
    2000 Miller Agrees to Drop Portland Malt Liquor Ads. Electronic document, http://www.jointogether.org/news/headlines/inthenews/2000/miller-agrees-to-drop-malt.html.
    2006a Budweiser Formula Evolved to Encourage Greater Consumption. Electronic document, http://www.jointogether.org/news/headlines/inthenews/2006/budweiser-formula-evolved-to.html.
    2006b Notorious Cali Cartel Leaders Face U.S. Prison Time. Electronic document, http://www.jointogether.org/news/headlines/inthenews/2006/notorious-cali-cartel-leaders.html.
Jones, A.
    1994 Health, Addiction, Social Interaction and the Decision to Quit Smoking. Journal of. Health Economics 13(1):93–110.
Jordan, Miriam
    2006 Cerveza, Si o No? Wall Street Journal, March 29: 1.
Just How Tainted Has Medicine Become?
    2002 Lancet 359(9313):1167.

Kane, Stephanie, and Theresa Mason
    2001 AIDS and Criminal Justice. Annual Review of Anthropology 30:457–479. Palo Alto, CA: Annual Reviews.
Kassirer, Jerome
    2006 How Drug Lobbyists Influence Doctors. Boston Globe, February 13: 1.
Katz, J., and J. Solomon
    2005 Frist AIDS Charity Paid Consultants. Washington Post, December 18: 1.
Kellestad, Brent
    2006 Florida Court Rejects Huge Penalty for Big Tobacco. The Washington Post, July 7: D1–D2.
Kessler, David
    1994 Statement on Nicotine-Containing Cigarettes to the House Subcommittee on Health and the Environment by the Commissioner of the Food and Drug Administration. Electronic document, http://www.fda.gov/bbs/topics/SPEECH/SPE00052.htm.
Khabir, Naeemah
    2004 Community Protests Proposed Liquor Store. Philadelphia Tribune, July 30: 1.
Khadem, Nassim
    2006 Australians Drink at Dangerous Levels. The Age, August 26: 5.
Khan, Shaila, Robert Murray, and Gordon Barnes
    2002 A Structural Equation Model of the Effect of Poverty and Unemployment on Alcohol Abuse. Addictive Behaviors 27(3):405–423.
Khantzian, Edward
    1985 The Self-Medication Hypothesis of Addictive Disorders: Focus on Heroin and Cocaine Dependence. American Journal of Psychiatry 142:1259–1264.
    1989 Addiction: Self-Destruction or Self-Repair? Journal of Substance Abuse Treatment 6(2):75.
    1990 Self-Regulation and Self-Medication Factors in Alcoholism and the Addictions: Similarities and Differences. Recent Developments in Alcoholism 8:255–271.
    1991 Self-Regulation Factors in Cocaine Dependence—A Clinical Perspective. NIDA Research Monograph 110:211–226.
    1999 Treating Addiction as a Human Process: A Plea for a Measure of Marginality. New York: Jason Aronson.
Kilbourne, Jean
    1988 Alcohol Advertising: A Call for Congressional Action. Statement to the Committee on Governmental Affairs of the United States Senate, June 29.
Kim, Jim Yong, and Joyce Millen, eds.
    2000 Dying for Growth: Global Inequality and the Health of the Poor. Monroe, ME: Common Courage Press.
Kirchgaessner, Stephanie
    2006 Huge Fine as Insurer Admits U.S. Stock Rort. The Australian, August 20: 39.
Kleinman, Arthur, Veena Das, and Margaret Lock, eds.
    1997 Social Suffering. Berkeley: University of California Press.
Kluger, Richard
    1996 Ashes to Ashes: America's Hundred-Year Cigarette War, the Public Health, and the Unabashed Triumph of Philip Morris. New York: Vintage Books.

Kopytoff, Ivan
  1986 The Cultural Biography of Things: Commoditization as Process. *In* The
    Social Life of Things: Commodities in Cultural Perspective. Arjun Appa-
    durai, ed. Pp. 64–91. Cambridge: Cambridge University Press.
Krieger, Nancy
  2005 Introduction. Health Disparities and the Body Politic. Harvard School
    of Public Health Symposium Series. Pp. 5–9. Boston: Harvard School of
    Public Health.
Kroop, R.
  2001 The Topsy-Turvy World of Tobacco. Electronic document, http://
    www.essentialaction.org/tobacco/qofm/0201/usca.html.
Kumar, Suresh, Shakuntala Mudaliar, and Desmond Daniels
  1998 Community-Based Outreach HIV Intervention for Street-Recruited Drug
    Users in Madras, India. Public Health Reports 113 (Supplement 1):58–66.
Kurian, George
  1998 History of the FDA. *In* A Historical Guide to the U.S. Government.
    George Kurian, Joseph Harahan, and Morton Keller, eds. Pp. 248–254.
    New York: Oxford University Press.
Landa, Victor
  2005 Alcohol Marketing a Frightening Trend. San Antonio Express-News.
    Electronic document, http://www.mysanantonio.com/opinion/columnists/
    vlanda/stories/MYSA103105.2O.landa.6640975.html.
Laszewski, Charles, and Janet Roberts
  2004 Frogtown Still Fighting Drug Crime. Pioneer Press, May 9: 2.
Law, Jacky
  2006 Big Pharma: Exposing the Global Healthcare Agenda. New York: Car-
    roll and Graf.
LeClézio, Véronique
  2002 Tobacco Industry Activities in Mauritius. Electronic document, http://
    www.essentialaction.org/tobacco/qofm/0201/mauritius.html.
Lee, D., J. Gaynor, E. Trapido
  2003 Secondhand Smoke and Earaches in Adolescents: The Florida Youth
    Cohort Study. Nicotine and Tobacco Research 5(6):943–946.
Leinwand, Donna
  2006 DEA Warns of Soft Drink-Cough Syrup Mix. USA Today, October 19: 2A.
Lenz, Widukind
  1992 The History of Thalidomide. Electronic document,
    http://www.thalidomide.ca/en/information/history_of_thalidomide.html.
Levin, M., H. Goldstein, and P. Gerhardt
  1950 Cancer and Tobacco Smoking: A Preliminary Report. Journal of the
    American Medical Association 143:336–338.
Levy, Barry, and Victor Sidel
  2006 Social Injustice and Health. Oxford: Oxford University Press.
Life Style Extra
  2006 Alcohol Deaths Double. U.K. News, July 18. Electronic document,
    http://www.lse.co.uk/ShowStory.asp?story=QO18272271&
    news_headline=alcohol_deaths_double.
Lindberg, R.
  2001 Origins and History of the Mafia "Commission." Search International.

Electronic document, http://www.search-international.com/Articles/crime/mafiaorigins.htm.

Lineberry, Timothy, and J. Bostwick
2006 Methamphetamine Abuse: A Perfect Storm of Complications. Mayo Clinic Proceedings 81(1):77–84.

Ling, P., and S. Glantz
2003 Why and How the Tobacco Industry Sells Cigarettes to Young Adults: Evidence from Industry Documents. *In* Tobacco and Public Health. Pp. 122–130. Washington, DC: American Public Health Association.

Livingstone, Grace
2002 Inside Colombia: Drugs, Democracy, and War. Piscataway, NJ: Rutgers University Press.

Logan, T., Carl Leukefeld, and D. Farabee
1998 Sexual and Drug Use Behaviors among Women Crack Users: Implications for Prevention. AIDS Education and Prevention 10(4):327–340.

Lovell, Anne
2006 Addiction Markets: The Case of High-Dose Burpenorphine in France. *In* Global Pharmaceuticals: Ethics, Markets, Practices. Adriana Petryna, Andrew Lakoff, and Arthur Kleinman, eds. Pp. 136–170. Durham: Duke University Press.

Lucas, Scott
1985 The Encyclopedia of Psychoactive Drugs. Amphetamines: Danger in the Fast Lane. New York: Chelsea House Publishers.

Luka, Ann
1999 The Tobacco Industry and the First Amendment: An Analysis of the 1998 Master Settlement Agreement. Journal of Law and Health 14(2):297–320.

Luke, Douglas, Emily Esmundo, and Yael Bloom
2000 Smoke Signs: Patterns of Tobacco Billboard Advertising in a Metropolitan Region. Tobacco Control 9:16–23.

Lupsha, P.
1992 Drug Lords and Narco-Corruption: The Players Change but the Game Continues. *In* War on Drugs: Studies in the Failure of U.S. Narcotics Policy. Alfred W. McCoy and Alan A. Block, eds. Pp. 177–195. Boulder: Westview Press.

Luthar, S.
2003 The Culture of Affluence: Psychological Costs of Material Wealth. Child Development 74:1581–1593.

Madigan, Lisa
2004 Landmark Settlement of "Kool MIXX" Lawsuits. Electronic document, http://www.naatpn.org/news/top_04_10_06.html.

Mann, David
2006 Alcohol and Money in U.S. Politics. Electronic document, http://drugscope.blogspot.com/2006/04/friday-focus-alcohol-and-money-in-us.html.

Mannino, D., R. Albalak, S. Grosse, and J. Repace
2003 Second-Hand Smoke Exposure and Blood Lead Levels in U.S. Children. Epidemiology 14(6):719–727.

Marin Institute
2004 Californians Pay the Price: Alcohol Abuse Costs Billion. Electronic document, http://www.marininstitute.org/alcohol_policy/hot/nov04.htm.

2006a Buying Influence: Alcohol Industry Campaign Contributions in California. Electronic document, http://www.marininstitute.org/alcohol_industry/contributions.htm.

2006b Money from Misery: Anheuser-Busch Uses Hurricane Katrina as an Opportunity to Increase Profits. Electronic document, http://www.marininstitute.org/alcohol_industry/money_from_misery.htm.

2006c New Booze Gets Youth Buzzed. Electronic document, http://www.marininstitute.org/alcohol_industry/AB_gets_youth_buzzed.htm.

2006d Latinos Say "Hands Off Our Holiday." Electronic document, http://www.marininstitute.org/take_action/hands-off.htm.

Marmot, Michael, and Ruth Bell
2006 The Socioeconomically Disadvantaged. *In* Injustice and Health, Barry Levy and Victor Sidel, eds. Pp. 25–44. Oxford: Oxford University Press.

Marshall, Mac
2004 Market Highs: Alcohol, Drugs, and the Global Economy in Oceania. *In* Globalization and Culture Change in the Pacific Islands. Victoria Lockwood, ed. Pp. 200–221. Upper Saddle River, NJ: Pearson/Prentice Hall.

2005 Carolina in the Carolines: A Survey of Patterns and Meanings of Smoking on a Micronesian Island. Medical Anthropology Quarterly 19(4):365–382.

Martens, Jens
2005 A Compendium of Inequality: The Human Development Report. Berlin: Friedrich-Ebert-Stiftung.

Martin, Susan Taylor
2001 Us versus Them: U.S. Policy Not Limited to Borders. St. Petersburg Times, July 29: 1.

Martineau, Kim
2006 Thief's Next 3½ Years Mapped Out. Hartford Courant, September 28: 1, 10.

Marx, Karl, and Frederick Engels
1848 The Communist Manifesto. London: The Communist League.

Massachusetts Department of Public Health
2002 Smokeless Tobacco Advertising Expenditures Before and After the Smokeless Tobacco Master Settlement Agreement. Electronic document, http://tobaccofreekids.org/pressoffice/release503/smokeless.pdf.

Mathews, Anna
2005 At Medical Journals, Paid Writers Play Big Role. Wall Street Journal, December 13: 1.

Mathews, Anna Wilde, and Barbara Martinez
2004 Warning Signs: E-Mails Suggest Merck Knew Vioxx's Dangers at Early Stage. The Wall Street Journal, November 1: A1.

Mattera, Philip, and Anna Purinton
2004 Shopping for Subsidies: How Wal-Mart Uses Taxpayer Money to Finance Its Never-Ending Growth. Washington, DC: Good Jobs First.

Mayko, M.
2005 Testimony: Arrest Didn't Stop Drug Deals. Connecticut Post, November 10: 1.

McClure, A., S. Dal Cin, J. Gibson, and J. Sargent
2006 Ownership of Alcohol-Branded Merchandise and Initiation of Teen Drinking. American Journal of Preventive Medicine 30(4):277–283.

McCoy, Alfred

    1995 Historical Review of Opium/Heroin Production. Electronic document, http://www.druglibrary.org/Schaffer/heroin/historic.htm.

McCubbin, Hamilton, Elizabeth Thompson, Anne Thompson, and Julie Fromer, eds.

    1998 Resiliency in Native American and Immigrant Families. Thousand Oaks, CA: Sage.

Mehrabadi, A.

    2005 Patients and Biotechnology: From a Satellite Looking Down at Our Use of Patents in the Great Planetary Scheme of Things. The Science Creative Quarterly 1(April–June):1.

Merlin, M.

    1984 On the Trail of the Ancient Opium Poppy. Rutherford, NJ: Fairleigh Dickinson University Press.

Merton, Robert

    1968 Social Theory and Social Structure. New York: The Free Press.

Mills, C. Wright

    1959 The Sociological Imagination. Oxford: Oxford University Press.

Mindell, Earl

    1999 Prescription Alternatives. New York: McGraw-Hill.

Mindus, Dan

    2003 Behind the Neo-Prohibition Campaign: The Robert Wood Johnson Foundation. Electronic document, http://www.consumerfreedom.com/article_detail.cfm/article/133.

Miner, R., and J. Crutcher

    2002 Second-Hand Tobacco Smoke in Oklahoma: A Preventable Cause of Morbidity and Mortality and Means of Reducing Exposure. Journal of the Oklahoma State Medical Association 95(3)135–141.

Mintz, Morton

    1962 "Heroine" of FDA Keeps Bad Drug Off of Market. The Washington Post, July 15: 1.

Mintz, Sidney

    1985 Sweetness and Power: The Place of Sugar in Modern History. New York: Penguin.

Modern Drunkard Magazine

    2004 Forty Ounces of Fury. Electronic document, http://www.moderndrunkardmagazine.com/issues/03_03/03-03_forty_fury.htm.

Mokhiber, Russel

    2005 Top 100 Corporate Criminals of the Decade. Electronic document, http://www.sorporatecrimereporter.com/top100.html.

Morrison, Toni, ed.

    1993 Race-ing Justice, En-gendering Power: Essays on Anita Hill, Clarence Thomas and the Construction of Social Reality. London: Chatto and Windus.

Mosher, James, and Diane Johnsson

    2006 Flavored Alcoholic Beverages: An International Marketing Campaign that Targets Youth. Journal of Public Health Policy 26:326–342.

Moyer, L.

    2005 The Most Charitable Companies. Electronic document, http://www.forbes.com/personalfinance/philanthropy/2005/11/11/charities-corporations-giving-cx_lm_1114charity.html.

Moyers, Bill
    2002 Tobacco Traffic. April 19. Electronic document, http://www.pbs.org/
        now/transcript/transcript114_full.html.
Muntaner, Charles, and Jeanne Greiger-Brown
    2005 Mental Health. *In* Social Injustice and Health. Barry Levy and Victor
        Sidel, eds. Pp. 277–293. Oxford: Oxford University Press.
Murray, C., and A. Lopez
    1996 Evidence-Based Health Policy—Lessons from the Global Burden of
        Disease Study. Science 274(5293):1593–1594.
Murray, D.
    1993 Migration, Protection and Racketeering: The Spread of Tiandihui in
        China. *In* Secret Societies Reconsidered: Perspectives on the Social His-
        tory of Modern South China and Southeast Asia. D. Ownby and M. Som-
        ers, eds. Armonk, NY: Sharpe.
Musto, D.
    1987 The American Disease: Origins of Narcotic Control. Oxford: Oxford
        University Press.
Myers, M.
    2002a California Judge Finds R.J. Reynolds Guilty of Marketing to Kids in
        Violation of 1998 Settlement Agreement. Electronic document, http://
        www.tobaccofreekids.org/Script/DisplayPressRelease.php3?Display=506.
    2002b United States Smokeless Tobacco Caught Increasing Marketing to
        Kids after Signing Agreement to Stop. Electronic document, http://
        www.tobaccofreekids.org/Script/DisplayPressRelease.php3?Display=503.
National Association of African Americans for Positive Imagery
    2004a Defeat of PowerMaster Malt Liquor. Electronic document, http://
        www.naaapi.org/documents/powermaster.asp.
    2004b X Cigarette. Electronic document, http://www.naaapi.org/campaigns/
        1995.asp.
National Cancer Institute
    1999 Health Effects of Exposure to Environmental Tobacco Smoke: The
        Report of the California Environmental Protection Agency (Smoking and
        Tobacco Control Monograph No. 10, NIH Publication No. 99-4645).
        Bethesda, MD: U.S. Department of Health and Human Services, National
        Institutes of Health.
    2005 Fact Sheet: Quitting Tobacco: Handling Stress . . . Without Smoking.
        Electronic document, http://www.cancer.gov/cancertopics/factsheet/
        Tobacco/stress.
National Center for Health Statistics
    2003 National Vital Statistics Reports 52(3), September 18.
National Center for Injury Prevention and Control
    2005 10 Leading Causes of Death, United States: Black, Non-Hispanic, Both
        Sexes. Electronic document,
        http://webapp.cdc.gov/sasweb/ncipc/leadcaus10. htmlin.
National Coalition for LGBT Health
    2004 New Campaign Addresses Crystal Meth Use in New York's African-
        American Community. Press Release. Pp. 1–2. Washington, DC: National
        Coalition for LGBT Health.

National Highway Traffic Safety Administration
    2005 Traffic Safety Facts: Young Drivers. Electronic document, http://www-nrd.
    nhsta.dot.gov/pdf/nrd-30/NCSA/TSF2005/810630.pdf.
National Institute on Drug Abuse
    2003 Monitoring the Future 2003 Data From In-School Surveys of 8th-, 10th-,
    and 12th-Grade Students. Washington, DC: National Institute of Health.
    2004a NIDA Info Facts. Electronic document, www.drugabuse.gov.
    2004b Monitoring the Future Study: National Results on Adolescent Drug
    Use. Washington, DC: National Institute of Health.
    2005 Drug Use among Racial/Ethnic Minorities. Rockville, MD: National
    Institute of Health.
National Library of Medicine
    2004 Biography: Dr. Frances Kathleen Oldham Kelsey. Electronic document,
    http://www.nlm.nih.gov/changingthefaceofmedicine/physicians/
    biography_182.html.
Navarro, Vicente
    2002 Neoliberalism, "Globalization," Unemployment, Inequalities, and the
    Welfare State. In The Political Economy of Social Inequalities: Conse-
    quences for Health and Quality of Life. Vicente Navarro, ed. Pp. 33–108.
    Amityville, NY: Baywood.
Neighbors, C., C. Spieker, L. Oster-Aaland, M. Lewis, and R. Bergstrom
    2006 Celebration Intoxication: An Evaluation of 21st Birthday Alcohol Con-
    sumption. Journal of American College Health 54(5):305–306.
NeSmith, Georgia
    2006 Taking Back the Neighborhood. Electronic document, http://
    www.homepage.mac.com/georgia.nesmith/iblog/C44378635/
    E20060616202502/index.html.
Newman, Andrew Adam
    2006 Overage Logos, Underage Market. New York Times, October 16. Elec-
    tronic document, http://www.nytimes.com/2006/10/16/business/media/
    16beer.html?ex=1318651200&en=fca11dfc9622e341&ei=
    5088&partner=rssnyt&emc=rss.
Nichols, John
    1974 The Milagro Beanfield War. New York: Henry Holt & Company.
Nichter, Mark, and Elizabeth Cartwright
    1991 Saving the Children for the Tobacco Industry. Medical Anthropology
    5:236–256.
Night Club and Bar Magazine
    2006 Beverage Bosses: Top Minds in the Industry Shared Insight on How to
    Reach the New Customer, May. Electronic document,
    http://www.nightclub.com/NCB_Magazine/NCB_May_2006/
    Beverage_Bosses.
Norr, Roy
    1952 Cancer by the Carton. Reader's Digest, July: 7–8.
Nusbaum, M., R. Wallace, L. Slatt, and E. Kondrad
    2004 Sexually Transmitted Infections and Increased Risk of Co-Infection
    with Human Immunodeficiency Virus. Journal of the American Osteo-
    pathic Association 104(12):527–535.

NZPA
  2005 Tobacco Companies "Target Poor." New Zealand Herald, May 25. Elec-
    tronic document, http://www.nzherald.co.nz/organisation/story.cfm?o_id=
    351&ObjectID=10358487.
Office of Applied Studies
  2005 National Survey on Drug Use & Health. Electronic document, http://
    www.drugabusestatistics.samhsa.gov/nsduh/2k5Results.htm#TOC.
Oligopoly Watch
  2004 Wal-Mart the Welfare Queen. Electronic document,
    http://www/oligopolywatch.com/2004/09/25.html.
Ong, E., and S. Glantz
  2000 Hirayama's Work Has Stood the Test of Time. Bulletin of the World
    Health Organization 78(7):938–939. Electronic document, http://
    www.economist.com/world/na/displaystory.cfm?story_id=4403338.
Owen, Frank
  2000 No Man is a Crystal Meth User Unto Himself. New York Times,
    August 29: 4.
Pacific Institute for Research and Evaluation (PIRE)
  2001 Impaired Driving in Colorado. Electronic document, http://
    www.nhtsa.dot.gov/people/injury/alcohol/impaired_driving_pg2/CO.htm.
Page, J. Bryant, and Sian Evans
  2003 Cigars, Cigarillos, and Youth: Emergent Patterns of Subcultural Com-
    plexes. Journal of Ethnicity in Substance Abuse 2(4):63–76.
PakTribune
  2006 Heroin Lab Workers Suffering from Different Diseases. Pakistan News
    Service, July 16.
Pappas, G., F. Hadden, S. Queen, W. Hadden, and G. Fisher
  1993 The Increasing Disparity in Mortality between Socioeconomic Groups
    in the United States, 1960 and 1986. The New England Journal of Medi-
    cine 329(2):103–109.
Parenti, Michael
  1980 Democracy for the Few. New York: St. Martin's Press.
Parker, Robert, and Linda-Anne Rebhun
  1995 Alcohol and Homicide: A Deadly Combination of Two American Tradi-
    tions. Albany: State University of New York.
Parrott, A. C.
  1999 Does Cigarette Smoking Cause Stress? American Psychologist
    54(10):817–820.
Patten, C.
  2001 Never the Twain Shall Meet? Adapting Kipling to a Globalised World.
    Electronic document, http://www.europa.eu.int/comm/external_relations/
    news/patten/sp01_461.htm.
Pepples, E.
  1976/1996 Industry Response to the Cigarette/Health Controversy, 1976,
    Internal Memo #2205.01. In The Cigarette Papers. Stanton Glantz et al.,
    eds. P. 392. Berkeley: University of California Press.
Petryna, Adriana, and Arthur Kleinman
  2006 The Pharmaceutical Nexus. In Global Pharmaceuticals: Ethics, Markets
    and Practices. Adriana Petryna, Andrew Larkoff, and Arthur Kleinman,
    eds. Pp. 1–32. Durham: Duke University Press.

Pettegrew, J., K. Panchalingam, A. Stanley, R. McClure, P. Mandal, and K. Perkins
2006 Neuromolecular Effects of Nicotine. Presented at Neuroscience, Atlanta, GA.

Philip Morris
2006a Smoking and Health Issues. Electronic document, http://www.philipmorrisusa.com/en/health_issues/?source=home_fca1.
2006b Legislation and Restriction. Electronic document, http://www.philipmorrisusa.com/en/legislation_regulation/smoking_restrictions.asp.

Philip Morris International Management
2006 Counterfeiting. Electronic document, http://www.philipmorrisinternational.com/PMINTL/pages/eng/busenv/Counterfeiting.asp.

Pierce, J., J. Distefan, C. Jackson, M. Martha, A. White, and E. Gilpin
2002 Does Tobacco Marketing Undermine the Influence of Recommended Parenting in Discouraging Adolescents from Smoking? American Journal of Preventive Medicine 23(2):73–81.

Pines, Wayne
2006 FDA: A Century of Consumer Protection. Washington, DC: Food and Drug Law Institute.

Pinkerton
2006 Company Web Site. Electronic document, http://www.ci-pinkerton.com/history.html.

Pletcher, Mark, Benjamin Hulley, Thomas Houston, Catarina Kiefe, Neal Benowitz, and Stephen Sidney
2006 Menthol Cigarettes, Smoking Cessation, Atherosclerosis, and Pulmonary Function: The Coronary Artery Risk Development in Young Adults (CARDIA) Study. Archives of Internal Medicine 166:1915–1922.

Pollay, R., J. Lee, and D. Carter-Whitney
1992 Separate but Not Equal: Racial Segmentation in Cigarette Advertising. Journal of Advertising 21:1.

Porter, B.
1991 Where to Get Some (Drug) Money. Electronic document, http://www.archives.cjr.org/year/91/5drug_laundering.asp.

Prideau, Michael
2004 Corporate Social Responsibility: Mainstream or Sidestream? Speech at the World Tobacco Symposium & Exhibition, Kunming, China. Electronic document, http://www.bat.com/oneweb/sites/uk__3mnfen.nsf/vwPagesWebLive/DO52A.

Project Censored
2004 Wealth Inequality in 21st Century Threatens Economy and Democracy. Electronic document, http://www.projectcensored.org/publications/2005/1.html.

Public Citizen
2004 The Medicare Drug War. Electronic document, http://www.badfaithinsurance.org/reference/HL/0098b.pdf.

Rabasa, Angel, and Peter Chalk
2001 Colombian Labyrinth: The Synergy of Drugs and Insurgency and Its Implications for Regional Instability. Santa Monica, CA: RAND.

Rajan, Kaushik Sunder
    2006 Biocapital: The Constitution of Postgenomic Life. Durham: Duke
        University Press.
Ramsden, I.
    1990 Whakaruruhau: Cultural Safety in Nursing Education in Aotearoa.
        Auckland: Maori Health and Nursing, Ministry of Education, Government
        of New Zealand.
Rannazzisi, Joseph
    2006 Prescription Drug Abuse: What is Being Done to Address This New
        Drug Epidemic? Testimony before the Subcommittee on Criminal Justice,
        Drug Policy, and Human Resources of the House Government Reform
        Committee, July 26. Electronic document, http://www.dea.gov/pubs/
        cngrtest/ct072606.html.
Ratner, Mitch, ed.
    1993 Crack Pipe as Pimp: An Ethnographic Investigation of Sex-for-Crack
        Exchanges. New York: Lexington.
Reiman, Jeffery, ed.
    2003 The Rich Get Richer and the Poor Get Prison: Ideology, Class, and
        Criminal Justice. 7th edition. Boston: Allyn & Bacon.
Reiman, Jeffery, and Leighton, Paul
    2003a A Tale of Two Criminals: We're Tougher on Corporate Criminals, But
        They Still Don't Get What They Deserve. In The Rich Get Richer and the
        Poor Get Prison: Ideology, Class, and Criminal Justice. 7th edition. Jeffery
        Reiman, ed. Boston: Allyn & Bacon.
    2003b Getting Tough on Corporate Crime? Enron and a Year of Corporate
        Financial Scandals. In The Rich Get Richer and the Poor Get Prison: Ideol-
        ogy, Class, and Criminal Justice. 7th edition. Jeffery Reiman, ed. Boston:
        Allyn & Bacon.
Reinarman, Craig, and Harry Levine, eds.
    1997 The Crack Attack: Politics and Media in the Crack Scare. In Crack in
        America: Demon Drugs and Social Justice. Pp. 18–51. Berkeley: Univer-
        sity of California Press.
Reno, J.
    1999 Statement by Attorney General Janet Reno on the Filing against the
        Major Tobacco Companies, September 22. Electronic document, http://
        www.usdoj.gov/opa/pr/1999/September/430ag.htm.
Rettig, Richard
    1999[1977] Manny: A Criminal-Addict's Story. Long Grove, IL: Waveland
        Press.
Richardson, Karen
    2001 Smoking, Low Income and Health Inequalities: Thematic Discussion
        Document. Report for Action on Smoking and Health and the Health
        Development Agency. Electronic document, http://www.renewal.net/
        Documents/RNET/Research/Smokinglowincome.pdf.
Richter, L., R. Vaughan, and S. Foster
    2004 Public Attitudes about Underage Drinking Policies: Results from a
        National Survey. Journal of Public Health Policy 25(1):58–77.
Robinson, Charyn, and Robert Sutton
    2004 The Marketing of Menthol Cigarettes in the United States: Popula-

tions, Messages, and Channels. Nicotine and Tobacco Research 6(Supplement 1):S83–S91.

Rogers, R., C. Nam, and R. Hummer
1995 Demographic and Socio-Economic Links to Cigarette Smoking. Social Biology 42(1–2):1–21.

Romero-Daza, N., M. Weeks, and M. Singer
2003 "Nobody Gives a Damn If I Live or Die": Violence, Drugs and Street-Level Prostitution in Inner City Hartford, Connecticut. Medical Anthropology 3:233–239.

Roux, Ana Diez, Sharon Merkin, Donna Arnett, Lloyd Chambless, Mark Massing, F. Javier Nieto, Paul Sorlie, Moyses Szklo, Herman Tyroler, and Robert Watson
2001 Neighborhood of Residence and Incidence of Coronary Heart Disease. The New England Journal of Medicine 345(2):99–106.

Roy, A.
1997 Civil Society and the Nation State in the Context of Globalization. In Globalization and SAP: Trends and Impact—An Overview. A. Muricken, ed. Pp. 81–96. Mumbai, India: Vikas Adhiyayan Kendra.

Rubin, Rita
2006 In Tim Ryan's Family, He is the Addict. USA Today, July 26: 1.

Rumble, Eric
2006 Business as Usual. Adbusters: Journal of Mental Environment. July/August:46–47.

Russell, Faith
2005 Alcohol and Tobacco Taxes: Informational Paper 8. Madison: Wisconsin Legislative Fiscal Bureau.

Saffer, Henry
2006 The Effect of Advertising on Tobacco and Alcohol Consumption. National Bureau of Economic Research. Electronic document, http://www.nber.org/reporter/winter04/saffer.html.

Saffer, H., and M. Dave
2006 Alcohol Advertising and Alcohol Consumption by Adolescents. Health Economics Early View, February 13.

Salinger, Lawrence
2004 Encyclopedia of White-Collar & Corporate Crime. Thousand Oaks, CA: Sage.

Schaeffer, R.
2003 Understanding Globalization: The Social Consequences of Political, Economic, and Environmental Change. Lanham, MD: Little Brown and Company.

Schensul, Jean, Sarah Diamond, William Disch, Rey Bermudez, and Jule Eiserman
2005 The Diffusion of Ecstasy through Urban Youth Networks. In New Drugs on the Street: Changing Inner City Patterns or Illicit Drugs. Merrill Singer, ed. Pp. 39–72. Binghampton, NY: Haworth Press.

Scott, James
1998 Seeing Like a State: How Certain Schemes to Improve the Human Condition Have Failed. New Haven: Yale University Press.

Seabrook, Jeremy
1999 Smoking and the Poor. Third World Network. Electronic document, http://www.pnews.org/art/2art/tobacpoor.html.

Seay, Gregory
    2005 Raids Stoke Fears of Meth. Hartford Courant, June 10: 1, 5.
Seltzer, Michael
    2004 Haven in a Heartless Sea: The Sailors' Tavern in History and Anthropology. The Social History of Alcohol and Drugs 19:63–93.
Shapiro, Mark
    2002 Is Smuggling a Patriotic Act? The Nation, April 18. Electronic document, http://www.thenation.com/doc/20020429/schapiro20020418.
Sharpe, Tanya Telfair
    2005 Behind the Eight Ball: Sex for Crack Cocaine Exchange and Poor Black Women. New York: Haworth Press.
Sheridan, B.
    1995 Fed's Big Catch: Man at Center of Cali Cartel. Miami Herald, October 5: 24A.
Shishkin, Philip, and David Crawford
    2006 In Afghanistan, Heroin Trade Soars Despite U.S. Aid. Wall Street Journal, January 18: 1.
Short, P.
    1977 Smoking and Health Item 7: The Effect on Marketing, April 14. Minnesota Trial Exhibit #10,585.
Siahpush, M., G. Heller, and G. Singh
    2005 Lower Levels of Occupation, Income and Education are Strongly Associated with Longer Smoking Duration: Multivariate Analysis Results from the 2001 Australian National Drug Strategy Survey. Public Health 119:1105–1110.
Siegel, Larry
    1998 Criminology. Belmont, CA: Thomson.
Singer, Merrill
    1996 A Dose of Drugs, a Touch of Violence, a Case of AIDS: Conceptualizing the SAVA Syndemic. Free Inquiry in Creative Sociology 24(2):99–110.
    1999 Why Do Puerto Rican Injection Drug Users Inject So Often? Anthropology and Medicine 6(1):31–58.
    2004a Why it is Easier to Get Drugs than Drug Treatment? In Unhealthy Health Policy: A Critical Anthropological Examination. Arachu Castro and Merrill Singer, eds. Pp. 287–303. Walnut Creek, CA: AltaMira Press.
    2004b Tobacco Use in Medical Anthropological Perspective. In Encyclopedia of Medical Anthropology: Health and Illness in the World's Cultures. Carol Ember and Melvin Ember, eds. Pp. 518–527. New York: Kluwer.
    2006a Something Dangerous: Emergent and Changing Drug Use and Community Health. Long Grove, IL: Waveland Press.
    2006b The Face of Social Suffering: The Life History of a Street Drug Addict. Long Grove, IL: Waveland Press.
    2006c A Dose of Drugs, a Touch of Violence, a Case of AIDS, Part 2: Further Conceptualizing the SAVA Syndemic. Free Inquiry in Creative Sociology 34(1):39–51.
Singer, Merrill, and Hans Baer
    In press Hidden Harm: An Introduction to the Complex World of Killer Commodities. In Killer Commodities: A Critical Anthropological Examination of Corporate Production of Harm. Merrill Singer and Hans Baer, eds. Thousand Oaks, CA: AltaMira Press.

Singer, Merrill, and Scott Clair
  2003 Syndemics and Public Health: Reconceptualizing Disease in Bio-Social Context. Medical Anthropology Quarterly 17(4):423–441.
Singer, Merrill, Pamela Erickson, Louise Badiane, Rosemary Diaz, Dugeidy Ortiz, Traci Abraham, and Anna Marie Nicolaysen
  2006a Syndemics, Sex and the City: Understanding Sexually Transmitted Disease in Social and Cultural Context. Social Science and Medicine 63(8):2010–2021.
Singer, Merrill, and Greg Mirhej
  2004 The Understudied Supply Side: Public Policy Implications of the Illicit Drug Trade in Hartford, CT. Harvard Health Policy Review 5(2):36–47.
Singer, Merrill, Greg Mirhej, Claudia Santelices, Erica Hastings, Juhem Navarro, and Jim Vivian
  2006b Tomorrow is Already Here, Or Is It? Steps in Preventing a Local Methamphetamine Outbreak. Human Organization 65(2):203–217.
Singer, Merrill, Hassan Salaheen, Greg Mirhej, and Claudia Santelices
  2006c Bridging the Divide: Drinking among Street Drug Users. American Anthropologist 108(3):502–506.
Singer, P.
  2003 Corporate Warriors: The Rise of Privatized Military Industrial Complex. Ithaca, NY: Cornell University Press.
Sklar, Holly
  2006 It's Boom Time for Billionaires. The Hartford Courant, October 4: A11.
Slater, M., M. Long, and V. Ford
  2006 Alcohol, Illegal Drugs, Violent Crime, and Traffic-Related and Other Unintended Injuries in U.S. Local and National News. Journal of Studies on Alcohol 67(6):904–911.
Smalley, Suzanne
  2006 Opiate Fentanyl Gaining Foothold; Region's Overdose Rate on the Rise. The Boston Globe, July 16: 1.
Smith, E., and R. Malone
  2003 "Altria" Means Tobacco: Phillip Morris's Identity Crisis. American Journal of Public Health 93:553–556.
  2005 Altria Means Tobacco. University of California, San Francisco. Electronic document, http://www.altriameanstobacco.com.
Smith, George, Deborah Wentworth, James Neaton, Rose Stamler, and Jeremiah Stamler
  1996 Socioeconomic Differentials in Mortality Risk among Men Screened for the Multiple Risk Factor Intervention Trail: Part II-Results for 20,224 Men. American Journal of Public Health 86:497–504.
Smith, Jeffery
  2005 Big Tobacco Jets DeLay to Court. Washington Post, October 22: 1.
Smith, Larry
  2006 Carlos Lehder's Bahamian Legacy. Bahama Pundit. Electronic document, http://www.bahamapundit.com/2006/07/carlos_lehders_.html.
Snyder, L., F. Milici, M. Slater, H. Sun, and Y. Strizhakova
  2006 Effects of Alcohol Advertising Exposure on Drinking among Youth. Archives of Pediatrics and Adolescent Medicine 160:18–24.
Spector, M.
  2006 Dark Days are Nigh for MLB. National Post, March 8: 12.

Stead, M., S. MacAskill, A-M. MacKintosh, D. Eadie, and G. Hastings
    1999 An Investigation into Smoking Cessation in Disadvantaged Communities: Qualitative Focus Group Research. Centre for Tobacco Control Research, University of Strathclyde.
Stebbins, K.
    2001 Going like Gangbusters. Transnational Tobacco Companies "Making a Killing" in South America. Medical Anthropology Quarterly 15:147–170.
Sterk, Clare
    2000 Tricking and Tripping: Prostitution in the Era of AIDS. Putnam Valley, NY: Social Change Press.
Stoddard, J., C. Johnson, T. Boley-Cruz, and S. Sussman
    1997 Target Tobacco Markets: Outdoor Advertising in Los Angeles Minority Neighbors [Letter]. American Journal of Public Health 87:1232–1233.
Stopka, Thomas, Kristen Springer, Kaveh Khoshnood, Susan Shaw, and Merrill Singer
    2004 Writing about Risk: Use of Daily Diaries in Understanding Drug-User Risk Behaviors. AIDS and Behavior 8(1):73–85.
Stowe, Harriet Beecher
    1879 The Education of Freemen. The North American Review, June.
Sturm, R.
    2002 The Effects of Obesity, Smoking, and Problem Drinking on Chronic Medical Problems and Health Care Costs. Health Affairs 21(2):245–253.
Substance Abuse and Mental Health Services Administration
    2003 Results from the 2002 National Survey on Drug Use and Health: National Findings. Rockville, MD: SAMHSA.
    2005 The Dasis Report: Polydrug Use Admissions, 2002. Electronic document, http://www.oas.samhsa.gov/2k5/polydrugTX/polydrugTX.htm.
Sutherland, Edwin
    1985 White Collar Crime: The Uncut Version. New Haven: Yale University Press.
Swift, Mike, J. Dolan, and Helen Ubinas
    2001 Not Just a City Problem: Hartford's Drug Market Draws Participants from Wide Area, Statistics Show. Hartford Courant, July 29: 1, 7.
Szabo, Liz
    2006 Secondhand Smoke Debate is "Over." USA Today, June 28: 4A.
Szalavitz, M.
    1996 By Demonizing Drug Users, the Partnership for a Drug-Free America Worsens their Plight. Salon. Electronic document, http://www.salon.com/media/media960904.html.
Tamayo, Juan
    2001 Thriving Heroin Culture Alarms Colombian, U.S. Authorities. Miami Herald, August 18: A1.
Taussig, Doron
    2004 Cork and Battle: The Fight over a North Philly Liquor Store Will Hit Court Next Week. Philadelphia CityPaper.Net. Electronic document, http://www.citypaper.net.
Taylor, Frances
    2006 A Family Confronts its History. Hartford Courant, July 5: A1, A7.
Tedeschi, Gary
    2004 Stress and Smoking: A Cruel Paradox. Helpwire, Winter: 1, 4.

Temporal, Paul
   1999 Strategic Positioning. Oxford: Oxford University Press.
Thaqi, A., A. Franke, G. Merkel, H. Wichmann, and J. Heinrich
   2005 Biomarkers of Exposure to Passive Smoking of School Children: Frequency and Determinants. Indoor Air 15(5):302–309.
The Economist
   2004 The Price of Powder. Electronic document, http://www.cocaine.org/cokecrime/prices.html.
Thomas, G.
   2005 Rival Drug Gangs Turn the Streets of Nuevo Laredo into a War Zone. New York Times, December 14: 5.
Thomas, G. Scott
   2004 Where is the Best Place to Live in America? Electronic document, http://www.msnbc.msn.com/id/5023308.
Thomas, Pamela
   2006 Illicit Drugs and Development: Critical Issues for Asia and the Pacific. Development Studies Network Development Bulletin 69: 5–9.
Thomas, Piri
   1967 Down These Mean Streets. New York: Vintage Books.
Thun, Michael
   2005 When Truth is Unwelcome: The First Reports on Smoking and Lung Cancer. Bulletin of the World Health Organization 83(2):144–145.
Todis, Bonnie, Michael Bullis, Miriam Waintrup, Robert Schultz, and Ryan D'Ambrosio
   2001 Overcoming the Odds: Qualitative Examination of Resilience among Formerly Incarcerated Adolescents. Exceptional Children 68(1):119–139.
Tominaga, Gail, Garrett Garcia, A. Dzierba, and J. Wong
   2004 Toll of Methamphetamine on the Trauma System. The Archives of Surgery 139(8):844–847.
Torry, S.
   1998 Tobacco's Lobbying Outlays Soared in '98. Washington Post, October 30: A10.
Tuohy, L.
   2005a Kingpin Details Ruthless Reign. Hartford Courant, November 27: 1, 16.
   2005b Ex-Drug Lord Testifies. Hartford Courant, November 17: B1, B7.
UNICEF
   2004 State of the World's Children 2004. New York: UNICEF.
Union Carbide
   2005 Statement of Union Carbide Corporation Regarding the Bhopal Tragedy. Electronic document, http://www.ghopal.com/ucs.htm.
Union of Concerned Scientists
   2006 Voices of Scientists at the FDA. Electronic document, http://www.ucsusa.org/scientific_integrity/interference/fda-scientist-survey.html.
United Nations Development Program
   1999 Human Development Report. New York: Oxford University Report.
United Nations Office on Drugs and Crime
   2006 World Drug Report. Electronic document, http://www.unodc.org/unodc/en/world_drug_report.html.

Universal Corporation
2006 Company Web Site. Electronic document, http://www.universalcorp.com.

U.S. Census Bureau
2002 Poverty in the United States. Washington, DC: U.S. Department of Commerce.

U.S. Department of Health and Human Services.
1985 Report of the Secretary's Task Force on Black and Minority Health. HHS Publication, Vol. 1. Washington, DC: U.S. Government Printing Office.

U.S. State Department
2001 The Fight against Money Laundering. Economic Perspectives: An Electronic Journal of the U.S. Department of State 6(2). Electronic document, http://www.usinfo.state.gov/journals/ites/0501/ijee/ijee0501.htm.

USA Today
2005 Jamaica to Hire More Police to Curb High Crime Rate. USA Today, November 8: 11.

van Binsbergen, Wim, and Peter Geschiere, eds.
2005 Commodification: Things, Agency and Identities. Berlin: Muenste.

Van Munching, Philip
1998 Beer Blast: The Inside Story of the Brewing Industry's Bizarre Battles for Your Money. New York: Random House.

Van Schendel, Willem
2005 Illicit Flows and Criminal Things: States, Borders, and the Other Side of Globalization. Bloomington: Indiana University Press.

Venkatesh, Sudhir
1997 The Social Organization of Street Gang Activity in an Urban Ghetto. American Journal of Sociology 103(1):82–111.

Vigil, James
2002 A Rainbow of Gains: Street Cultures in the Mega-City. Austin: University of Texas Press.

Vivian, Jiam, Hassan Salaheen, Merrill Singer, Juhem Navarro, Greg Mirhej
2005 Under the Counter: The Diffusion of Narcotic Analgesics to the Inner City Street. Journal of Ethnicity and Substance Abuse 4(2):97–114.

Wacquant, Loïc
2002 Deadly Symbiosis: Rethinking Race and Imprisonment in Twenty-First-Century America. Boston Review, April/May. Electronic document, http://www.bostonreview.net/BR27.2/wacquant.html.

Wakeham, H.
1961 Tobacco and Health—R&D Approach, 1961, 15 November, Cipollone 608. Minnesota Trial Exhibit #10,300.

Waldorf, Dan
1973 Careers in Dope. Englewood Cliffs, NJ: Prentice-Hall.

Wallace-Wells, Ben
2003 The Agony of Ecstasy. Washington Monthly. May. Electronic document, http://www.washingtonmonthly.com/features/2003/0305.wallace-wells.html.

Walters, James
1985 "Taking Care of Business" Updated: A Fresh Look at the Daily Routine of the Heroin User. In Life with Heroin: Vices from the Inner City. Bill

Hanson, George Beschner, James Walters, and Elliot Bovelle, eds. Pp. 31–48. Lexington, MA: Lexington.

Warrick, Joby
2006 Safety Violations Have Piled Up at Coal Mine. Washington Post, January 4: A4.

Waters, W.
2001 Globalization, Socioeconomic Restructuring, and Community Health. Journal of Community Health 26(2):79–92.

Waterston, Alisse
1993 Street Addicts in the Political Economy. Philadelphia: Temple University Press.

Watson, Peter, and Cecillia Todeschini
2006 The Medici Conspiracy: The Illicit Journey of Looted Antiquities. Prahran, Victoria, Australia: Hardie Grant Books.

Weiss, Brad
2005 Coffee, Cowries, and Currencies: Transforming Material Wealth in Northwest Tanzania. In Commodification: Things, Agency and Identities. Wim van Binsbergen and Peter Geschiere, eds. Pp. 175–200. Berlin: Muenste.

Wells J., and E. Pepples
1981 Re: Smoking and Health—Tim Finnegan. Memorandum, Brown and Williamson, July 24. Electronic document, http://www.library.ucsf.edu/tobacco/docs/html.

West, Jean
2004 Slavery in America. Tobacco and Slavery: The Vile Weed. Electronic document, http://www.slaveryinamerica.org/history/hs_es_tobacco_slavery.htm.

Westbrook, J.
2006 AIDS May Settle Investigations Soon. Hartford Courant, January 14: E1, E8.

White, L.
1988 Merchants of Death: The American Tobacco Industry. New York: Beech Tree Books.

Whyte, S., S. Vander Geest, and A. Hardon
2002 Social Lives of Medicines. Cambridge: Cambridge University Press.

Wilson, N., S. Syme, W. Boyce, V. Battistich, and S. Selvin
2005 Adolescent Alcohol, Tobacco, and Marijuana Use: The Influence of Neighborhood Disorder and Hope. American Journal of Health Promotion 20(1):11–19.

Wolf, Eric
1982 Europe and the People without History. Berkeley: University of California Press.

Wolff, E.
1995 Top Heavy: The Increasing Inequity of Wealth in America. New York: The New Press.

Working Families for Wal-Mart
2005 Organizational Web Site. Electronic document, http://www.forwalmart.com.

World Association of Alcohol Beverage Industries, Inc. (WAABI)
2005 WAABI. Electronic document, www.waabi.org/index.htm.

World Bank
2005 Informal Sector in Transition Economies. Electronic document, http://www.gdrc.org/informal/1-is_concept.html.

World Health Organization
2001 Global Status Report on Alcohol. Vienna: World Health Organization.
2006 World Drug Report. Office on Drugs and Crime. Vienna: World Health Organization.

Wynder, Ernest
1998 The Past, Present, and Future of the Prevention of Lung Cancer. Cancer Epidemiology, Biomarkers and Prevention 7:735–748.

Wynder, Ernest, and Evarts Graham
1950 Tobacco Smoking as a Possible Etiological Factor in Bronchogenic Carcinoma: A Study of 684 Proved Cases. Journal of the American Medical Association 143:329–336.

Yi, Daniel
2006 Direct Ads Drove 50% Rise in Use of Sleeping Pills. Hartford Courant, August 8: A6.

Zajac, A.
2006 Ashcroft Breaks with Tradition: Ex-Attorney General Opens Lobbying Firm. Hartford Courant, January 11: 9.

Zalin, L.
2004 Binge Drinking, Harmful Drinking Linked to U.S. Death Rates. University of Washington. Electronic document, http://www.uwnews.org.

Zill, Oriana, and Lowell Bergman
2001 U.S. Business and Money Laundering. PBS Frontline. Electronic document, http://www.pbs.org/wgbh/pages/frontline/shows/drugs/special/us.html.

*All websites were accessed between June 2005 and October 2006.

Index

291